Democratizing Pension Funds

Ronald B. Davis

Democratizing Pension Funds

Corporate Governance and Accountability

UBCPress · Vancouver · Toronto

16 15 14 13 12 11 10 09 08   5 4 3 2 1

Printed in Canada on ancient-forest-free paper (100% post-consumer recycled) that is processed chlorine- and acid-free, with vegetable-based inks.

Library and Archives Canada Cataloguing in Publication

Davis, Ronald, 1947-

Democratizing pension funds: corporate governance and accountability / Ronald B. Davis.

Includes bibliographical references and index.
ISBN 978-0-7748-1397-6 (bound); ISBN 978-0-7748-1398-3 (pbk.)

1. Pension trusts – Investments. 2. Social responsibility of business. 3. Institutional investments – Social aspects. 4. Corporate governance. 5. Pension trusts – Management. 6. Institutional investors. I. Title.

HD7105.4.D395 2008   332.67'254   C2008-901770-6

Canada

UBC Press gratefully acknowledges the financial support for our publishing program of the Government of Canada through the Book Publishing Industry Development Program (BPIDP), and of the Canada Council for the Arts, and the British Columbia Arts Council.

This book has been published with the help of the K.D. Srivastava Fund.

UBC Press
The University of British Columbia
2029 West Mall
Vancouver, BC V6T 1Z2
604-822-5959 / Fax: 604-822-6083
www.ubcpress.ca

Contents

Acknowledgments

I would like to acknowledge the contribution of Michael Trebilcock, Edward Iacobucci, and Jennifer Nedelsky of the Faculty of Law, University of Toronto, who provided invaluable comments on various drafts, and of my colleague Janis Sarra of the Faculty of Law, University of British Columbia, for providing irreplaceable advice from an acknowledged corporate law scholar. Mary Condon, of Osgoode Hall Law School, provided insightful comments that helped to bring the book's major themes into clearer focus.

I want to acknowledge and express my gratitude for the financial support of this work by the Social Sciences and Humanities Research Council of Canada and the University of Toronto's Capital Markets Institute. My former colleagues in the law firm of Koskie Minsky, Barristers and Solicitors, provided support by allowing me to take a lengthy leave of absence. I also want to thank Jessica Metters of the Faculty of Law, University of British Columbia, for her valuable research assistance. I would like to thank the anonymous reviewers for their helpful comments and suggestions, and the participants at the Corporations, Markets, and the State: A Multidisciplinary Inquiry into the Future of Modern Global Business, Alfred P. Sloan Foundation Conference, George Washington University Law School, Washington, DC, for their comments on my paper dealing with one of the themes of this book. Of course, the foundation for my decision to embark on this project was the immeasurable support and encouragement provided by my partner, Janis, and my children, Samantha, Danielle, and Alexander.

Democratizing Pension Funds

Introduction

Employee Ownership, Pension Funds, and Economic Power

The "Socialist Revolution"

In 1976, Peter Drucker proclaimed that the United States had become the first truly socialist country because the ownership of the means of production by the workers had been achieved.[1] He claimed that employees in the private sector beneficially owned at least 25 percent of American businesses' equity capital through their pension funds, while employees in public and non-profit institutions beneficially owned another 10 percent. Collectively, this was sufficient to provide them with control. In 1993, Mark Roe reported that pension funds owned $1.5 trillion dollars in equities, representing about one-third of the value of all equity stock, and that, in aggregate, they owned a control block in every major corporation in the United States.[2] The Employee Benefit Research Institute reported on the historical increase in equity holdings of employment-related retirement plans in the United States from 1950 to 1998. It reported that these plans held 0.8 percent of all equities in 1950, 4 percent in 1960, 9.4 percent in 1970, 18.6 percent in 1980, and 25.9 percent in 1990. By 1998, that figure had risen to 27.3 percent of all equities held in the United States, with a value of $3.5 trillion.[3] The total value of all assets of employment-related retirement plans in the United States in 2001 was $8.3 trillion.[4]

In Canada, at the beginning of 2002, the total value of all assets in all types of employment-related retirement plans was $1.2 trillion,[5] the value of assets in trusteed pension funds was $568 billion, and the value of equities held by these funds was $220 billion, or 38.7 percent of the total value of pension fund assets.[6] Trusteed pension funds directly owned equities representing about 10.4 percent of the value of the Canadian corporations on the Toronto Stock Exchange, and these stocks represented 12.9 percent of the value of the TSE 300 stock index in 2001.[7] Globally, Robert Monks reviewed various estimates of the equity holdings of funded pension plans in

North America and the United Kingdom in 2001 and concluded that collectively pension funds owned up to 77 percent of the equity in the largest 1,000 companies in the world.[8] Yet William Simon concluded that, despite the extent of this "ownership," a number of factors acted to restrict the "democratic and egalitarian" aspirations of pension fund socialism to merely a modest realization in the United States.[9]

Among these factors is the history of the courts' failure to recognize personal proprietary rights over assets held for the benefit of all plan participants in the plan.[10] Another factor, first identified by Adolph Berle and Gardiner Means in 1932, is the separation of "ownership" and control inherent in equity investments in the modern corporation.[11] There are also the intergenerational conflicts between employees and retirees, as well as those between younger employees on the one hand and older employees and retirees on the other.[12] Finally, because the control arising from pension fund share ownership can be exercised only by aggregating the holdings of a number of different pension plans, problems and costs related to collective action will be encountered. Despite these problems, however, the alternatives seem even less palatable. In the first alternative, the potential for control is not exercised. In the second alternative, it is exercised but the decisions about when, how, and for what purposes are left in the hands of individuals who are not accountable to the plan participants in any meaningful way for these decisions.

My contention is that there are both normative and prudential reasons why plan participants ought to exercise a greater degree of democratic control over the corporate governance decisions of funds held for their benefit, and why accountability for those decisions must flow from the funds' managers to the plan participants. By corporate governance decisions I mean decisions concerning the exercise of shareholder rights to try to increase the responsiveness of the management of investee corporations to shareholder concerns. Some of these concerns would include any changes in the financial or control structure, the independence of directors from management, accounting and auditing practices, and management of environmental, social, and ethical risks.[13] While it may be argued that this control should extend to determining the types of investments the plan purchases, I will argue that there is a limited scope for control of this feature of trustee responsibilities due to the nature of the decision making in that area. However, pension fund managers should be accountable to plan participants for active engagement in pressuring corporations in which the plan is invested to better manage environmental risks, such as global warming.

There are limits to this control and accountability generated by the dual-agency nature of plan participants' relationships to a fund's equity investments. "Dual agency" refers to the beneficiary–trustee agency problems in the pension trust fund relationship and the stockholder–manager agency problems in the corporate equity investor relationship. Any agency relationship involves the attenuation of the principal's control merely from having to act through another human being's agency. The limits to control by and accountability to plan participants have not yet been tested to any real extent.

Instead, control over these decisions has been exercised primarily by large financial institutions without any formal or statutory obligations to account to the plan participants for their decisions. These institutions were granted this control by default, without any conscious or deliberate decision to do so, as a result of the uncertainty surrounding the proper locus of "ownership" early in the history of the Anglo-American pension system. In 1959, just a few years after the assets controlled by private pension plans funded through trusts began increasing dramatically, Paul Harbrecht wrote that control had been delegated to a few large financial institutions acting as financial trustees and investment managers.[14] He pointed to several factors that undercut plan participants' ability to exert any control over these trustees through court proceedings, including:

- employers' claims of ownership based on their discretion as to whether or not, and in what manner, to fund defined benefit pension promises
- the fact that employees' benefits typically did not "vest" until retirement or until after a lengthy period of service with the employer, if they vested at all
- employers' right to hire and terminate the trustees at will, and to amend and terminate the pension plan
- the courts' reluctance to grant employees standing to sue the trustee on a trust agreement between the employer and the trustee, or to recognize their property rights in the pension fund in the absence of vesting
- language in the pension plan and/or trust agreement that characterized the employees' pensions as gratuities granted by the employer.[15]

Many of these issues have been settled in the decades since Harbrecht wrote, either by legislation that imposed mandatory prefunding of pension promises and much earlier vesting of benefits or by court decisions recognizing the plan participants' legal and equitable interest in the assets of the pension fund.[16] It is also accepted today that the employers' contributions to pension plans are, in reality, deferred wages of the employees that are part of the total "package" of compensation paid for employees' services.[17] Yet, in his recent survey of decision making by Anglo-American pension fund investment managers, Gordon L. Clark notes that "[i]t is very rare for plan participants to have a voice in trustee investment decision making.[18]

Trustees and Investment Managers

A brief outline of the process followed in investing pension fund assets may provide some context with which to assess my proposal for beneficiary control. The description will be of a relatively large pension fund. Smaller pension funds may turn over all aspects of administration and investment to insurance companies, but the assets in such funds are relatively small compared with those in trusteed pension funds.[19]

Pension funds are usually held in a trust fund. A board of trustees appointed by the sponsoring employer administers the trust fund.[20] The trustees are typically mid-level managerial employees of the corporation. Pension funds receive contributions from the employer and invest them, either through asset managers employed by the fund or through investment management firms whose performance is assessed against investment return benchmarks, such as the average return earned on investments in a certain sector of the market. Failure to meet benchmarks may result in contract termination. Investment managers are typically given almost complete discretion to determine which corporate securities to purchase within the asset class(es) that they have been authorized to manage.[21] Earnings are returned to the trustees by the asset managers for either reinvestment or distribution to retired plan participants as regular pension payments.

Pension funds invest predominantly in corporate securities, both stocks and bonds, with the balance invested in fixed income government securities and real estate.[22] Among their purchases are stocks that carry voting rights on certain corporate governance decisions. When pension plans began to become major investors in voting stock, many pension fund trustees delegated the decision as to how to vote the fund's stock to the external investment managers, who initially were large commercial banks.[23] Although the use of the voting power of the pension fund's investments has become the topic of public discussion recently, the practice of delegating voting to investment managers continues to this day.[24] Thus, at best, the trustees retain some form of overall supervisory authority but have delegated to financial services industry experts the decision making about whether to invest in a particular project or security and how to exercise any voting rights that are included in an investment. Their decisions have an important impact on the economic, social, and political life of society.

The Potential Impact of Participant Decision Making

There are several dimensions along which the importance of participant decision making can be measured, including the economic, political, and social. These dimensions are, of course, able to affect one another in judgments about the importance of a particular kind of decision. For example, one way one can measure the political importance of a particular decision is to look at its potential economic impact and vice versa. One important factor in assessing the potential impact is the success that arguments in favour of what is often characterized as market-based regulation of corporate activity have enjoyed over the past few decades in North America. The arguments suggest that markets are better able than regulatory command and control to control harmful activity by corporations and/or their managers.[25] The successful promotion of "governance through markets" has thus increased the importance of participant decision making as one aspect of the use of markets to govern corporate activity. It represents one way in which a broader cross section of citizens can have a voice in market-based decision making, a voice that might otherwise be expected to be heard through the regulation of the corporation by governments in the name of the "public interest."

I am not suggesting that participant decision making is an acceptable or sufficient substitute for the "public interest" as expressed through the democratic process, but rather that it is the best that the market can provide, given the partial withdrawal of government from regulatory activity in favour of market efficiency. The biases and exclusion of important groups in our society that are inherent in the pension system's reliance on employment as the source of rights to participate have been discussed by other scholars and are not the focus of this book;[26] however, the representational weaknesses of pension plan participants as a decision-making body should be neither forgotten nor ignored.[27] Another indicator of relative importance is the relative size of pension fund assets in relation to other assets in the economy.

Size and Diminishing Role of the State

In 1976, Drucker predicted that pension funds would own at least 50 to 60 percent of US equity capital by 1985.[28] While the percentage of direct ownership of equity by pension funds has stayed relatively constant in the US market, pension funds' ownership of equity in the largest corporations has increased. As well, these percentages do not reflect their ever-increasing investments in global capital markets. For example, 1997 estimates of pension fund assets as a portion of annual gross domestic product (GDP) for the United Kingdom are 93 percent, while for the United States these assets represent 57 percent of its GDP.[29] By 2004, the UK pension fund assets were 125 percent of its GDP, with an estimated value of £1.63 trillion.[30] John Langbein calculated the value of US pension trust fund assets at $5.5 trillion in 1997.[31] By the fourth quarter of 2006, the Federal Reserve estimated that pension fund assets had grown to $9.75 trillion.[32] In Canada, the value of pension savings grew from $825 billion in 1993 to $1.33 trillion in 2003.[33]

The influence of pension funds is also connected to the distribution of their investments in various markets and how that distribution affects or can affect the operation of those markets. As they began to grow, pension funds tended to purchase the higher-priced equity issues of large established companies, so that their ownership stakes in these firms were relatively larger than the percentage of equity ownership measured against the value of all stocks in the market.[34] While this pattern has persisted in large US pension plans, the increase in the absolute size of the funds has led to Clark's claims that these large funds and their service providers sustain the national and international financial services industries of New York, London, Toronto, Melbourne, and Sydney.[35]

This concentration of power has social and political implications, as well as economic consequences. One consequence of the growth in the size of pension funds relative to the total assets in a particular nation is that pension funds' investment decisions can have profound effects on the relative rates of investment in particular economic sectors and geographic regions of that state. The fiduciary relationships that govern the investment choices of trustees or their investment managers subject investment decisions to the constraints of those relationships and the underlying pension liability structure that must be funded from those investments. These constraints, together with those arising from the nature of the investment management business, drive investment or corporate governance decisions in ways that may be contrary to the state's economic policy and/or the interests of plan participants as citizens of that state, locality, or community.[36]

Thus, economic power is concentrated in the hands of pension fund trustees appointed by corporate management in a few large pension funds. Many of these trustees depend on the corporation for their livelihood or for continued employment once their term as trustee has expired. This power is further concentrated in the hands of investment managers who control the investment and corporate governance decisions for a number of these large pension plans.[37] These individuals and firms in turn may have their employment or their investment management service contracts terminated by the trustees. The grant of this power to agents by a widely dispersed group of plan participants raises issues of legitimacy and the legitimate use of the power.[38] It also raises the issue of the mechanisms by which legitimacy should be determined, and how the interests of the plan participants and of the society affected by decisions ostensibly made in their interests are defined and taken account of in the decision-making process. Implicit in my treatment of these factors as issues is a claim that the present system of decision making concerning pension fund assets does not adequately define these interests, take them into account, or provide appropriate mechanisms of accountability.

Structure

Chapter 1 will introduce some of the normative and prudential arguments in support of accountability to plan participants and a redefinition of their interests in pension fund investment and corporate governance decisions.

The redefinition situates them as members of a society in whose well-being and social fabric they have an interest, instead of as isolated rational wealth maximizers whose agents' only concern is maximum immediate financial gain in an efficient corporate securities market. The concepts introduced include the issue of fairness in the locus of decision making at levels far removed from the beneficiaries, the value of democratic decision making, the contested nature of shareholder wealth maximization as a primary norm for corporate governance, and the need to balance the process of "externalization" of costs onto plan participants and other members of society with increasing shareholder wealth.

In Chapter 2, I then set out an outline of the tax-supported retirement savings regime in Canada, including the defined benefit and defined contribution pension plans, the Registered Retirement Savings Plan, and the recent decision to invest contributions to the Canada Pension Plan in equities. This outline forms the basis for a discussion of the beneficial "ownership" of the funds' assets based on an analysis of the economic burden of contributions, the ultimate incidence of investment risk, and case law. The implications of the public interest in the private pension system arising from the tax deferrals granted, and the implications for the public pension system of failures in private pensions, are also discussed. Chapter 2 concludes that plan participants have a claim that the assets of the plan, including any corporate governance rights or influence arising from the plan's ownership of corporate securities, ought to be exercised to further their interests. In addition, there is a public interest in the exercise of these rights arising from the tax support and the reliance on the private pension system to generate adequate retirement incomes for a large portion of the working population.

Chapter 3 reviews the legal regimes of trust law and pension law in order to discover the doctrinal support for and impediments to accountability to plan participants in these regimes. In particular, the review of trust law concludes that there are two distinguishing factors in the application of the law of trusts to pension funds. First, the distinctive nature of a pension trust in which the employee is both settlor and beneficiary justifies an expansive interpretation of the trustees' fiduciary duties to include a requirement to account for corporate governance activity, as well as to accept a certain level of instruction from plan participants. Second, a more detailed scrutiny of the pension fund investment decision-making process and the roles of financial services industry professionals in that process leads one to conclude that participant involvement is a necessary antidote to the processes' agency problems. Court decisions that interpret the plan beneficiaries' interests as restricted solely to maximizing return on investments will be analyzed, as well as those that appear to have expanded the interests that can be recognized and acted on by pension fund trustees.

Pension law codifies much of common law trust law doctrine, while vindicating the public interest in adequate pension income by imposing minimum funding, vesting, and portability standards on private pension plans. These standards also support plan participants' claims to beneficial ownership of the funds. Further recognition of these claims is granted by requiring vesting of benefits after two years of service and permitting terminated employees to transfer an amount of the fund equal to the actuarially calculated value of these vested benefits to another retirement savings plan following their termination. Pension law has also codified investment standards that require diversification and impose standards of prudence that are consistent with a portfolio theory of investment, with its emphasis on acceptance of risk with appropriate compensation.

This standard can be contrasted with the traditional standard for assessing trustee investments, in which risk is to be avoided or minimized in order to preserve the trust's capital. This analysis of the effects of trust and pension law provides part of the context in which the claims for participant involvement in investment and corporate governance decision making can be evaluated. Further context is provided by the results of studies of the performance of pension fund investments, which indicate that the primary variable affecting return on assets appears to be the relative weighting of different classes of assets in the total investments of the fund. Thus, viewed in this context, the choice of investment and/or corporate governance decisions made by trustees is not so much a choice between investments/decisions that provide lower returns (but increased collateral benefits to participants) and those providing higher returns (but no benefits or collateral "costs" in the form of corporate "externalization"). Rather, they are choices among highly contested normative views of the role of corporate social responsibility, in which the effects of the choice on the long-term returns to the pension fund are also highly contested.

Chapters 4 and 5 review the impediments and incentives arising from corporate and securities law. Corporate law brings another set of agency relationships into the picture, that between the shareholders and the managers of the corporation. As has been pointed out by scholars, however, this is not a classic agent/principal relationship because the purported principals, the stockholders, are not able to give directions to the agent as to the agent's conduct. Of course, this lack of control can be offered as one justification for limiting to the amount invested in the firm the stockholder's liability for any damages that result from corporate activity.[39] Thus the corporate governance activities of pension funds are necessarily limited to the influence the pension funds can exert on management through persuasion, backed by the threat of exit from the pension funds' investment, and those matters on which shareholder votes are binding on corporate management, including the election of the board of directors. A single pension fund's investments in a corporation are unlikely to be large enough to win a vote, or even to persuade a reluctant management to change its practices; thus, it may require the coordination of a number of pension plans' votes or influence to accomplish a particular change.

Such coordination may impinge upon the arena of securities law, which governs the offer for sale of corporate securities and certain types of communication about the corporation and its securities. Securities law also regulates the conduct of votes among shareholders through its proxy voting rules. In addition, forming alliances among shareholders may be considered a change of control activity that is also subject to regulation under securities legislation.

Chapter 6 will summarize the present state of the rights and norms concerning the participation of plan participants in corporate governance decision making by trustees or their agents using corporate assets held for the benefit of those participants. Various initiatives to increase active corporate governance by pension plans in Canada, the United States, and the United Kingdom will be reviewed. While these initiatives are making progress, their voluntary nature and the conflicts inherent in the ability of plan sponsors to unilaterally control the nomination and terms of trustees and investment managers necessarily limits the potential scope of success for the initiatives. Several potential regulatory and administrative changes in the pension regulation and corporate and securities law regimes are then reviewed. With respect to pension regulation, these changes may include: setting a minimum standard of joint trusteeship; independent chairpersons of boards of trustees; enforcement activity requiring the exercise of proxy votes and accounting to plan participants; and prohibition on continued registration of plans that do not require socially responsible corporate governance guidelines to be followed by investment managers.

In the corporate and securities law field, the proposed changes include: changes to voting rules; easier nomination of directors; cumulative voting; mandatory outside directors; and express recognition of social responsibility as part of the directors' mandate. In the securities law field, the expansion of mandatory disclosure to include corporate policy and activity with reference to certain standards in the employment, human rights, environmental, and social fields is discussed as being justified as disclosure of material facts affecting long-term value.

Chapter 6 will also discuss the issues that arise in determining the manner in which plan participants will provide direction to the trustees regarding corporate governance activity. It will provide a framework for resolving the issues of representative democracy versus direct participation through referenda. A tentative conclusion is offered that a combination of direct policy setting together with representatives serving on the board of trustees may best serve to maximize the democratic potential while allowing for effective decision making. It will also be necessary, however, for the government to retain some limits on the scope of decision making in order to vindicate the public interest when it is threatened by majoritarian self-interest.

The Conclusion affirms that the normative basis for the proposal for beneficiary control is the challenge of providing meaningful participation in decisions that affect the economic direction of our society without utilizing the somewhat discredited electoral machinery of the state. It is based on a vision of the citizen as a member of a community, not as an atomistic self-regarding utility maximizer whose bonds with the community are those that serve to maximize utility and no more. Rather, the bonds themselves and the process by which they are defined and agreed upon have a moral value in the concept of reciprocity and a social contract that is based on a long-term relationship. While "ownership" has often been identified with neoliberal individualism, the collectivization of property in the pension fund may provide an avenue for plan participants to utilize their "ownership" to enhance reciprocal relationships in a social contract. It also provides a means by which this social contract can touch those who often seem most removed from its concerns – the management of large corporations, whose decisions affect whole communities and nations. These managers often appear to be responding to the imperatives of abstract shareholders, unconnected to any specific community, abstractions that apparently demand immediate wealth maximization. Involvement of pension plan participants in corporate governance activity will provide an opportunity for these managers to hear the views of actual shareholders situated in communities and their social contracts, rather than always responding to an abstract version of these shareholders. In sum, hopefully it will permit a further realization of the democratic and egalitarian aspirations of "pension fund socialism."[40]

1
Corporate Investment by Employee Pension Funds: A Deal with the Devil?

A Normative Theory for Beneficiary Control

A Summary of the Background: Limited Liability and Corporate Social Responsibility

There often appears to be a conflict between corporations and the public over the issue of corporate "social responsibility." This is interesting because for individual members of a social grouping, the issue does not arise in the same manner. That is, even though we are inundated by stories about numerous individuals who act in ways that we find socially irresponsible, there are few basic questions about whether or not individuals ought to be "responsible" for their actions.[1] In contrast, all dimensions of the concept of corporate "social responsibility" are deeply contested among scholars who have written on the issue, yet a blue ribbon commission issued a report outlining the concern among members of the public over a perceived lack of social responsibility being exhibited by corporations.[2] The concern stems from the lack of accountability through democratic institutions of corporations, whose scale of economic activity often surpasses that of many governments.[3] Instead, the individuals who manage the corporations are often said to be accountable only to the corporation's shareholders, and only to the extent they fail to maximize shareholder wealth.[4]

Yet the shareholders are not personally accountable for any legal wrongs arising from the decisions of the corporation in the same manner that an individual might be accountable. Their potential liability to those who may legally claim compensation for the consequences of those corporate decisions is limited to the extent of their financial investments in the corporation. The corporation's managers have a duty to promote the shareholders' interests and thus are not accountable to any other constituency affected by the corporation's decisions. Thus, the corporation, even though it has been granted the status of a legal person under the law, is not accountable to anyone other than the shareholders.[5] This apparent lack of accountability on the part of corporate management may not be a problem, however, since they are bound to advance the interests of shareholders. Shareholders are members of society and, as such, will be adversely affected by socially irresponsible corporate decisions along with other members of that society. Some of the concerns about the negative effects on society might be assuaged if shareholders could require management to act in socially responsible ways.[6] However, the duty of corporate managers to advance shareholder interests does not extend to their actual interests as members of society, but rather only to the interests imputed to shareholders through legal doctrines and the operations of securities markets.

Corporate Accountability: Answering the Demands of the Legally Constructed Shareholder

On closer examination, the accountability of management to the actual individuals who own the shares, or for whose benefit they are held, is rather fictional. Instead, the shareholders to whom the directors are accountable are artificially constructed by the perceived requirement that managers must maximize share prices and by the operation of securities markets as immortal beings whose only desire is that the value of their shares be maximized. These artificially constructed shareholders desire share value maximization irrespective of any interests, desires, or needs of the actual "shareholders," and, where necessary, in opposition to the shareholders' actual desires.[7] The securities markets provide the immortality for the fictional shareholder because an individual shareholder's death does not destroy the fictional shareholder's status, but merely changes the identity from the individual to the individual's estate or beneficiary. This change of identity makes no difference to the fictional shareholder's relevant characteristics. This situation leaves us with powerful economic organizations whose primary accountability is not to a human being or even a group of humans, but rather to the one-dimensional construct of the wealth-maximizing shareholder. Scholars have recognized the dangers to society and its well-being from the inexorable demands of share price maximization, and have proposed that corporate management be released from strict compliance with the logic of share price maximization. Some have proposed that managers be required to exercise their human judgment through a broader recognition of a duty to consider the interests affected by the corporation.[8]

Thus, the exclusion of all of the attributes, needs, and desires of human beings, except one, from the motivating force for corporate activity is certainly an important source of the concern about corporate social responsibility. Daniel Greenwood has expressed this concern as follows:

> Specifically, I contend that the fictional shareholder is fundamentally different from the human beings who ultimately stand behind the fiction.

> The law and the legally created structure of corporation and market filter out all the complexity of conflicted, committed, particularly situated, deeply embedded and multi-faceted human beings, leaving only simple, one-sided monomaniacs. Human beings have short lives, spent in particular places with particular relationships to other human beings; they constantly confront the problems of finitude and commitment. Shareholders, in contrast, are in significant senses immortal, uncommitted and universal: They are indifferent as to time and place, language and religion. They are indifferent between projects and personalities. They are understood to care deeply about one important and vital human aim – profit maximization – but not at all about numerous others. While the ultimate owners of the shares are specific, situated, conflicted and committed human beings, shareholders in most instances may be thought of more appropriately as a "large, fluid, changeable and changing market."[9]

Lawrence Mitchell noted the dehumanizing effects of the shareholder profit maximization duty on the directing minds of the modern corporation, and the dangers of permitting corporations to enjoy all of the rights and powers of a natural person in liberal society:

> But the limiting condition of the corporation is that while the directors, officers and employees might well look and sound like the natural people of liberalism's ideal, the reality is otherwise. Instead of animating the corporation, the corporation animates them ...
>
> Outside of the boardroom or the office they may be regular people, churchgoing, good parents, members of the country club, and respectable people in their community who balance their various roles and obligations in life against one another in ways they find both fulfilling and consistent with their systems of values. But once they act under color of their offices ... they take on a single function, a single form: to cause the corporation to maximize its profits ... And as such they forgo the capacity of people so prized by liberalism – the capacity for self-determination.
>
> This might not be such a bad thing if we treated the corporation as the artificial legal construct that it is, if we understood it to exist for a narrow purpose and that the consequence of that limitation was that we carefully watched and regulated what the corporation did, that we carefully watched and regulated the way their directors, officers and employees behaved.[10]

Others have expressed concerns about the unlimited licence granted to corporations because of the separation of the power to exercise that licence from the responsibility of any individual human for the consequences of that exercise.[11] This concern about the exercise of unaccountable power is not confined to academics and commentators. A recent survey of Canadians found that 72 percent of those surveyed wanted corporate executives to take social responsibility issues into account in corporate decision making.[12]

The Dual Nature of Plan Participants: Stockholders or Externalities?

The issue of the social responsibility of corporations is not new and has been the subject of earlier debates over the ability and desirability of corporations' "externalizing" the costs of their activities. Some scholars have advocated expanding the scope of directors' duties to include consideration of the interests of stakeholders, such as employees, creditors, suppliers, consumers, and the communities in which the corporations conduct their activities, in order to determine the appropriate level of externalization. Much of the early debate centred on the devastating effects on employees who lost their jobs during the takeover boom in the 1980s and the subsequent era of firm failure and restructuring resulting from excessive leveraging.

Gordon L. Clark explored this issue in his detailed examination of the restructuring activities of three large US corporations that centred on their efforts to shed large, unfunded pension liabilities to long-service employees as part of the restructuring strategy.[13] He described the issue as determining the appropriate boundaries between the economic interests and social obligations of corporations, and documented what he described as a crisis of regulation in the American political economy, illustrated by the inability of the regulatory regime to adequately protect workers' pension benefits.[14]

In two of the cases, the corporations were involved in secret keeping and deception in its relations with the employees, their unions, and federal pension regulators in order to gain their cooperation in and/or acquiescence to some of the steps in the strategy. In one case, the corporation provided altered documents and resisted disclosure in subsequent litigation. One scheme involved the corporation management's targeting of certain plants, production lines within plants, and individual employees for either permanent layoff or retention. The decision between these options was based on whether they would be eligible for plant-closing pensions in the near future (layoff) or were already eligible (retain). The strategy meant that employees who lost their jobs and would otherwise have been eligible for plant-closing pensions were both out of a job and denied any pension rights until they reached age sixty-five. The second corporation engaged in a sham transaction in which it ostensibly "sold" its steel-making division to a near-insolvent corporation with no experience in the industry, while retaining control of the valuable assets through security on the loan used to finance the sale. After the inevitable bankruptcy of the steel-making division, the second corporation disclaimed all responsibility for the pension liabilities of the employees because the purchaser had assumed the liabilities. This strategy meant that employees who qualified for pensions or were in receipt of pensions received only the (much lower) maximum pension benefits guaranteed by the US federal Pension Benefit Guarantee Corporation.[15] In both cases, the strategies were found to be unlawful many years after the events took place, due to the concealment of the strategy and the length of the litigation. As a result, Clark concludes that in these cases the public welfare in protecting private pension schemes was not advanced because by the time judgment was rendered, both the workers and executives involved had long departed. In addition, the penalties were either unenforceable, because the corporation's assets were highly leveraged, or less than the benefits that accrued from the shedding of the pension liabilities.[16]

Clark's concern about both the corporate strategy and the outcomes of regulatory efforts is that they were the result of and reinforced a mode of corporate behaviour that treated compliance with public regulation as just one more factor to be considered in the cost/benefit analysis of corporate strategy. He suggests that such corporate behaviour can lose its claim to legitimacy only when it is evaluated on the basis of moral sentiments rather than prices. He offers Fried's view that the dependence of contractual relations on social norms of trust and honesty makes contractual relations a social institution that "provides the basis for a procedurally just society" as one example of regulation based on the maintenance of social institutions rather than individuals' assessment of costs and benefits.[17]

Clark's prescription for the crisis of regulation envisioned a renewed regulatory regime explicitly claiming legitimacy for the moral foundations of public regulation of economic imperatives. He saw the average citizens' abhorrence of certain aspects of economic life as providing the force for such regulation. The renewed regime would emphasize individual responsibility of corporate management through increased use of criminal sanctions instead of corporate fines, and through the shaming of executives in the criminal courts, in a manner similar to the treatment of professionals who are disbarred or have their licences to practise their profession revoked.[18] In evaluating this suggestion and some of the regulatory initiatives following Enron, one must clearly consider and balance the effects on plan participants from both the dangers of deterring profitable corporate activity, as discussed by Ronald Daniels,[19] and the incredibly devastating consequences of market corrections following events such as the failure of Enron.[20] Further detail on the Enron failure is provided later in this chapter, in the section entitled "The Enron Pension Story: The Triumph of Perverse Incentives."

Thus, in Clark's view, corporate management will not serve as the source of meaningful implementation of considerations of justice and fairness in the corporation's dealings with its stakeholders or society. Only an outside force grounded in the moral claims of society on the one hand, and with sufficient legitimacy to intrude on the "private" sphere of managerial decision making on the other, may be able to set appropriate boundaries to the economic imperatives of corporate management. While Clark views this as a legitimate role of government, he notes that the US Congress has shown no willingness to assume such a role.

This book grew out of a realization that pension plan participants straddle both sides of the social responsibility debate, as they are both stakeholders (as workers, retirees, and community members) and stockholders (as the beneficial owners of the equity investments of their pension funds). The insight at the book's foundation is that in this dual aspect of the plan participant stakeholder may lie the answer to two related problems in corporate governance, namely, social responsibility and the need for an alternative to share price maximization as the measure of corporate performance.

In order to address these problems, however, the artificially schizophrenic existence of the plan participant stakeholder/shareholder must be broken down. That is, the plan participants' actual needs, desires, and preferences must be reflected in the corporations' decision making, rather than only the share price maximization preferences imputed to the artificially constructed shareholder. Janis Sarra provides a compelling argument that even where employees are not both stockholders and stakeholders, their investments in the firm give rise to residual claims on the value of the corporation's assets, and thus are such that directors should be required to take employees' interests into account in corporate decision making.[21] Where the stakeholder/shareholder preferences diverge with respect to the "externalization" of some costs of corporate activity, consent, an important normative value in a liberal, democratic society, becomes engaged in the decision about which set of preferences will govern. Thus, when employees' jobs, benefits, and pensions are being eliminated by the corporations' managers, it is often said that these losses are inflicted because it is in the best interests of the corporations' shareholders (or, to put it another way, the law has given the shareholders the right to terminate the employees' jobs with relatively little compensation). Yet, these decisions are made without reference to the actual preferences of the shareholders, other than the imputed preference that shareholders consent to any action that increases the price of their shares.

I should be clear at this early stage that, in the paragraphs above, I am not referring to the situation in which the employees of the corporation own a significant proportion of the corporation's voting stock. Most applicable pension legislation restricts the percentage of the plan's assets that can be invested in a single corporation's securities to 10 percent, and prudence would ordinarily require investment at a much lower percentage than the maximum. I am therefore referring instead to a situation in which corporate managers are eliminating employees' jobs, benefits, and pensions in a manner similar to that described by Clark, *supra* note 13. In such circumstances, the actual preferences of the stockholders (a significant proportion of whom may be pension funds) ought to govern. If they find the proposed method of elimination socially irresponsible and repugnant because, for example, it destroys the trust implicit in the promise of pension benefits, they may reject such a course of action, either prospectively or retrospectively through a change of management.

An early example of preference for the imputed rather than actual preference is found in a 1973 debate between Milton Friedman, the economist of profit-not-social-responsibility fame, and Eli Goldston, chairman of the board of Eastern Gas and Fuel Associates.[22] In response to Friedman's claim that a truly competitive enterprise had to choose between social goals and profit to survive, or else be able to exercise monopoly market power, Goldston responded with three claims. First, he stated that Eastern Gas had polled its shareholders and received 87 percent support for its practice of donating 1 percent of pre-tax income to charitable contributions. Second, he said that the path to maximizing profits was a difficult one to chart and that in the real business world, "you're lucky if you have a plus or minus 10 percent fix on things." Finally, he claimed that corporations were made up of people who "are not detached from society" and that society expected corporations to do more than maximize profit. Friedman's response emphasized that the only efficient role for corporations in achieving social progress was in engaging in competition to eliminate monopolistic profits and in paying the unsubsidized price for resources used and charging these costs to consumers in the prices of the goods they distribute. When Goldston objected that overemphasizing the maximization of profit let the lowest common denominator, "the cheapest louse in every operation," determine what was good for the country, Friedman responded with his view that it was wrong of corporate executives to make such decisions with other people's money; they could only legitimately do so using their own money.[23] What neither Friedman nor Goldston dealt with any further were the implications of Goldston's corporation's having the support of an overwhelming majority of the stockholders for at least some of the social goals that stockholders' money was utilized to support.

Pension Fund Corporate Governance: Why It Must Be Exercised in the Interests of Plan Participants

Is There a Conflict between Shareholder and Stakeholder Interests?

My claim is that the corporate governance rights attached to the equity investments of pension funds must be exercised in the best interests of the pension plan's participants and those spouses and dependents who are also beneficiaries of those funds. In particular, they ought to be exercised to protect and enhance participants' interests as employees, retirees, members of communities, and parents of children where these interests are at risk in corporate decision making, and where doing so does not clearly conflict with the goal of providing adequate retirement income for the participants. The seeming conflict between the goals of protecting the interests of plan participants as workers, retirees, or community members and providing an adequate retirement income is more apparent than real. There is no direct trade-off between these goals once the unique characteristics of pension fund investments with respect to timelines and liquidity are taken into account. In fact, corporate strategies that maximize share prices in the short term may actually harm the investments by pension funds over the medium and long term. Serious questions have been raised about the nature of the connection between stock prices and the value of the corporate investment. Thus, the exercise of corporate governance rights is required, not merely permitted, by the fiduciary duty to act in the best interest of the beneficiaries imposed by the common law and by pension statutes on those who hold the equity investments in trust for the employee-beneficiaries.

In addition to the benefits that may flow directly to the employee-beneficiaries from this exercise of corporate governance rights, both the employee-beneficiaries and civil society may receive indirect benefits in the form of increased democratic participation and accountability. The need for pension fund fiduciaries to consult with plan participants about their interests as employees, community members, and parents and the potential conflicts with the adequate retirement income goals of a pension fund (adequate investment income flows) may lead to democratization of important aspects of civil society. David Sciulli has emphasized the potential for corporate boards of directors to be sites of forms of decision making that support democratic societies by preventing abusive exercise of positional power within the corporation.[24] Amartya Sen argues that decisions about what human capabilities are to be privileged over others can be legitimized only by public discussion and democratic acceptance.[25] Attempts to use the corporate governance rights of the employee-beneficiaries to raise the protection of their interests as both stakeholders and stockholders can put the issues of corporate social responsibility and the appropriate measure of corporate performance on the agenda of corporate boards. The employee-beneficiaries' dual aspects of stakeholder and shareholder situate these debates over corporate social responsibility and measurement of corporate performance in a broader context, more conducive to the types of discussion envisioned by Sciulli and Sen, than the discussions of directors bound to promote the maximization of share price.

Objections to the Introduction of Shareholders' Actual Desires into the "Pure" Shareholder Construct

Undoubtedly, a major objection to this proposal will be that implementation of this conceptual framework will lead to undue interference in the "market" for the corporation's securities by introducing concepts and values that are irrelevant to the present value of the future stream of income discounted for the risk involved (the "price" of the security), which is the only reliable measure of corporate performance. Cynthia Williams analyzes this claim of interference in the context of her proposal that the US Securities and Exchange Commission (SEC) require expanded disclosure of social factors in corporate operations, and rejects it because expanded disclosure would support the free and knowledgeable exercise of consumer preferences in the market.[26] In the context of using shareholder proxy votes to try to change management's policies, however, the justification must necessarily extend beyond consumerism as the source of legitimacy for shareholders' influence over management's policy making. Nevertheless, it is important to keep in mind that decisions on social policy issues are continually being made by corporate management. Therefore, the contest for legitimacy between corporate management and shareholders is over who should decide social policy, not whether or not a social policy decision must be made. As well, the objection will be that incorporating stakeholder preferences into directors' decision making merely dilutes the directors' loyalty to shareholders and thereby increases agency costs by substituting an inherently incoherent duty for a coherent one.[27] Another possible objection is that the issues of social responsibility and the protection of stakeholder interests are really issues of market failure that are more properly dealt with through the political process, rather than through the use of private law rights.[28] The economic efficiency of share price maximization has come under increasing scrutiny, however, because the use of fiduciary duty as a means of filling "gaps" in the incomplete contracts that are the hallmark of the corporate form does not inexorably require the duty to be to maximize share prices. Rational investors would prefer a rule to maximize the value of all of the financial claims against the corporation rather than just the share prices, because as rational investors, their investments are diversified across all classes of available corporate investments.[29]

The coherence of the shareholder wealth maximization standard has also come under question. Scholars have raised questions about the coherence of the concept with respect to the timing of shareholdings; that is, is it a duty to today's shareholders or to tomorrow's?[30] Other commonly used measurements of pecuniary benefit to shareholders – corporate earnings and share prices – have come under scrutiny due to the potential for destruction of shareholder wealth that can also occur using these measures. Henry Hu points out that the traditional measure of shareholder benefit – earnings or earnings per share – can increase while shareholder wealth is actually reduced.[31] He then points out that an increasingly accepted alternative, share price maximization, also suffers from the inability of corporate management to control the influence of irrational factors on stock prices, and the discounting effects on stock prices of information asymmetry between managers and market participants. The effect of these factors is that actions that may increase the stock price may be harmful to the intrinsic value of the investment, and even if corporate management could control these factors, we would not want them to do so. Hu explains as follows: "Managers would be encouraged – indeed required – to take whatever actions are legally permissible to drive the trading price up, even if it were to destroy the true, intrinsic value of the shares. The cart is put before the horse; the ability to manipulate share prices within the bounds of the securities laws becomes the test of management rather than the ability to produce widgets."[32]

Scholars have also noted that the shareholders of any corporation consist of those that are diversified and those that are undiversified. These two groups of shareholders have quite different and conflicting interests with respect to management's risk assumption strategies: the former is indifferent to the risk of bankruptcy, while the latter is risk-averse with respect to bankruptcy. Many scholars have measured the duty to maximize shareholder wealth with reference to the risk preferences of diversified shareholders. Richard Booth argues that adopting the risk preferences of diversified shareholders is not a self-evident choice for management because diversified shareholders would prefer that corporate management's risk preferences were the same as undiversified shareholders because: (1) management must guess at the preferences of diversified shareholders, given the different forms of diversified investing they utilize; (2) shareholders can diversify away from company-specific risk more cheaply than management can through conglomeration; and (3) diversified shareholders are more likely to be bondholders as well, and therefore oppose diversion of wealth from other asset classes.[33]

In addition, the functional coherence of shareholder wealth maximization has been questioned as a result of the invention of new financial products that "unbundle" rights traditionally attached to shares into separately owned voting rights, rights to receive dividends, and rights to the residual value of corporate assets. This raises the question of which set of rights management ought to maximize.[34] Finally, the participation of corporations in the political process may make illusory the idea of the political process as the proper forum for correcting market failures. Corporate directors are duty-bound by the shareholder wealth maximization norm to utilize the corporation's considerable resources to oppose any attempt to use the political process to impose the cost of externalities on them.[35]

Consistency with Norms of Justice and Democratic Decision Making

Thus, the "deal with the devil" aspect of pension fund equity investments has hopefully become clearer. The nature of the share price maximization norm is such that the corporation imposes as many costs of corporate activity as legally possible on the plan participants as citizens (externalizing all possible costs), while utilizing their money to vigorously oppose any attempts to regulate this externalization in the political forum, and proclaiming that the directors are doing so in the plan participants' interests as share price-maximizing shareholders. This subordination of the shareholders' actual interests need not be so, however, and it is both just and consistent with democratic values that pension funds engage their beneficiaries in a dialogue about the appropriate limits to the actions of the corporations that they "own." Justice is implicated in such a dialogue first through justice's consistency with notions about the illegitimacy of alienating another's property without their consent. Where the use of (or failure to make use of) that property can result in both benefits and costs to the beneficial owners and/or their social or economic environment, then it is just that the owner be consulted about the appropriate trade-off in the circumstances, rather than have their consent implied from membership in the pension plan.

Pension plans are not merely the beneficent acts of grateful employers toward their faithful servants. Rather, on the one hand, they represent a form of mutual commitment between the employer and employees to contribute to and maintain a fund to provide pension benefits. On the other hand, pension plans also involve mutal commitment between employees to share the investment risks of the pension fund, as well as pooling the risks of funding benefits based on the life expectancies of the plan members. The use of the trust as a funding tool is an important part of this commitment as it involves mutual sharing of the benefits and risks of the fund's investments. Merely offering money to buy shares would deprive the employer of one of the most important benefits a defined benefit pension plan provides – loyalty energized by the increased benefits that typically accrue near the end of an employee's career. There are certain characteristics of pension funds that impart more of a collective or social character to their ownership than individualized private ownership. These characteristics will be discussed in greater detail in the section "Implications of the Public Origins of Today's Pension Schemes" in Chapter 2. As one example, by combining their assets in defined benefit plans, employees can obtain more pension benefits per dollar in the fund because monies that are not used to provide benefits to shorter-lived retirees can be used for the longer-lived, unlike the case in more individualized schemes. In a individualized defined contribution plan, those funds that are not used to provide pension benefits for the individual and spouse become part of the estate on their death and are no longer earmarked for pension benefits.[36] This social character of ownership does not justify the appropriation of those rights without consultation or consent.

Second, a dialogue between pension funds and their beneficiaries about the appropriate limits to the actions of the corporations that they "own" is consistent with democratic values. Democracy is consistent with the understanding that human development is a process that requires debates about the choices to be made in a particular society and that the participation of those affected is a source of legitimacy and authority for the resulting decisions.[37] The legal construction of the corporation as the economic organization whose sole goal is that of shareholder wealth maximization has, to a large degree, insulated it from such debates by practically excluding all other considerations as legitimate sources of justification for corporate actions.[38] Third, the dialogue between pension funds and their beneficiaries can function as a countervailing force to the allocative effects of markets on the distribution of resources and opportunities in society. It will thus counter the injustice of the markets' pricing mechanisms' effect of redistributing resources to those who enter the markets with the greatest entitlements.[39] Fourth, this dialogue counters, to some extent, the relations of subordination (to the corporation as the employer) that otherwise dominate the constellation of economic relations within the corporation, and, in doing so, furthers norms of equality among economic actors.[40]

This is not to say that pension funds should take over the day-to-day operation of the corporations in which they invest, but they can and should raise, as matters of general policy, human resource, ecological, political, and human rights issues on behalf of their beneficiaries. This does not mean that the pension funds must forgo investment income in the name of protecting other interests of their beneficiaries. It does mean, however, that where corporate management is faced with choices between these goals, it may no longer be able to automatically choose share price maximization as the only legitimate alternative, invoking their fiduciary duty to shareholders, because many of those shareholders may object vociferously.

Prudential Reasons for Employees to Oppose Share Price Maximization as a Corporate Norm

Diversification and Externalities

There are also a number of prudential reasons why maximization of share prices should not be supported by beneficiaries of pension funds and retirement savings plans as the norm for corporate management. They include the effects of diversification of investments and the fragility of a finance-based economic system. Diversification of investment among different asset classes in order to reduce the portion of the risk that arises from the specific attributes of a particular asset or class of assets is a well-established investment strategy for pension funds.[41] Thus, a fully diversified pension fund investment strategy would involve investment in both equities and corporate bonds or other forms of non-equity securities. As a result, to the extent that maximizing share prices is achieved at the expense of the value of other claims to corporate assets, such as bonds, commentators have suggested that utilizing share prices as a measure of the economic efficiency of certain corporate transactions is not suitable. The increase in share prices may be a result of a transfer from other claimants to the shareholders.[42] Clearly, for a pension fund that is invested in a diversified manner, it is not efficient for the increase in the value of one investment to come at the cost of the value of another.

Robert Monks has utilized a similar reasoning with respect to global investment by pension fiduciaries. In his view, fully diversified pension funds (Global Investors) cannot encourage corporate managers to engage in the process of externalization of costs. He comments:

> The Global Investor is likely to make good decisions for the long-term of society, because it can afford in most cases to take a long-term view, and a diversified view. An ordinary domestic investor may choose to invest in a corporation that externalizes the brunt of the harm that it is doing. But importantly, *nothing is external to a global shareowner.* Institutions having investments in all countries have virtually no incentive to permit environmental and hiring practices in the poorest countries that can only have the impact of competing with their own investments elsewhere.[43]

If one accepts Monks' reasoning, then it could also apply to investments within national markets by such investors.[44] Ronald Gilson and Reinier Kraakman suggest that the only rational expenditure for all indexed portfolios is to design corporate governance strategies that enhance the value of the entire portfolio rather than the value of individual firms in the portfolio.[45] Of course, it may be an overstatement to say that nothing is external to a global shareowner, given the much deeper problems of informational asymmetry, thin capital markets, and opaque legal systems that are part of a global investor's realities. These factors may mean that some costs from corporate activities may not be reflected in the overall pricing of investments in the affected market. Perhaps the claim could be rephrased as one that global shareowners have to be alive to the adverse effects on their portfolios of investing in exploitation. This is especially so in the case of pension funds, as their investments have tended to be concentrated in the higher-value stocks in the market.

Share Price Maximization Creates Perverse Incentives for Managers

Another concern that has been expressed is that the installation of share price maximization as the norm of corporate governance has created perverse incentives for corporate management through the divergence between capital market expectations and the actual earnings that can be delivered in competitive product markets.[46] These incentives have been exacerbated by compensation practices that generate extreme rewards for managers who increase these prices over the short term.[47] Henry Hu recognized the moral hazard created by these practices and described it as follows:

> Although not widely noted in the academic literature, managerial compensation can have the opposite effect as well, as may occur when compensation is highly sensitive to perceived performance, and true, risk-adjusted performance is difficult to measure. The moral hazard is obvious when such a monitoring problem exists. If the individual's superior were not cognizant of the full extent of the risks being assumed, the superior might overestimate performance of the individual and thereby overpay the individual. In an environment involving both this sort of informational asymmetry and highly variable compensation, the individual will be sorely tempted to take large, unrecognized risks. A corresponding argument can be made for the moral hazards facing an entire management team relative to its stock market superior when the stock market does not recognize the full extent of the risks a corporation's management team has elected to have the corporation assume.[48]

Management has also adopted a number of strategies aimed at the balance sheets, such as cost cutting, labour shedding, divestment and acquisition of product lines, and increasing of leverage in order to increase the return on equity above that provided in the products and services markets.[49] Commentators have pointed to two trends that have contributed to the ability to sustain an apparently endless asset-price appreciation in financial markets despite the divergence between earnings and market expectations. First, a high degree of leverage has enabled corporate management to distribute cash flow to shareholders instead of reinvestment.[50] The value of highly leveraged equity can be eroded quickly, however, if the liquidity of the stock is threatened or the flow of earnings that support its value suffers a shock.[51] The second trend is that the increase in the amount of retirement savings available to be invested in a shrinking pool of equities has bid up the price of those shares.[52] This development, however, may result in a financial bubble in which stock prices are overinflated.[53]

These trends pose dangers to both the ability of the pension system to deliver the promised benefits and the ability of the corporate sector to continue its participation in the productive sector of the economy. The seeming failure to invest for the future while maximizing cash flow to shareholders has raised concerns that the core function of the corporation – to bring together assets and labour to produce goods and services efficiently – is being ignored and that the economy will suffer for it. Teresa Ghilarducci summarizes the problems of short-term investment for pension plans as arising from market failures on the one hand (particularly the gaps in market coverage) and the regulatory regime, which fails to distinguish the interest of pension funds in continuing employment and contributions from the interests of ordinary income trusts.[54] One shorthand term for this phenomenon is "short-termism." Robert Monks and Allen Sykes have suggested that the short-term stock price maximization pressure actually forces management to act in ways that are harmful to the value of the corporation over the long term, and therefore to investors with longer-term investment horizons.[55] A recent review of institutional investors in the United Kingdom noted that pension fund investment managers perceived that their performance was being judged over very short periods, and expressed concerns about the potential distortion from such managers' failure to invest in long-term wealth creation.[56] Michel Aglieta has pointed out that pension funds cannot accept the nominal financial returns generated through asset-price appreciation and must seek long-run economic return that increases labour productivity in order to have an increase in real wages that will support the present mixed public/private pension system with the much smaller workforce in place following the retirement of the baby boom generation.[57] If capital markets are consistently outperforming the growth rate of the economy, then there is a transfer of the benefits of that growth from labour to capital, in the form of reduced wages and employment.[58] However attractive this may seem over the short term, the long-term effects of such a transfer in conditions of low rates of economic growth may be harmful to pension plan beneficiaries. Someone must be willing to pay prices for future retirees' financial assets at a level that will provide an adequate retirement income, and without economic growth the next generation may not be able to pay those prices.[59]

Recently, a number of authors have reviewed attempts by labour unions in the United States to mobilize the corporate governance activities of those pension funds where union members have trustees and to extend worker representation into other funds.[60] The unions' aim is to align the decisions about the allocation of workers' savings and the strategic directions of the firms where they invest and work with what is defined as "long-term value."[61] Long-term value is achieved through the cooperative efforts of various corporate stakeholders, and is contrasted with short-term value, extracted through capital market pricing that encourages a strategy of value stripping and zero-sum approaches by management.[62] As the some of the authors acknowledge, the union movement faces significant hurdles, particularly with respect to 401(k) plans,[63] and will require regulatory initiatives to allow participants to gain access to the governance levers of such plans.[64]

The potentially infinite lifespan of pension funds (as long as employees continue to work for the corporation) together with their relatively long-term liquidity requirements can potentially combine to overcome the pressures generated by the use of the short-term share price as the primary measure of the economic value of the investments.[65] The hollow nature of the promise of share price maximization as a measure of corporate performance could not be clearer than in the Enron saga. One firm, even one that, at one point, had the seventh largest capitalization in the US, may not be the basis for conclusions about share price maximization, but there are also instances of the very same kind of earnings management aimed at supporting the short-term stock price at Sunbeam, WorldCom, Qwest, and Global Crossing.[66] Enron's management were motivated by options and bonuses that provided incentives to increase short-term stock prices, leading them to disregard everything else, including the corporation's survival and the retirement benefits of its employees.

The Enron Pension Story: The Triumph of Perverse Incentives

Enron sponsored a "defined contribution" 401(k) plan for its employees, to which they could contribute up to 15 percent of their salary, subject to a maximum yearly contribution.[67] Enron contributed one-half of the amount donated by the employee in the form of its own stock. The employee was allowed to choose how his or her contributions were invested among various investment options, including the purchase of more Enron stock. The stock contributed by Enron had to be held in the individual employee's account until the employee was fifty years old.

By the end of 2000, 62 percent of the Enron 401(k) plan's assets were invested in Enron's common stock.[68] Of that amount, 89 percent was stock purchased voluntarily by employees.[69] Employees at other large corporations in the United States are even more committed to employer stock in their 401(k) retirement savings plans. In her statement to the Senate Governmental Affairs Committee, Susan Stabile pointed out that approximately 20 percent of 401(k) plans had invested at least 50 percent of their assets in employer stock, with Procter & Gamble (94.7 percent), Sherwin-Williams (91.6 percent), Abbot Laboratories (90.2 percent), and Pfizer (85.5 percent) being among the large corporations in the lead.[70] When Enron entered bankruptcy protection, the stock ceased to be available for public trading. In testimony before the Senate Committee on Health, Education, Labor and Pensions, Enron employees related how their 401(k) accounts went from six figures to a few hundred dollars while they received assurances that the company's prospects were good. In addition, they were unable to sell the portion of stock purchased with their contributions during the crucial phase of Enron's collapse, due to a hold on trading activity because the Enron plan was changing administrators.[71]

For many employees at Enron, the 401(k) plan was not the only source of potential retirement income; they also had benefits available from a defined benefit pension plan. The latter, however, had also been eroded over the years through a combination of factors, including the use of Enron stock in its employee stock ownership plan (ESOP) to offset a significant portion of the defined benefits.

Up to 1 January 1987, employees at Enron and its predecessor companies participated in a traditional defined benefit pension plan that provided retirement benefits based upon the final average salary of employees and their years of service.[72] Effective 1 January 1987, the pension plan was amended to provide a "floor-offset" benefit, in which the benefit provided from the pension plan's assets was "offset" by the amount of that benefit that could be generated from Enron's ESOP program. That is, if an employee was entitled to $600 per month on retirement under the benefit formula, and his or her ESOP account would generate $400 per month, then the employee would receive only $200 of the monthly benefit from pension fund assets. The remainder of the $600 benefit was paid from the ESOP account's assets.[73]

While this type of pension fund arrangement was not unusual, the steps that Enron took when it ended the "floor-offset" benefit in 1994 appear to be unique in that they effectively transferred the future investment risk of the ESOP portion of the benefit to the individual non-retired employees.[74] Once the "floor-offset" benefit was discontinued, Enron began to "release" the stock in the ESOP to the participants at the rate of 20 percent per year, and in doing so used the current market value of the stock that was released to fix the offset of their benefits earned for the 1987-94 period. This fixed offset was used in calculating the benefits owed from the defined benefit plan, irrespective of the future performance of the stock.[75] According to one news article, an unidentified former employee claimed that this employee's pension benefit summary issued in June 2001 indicated that no benefits were payable for the 1987-94 period as they were all offset by the market value of the ESOP's Enron stock, which the statement indicated was worth $385,000.[76] While the $385,000 amount may seem small, it represents the value of five of a potential total of thirty years of benefits (approximately 17 percent of the total benefits that could be earned by the employee). In a defined benefit pension plan, the current value of those five years of benefits would gradually increase until an employee became eligible for early retirement benefits under the plan, at which point the current value would increase dramatically until the mandatory retirement age. The offset of the 1987-94 pension benefit was computed at the prices for Enron stock in effect from 1996 to 2000 (when the ESOP stock for the offset was being "released" to the participants and the offset was "fixed"). Thus, if the method of "fixing" the employees' offset holds up to legal scrutiny, then this employee and many others will receive no pension benefits from the Enron defined benefit pension plan for their service from 1987 to 1994, as a result of the Enron stock price crash.[77]

The Enron story provides one illustration of how the interests of employers and pension plan participants conflict with respect to the design and administration of the pension plan.[78] There are also conflicts of interest, however, with respect to corporate governance activity by the pension fund's fiduciaries.

Reasons to Increase Accountability: Conflicts of Interest with Respect to Corporate Governance

It is important to remember that for many private sector pension funds, the employers' management, not the employee-beneficiaries, appoints the trustees. Those managers have little or no interest in encouraging the practice of active intervention by pension fund trustees in corporate governance. Mark Roe points out that private sector managerial control of the bulk of the pension funds involved in equity investments is a core structural problem for any program of active corporate intervention by institutional investors. He states: "Those calling for greater institutional involvement in corporate governance must face the complicating fact that the institutions, primarily controlled by corporate managers, are being asked to monitor corporate managers. Such a circle of control makes monitoring difficult, perhaps impossible."[79]

The potential for conflicts of interest is present in managerial control over pension funds, and recent history with respect to conflicts arising when financial markets analysts are employees of investment banking firms has shown that pressure will be exerted despite analysts' ostensible independence. These conflicts have been the subject of a number of newspaper stories.[80] Roe reviews the reports of similar pressure being exerted by managers on pension fund fiduciaries to vote with management in proxy fights, as well as the attempts by investment management firms to keep from having to cast proxy votes in order to avoid giving offence to potential clients.[81] In Canada, Jeffrey MacIntosh has described these counter-incentives as arising from the pressure on fund managers from corporate management to maintain or obtain the pension fund's investment business, the distribution of which is controlled by management.[82] For an illustration of these conflicts, see Chapter 3 for the story of the change in its vote on the Hewlett-Packard/Compaq merger by Deutsche Bank's proxy voting division after the investment banking division arranged a meeting with the management of Hewlett-Packard.[83]

These conflicts have led scholars to call for changes in the manner in which pension fund trustees are appointed. Following their review of a number of studies of the state of corporate governance activity in Canada,[84]

Ronald Daniels and Randall Morck suggested that the beneficiaries of pension funds should elect senior managers of corporate and public pension funds. The suggestion was made in order to deal with concerns about the managers' commitment to the beneficiaries' interests arising from their employment by fund sponsors. They also recommended that any breach of their fiduciary duty to the beneficiaries should make them liable to class action lawsuits by the beneficiaries.[85] Recently, another author from the US has suggested that an appropriate response to problems of corporate governance following the Enron and WorldCom revelations would be to combine Gilson and Kraakman's concept of independent directors recruited by associations of institutional investors with the notion that instructions on choice of directors would be provided directly by plan participants.[86]

Beyond Conflicts: Public Sector Pension Plans and the Struggle for Legitimacy

Public sector pension plans are in the forefront of corporate governance activity among institutional investors. Many of these plans are also in the vanguard of new global initiatives by institutional investors to enhance the use of environmental, social, and governance factors in their fund's investment activities pursuant to United Nations Principles for Responsible Investment or to encourage disclosure of climate change risks by the large corporations in which they are invested, through the Carbon Disclosure Project. These initiatives are discussed in more detail in Chapter 5.[87] The pension funds involved in these initiatives are predominantly from the public sector.[88] Indeed, when the United Nations Environment Programme Finance Initiative and the United Kingdom Social Investment Forum decided to publish a study of how pension funds are taking environmental, social, and governance issues into consideration in their investment process, only public sector pension funds were used as case studies.[89]

The case studies reveal the struggle that even pension funds willing to consider environmental, social, and governance issues are having in describing their actions in a way that indicates the impact they are having on the companies in which they invest and on the return on their investments. The following quote from the case study of ABP, the pension fund for the Dutch government and education employees that is the second largest pension fund in the world, illustrates the dilemma:

> ABP believes that companies with strategies that encompass both financial and environmental, social and governance issues will deliver better long-term performance. As a result, the pension fund considers the integration of ESG information throughout its mainstream investment analysis to be essential and promotes the integration of material issues into its investment decision-making by both internal and external fund managers. Ultimately,

> ABP believes capital markets will appropriately value and reflect environmental, social, governance risks and opportunities in stock prices. However, while progress is being made, good quality data and research on extra-financial ESG issues is broadly lacking.

This concern is reflected in a survey of UK pension trustees in 2006, in which they reported that the barriers to the integration of social, environmental, and ethical factors into investment practices clustered around cost versus benefit and the ability to evaluate the financial impact on investee companies.[90] It will clearly take some time and the investment of considerable resources to develop tools that evaluate both the impact of ESG factors on investee companies and the impact of various ESG strategies by pension funds on the companies and the funds' returns.[91]

Given the lack of immediately quantifiable data, trustees recognize that any measurable impact will probably occur over the long term.[92] This leaves the decision to incorporate ESG factors into pension funds' investment strategies vulnerable to challenge, and this possibility may inhibit trustees from commencing or continuing with a responsible investment strategy. Seeking members' support for this initiative would assist in sustaining and legitimizing public sector pension funds' expenditure of resources on responsible investment strategies.

The Potential of Democracy and Accountability

The benefits for pension plan participants of implementing accountability for corporate governance activity are the ability to effect change in the behaviour of the corporation that will improve the social and physical environment in which they live, and the ability to control potential abuses of corporate power by management that may adversely affect the financial returns of their pension funds. The potential economic and social devastation of global warming has been extensively analyzed in the report by Sir Nicholas Stern to the Prime Minister of the United Kingdom, *The Economics of Climate Change*.[93] Stern reports that the benefits of present expenditures to reduce greenhouse gas emissions outweigh the long-term costs of not doing so by a margin of at least 5 to 1.

Pension plans, as major sources of capital for industries that are major emitters of greenhouse gases, can play a role in encouraging the investment in technology and processes that reduce emissions in their investee companies. As outlined above, public sector pension plans are active in initiatives to define the scope of the problem and the risks in particular industries and corporations, refusing to wait until some governments finally decide to act. Yet, where are the major private sector pension plans? In its 2006 Key Proxy Vote Survey of thirty-four Canadian investment management firms that collectively manage $371.6 billion in pension assets, of which $88.5 billion are invested in Canadian equities, the Shareholder Association for Research and Education found that 73 percent of the firms participating in the survey indicated that their pension plan clients had given them *complete* discretion to vote the proxies for more than 85 percent of the pension fund assets they manage.[94] Clearly, these plans have not yet taken seriously their fiduciary responsibility to exercise their corporate governance rights.

In a recent speech to the Conference Board of Canada conference on corporate social responsibility, a senior official of the Canada Pension Plan Investment Board made it clear that one of the considerations in the allocation of capital by the Board is the assessment as to whether or not a particular corporation is likely to be a loser in the market shift in response to climate change.[95] If plan members were members of the board of trustees of private sector pension plans, it would be possible to for them to challenge the plan's inactivity on this major risk to the long-term financial return of the plan and to the future well-being of its members.

Plan members can also benefit from accountability for their pension funds' corporate governance activity by being able to galvanize the fund to engage corporations' directors concerning matters such as management compensation arrangements that are unconnected to performance. The problems of corporate executives' compensation have been well documented.[96] In response, institutional investors have sponsored resolutions to amend the bylaws to give shareholders a non-binding vote on executive compensation packages. These resolutions have recently begun receiving enough votes to pass at the annual shareholder meetings of some publicly traded companies in the US.[97]

These are two examples of corporate governance activities that pension funds might pursue if plan governance activities were a matter for which the trustees were accountable to the plan members. It should be clear, however, that the determination of what environmental, social, and governance matters, if any, the pension plan ought to pursue will and ought to be in the hands of the plan members. They will determine the agenda following a discussion of the issues. I set out a more detailed proposal for this process of accountability in Chapter 6.

Pension Plan Corporate Governance Is a Matter of Public Policy

Enron is not just a story about out-of-control managers and the devastating effect on employees and retirees. Many would argue that the choices of employers and employees about their pension savings are private and should not be the concern of policy makers. There are two arguments that counter this position. First, private pension plans receive tax subsidies in order to support a public policy that employees who retire should have an adequate income. Second, any failures of the system are borne by the general public, who will have to provide substitute income for inadequate pensions generated through tax-subsidized private employers. Lastly, the choices that undermine the publicly funded policy of providing adequate retirement income through a combination of public and private pension schemes appear to benefit employers only. The hundreds of millions of dollars of Enron stock in these retirement savings and pension plans represented an immense tax subsidy to the corporation for its employee benefit plan.

The following chapter discusses the tax-supported scheme for retirement savings and pension plans in Canada, together with the law concerning the beneficial ownership of the funds, including their investments in corporate securities. It concludes that the law supports the view that fiduciaries who control these funds are under an obligation to exercise the funds' corporate governance rights in the interests of the employee-beneficiaries.

2
Pension Fund Assets and Plan Members: A Question of Ownership?

Employee Retirement Investments as Creations of Public Policy

In North America, the concept of providing for retirement income was a latecomer to the area of public policy, arriving in Canada after the Second World War. As public policy, it has taken two forms: direct sponsorship by the federal and Québec governments of a pension plan for all employees (which was combined with an earlier government subsidy provided to all retirees) and tax-driven incentives for employers and their employees to engage in some form of retirement savings plan.

The creation of both forms of retirement savings initiatives was justified on the grounds that it was in the public interest that older workers be provided with a means of leaving the workforce without being driven into abject poverty and becoming clients of their communities' welfare system. In addition, providing for adequate income upon retirement enabled employers and employees to plan for retirement on a fixed date, and thus enabled employees to plan their financial arrangements and employers to plan their staffing and training requirements. It also provided a relatively predictable demand for new employees based on mandatory retirement ages rather than on individual employers' decisions to dismiss individual workers when they were no longer capable of performing their duties. The important public policy goals of a mandatory retirement age policy were recognized by the Supreme Court of Canada in its decisions upholding the exclusion of such policies from the definitions of discrimination on the basis of age in various provincial human rights legislation.[1] Typically, the human rights legislation prohibited discrimination on the basis of age only between the ages of eighteen and sixty-five. Recently, some provincial governments have begun to reverse the mandatory retirement policy by amending their human rights legislation so that it prohibits discrimination on the basis of age for those eighteen years of age and older, without any upper age limit.[2]

A Government Pension Plan

Prior to the Second World War, the only form of government involvement in the retirement income arrangements of Canadians was the Old Age Pension. It was initiated in 1927 as a form of federal cost sharing with the provinces in a means-tested welfare program for those who were too aged and infirm to take part in the usual work-for-welfare programs applicable to younger unemployed individuals during that era.[3] In 1952, the federal government initiated the Old Age Security program.[4] It was originally a universal program of flat benefit payments available to anyone on the basis of age and residence criteria alone. It has now been supplemented by a Guaranteed Income Supplement that is provided on the basis of age and financial need.[5] Both programs are funded through general tax revenues, however, and are not part of the retirement savings programs that form the subject of the central part of this book.

The Canada Pension Plan (CPP) (in Québec, the Québec Pension Plan) is a mandatory payroll taxation pension plan that provides pensions to employees at the normal retirement age of sixty-five.[6] Both employees and their employers make contributions to the plan, with the level of contributions being based on the employee's wages up to a maximum. No further contributions are required on earnings above the maximum. The level of benefits is determined based on the average earnings and numbers of years the individual contributed to the CPP.[7] All contributions to the CPP are not subject to taxation when they are made, and any earnings on those contributions accumulate in the CPP fund without taxation. Once the employee begins to receive the CPP pension benefits, however, they are treated as income to the employee and subject to taxation at the appropriate rate.[8]

Thus, requiring mandatory contributions supports the public policy that employees should have a source of retirement income. This policy is also supported financially through a tax-deferral program that usually results in lower tax revenues due to the lower income level of the CPP recipient compared with that of the employee at the time the contributions were made. The fund created by these mandatory contributions has just recently commenced investments in equity securities, and intends to increase the percentage of its investments each year. In a later section, I will discuss the implications of these investments for my argument, particularly the implications for corporate "social responsibility" and democratic accountability.[9]

"Private" Pension Plans and Tax Incentives

It is an accepted fact that the CPP pension, even when augmented with the Old Age Pension and its supplement is intended to provide only a minimum level of retirement income.[10] In order to receive a comfortable retirement income, employees require an additional source of income during their retirement. They must either receive a pension from another source or have saved sufficient funds to produce the investment income needed after their retirement. The federal government introduced tax legislation allowing employers and their employees to make contributions to an employer-sponsored pension plan without paying any tax on the contributions.[11] In addition, the investment income of the pension plan was not taxable while it remained in the pension fund. Once an employee retired and began receiving benefits, however, the benefits were treated as taxable income. As in the case of the CPP, the government supported the adequate retirement income policy financially by deferring taxation until the benefits were paid to a retiree. Unlike the CPP, however, the provision of an employer-sponsored pension plan was not made mandatory for employers.[12]

Instead, the government made provision for the employees of an employer who provided either no pension plan or a woefully inadequate plan to set up their own retirement savings accounts on a tax-deferred basis. The Registered Retirement Savings Plan (RRSP) provisions allow employees to contribute on either a tax-deferred or tax-refundable basis to a locked-in retirement savings account at a financial institution approved by the government.[13] These contributions are subject to the same annual maximum amounts as those made to private pension plans, and where there is both a private pension plan and the RRSP, the RRSP limits are lowered by the value of the contributions to the private pension plan. Employees can continue to contribute to their RRSP until they reach age seventy, at which time they must convert the account to an income-producing annuity or fund from which they withdraw a minimum amount of income each year.[14]

Implications of the Public Origins of Today's Pension Schemes

The public origins and funding support for the CPP, employer-sponsored pension plans, and employee RRSPs are such that the use of these funds does not fall exclusively within the private half of the public/private divide. When the issue of whether or not the corporate governance rights that accompany the investments of these funds ought to be used to promote corporate social responsibility arises, its resolution is not just a matter of the preferences of the funds' "owners," however defined. At present, the preferences of the plan participant with respect to this issue are not required to be canvassed or taken into account in a systematic way.

While it is the purpose of this book to argue that these preferences must be taken into account, it should not be forgotten that there is also the public interest to be considered. The public interest lies in both providing adequate income through tax-deferred contributions and investment earnings, and ensuring that investments that have received substantial public support are used to promote corporate social responsibility.[15] That public interest must be implicated in the resolution of the corporate social responsibility issue for pension fund trustees, investment managers, and mutual fund managers whose clients include RRSP accounts.

Considering the public interest will also extend the reach of democratic decision making into an arena from which it has been absent for the most part. It should not be forgotten that many Canadians want corporate social responsibility and wish their pension funds to be invested in ways that promote it. As mentioned earlier, the Canadian Democracy and Corporate Accountability Commission commissioned a survey of over 2,000 Canadians concerning the issues that the Commission was going to investigate. A summary of the poll by Vector Research reported the following responses:

- 72 percent say that business should pursue social responsibilities, not just profits.
- Most want pension funds invested in responsible companies.
- 80 percent say that government should set social responsibility standards.
- 75 percent say that governments should boycott firms that don't comply.
- Most doubt that people would pay more for socially responsible products.
- 84 percent say to go it alone on a corporate ethics code if other nations stall.
- Most [respondents] back trade deals with worker and environmental rights.
- Half say that firms have become more socially responsible.
- Most want a federal ban on union and corporate political donations.[16]

This public interest serves to counterbalance the view that the governance of the corporations in which retirement savings are invested is a completely private matter for the employee-beneficiaries and/or the employer-sponsor of the pension plan. It also counterbalances the argument that the private decisions of beneficiaries and/or sponsors concerning whether or not to pursue corporate social responsibility with "their" pension investments should trump all other considerations. In making this statement, one ought not to forget that one of the aspects of the public interest in retirement savings is the need to ensure that employees and their spouses will receive an adequate income following their retirement. It is important to keep both the adequate income and corporate social responsibility aspects of the public interest in mind during the following discussion of pension plan design and its effects on the issue of the "ownership" of plan assets.

The Structure of Tax-Supported Employee Retirement Investments

Pension plans can be roughly divided into defined benefit and defined contribution plans, with some plans that contain elements of both.[17] They represent different approaches to the basic issue of pension plan design: how current contributions can be utilized to fund an adequate stream of income for retirement that will commence decades in the future. The issue of funding is crucial because it is this aspect that distinguishes a pension plan from an unfunded promise that on retirement the employer will pay the promised benefit from its current income stream at the time of retirement. The rationale for this distinction has been described as follows:

> Registered pension plans can be distinguished from other terms of the employment contract in two ways. First, all pension promises require pre-funding, that is, the pension benefits are not paid out of the employer's current revenues as the pension benefits begin, but rather they are paid from funds set aside for that purpose years, often decades, earlier ... Second, and certainly one reason for requiring the pre-funding, pension benefits only commence after the employment relationship has terminated and the employee has rendered full consideration for the pension benefit. Obviously, without pre-funding, employees would be completely dependent on the employer's continued solvency in order to receive the promised pension benefit.[18]

The rationales for prefunding are part of the debate concerning the relationship between the employee-beneficiaries of a defined benefit pension plan and the funds of that plan that will be discussed in a later section concerning the "ownership" of these funds while they are held in the plan.

Defined Benefit Pension Plans

The distinguishing feature of a defined benefit plan is that the pension promise is "defined," that is, the plan provides that an employee is entitled to a specified level of monthly payments on retirement, the amount of which is defined according to a formula (often based on length of service and salary) set out in the pension plan documents.[19] The employer regularly contributes an amount calculated to pay its current pension obligations when they become due.

Since the funding is occurring years, or even decades, before the obligations become due, however, the amount contributed is much less than the actual amount owed at that future date. The balance of the pension obligation is funded by the investment earnings generated by the original contribution over the years (or decades) that it is being held in the fund, pending retirement. The amount the employer contributes each year is based upon a calculation by an actuary of the present cost of providing the pension benefits earned by employees over the course of that year. In making this calculation, one of the factors the actuary takes into account is an estimate of the amount of future income that may be generated by investing the contributions until they are paid as benefits, using an assumed rate of return.[20]

Defined Contribution Pension Plans

In contrast to the defined benefit plans, in a defined contribution plan, it is the input (the contribution), rather than the output (the pension benefit), of the pension fund that is defined. A typical defined contribution plan is one in which the level of employer (and sometimes employee) contributions into the plan is defined, often as a percentage of the employee's wage. These contributions, plus the earnings generated by their investment until retirement, will be the amount of funds available to provide an annual pension benefit upon the employee's retirement. Thus, the defined contribution plan promises no particular level of benefits on retirement, only a particular level of contributions over the course of an employee's working life.[21]

Since each employee will be entitled to differing levels of contribution as a result of differing salaries and employment history, the defined contribution plan tracks the contributions made on each employee's behalf and the investment earnings on those contributions separately in an "account" in that employee's name. This procedure also enables the plan administrator to calculate the amount of the fund to which the employee is entitled on retirement.

Thus, in a defined contribution plan, the fulfillment of the employer's pension promise is not deferred until the employee's retirement, as it is in the defined benefit plan. The employee receives the promised benefit (the contribution) almost concurrently with the employee's provision of the promised consideration (the services provided to the employer). Accordingly, the employer has no further claim on the assets in a defined contribution plan once those contributions have been remitted to the plan and the beneficial "ownership" of the assets has been transferred to the employees.[22]

Some pension plans contain elements of both of these types of plans, that is, they provide a defined benefit and require a defined contribution from the employer (and at times from the employees as well). While such plans may be treated as defined benefit plans in many respects, for the purposes of determining the beneficial ownership of the plan's assets, it is likely that the defined contribution aspect will become a primary consideration, especially if the plans' assets are held in trust. Therefore, it is likely that the beneficial owners will be the employee-beneficiaries.[23]

Registered Retirement Savings Plans (RRSPs)

RRSPs are tax-deferred retirement income vehicles whose sole source of funding is employee contributions.[24] Investment income earned on RRSP contributions is also tax-deferred. Employees may make contributions to an employer-sponsored "group RRSP" through payroll deductions if their employer provides such a plan, or may make a tax-refundable contribution to their own RRSP account with an approved provider of such services. With respect to the ownership issue, in both cases the contributions, together with any investment earnings, are held solely for the benefit of the individual employee and these funds are not subject to any claims by the employer once the contributions have been made.

Canada Pension Plan (CPP)

The CPP is a mandatory program providing retirement, disability, and survivor benefits to eligible contributors and their families. It was introduced in 1966 at a time when Québec and Ontario, the two largest provinces, were considering mandating minimum levels of pension coverage for employees that would have required employers to sponsor pension plans providing at least the minimum coverage in those provinces.[25] The benefits are funded by mandatory employer/employee contributions and investment income on the fund created by those contributions. Contribution levels have recently increased and will continue to do so as the CPP moves towards greater funding of the benefits from a reserve fund created through investment of the current contributions.[26] The increases and the decision to increase the reserve were implemented to deal with a funding shortfall resulting from longer life expectancy, slower economic growth, increased benefits, and increased utilization of the disability benefit.[27] Benefits are provided on a defined benefit basis, based on the Yearly Maximum Pensionable Earnings ("YMPE") subject to the contribution requirement multiplied by the ratio of the contributor's annual earnings to the YMPE over the course of the contributor's working life.[28]

Now that we have briefly described the funding and benefit structures of these various forms of publicly supported employee retirement income plans, a key issue now arises. The issue is whether the structure of these plans will support a legal framework that requires those who exercise actual control over the investments of these plans to respond to the preferences of the plans' beneficiaries. It is common for these funds to be controlled by pension trustees, pension committees, trust companies acting as investment managers, professional investment managers, and mutual fund managers, all of whom may hold the funds' investments in their own names. The first component of that framework is the question of "ownership" of the plan's assets. Since those assets are property, determining the legal interests attached to them is a fundamental step in defining whose interests will be the controlling factor in the use of the property.

The Question of "Ownership" and Conflict of Interest

The issue of the beneficial ownership of the funds held in various types of employee retirement savings vehicles is relevant to my argument because the investment managers, trustees, and mutual fund managers are fiduciaries of the beneficial owners of the funds. They also have control over the investment of these funds and the exercise of the corporate governance rights attached to the fund's securities. Unless the employee-beneficiaries can be clearly identified as the beneficial owners to whom the fiduciary duties are owed, there will be little incentive for those in control of the pension funds to take any action to further the employee-beneficiaries' interests. These fiduciaries are already subject to powerful counter-incentives that have resulted in many of them (especially in private sector pension funds where corporate managers are the trustees) refusing to take even the most innocuous steps to discipline the management of the corporations in which the pension funds are invested. Jeffrey MacIntosh has described these counter-incentives as arising from the pressure on fund managers from corporate management to maintain or obtain the pension fund's investment business, the distribution of which is controlled by management.[29] In addition, the employee-beneficiaries will lack the standing necessary to enforce the fiduciaries' duty to exercise the corporate governance rights in a manner that ensures both adequate retirement income and corporate social responsibility.

Defined Contribution Plans and RRSPs

There is very little controversy over beneficial ownership of the assets of defined contribution plans, and no controversy over that issue for an RRSP. The latter is clearly owned by the employee-beneficiary, and the only restrictions on the exercise of the ownership rights come from the applicable provisions of pension legislation and income tax statutes.

Defined contribution plans become most controversial when there is also a defined benefit aspect to the plan. When the plan is one that merely provides for defined employer contributions and a benefit payable from the funds resulting from those contributions plus investment income, there is no basis on which an employer may claim entitlement to any part of the funds.[30] The employees are merely receiving the agreed-upon benefits, regardless of the performance of the investments. When the plan provides for a defined benefit, however, instead of a benefit contingent on the funds generated by contributions plus investment income, then controversy arises whenever the plan's actuary determines that there is a "surplus" in the plan.

The status of that surplus and its relationship to the defined benefit will be discussed in the next section. One important factor must be kept in mind concerning the "ownership" issue, however. That factor is that whatever the status of the "surplus," the bulk of the funds in the plan are held for the benefit of the employee-beneficiaries, not the employer. The Supreme Court of Canada has ruled that where a pension plan is subject to a trust, the pension fund is presumptively held for the exclusive benefit of the employee-beneficiaries. Mr. Justice Cory, writing for the majority, found that a pension trust is a transfer of property, and in view of the dynamics of the employment relationship concerning pension plans, it would be inequitable to grant the employer the power to take the funds back by a subsequent amendment. He wrote:

> One of the most fundamental characteristics of a trust is that it involves a transfer of property ...
>
> The judgment of the B.C. Court of Appeal in *Hockin*, if followed to its logical conclusion, would mean that the presence of an unlimited power of amendment in a trust agreement entitles a settlor to maintain complete control over the administration of the trust and the trust property. That result is inconsistent with the fundamental concept of a trust, and cannot, in my opinion, be sustained without extremely clear and explicit language. A general amending power should not endow a settlor with the ability to revoke the trust. This is especially so when it is remembered that consideration was given by the employee beneficiaries in exchange for the creation of the trust. In the case of pension plans, employees not only contribute to the fund, in addition, they almost invariably agree to accept lower wages and fewer employment benefits in exchange for the employer's agreeing to set up the pension trust in their favour. The wording of the pension plan and trust instrument are usually drawn up by the employer. The employees as a rule must rely upon the good faith of the employer to ensure that the terms of the specific trust arrangement will be fair. It would, I think, be inequitable to accept the proposition that a broad amending power inserted unilaterally by the employer carries with it the right to revoke the trust. The employer who wishes to undertake a restricted transfer of assets must make those restrictions explicit. Moreover, amendment means change, not cancellation, which the word "revocation" connotes.[31]

Thus, the pension fund should be considered as trust property held for the benefit of employees and retirees who are entitled to pension benefits under the plan.

Defined Benefit Plans: The Employment Contract, "Risk," Deferred Compensation, and Trust Law

It is important to re-emphasize a point made in the previous section. The bulk of the assets in a defined benefit pension plan are clearly dedicated to the provision of the pension benefits for the employee-beneficiaries; thus, the securities in which those funds are invested are held for their benefit. Accordingly, the corporate governance opportunities attached to those securities ought to be exercised to provide an adequate retirement income and to further corporate social responsibility. One of the factors that may be advanced in opposition to this position is a claim that a portion of the pension fund's assets are surplus assets and represent an overpayment by the employer in which the employer has an ownership interest. However, the nature of a "surplus" in an ongoing pension plan, as defined in an authoritative decision of the Supreme Court of Canada,[32] means that such a claim by the employer cannot be the foundation for control of the corporate governance rights of the funds of an ongoing pension plan.

A "surplus" in an ongoing defined benefit plan occurs when the value of the assets exceeds the actuarial calculation of the liabilities of the plan at the time the calculation is made.[33] Both of these values are variables, however, and their values can change dramatically as a result of exogenous factors. Obviously, the value of the assets of the fund will vary with the market value of the securities that constitute those assets.[34] At times, the values of these securities may be extremely volatile, and a surplus today may be eroded or vanish tomorrow.[35] As well, the assumptions about future returns on assets may become too conservative as a result of inflation's increasing the returns. Of course, while inflation will increase the investment returns of the pension fund, it also erodes the purchasing power of the defined benefits promised to the employees under the plan. One of the options facing an employer in this situation is to use the increased earnings to increase the promised pension benefits in order to offset the erosion of purchasing power as a result of inflation. If the employer does not use the increased investment returns from inflation to counter the erosion of the pension benefits' purchasing power, a surplus may emerge.[36]

Similarly, the actuarial calculation of liabilities is founded upon assumptions about the future conduct of the corporation's business, including the dates at which employees will be seeking to retire, the turnover rate among employees, and the timing and amount of future wage increases. Obviously, changes in the actual experience (for instance, a plant shutdown) can affect the value of the liabilities of the plan by leading to early terminations of a significant number of employees and perhaps an increase in the number of employees choosing early retirement.[37] Moreover, a corporate merger, with an accompanying merger of the pension plans, can dramatically increase the liabilities of the merged pension plan.

All of these factors combine to emphasize the contingent nature of any "surplus" in an ongoing plan. It is not until a plan is terminated with all assets liquidated and all liabilities paid out that one can determine with certainty the existence and amount of any surplus. The Supreme Court of Canada clearly accepted this characterization of a pension surplus in *Schmidt v. Air Products* when Mr. Justice Cory wrote:

> Once funds are contributed to the pension plan they are "accrued benefits" of the employees. However, the benefits are of two distinct types. Employees are first entitled to the defined benefits provided under the plan. This is

> an amount fixed according to a formula. The other benefit to which the employees may be entitled is the surplus remaining upon termination. This amount is never certain during the continuation of the plan. Rather, the surplus exists only on paper. It results from actuarial calculations and is a function of the assumptions used by the actuary. Employees can claim no entitlement to surplus in an ongoing plan because it is not definite. The right to any surplus is crystallized only when the surplus becomes ascertainable upon termination of the plan. Therefore, the taking of a contribution holiday represents neither an encroachment upon the trust nor a reduction of accrued benefits.
>
> Similar reasoning explains why I cannot accept the proposition that an employer entitled to take a contribution holiday must also be entitled to recover surplus on termination.
>
> While a plan which takes the form of a trust is in operation, the surplus is an actuarial surplus. Neither the employer nor the employees have a specific interest in this amount, since it only exists on paper, although the employee beneficiaries have an equitable interest in the total assets of the fund while it is in existence. When the plan is terminated, the actuarial surplus becomes an actual surplus and vests in the employee beneficiaries. The distinction between actual and actuarial surplus means that there is no inconsistency between the entitlement of the employer to contribution holidays and the disentitlement of the employer to recovery of the surplus on termination. The former relies on actuarial surplus, the latter on actual surplus.[38]

Thus, the employer's interest in surplus, if any, is restricted solely to any surplus that may exist after the plan is terminated. Until that time, it is the employees who, in the words of the Court, have an "equitable interest in the total assets of the fund." However, employers have another claim that is used to justify their control over the investment decisions in an ongoing defined benefit plan. The claim is that because the benefit levels are "defined" regardless of the actual earnings on the pension fund's investments, the employer bears all the "risk" of investment performance that falls below the rate of return assumed in the actuarial calculations of the level of contributions required. The claim is that the employer thus assumes the burden of any additional contributions required to make up the funding shortfall from investment earnings below assumed rates.

The Question of "Risk" in a Defined Benefit Plan

On closer examination, however, the employer's claim is not as straightforward as it may initially appear. The employees may bear the ultimate incidence of the costs of both the initial contribution and any additional contributions required to fund the promised benefit. This is because the costs of these contributions can be passed on to employees in the form of reductions in the amount of future increases in the cash portion of the employees' total compensation. In addition, the employer receives a reward for bearing this "risk" in the form of "contribution holidays" during periods when the fund has a surplus sufficient to fund the costs of current pension obligations. Finally, most defined benefit plans do not require the employer to use surplus funds to protect the defined benefit from the erosive effects of inflation; thus, the employees' benefits in real purchasing power may be much lower than the benefit they bargained for originally.

The issue of "risk" arises only when the question of the employer's obligation to make subsequent contributions required by pension legislation to maintain benefits is under discussion. It does not arise with respect to the initial contribution because it is well recognized that such contributions are merely a portion of the total compensation package provided by the employer in return for employees' services. Such contributions, provided they earn exactly the rate of return assumed by the actuary in calculating the cost of benefits earned in the year the contributions were made, can be considered only "deferred compensation" for those services. They are deferred compensation because the employee chose to receive compensation for current services rendered at some future date in the form of the contribution + earnings formula implicit in the defined benefit pension plan promise. Clearly, the employee could have received the amount of the contribution as wages instead, and invested it in order to defer it in the same fashion.

But what happens if the contributions earn less than the assumed rate of return? Under applicable pension legislation, a plan sponsor of a defined benefit plan must contribute additional amounts in order to eliminate any deficiency in the plan's funding revealed by comparing the value of the plan's assets with its payment obligations.[39] Where the current value of the assets is less than the amount required to pay all benefits if the plan was terminated, the pension plan is said to have a "solvency deficiency". However, the legislation does not require that the contribution be made in one lump sum; rather, it may be amortized over a number of years.[40] Thus the "shock" of additional payments is ameliorated by the ability to spread them out over time. In addition, there is some evidence that, just like the initial payments, the additional payments may be eventually offset through concessions in future increases in wages or benefits.[41]

The second way in which employees bear the risk of lower than expected investment returns in defined benefit plans is the risk of the employers' insolvency while the plan is underfunded. In such a case, employees will receive only that portion of the pension benefits for which there is funding available at the time of the insolvency. Even in jurisdictions in which a form of pension benefit insurance is provided, the amount of benefit insured is limited, and the level of insured benefit may be much lower than the benefits provided by the pension plan of the insolvent employer.[42] In recent cases where the employer undertook a restructuring process under insolvency legislation, employers have gained a concession from regulators and plan members in which the solvency deficiency in the pension plan is liquidated over a longer period than the five years provided for under pension legislation. Thus, employees assume a greater level of risk (because of the delay in liquidating the solvency deficit) than provided for under legislation.[43]

Pensions and the Risks of Erosion Following Retirement

Very few private sector pension plans have benefits that are indexed to inflation. This leaves retirees' benefits vulnerable to erosion by inflation. While nothing prevents plan sponsors from using surplus funds in the plan to increase benefits for retirees, there are few economic benefits for an employer who follows such a course of action. Employers may also use surplus pension funds to fund the cost of their pension obligations to current employees and/or to fund increased benefits for such employees. Thus, it is possible to have retirees whose pensions have sharply reduced purchasing power due to inflation, while at the same time employers are utilizing surplus pension funds generated by that same inflationary trend to pay their current contribution obligations to the pension plan. To the extent that one accepts that there is an initial trade-off between the wage portion of the compensation package and the cost of the pension contribution, then the employers' claim to be able to utilize the gains from investment performance is weakened.[44] Of course, the reduction in the employer's current pension contributions may lead to increased cash compensation to current employees, if the labour market is efficient in preventing the employer from extracting rents from the situation. Thus, the risks of inflation are likely to be borne by retiree-beneficiaries in the defined benefit plan, not employers.

All of these risks undercut the claim by employers that they are the ultimate risk-bearers with respect to the investment performance of a defined benefit pension fund. An employer can transfer the burden of the extra payments it must make to keep the pension fund solvent to its current employees in determining the amount of future compensation increases. If the employer is unable to make the payments due to its own insolvency, then it is the employees whose benefits are reduced as a result. The second basis for employer claims of a voice in the investment of the fund is that when the pension funding arrangement is viewed through the lens of economic analysis, both employers and employees are beneficiaries and settlors of the pension fund. Fischel and Langbein contrast the pension trust with the classic trust by constructing a model in which, because the arrangement is mutually beneficial, both parties must be treated as trust beneficiaries.[45] However, their model appears to confuse two differing types of benefits and treat them as if they both arose from the administration of the trust. In fact, the benefits that accrue to the employer (decreased costs for recruitment and training arising from greater employee retention through the provision of defined pension benefits, and the tax benefits accruing to registered pension plans) arise from the existence of the pension plan, not from its investment performance. In contrast, the benefits transferred to employee-beneficiaries through the pension trust fund (benefits funded by the earnings on the investment of contributions made on their behalf in the form of deferred wages) arise directly from the trust's administration and require that they be considered its only beneficiaries.

The Case for Beneficial Ownership in the CPP

This equitable interest in pension funds discussed in *Schmidt* is even clearer in the case of the CPP funds. They are contributed to the CPP fund for the sole purpose of providing the benefits under the CPP legislation. Although individual contributors may not be able to claim individual property rights in the funds' assets, the situation is similar to that of any other defined benefit pension plan in which the employee-beneficiaries have an equitable claim on the funds' assets.[46] The legislation creating the CPP fund requires that all contributions be deposited into the CPP Account in the Consolidated Revenue Fund of Canada.[47] The legislation also makes it clear that the amounts available for benefits under the CPP are limited to the funds in the CPP Account.[48] Thus the CPP is not an open-ended commitment by the government to fund the CPP benefits, but rather a benefit plan funded entirely by contributions and investment income. As such, it is more akin to the private sector pension plans than to a government benefit program funded from general tax revenue. In view of the discretion granted to the federal Minister of Finance and the Canada Pension Plan Investment Board (CPPIB) over the investment of the fund, it is likely subject to a trust, whose beneficiaries are the plan participants whose contributions fund the benefits.[49]

Now that these funds are beginning to be invested in securities other than the non-marketable fixed rate provincial bonds in which they were invested until 1998, the issue of the corporate governance stance of those CPP funds that invested in corporate securities will become increasingly important. The decision to broaden the investments of the CPP to include marketable securities was accompanied by legislation that put the investments of the CPP fund in the hands of an appointed board, the CPPIB.[50] The CPPIB is a federal Crown corporation whose board of directors is appointed by the federal Minister of Finance in consultation with the provinces.[51]

The *Canada Pension Plan Investment Board Act* provides the following limitation on the CPPIB's investment discretion:

5. The objects of the Board are
   (a) to manage any amounts that are transferred to it under section 111 of the Canada Pension Plan Act in the best interests of the contributors and beneficiaries under that Act; and
   (b) to invest its assets with a view to achieving a maximum rate of return, without undue risk of loss, having regard to the factors that may affect the funding of the Canada Pension Plan and the ability of the Canada Pension Plan to meet its financial obligations.[52]

This language clearly indicates that the CPPIB owes a fiduciary duty to the plan participants with respect to its investment activities, and that the plan participants have an equitable interest in those funds and their investment.

Following this review of the "ownership" interests of the plan participants in the assets of the various forms of retirement savings plans, another key issue arises. Is the exercise of the corporate governance rights attached to the securities held by the plan an asset of the plan?

Corporate Governance Rights as Plan Assets

Pension Plans

In the United States, the Department of Labor takes the position that fiduciaries of employee benefit plans must exercise their voting rights as part of their fiduciary duty to manage the assets of the plan.[53] While the legislation and pension regulators in Canada are not quite so blunt, it is likely that the United States position properly reflects the scope of the fiduciary duties of pension plan trustees or administrators.[54] At present, the express requirements in Canadian legislation applicable to private pension plans is that the fiduciaries exercise due care in the investment and management of fund assets.[55] Pension regulators also require that these trustees or administrators formally adopt a written statement of investment policies and procedures (SIPP) that sets out the plan's asset allocation strategy and the categories of assets in which investments may be made. These SIPPs generally must also set out the plan's proxy voting policies.[56]

Ordinarily, a pension plan's trustees or administrators do not make specific investments on behalf of the plan, but rather delegate those duties to professional investment managers. However, the agreement with the investment managers must clearly delegate the responsibility for exercising the voting rights attached to the investments, otherwise that responsibility remains that of the trustees or administrators. Even where the voting responsibility is delegated, the trustees or administrator maintain the responsibility of monitoring the voting activities of the investment managers, who act as their agents.[57] There are limits to the fiduciary obligation to exercise the voting rights of securities, however, and those limits are effective at the point where the cost of exercising the vote outweighs the potential benefits.[58] Thus, the fiduciary of a registered pension plan in Canada is likely to be obligated by fiduciary duty to exercise the voting rights attached to the plan's investments, unless the costs outweigh any reasonable expectation of benefits to the plan's participants.

The CPP Investment Fund

The CPPIB has evolved over time. Originally, it invested only in equities and delegated its voting rights to the external investment managers who manage its investments. The CPPIB instructed these managers to vote for shareholder proposals on the basis of whether they are likely to add value to a company and its shareholders.[59] As the CPP Investment Fund has grown, however, so has its willingness to take a more active role in corporate governance and the assessment of the role environmental, social, and governance (ESG) factors play in the value of its investee companies. This willingness is reflected in the recent decision of the CPPIB to sign the United Nations Principles for Responsible Investment and in its new "Responsible Investment" Policy.[60]

Until February 2007, the CPPIB's Social Investing Policy was that it would not exclude any investment that was lawful to invest in from consideration; it would not prefer or exclude investments based on non-investment criteria; and it would take corporate behaviour concerning ESG factors "into account" in its investment decisions.[61] The new Responsible Investment Principles are a much more sophisticated and nuanced statement of engagement with investee corporations on a number of issues:

- The overriding duty of the CPP Investment Board, consistent with its mandate, is to maximize investment returns without undue risk.
- Portfolio diversification is an effective way to maximize long-term risk-adjusted returns.
- Portfolio constraints either increase risk or reduce returns over time.
- Recognizing that the importance of environmental, social, and governance (ESG) factors varies across industries, geography, and time, responsible corporate behaviour with respect to ESG factors can generally have a positive influence on long-term corporate performance.
- Disclosure is the key that allows investors to better understand, evaluate, and assess potential risk and return, including the potential impact of ESG factors on a company's performance.
- Investment analysis should incorporate ESG factors to the extent that they affect long-term risk and return.
- There should be a clear division of authority and responsibilities among shareholders, directors, and managers.

- Employees, customers, suppliers, governments, and the community at large have a vested interest in positive corporate conduct and long-term business performance.

Unlike previous policies, the Policy on Responsible Investment provides guidance to CPPIB employees and investment managers about the defining characteristics of ESG factors, thus enabling them to defend their decisions on whether or not to take action on the grounds specified in the policy. The characteristics of environmental, social, and governance factors are that they:

- are the focus of public concern
- have a medium to long-term horizon
- are qualitative and are not readily quantifiable in monetary terms
- reflect externalities not well captured by market mechanisms
- are often the focus of a tightening policy and regulatory framework
- arise throughout a company's supply chain.[62]

The CPPIB issued new proxy voting guidelines together with its Policy on Responsible Investment. It reports that the CPPIB has contracted with Institutional Shareholder Services (ISS) to vote its shares in accordance with the guidelines based on ISS proxy research on the issues in a particular corporation. ISS makes a recommendation to the CPPIB based on the research and guidelines, and CPPIB may change the vote if it disagrees with the recommendation.[63] The issue still plaguing the Policy on Responsible Investing is the absence of detailed criteria as to the elements of responsible corporate behaviour in such areas. Is it sufficient that corporations merely abide by minimum legal standards?

The absence of explicit criteria for measuring responsible behaviour threatens to render the policy meaningless, or at least make it difficult to assess compliance.[64] The policy does make it clear, however, that the CPPIB is responsible for both the decisions about whether a corporation has exhibited responsible behaviour and how the corporation's behaviour is "taken into account" in various decisions, which is an improvement on earlier practice, in which the CPPIB had delegated decisions about proxy votes to various investment managers with whom it had contracted, with only the most general of instructions to vote for proposals that would add value to the corporation and its shareholders.[65] It has thus removed these intensely value-laden decisions from essentially unaccountable financial sector companies. These companies and their employees are driven by the incentives of the capital markets to maximize short-term stock prices. Thus, when "taking into account" the long-term beneficial effects of responsible corporate behaviour, their incentive is to apply a deep discount to those effects versus the short-term downward pressure on stock prices generated by recording the costs associated with responsible behaviour on the corporate balance sheet.[66] In the new Proxy Voting Principles, the CPPIB has expressly recognized that these two factors may lead to widely differing decisions: "We oppose resolutions that are likely to diminish long-term shareholder value even though they may produce short-term gains. It is profit growth that ultimately drives returns on equities. Management's priority should be to enhance sustainable long-term profitability."[67]

The evolution of the CPP Investment Board from a body that was wary of "non-investment criteria" in its investment decisions to one that has signed the UN Principles for Responsible Investment and agreed to pursue environmental, social, and governance issues with its investee corporations occurred without any substantial public debate. If one accepts that this transformation involved implicit choices that privileged certain normative considerations over others, such choices ought to have been made after a full public debate. Neither the interests of employee-beneficiaries and the public in corporate social responsibility nor the public's interest in the effects of investment decisions of large institutional investors on the domestic economy have been provided a voice in the CPPIB's deliberations. There is still no means by which the CPP Investment Board is required to be accountable to these interests, in addition to its statutory obligation to obtain the maximum rate of return without undue risk of loss

The next chapter reviews the legal regime applicable to the investment and corporate governance activities of retirement savings funds. It analyzes the legal impediments and incentives created by the regime that affect the employee-beneficiaries' ability to require trustees and fiduciaries to be accountable to them for corporate governance decisions.

3

The Duties of Pension Fund Managers towards Plan Members with Respect to the Governance of Investee Corporations

Trust Law

Trust law is at the heart of the funding arrangements that have driven the pension funds and other retirement savings arrangements to their present position as major forces in the capital markets of North America, and increasingly in global capital markets. Its strong fiduciary obligations provide the necessary binding force to the promises from the employer of future benefits in return for present service. Trust law, however, also contains doctrinal strands that are inconsistent with a desire that the wishes of the beneficiaries concerning the management of the trust should be considered by the trustees. These doctrines stem from its origins as a law designed to protect the intentions of the (usually deceased) settlor with respect to a gratuitous transfer of wealth through the trust to vulnerable (and often unborn) beneficiaries.[1] These doctrines allow the trustees to ignore the beneficiaries' wishes or even to cause them harm, where such harm is required by the express provisions of the trust.

Before discussing these doctrines, it is important to reiterate that my principal argument is that the corporate governance tools provided by the pension funds' investments ought to be exercised so as to further the employee-beneficiaries' interests, both economic and non-economic. It is difficult to conceive of a pension fund, or mutual fund trust agreement or trust declaration, in which it was expressly required that the trustees must exercise the trust funds' corporate governance tools so as to harm the non-economic interests of the employee-beneficiaries. It is much more likely that the trust agreement or declaration and the applicable legislation will be silent, or require that the trustees perform their fiduciary duties with respect to the investment and administration of the trust fund. Thus, the real issues are whether or not trustees are required to exercise the trust funds' corporate governance tools to further the non-economic interests of the employee-beneficiaries and, if so, whether and how they must be accountable to employee-beneficiaries for their decisions.

Trust law does not provide a complete answer to these issues. The main trust law fiduciary duties that are said to create barriers to the use of pension funds to further the interests of their beneficiaries in socially responsible corporate governance are the duties of loyalty and prudence.[2] The argument based on these duties is that they require that trustees not sacrifice the financial interests of the employee-beneficiaries in order to further other interests of some, a majority, or all of the beneficiaries by embarking on a program of socially responsible corporate governance activities.

There are several assumptions in this argument that are contestable. First, there is the assumption that furthering the financial interests is incompatible with furthering the non-financial interests of employee-beneficiaries. The second assumption is that at the time the investment or corporate governance decision is being contemplated by the trustees, the impact of that decision on the employee-beneficiaries' financial interests is completely predictable. Finally, there is the assumption that the financial interests of the employee-beneficiaries in a pension trust fund are capable of being clearly defined separately and in opposition to their other interests at the time the fund is contemplating the particular decision or investment. If all of these assumptions are contestable, then the issue arises as to whether it is more appropriate that the employee-beneficiaries provide the guidelines on these choices to the trustees, or that the trustees or the investment managers decide without any input from the employee-beneficiaries.

Clark, in his extensive study of the Anglo-American pension fund investment industry, makes this point clearly in discussing the debate over Economically Targeted Investments (ETI) of pension funds in the United States during the Clinton presidency:

> While Langbein and others are right to emphasize the fiduciary duties of trustees, this particular institution is not now an adequate or realistic depiction of the scope of the relationships normally encompassing investment decision making. It is *inevitable* that pension funds take into account the social and political consequences of their investments. The real issue is how to regulate such accounting practices given the interests of the plan beneficiaries, the overarching social importance of protecting the integrity of private pension systems, and the threats of recklessness and corruption which pervades the investment management industry in general.[3]

Clark points out that there is a fundamental problem in the agency relationships between trustees and investment managers that undermines any claims that determining what the trustees' fiduciary duty requires with respect to investment choices is a relatively simple matter. The problem is that the very foundation of the investment management industry, predictability of future performance based on past performance, is implausible.

Clark cites evidence that average investment manager performance lags behind overall market performance, once fees are taken into account.[4] He also points out that trustees are risk-averse, given the enormous disparity between their personal wealth and the investments for whose returns they are accountable. Trustees must operate in a decision-making framework in which risk and uncertainty must be managed, while taking what in reality amounts to a gamble. Thus, he argues that trustees' decision making cannot reproduce the decision making of the risk-neutral rational market portfolio investor.[5]

As discussed in Chapter 1, these trustees are also subject to the pressures of interests that conflict with those of the beneficiaries. It is important to remember that for many private sector pension funds, the employers' management, not the employee-beneficiaries, appoints the trustees. Those managers have little or no interest in encouraging the practice of active intervention by pension fund trustees in corporate governance. To reiterate the points made in Chapter 1, Mark Roe points out that a core problem for active corporate intervention by institutional investors is managerial control of the bulk of the private sector pension funds.[6] The potential for conflicts of interest is present in managerial control over pension funds, and recent history with respect to conflicts arising when financial markets analysts are employees of investment banking firms has shown that pressure will be exerted despite analysts' ostensible independence.[7] Roe reports instances of similar pressure being exerted by managers on pension fund fiduciaries to vote with management in proxy fights, as well as the attempts by investment management firms to keep from having to cast proxy votes in order to avoid giving offence to potential clients.[8] One case that gained some notoriety involved the change by Deutsche Bank of its vote on the merger between Hewlett-Packard and Compaq after the bank's proxy voting division was told by Hewlett-Packard management that the vote was of great importance to their ongoing relationship.[9] At the time of the vote, the investment banking division of Deutsche Bank was advising on the merger and receiving fees for that advice from Hewlett-Packard. Although the Securities and Exchange Commission (SEC) ultimately fined Deutsche Bank $750,000 for failing to disclose a material conflict of interest to its investment clients, a subsequent challenge to the validity of the vote in favour of the merger was dismissed in Delaware Chancery Court.[10] The Court held that, while it was "troubling" that the discussion between the proxy voting division and Hewlett-Packard management was arranged by the investment banking division, the discussion itself contained no threats or coercion and the decision of the proxy voting division was based on consideration of the best interests of the beneficial shareholders. However, the foundational doctrines of fiduciary duties to the beneficiaries and compliance with the settlor's intention do provide a legal basis for the claim that trustees' obligations include accounting to the employee-beneficiaries for corporate governance decisions.

The Conflict over the Duties of Loyalty and Prudence

The duty of loyalty requires trustees to act in the best interests of the beneficiaries and to treat all beneficiaries in an evenhanded fashion. The duty of prudence (sometimes called the duty of care) requires that the trustees invest the fund in the same manner as a prudent individual investing the property of another person.[11] Much of the commentary and the judicial decision making over whether or not these duties have been breached has occurred with respect to "socially responsible investing," in which trustees screen out potential investments on social grounds, or, alternatively, choose their investments based on social grounds.[12] Another form of socially responsible investment practice is the economically targeted investment, where the investment generates some form of indirect financial benefit for the employee-beneficiaries, perhaps in the form of increased employment opportunities, job security, or economic development of their local community. A third type of activity that may conflict with the duties of loyalty and prudence is shareholder advocacy, where the trustees seek to bring about changes in the corporation's activities that provide (usually) indirect benefits to the employee-beneficiaries through the use of influence over management derived from their powers and rights as shareholders.[13] These benefits may range from improvements in socially responsible behaviour that internalize some of the costs that would otherwise be externalized through negative social, human resources, or environmental practices to improved long-term economic results generated by encouragement of investment in projects with longer timelines for generating returns.

The first point that needs to be made regarding these socially responsible investment and shareholder advocacy activities is that they do not necessarily conflict with the duties of loyalty or prudence, however strictly construed.[14] If the use of social or non-financial criteria is reasonably connected to the financial benefit of the trust fund, then the investment decision or advocacy will probably not be a breach of these duties.[15] In fact, prudence may dictate an evaluation of a corporation's performance on grounds that traditionally have been viewed as socially responsible criteria, such as the environment or employment practices, which are examples of such criteria considered by the CPPIB in its social investment policy and proxy voting guidelines.[16] Pension regulators have not taken the position that socially responsible investing is imprudent *per se,* but rather have contented themselves with reminding trustees of their fiduciary duties in relation to investments in discussing the issue.[17]

Notwithstanding the foregoing discussion, the trust law doctrines that are the source of the greatest objection to the utilization of pension fund investments to further the interests of the employee-beneficiaries are those concerning the trustees' duty to productively invest the funds. Quite simply, the objection is that investing with a view to any goal other than the maximization of return on investment is a breach of the trustees' fiduciary duties of prudence and loyalty.[18] Despite the apparently simple nature of this objection, however, there are complicating factors that detract from its initial simplicity.

First and foremost, as discussed above in the context of including or excluding potential investments on socially responsible criteria, the goals of maximization of return and socially responsible corporate activity are not necessarily mutually exclusive. Langbein and Posner note that certain investments based on social investing criteria have been accepted by US regulators on the grounds that they were economically equivalent to those that might have been chosen without reference to such criteria, and their substitution was costless in relation to these alternatives. The authors point out that such costless alternatives are limited.[19] However, their economic objections to social screening of initial investments is that the resulting portfolios are underdiversified in relation to an unscreened portfolio, and thus the undiversified risk is increased, as is the administrative cost. Their argument would have more force if the legal standard for pension fund investments was the passive portfolio of diversified investments, a standard that they had earlier argued was the only rational standard for prudent trust investments.[20] Instead, it appears that many pension fund investment managers are engaged in active stock trading strategies, holding an average share less than two years and losing money in comparison with the performance of major indexes, according to a 1992 study.[21] In a study undertaken in the 1980s of the costs of divesting South Africa–related corporate securities in the portfolio of a large public service pension plan, the authors claimed that, using a computer program, they were able to construct an efficient portfolio from remaining securities. They concluded that the only increase in the anticipated costs of the retirement plan would be a fraction of a percent increase as a result of the transaction costs of divestment and the slight increase in the worst-case scenario pension costs from a small increase in the portfolio risk of the plan's corporate securities investments.[22]

Even if there were some losses to the fund rate of return as a result of the use of socially responsible criteria in screening investments, some scholars have argued that their use can be justified on the same grounds that the courts have used to justify permitting corporate management to make charitable gifts. Edward Adams and Karl Knutsen point out that the courts gradually expanded the scope of corporate management's power to utilize corporate resources to make charitable gifts on the grounds that such giving constituted a direct benefit to the corporation.[23] In later years, the courts also adopted the rationale that such behaviour was consistent with corporate citizenship obligations that accompanied the shift in the concentration of wealth from individual to corporate control. They argued that the more recent shift of wealth from corporate shareholders to pension fund investments justifies allowing the funds to undertake socially responsible investment practices in a manner that is consistent with their fiduciary duties. By recognizing that the beneficiaries are also part of a community and thus would share in the benefits of socially responsible investment, the courts could extend the permissible boundaries of fiduciary duty as they did in the case of corporate charitable giving. Permitting socially responsible investing enables the communities to access to some of the benefits of the investment of pension funds to which these communities have granted significant tax concessions, in the same way that extending charitable corporate giving gave society access to the wealth controlled by corporations.[24]

This is especially so in the case of a decision about how to exercise one's vote, once a decision to invest has been made. The ease with which one can disentangle the issues of maximization of return and responsible corporate behaviour may decrease as the time period over which the investment will be held increases.[25] That is, a case can be made that responsible corporate behaviour is costly in relation to irresponsible behaviour provided one restricts one's measurement of the costs and benefits to the period of the first quarter after the decision.[26] It is in that quarter that the costs of responsible behaviour will likely show up on the balance sheet, as will the supposed benefits of irresponsible behaviour. The costs of the irresponsible behaviour, whether it is polluting the environment or destroying the trust of your workforce by misleading them about job security, will show up only later, and perhaps late enough that the connection with the earlier irresponsibility is difficult to make. Analyzing the opposite hypothesis, Marc Orlitzky and colleagues found a positive relationship between corporate social performance and corporate financial performance in a meta-analysis of fifty-two previous event studies.[27] They concluded that reputation was an important mediator of the relationship. Thus, it would be wrong to characterize the relationship between socially responsible behaviour by a corporation and corporate financial performance as a trade-off. A better view would be that corporate social responsibility goals ought to be pursued by pension plan trustees because they are likely to benefit the plan members' social and physical environment without posing a substantial risk to their retirement security.

Finally, there is the issue of the legitimacy of considering benefits to the employee-beneficiaries in addition to the financial benefits to the fund when making investment and corporate governance decisions. Gil Yaron reviews a number of US and United Kingdom cases that have come down on both sides of this issue. Much seems to depend on whether the courts perceived an immediate connection between the proposed investments and the benefits to be provided to the beneficiaries, as well as whether the trustees exercised diligence in investigating the economic consequences of the investment.[28] These benefits can vary from investment in the geographic region in which the employee-beneficiaries reside that increases the general economic health of that region to investments that will generate increased or continued employment opportunities for employee-beneficiaries.[29] They will also involve consideration of the collateral effects of proposed leveraged buyouts or mergers and acquisitions to the extent that shareholders, including pension fund investment managers, have a voice in the decision.[30]

Do the Cases Require Trustees to Ignore Considerations of Social Responsibility and Collateral Benefits to Plan Participants?

Two cases are most often cited for the proposition that consideration of any criteria other than the maximization of return on investments is a breach of the trustees' fiduciary duties of prudence and loyalty. They are *Cowan v. Scargill*[31] from the English Court of Chancery and *Blankenship v. Boyle*[32] in the United States federal court system. While both of these cases dealt with trustee actions at the behest of the unions who represented the active employee-members of the benefit plans, another case in the US federal courts, *Donovan v. Bierworth,* set limits on the actions of trustees that the court found to be advancing the interests of corporate management rather than those of the plan members.[33]

Cowan v. Scargill was a case brought against union-appointed trustees of a coal miners' pension plan by the management-appointed trustees because the union-appointed trustees wished to freeze investments in foreign companies, divest existing foreign investments when it was opportune, and cease investments in energy companies that competed with the coal industry. The pension plan was funded by both employee and employer contributions. The union-appointed trustees' position reflected the position expressed by the union's members through their national convention. At the hearing, the union's president, Arthur Scargill, acted as spokesperson for the union trustees. According to the Court, Scargill never provided any specific justification for the ban on foreign investment, other than the most general claim that it would be for the benefit of the plan's beneficiaries.[34] The defendants did, however, file affidavits of experts with respect to the effects of investment in the United Kingdom that the court summarized as follows:

> The general thrust of the defendants' evidence in support of the restrictions that they seek to impose was along the following lines. Pensions funds in Britain have enormous assets. If all, or nearly all, of these assets were invested in Britain, and none, or few, were invested overseas, this would do much to revive this country's economy and so benefit all workers, especially if the investments were in the form not of purchasing established

> stocks and shares but of "real" investment in physical assets and new ventures. For the mineworkers' scheme, the prosperity of the coal industry would aid the prosperity of the scheme, and so lead to benefits for the beneficiaries under the scheme. This point was put in various ways, and a short summary necessarily omits many facets; but in the end the approach seems to me to have been along these general lines.[35]

The Court found that the possibility of benefits that might accrue to the plan's members from the potential economic upturn "too speculative and remote" to justify the restrictions on investments in whole classes of assets. It also rejected the argument that restricting investments in coal industry competitors would benefit the plan members because the plan was fully funded and therefore benefits would be paid to retirees regardless of the future economic health of coal mining in the United Kingdom.[36] Therefore, a substantial portion of the plan's members (the retirees) had no direct interest in the economic health of that industry and would not share in any benefits that might arise from refusing to invest in competing industries. The Court's reasoning appears to break down at this point, however.

If retirees were disinterested in the financial health of coal mining because the coal industry plan was fully funded and a defined benefit plan, then the union-appointed trustees' investment scheme would not adversely affect their financial interests. Their benefits would not be affected by either adverse or favourable financial returns because their benefits were guaranteed in either event. It would be the interests of the coal industry and current employees that would be adversely affected by poor financial results due to restrictions on investments in competitors and foreign companies, as they would have to increase contributions in order to maintain full funding of future benefits.[37] Now it appeared from the Court's decision that Mr. Scargill claimed that the union's members supported the policy on investment from the local membership through to the national convention. Nevertheless, the Court felt that the benefits that were supposed to accrue to either the coal industry or the national economy from the union's policy were extremely unlikely to result from the investment activity of only one (albeit large) pension fund, when balanced against the risk of loss from excluding investment in a whole sector of the economy.[38]

Blankenship v. Boyle involved another coal-mining fund. It was not only a pension fund, however, but also provided payments for sickness, accidents, medical expenses, hospital expenses, and workers' compensation payments. It was funded by a royalty on each ton of coal mined by union coal operators, and its yearly royalty payments of $163.1 million only exceeded its welfare and pension expenditures of $152 million by $11.1 million in 1968. The court found that the fund was held in cash in a union-owned bank instead of being invested in securities that would have earned more income while still providing any needed liquidity. It also found that the fund had made certain investments in utility companies in order to advance the interests of the union and coal operators in having these utilities use union-mined coal, and thus the investments were a breach of trust. The trustees' duty was to invest in the sole interest of the beneficiaries, and considering the interest of the union and coal operators in making investment decisions was not complying with that duty. The court did not discuss the fact that increased coal sales would also increase the royalties paid to the fund.[39]

The case law does not discuss the effect of an investment on the income of the fund until the case of *Withers v. Teachers' Retirement System of the City of New York*.[40] This retirement plan was designed to be fully funded, but in 1970 substantial retroactive benefits were granted that created an unfunded liability in the plan. The amount of the city's annual contributions far exceeded the amount of employee contributions and investment earnings, and without the city's contributions, the retirement plan would use up its assets within seven to ten years. The City of New York was about to go bankrupt unless the Retirement System agreed to buy $860 million of its below investment-grade bonds. After insisting on some conditions that slightly enhanced the potential payments that would be made, the trustees agreed, being convinced that the alternative was the end of city contributions. After they agreed to do so, some retirees, who claimed that the trustees were acting to preserve the active teachers' jobs by sacrificing the financial security of retirement benefits, sued the trustees. The court held that the trustees did not breach their duties because continued contributions were essential to the interests of all beneficiaries of the fund. The court found that there was no priority of duties to the retirees, a substantial proportion of whom would have been adversely affected if the retirement plan funds were exhausted in the next seven to ten years. Thus, *Blankenship v. Boyle* is modified to the extent that the availability of continued employer contributions, where those contributions are a key factor in the continued provision of benefits, may be considered by trustees in their investment decisions without breach of their fiduciary duties.

In *Donovan v. Bierworth*,[41] corporate management, sitting as the pension plan trustees, responded to a hostile takeover bid by refusing to tender the plan's shares to the bidder at a $20 per share premium. They also purchased even more of the corporation's shares on the open market at the higher prices that followed the announcement of the bid. The trustees claimed that they acted out of concern for the potential fate of the pension plan in the hands of a highly leveraged bidder and the fact that the bid made the stock a good buy. Although the court did not say that these were improper considerations, it refused to believe that the trustees gave the matter sufficient consideration during a two-hour meeting in which they received no expert advice from investment advisors or independent legal advisors.[42]

The courts, however, have permitted pension fund trustees to undertake controversial investment strategies where they were able to demonstrate careful consideration of all the relevant factors before deciding on the strategy. In *Donovan v. Walton,* the US Secretary of Labor charged union trustees with breaching their fiduciary and statutory duties as union-appointed pension fund trustees by constructing a building on property owned by the pension fund and leasing part of it to the union, as well as by providing mortgages with the fund's assets to plan participants at rates 2 percent below those charged by banks. [43] The court found that the building project was thoroughly researched and that the rental to the union was designed to obtain a reasonable rate of return, while the benefits to the union were merely the result of a mutually beneficial transaction.[44] With respect to the mortgage loans, the court noted that plan participants had to be creditworthy and provide insurance in appropriate circumstances, and that the *Employee Retirement Income Security Act* (ERISA) provided only that loans to plan participants had to receive a reasonable rate of interest, not the prevailing rate. In addition, the mortgage loans earned the highest rate of return of the assets in the portfolio.[45]

The Maryland Court of Appeals also approved a plan by the City of Baltimore to require the trustees of its employee pension plans to divest their investments in companies that did business in South Africa during the apartheid era.[46] The Court found no violation of the trustees' fiduciary duties by using social criteria as the basis for excluding investments, provided the costs for doing so were minimal, despite the need to divest 47 percent of the plans' equity portfolios and 10 percent of their fixed income portfolios. The Court emphasized that the plans' trustees were given the power to suspend divestment if they believed that it was becoming imprudent to continue to divest. It accepted evidence that it was possible to construct a portfolio of South Africa–free investments with a comparable risk/return profile at minimal costs.[47] However, in another case in which a city council sought divestment of South African investments in its various trust funds, the court found a breach of the requirement to be prudent.[48] Even though the trust funds' investments were profitable after divestment, the court found a breach because the decision was made without an express consideration of whether or not the divestment was in the best interests of the beneficiaries, and without the advice of experts on that issue. The court did find, however, that trustees were not required to pursue maximized returns without consideration of other factors:

> I accept that the most profitable investment of funds is one of a number of matters which trustees have a duty to consider. But I cannot conceive that trustees have an unqualified duty, in terms of the first two propositions

> which counsel for the pursuer sought to draw from Cowan, simply to invest trust funds in the most profitable investment available. To accept that without qualification would, in my view, involve substituting the discretion of financial advisers for the discretion of trustees.[49]

Thus, divestment of South African investments was not *per se* a breach of trust, provided that the best interests of the beneficiaries were considered and protected in both the divestment decision and procedure.

Limitations from the Case Law

One can reach two conclusions from this brief review of some of the major cases. First, the courts have not set out a complete code on the factors that trustees of pension funds may take into account and the proper relationship among the different factors. Second, the courts will require that trustees provide proof that they considered all relevant factors and received expert advice on issues where they lacked expertise, regardless of the eventual performance of a particular investment or investment strategy. Despite somewhat sweeping and restrictive language in the early cases, however, later decisions appear more open to evidence that considering factors other than the return on the investment will not automatically be a breach of the trustees' duties.

Gil Yaron argues that the case law indicates that the duties are "flexible and open to interpretation" and that "consideration of non-financial criteria does not violate the principles of prudence and loyalty, provided that the investment decision adheres to the pension plan's investment policy and independent expert advice."[50] Freya Kodar completes her review of the case law with the conclusion that "shareholder activism, screening and economically targeted investing, often referred to collectively as socially responsible investment (SRI) can be pursued as long as the rate of return to the fund is not negatively affected."[51] Hutchinson and Cole earlier reached a similar conclusion, assigning a greater range of trustee discretion with respect to voting on social issues in corporate proxy contests.[52] The decision concerning the effects of these activities is necessarily an *ex ante* decision, and thus the judgments about the effects of considering various criteria on the rate of return will be subject to the uncertainty that accompanies estimates of future results. My point is that since these are not straightforward cause-and-effect decisions, those who will be most affected by the eventual results, the plan participants, ought to determine the policies that guide the decisions.[53] However, these scholars are merely considering the use of non-financial criteria in investment and voting decisions as a permissible activity by pension fund trustees, not a mandatory requirement of their fiduciary duties of loyalty and prudence. Benjamin Richardson concludes that the failure to consider and act on environmentally and socially related information is "not prudent in the financial sense of the word and should not be treated as prudent in the legal sense either."[54]

In order to try to clarify the legal situation of trustees asked to consider and act on environmental, social, and governance issues in their management of investments, the United Nations Environment Programme Finance Initiative Asset Management Working Group requested an opinion from Freshfields Bruckhaus Deringer, a leading global law firm, on the following question:

> Is the integration of environmental, social and governance issues into investment policy (including asset allocation, portfolio construction and stock-picking or bond-picking) voluntarily permitted, legally required or hampered by law and regulation; primarily as regards public and private pension funds, secondarily as regards insurance company reserves and mutual funds?[55]

The Freshfields opinion concludes that, given the growing recognition that ESG factors influence financial performance, consideration of these factors to more reliably predict financial performance "is clearly permissible and is arguably required in all jurisdictions."[56] It also suggests that ESG considerations must be integrated into investment decisions where there is a consensus to that effect among beneficiaries, and that ESG factors may be used as deciding factors in a choice among value-neutral alternative investments.

In order for the trustees to be truly accountable, however, they must be required to report to the plan participants on their activities in this area. In addition, they must be responsive to the plan participants' instructions with respect to the general direction of the pension fund's investment and voting activity. The seven reasons why fiduciary accountability for the exercise of corporate governance powers ought to be mandatory are as follows:

1. the need for fund fiduciaries to use corporate governance tools ("voice") rather than merely selling the securities in the market ("exit") as a means to enhance the value of the fund's securities
2. a growing recognition that corporate governance powers are a valuable asset that must be exercised for the benefit of the participants
3. the permissibility of fiduciaries' consideration of collateral benefits to participants where expected investment returns are equivalent
4. the incompatibility of individual corporate irresponsibility with the financial health of the funds' overall investment portfolio
5. the ability of pension funds as broadly diversified portfolio investors to capture a greater proportion of the benefit of public goods and positive externalities than an individual corporation

6 a growing acceptance of socially responsible corporate behaviour as an indication of firm quality
7 the presence of fundamental conflicts of interest between fiduciaries and their professional advisors, on the one hand, and plan participants, on the other, with respect to active intervention in the management of corporations.

In light of these reasons, is there anything in trust or pension law that would act as a barrier to such a mandatory rule?

Potential Barriers to Accountability

Several doctrines might have that effect. Some require fiduciaries to obey the settlor's wishes over the desires of the beneficiaries, while others require that they administer the benefits evenhandedly or require that they exercise their own judgment and not delegate certain decisions to others.

Preference for the Settlor's Express Wishes over Beneficiary Desires

The first of these doctrines is that the trustees are bound by the express intentions of the settlor with respect to their administration of the trust property, and cannot consider the wishes of the beneficiaries where they conflict with those expressed by the settlor. Even the courts do not have jurisdiction, absent legislative authority, to change the trust's terms, with a few minor and strictly construed exceptions.[57] In cases where these exceptions have been successfully invoked, however, the courts have used the device of the settlor's presumed intent as the justification for their alteration of the trust, and described their role as acting as the settlor would have acted if the settlor had foreseen the circumstances.[58]

Impartiality in the Treatment of Beneficiaries

The second doctrine is that trustees must remain impartial and not grant greater advantage or impose greater burden on one beneficiary or class of beneficiaries over another unless the terms of the trust require such treatment.[59] There are a number of ways in which plan participants may be differentially affected by corporate governance and investment decisions. The classic case involves the intergenerational conflicts that can arise between retirees and active employees over a particular investment or corporate governance decision on the grounds that it increases the risk to the retirees' benefit security in order to protect the employment security of active employees.[60] Another potential conflict may occur during a takeover of the employer's corporation. The conflict concerns whether or not to tender a pension fund's shares when the interests of those employees whose compensation includes stock options may conflict with those of employees whose compensation does not include stock options and whose jobs are at risk.[61] However, unlike the classic case where the conflicts are between life interests and those entitled to whatever portion of the trust fund remains after those entitled to a life interest have died, the conflicts inherent in pension funds in relation to corporate governance issues are part of the funds' fundamental design, in which the employer (or designated manager) acts as trustee on behalf of the employee-beneficiaries. Their interests in corporate governance by pension funds are conflicting, with the employer (as a potential subject of corporate governance activity by pension funds) adopting a policy generally supportive of the fund's portfolio companies' management.

Restrictions on Delegation of Decision-Making Responsibility

Finally, where discretion is granted, the trustees are required to exercise their own judgment in determining what course of action is in the best interests of the beneficiaries without considering or being influenced by the desires of the beneficiaries. This is consistent with the classic understanding of trusteeship as a personal obligation, one that the trustee cannot hand over to another individual unless the trust document so provides.[62]

Doctrines Applied to Pension Plans Lead in the Direction of More, Not Less, Accountability

When these doctrines are applied to pension or retirement savings trusts, however, several incongruities arise. First, the employees are the settlors (or at the very least one of the settlors) as well as the primary beneficiaries of the trust. Employees make contributions to many pension plans directly. Even where they do not contribute directly, the employer's contributions are merely that portion of their compensation package that the employees have agreed to defer through the pension plan. Thus, employees are also the settlors of the employer portion of the contributions to the plan, since the cost of these contributions is borne through reductions in their future compensation. This settlor/quasi-settlor status provides a trust law basis for requiring fiduciaries be accountable.

Second, the pension plan or retirement savings trust has been created as part of a contractual scheme in which the employees agree to perform their services for the employer and the employer promises to provide retirement income at some future date.[63] Once the employees' portion of the contract has been performed, their collective claim to an exclusive interest in the funds is sufficient for them to insist on an implicit right to control the corporate governance decisions of the fund.[64] This is especially so in light of the conflicts between their interests and the interests of corporately appointed fiduciaries and their professional advisors with respect to corporate governance activity. If the claims by pension regulators that the active exercise of corporate governance powers is a fiduciary obligation are to be taken seriously, then beneficiary accountability seems to be the only means by which fiduciaries can be stimulated into active involvement.[65]

Third, the participants of pension funds are primarily adults (although some beneficiaries may be children who are entitled to benefits resulting from their parent's participation in the plan). They are clearly capable of listening to reasoned advice and deciding on an appropriate policy. In addition, the types of decisions at issue – the corporate governance policies that should determine how proxy votes attached to the fund's investments should be exercised – are not decisions in which a particular form of specialized expertise is required, nor are they likely to have a profoundly negative effect on the fund's rate of return. Thus, they are not as crucial to the trustee's primary concern, the fund's rate of return, as are the decisions regarding the percentage of the fund's assets to be allocated to investments in stocks versus real estate.[66] Accordingly, it is inappropriate for trustees to assume a protective role with respect to proxy voting policy that insulates their decision making from guidance by the participants' interests and desires in the area of corporate governance. This is particularly the case where the potential impact on the long-term returns of the fund of corporate governance initiatives with respect to corporate social responsibility is not completely transparent to either the trustees or the plan participants.

The choice of investment and/or corporate governance decisions made by pension fund trustees is not so much a choice between investments or decisions that provide lower returns (but increased collateral benefits to participants) and those providing higher returns (but no benefits, or collateral "costs" in the form of corporate "externalization"). Rather, they are choices among highly contested normative views of the role of corporate social responsibility, in which the effects of the choice on the long-term returns to the pension fund is also highly contested. It is inappropriate that the results of these contests should be determined by the decisions of those (corporate management and investment managers) who have interests that conflict with those of the participants on the issue of corporate governance intervention in opposition to corporate management. These conflicts are compounded by the fiduciaries' personal risk aversion, which finds a refuge from that risk in the fiduciaries' traditional relationship with the investment management industry and its "expertise." By doing nothing extraordinary, the fiduciary cannot be accused of departing from the norm and thus incurring undue risk. Besides these reasons why trust doctrines that would otherwise restrict beneficiary participation ought not to operate in that fashion with respect to corporate governance issues, there are also doctrines that recognize the legitimacy of beneficiary participation in trust decision making.

Doctrines that Require the Trustee to Listen to Beneficiaries

There are two elements in the law of trusts that allow beneficiaries a voice in the administration of a trust. Their presence in the law provides another basis for the claim that trustees ought to be expressly accountable to them for voting decisions. The first is the "Rule in *Saunders v. Vauthier,*" which permits the beneficiaries of a trust to terminate the specific performance of a trust and modify or extinguish the trust, provided they are all adults capable of providing their consent and the consent is unanimous.[67] The second is legislation permitting the courts to vary the terms of a trust, on the application of some of the trust's beneficiaries, provided that the court is convinced that the proposed change is in the best interests of the beneficiaries. There is no requirement of unanimity or that all of the beneficiaries be adults before the court will grant the application.

In many jurisdictions in Canada, the variation of trust powers has been codified. The recognition of the variation of trust powers implicitly undermines the settlor's intention–dominated view of the administration of gratuitous trusts, where such a viewpoint may have some legitimacy. In the context of a pension trust, however, relying on the settlor's intention as a ground for ignoring the wishes or interests of the employee-beneficiaries has little or no legitimacy (since to all intents and purposes they are the settlors). Some concerns have been expressed about potential negative effects on the employer if the funding of pension promises in defined benefit pension plans is adversely affected by adoption of non-financial criteria and consequent poor investment performance.[68] Thus, it is assumed that an employer could legitimately object to the use of non-financial criteria by a defined benefit pension fund on the grounds that this increased its risk of having to make additional contributions. As Langbein and Posner acknowledge, however, the costs of additional contributions will be passed on to the employees through lower future wage rates. Those who actually bear the risk are current employees (whose future earnings may be reduced) and those future employees who are not currently employed but whose future earnings will be affected.

There is, however, what appears to be legitimate concerns that there may be conflicting views among the beneficiaries about the exercise of the proxy. The concern is that being subject to the rule of the majority would oppress minorities who feel strongly about some decision concerning the use of corporate governance powers. Before analyzing this concern further, it is important to be clear about the types of decisions that would be subject to beneficiary control.

First and foremost, they would be decisions about how to vote the shares in a particular corporation where an issue had arisen regarding the corporation's activities, such as discriminatory hiring practices or a policy of monitoring compliance with international labour standards by its foreign suppliers. The issue would be coming to a vote only because corporate management did not agree with the dissident shareholders' position. If there was conflict among the beneficiaries on these issues, between those who wished to support current management and those who did not, abstention would not be a third, neutral option. Abstention would, in effect, support management, since all proxies that are not returned are treated as votes for the management's position. Therefore, a decision by a majority of the beneficiaries about how the proxies should be voted in their best interests ought to govern the way the shares are voted. Since variation of trust powers allows the courts to balance conflicting interests even where some of the beneficiaries disagree, such disagreement concerning the exercise of corporate governance proxy votes ought not to allow the minority to determine the result.[69]

There are important limitations on the majority vote rule, however. These are found in the courts' supervisory powers over the administration of trusts, including their supervision of the continuing obligation of the trustees to ensure that the financial position of the fund is not sacrificed. These supervisory powers would allow either trustees or the minority of beneficiaries to apply to the court if they could show that the policy or voting instructions of the majority of beneficiaries was harmful to the long-term financial interests of the fund.

Pension Law

In many ways, pension law is a codification of trust law. However, it also provides its own incentives and impediments to the project of making pension trustees accountable to the plan's participants for their corporate governance decisions. The impetus for the creation and revision of pension law over the years has been the fundamental conflicts that exist between employees and their employers with respect to the pension promise and the funds that are used to implement that promise. Harbrecht provides a carefully researched glimpse into the sources of modern pension legislation in his review of the private pension system in the United States at the end of the 1950s.[70] There were extremely lengthy vesting periods, the employer's discretion as to whether to terminate the trust and use some other method of funding prior to vesting, pension plans that permitted employers to terminate or reduce promised benefits, and even pensions that were vested and being paid. In addition, there were few regulatory standards for funding; as a result, many pension plans' liabilities were not adequately funded.

Vesting and Funding: The Creation of the Employee-Beneficiary

In Canada, legally enforceable pension benefits were created in 1942 through income tax rules concerning tax deductibility of employer contributions to a pension plan. The contributions had to be supported by an actuarial statement that confirmed that the contribution was required to fund the pension. In addition, pension benefits had to vest once the employee retired and began to receive payments, and could not be revoked by the employer after retirement.[71] Later legislation imposed pre-retirement vesting standards and minimum funding requirements on pension plans funded through trusts. Most pension legislation now requires that employees' pension benefits vest after two years of participation in the pension plan.[72] The legislation also provides that following vesting, an employee whose employment is terminated may elect to transfer the cash value of the employee's accrued pension benefits to a personal retirement account or to the pension plan of the employee's new employer.[73] Prior to the passage of ERISA in the US in 1974, employees' claims to an interest in the funds set aside to fund their pension benefits were often denied in the courts on the grounds that their interest in the funds was merely contingent because their right to a pension benefit would not vest until their retirement.[74] Thus, the legislation has both resolved the conflicts over pension security between the employer and plan participants in favour of the participants and provided a legal foundation for their claims to an interest in the pension plan's funds.[75]

The imposition of minimum funding requirements in pension legislation has also generated the concentrated economic power of pension plans by forcing the aggregation of large amounts of capital that must be invested for the benefit of an identifiable group of beneficiaries. Yet the claims of individuals among this group must necessarily remain contingent because the nature of the pension promise is that a defined benefit would be provided for the participant and, where applicable, surviving spouse from the date of retirement until death. Since neither of these dates is known, nor are a number of other factors that would be necessary for an exact calculation of each individual's "share" of the plan's funds, the only certainty is that the entire fund is held for the benefit of all the participants collectively. Individuals' shares can only be estimated, using actuarial calculations of the probabilities of various events. Pension legislation may prescribe the parameters of some of the actuarial variables used in such calculations for determining the value of individuals' shares following their termination, since such a calculation is necessary to permit individuals to transfer the current value of their pension benefits to another retirement savings vehicle. In that case, however, one of the crucial variables – length of service – is known, unlike in the case of participants in an ongoing plan.[76]

Pension Law and Investment Policy

Pension law also sets minimum standards for the conduct of a pension plan's investments by its fiduciaries. These standards do not restrict the categories of investments that may be purchased but rather impose a due diligence standard on the trustees' choices of investments and professional advisors. Pension legislation limits the maximum amount of a single corporation's securities that a pension fund can retain in its portfolio, however.[77] These provisions prevent the corporate managers appointed as pension fund trustees from investing a major portion of the plan's assets in the corporation's securities. These controls on concentration of the plan's assets in a single corporation's securities are not restricted only to the securities of the sponsoring corporation. The same restrictions apply with respect to securities of any other corporation, and thus provide incentives to adopt a diversified investment strategy, incentives that are reinforced by the trust law duties of prudence and loyalty. These duties require that pension investments should be diversified so as to reduce the uncompensated risk to the extent possible.[78]

These provisions are also important because they recognize that the traditional trustee/beneficiary relationship and the common law of trusts does not provide sufficient protection from the conflicts of interest between the duties trustees owe to the pension fund beneficiaries and their incentives to promote their employer's conflicting interests. These conflicts of interest are most likely to arise in areas in which the law of trusts grants trustees virtually unlimited discretionary decision-making power.

Recognizing Employer/Trustee Conflicts

One area in which pension legislation has overcome the shortcomings of trust law is with respect to information disclosure to beneficiaries. Gillese points out that the law of trusts provides that a trustee exercising discretionary decision-making power cannot be compelled by the beneficiary to give reasons for the decision.[79] Pension legislation, however, imposes a duty on trustees to disclose information concerning their decision making regarding investments in a "statement of investment policies and procedures" (SIPP) that sets out the guidelines utilized by the trustees and investment managers in their investment and corporate governance decisions.[80] The SIPP must be made available to participants, as must the plan's constitutive documents and financial reports.[81]

Thus, conflicts may arise in the context of pension plans that may prevent pension plan trustees from fully complying with their fiduciary duties to the participants. In such circumstances, pension legislation has imposed duties in addition to those imposed by the law of trusts, in order to resolve the conflict in favour of the participants. Similar conflict-resolving legislation may be required to deal with the conflicts that prevent many trustees of private pension plans from exercising their corporate governance powers to further the participants' interests in both enhanced returns from the plans' investment portfolios and collateral benefits from corporate social responsibility.

Why Not Institute Trustee Election?

Aside from the fact that the relevant pension legislation permits an employer to both sponsor and administer a pension plan, the only justification for not allowing the participants to elect the plan's trustees is expertise.[82] The concern is that the plan participants will choose those who are incapable of meeting their fiduciary obligations by properly investing the assets of the plan due to their lack of understanding of the requirements of such activities. This concern was expressed by the Senate Committee on Banking in its report on institutional investor governance in Canada.[83] Roberta Romano has pointed out, however, that the presence of trustees elected by the plan participants on public pension plan boards does not seem to affect their investment returns. There are a number of practical and theoretical issues concerning frequency of election/appointment and the appropriate decision rule for participant participation that will be discussed further in Chapter 6. First, however, the potential for, and limitations to, implementing a system of trustee accountability to participants for corporate governance decisions in our system of corporate law and securities regulation will be analyzed.

4
Corporate Law's Opportunities and Limitations for Pension Fund Corporate Governance Activity

Corporate law has a profound impact on the issues of trustees' accountability to pension plan participants and the ability of participants to exercise control over corporate decision making. The fundamental concept on which a resolution of these issues will turn is the nature of the corporation in our society. Although much of the legal analysis of the issue treats share ownership as equivalent to classic property ownership of the corporation, this is in fact not the legal paradigm that informs corporate law. Thus, when we speak of the exercise of corporate governance rights by pension fund trustees on behalf of participants, these rights are not rights to control the corporation or its assets in the manner of an owner. Rather, they are more akin, in many respects, to the rights of a member of a club or association to participate in the choice of the responsible officers and fundamental amendments to the corporation's legal rules.

Of course, a business corporation is not a club. The economic assets invested by shareholders are considerably greater than the monetary investments of most members of clubs or voluntary associations, and corporations serve as the site where the vast majority of goods and services are produced in our society. The legal analysis of the corporation has been undertaken from both an internal viewpoint[1] and an external viewpoint.[2] The internal analysis focuses on "the legal rules that directly concern the internal organization of the corporation and the conduct of corporate actors."[3] The external analysis focuses on the effects of the legal rules concerning corporations on the citizens of the wider society who are not corporate "actors." Much of the debate in corporate law has been over where one draws the line between the internal and external for the purposes of the analysis, and the description of duties owed by corporate management to various groups that follows from the line drawing. The debate over corporate constituency statutes and stakeholder analysis provides a classic illustration of this type of analysis.

Managerial "Control" of the Corporation and the Concept of "Governance" by Its Shareholders

Corporate law must account for two different kinds of phenomena that result from the corporation's legal construction. First, corporate managers exercise "control" over corporate assets, even though they do not "own" the assets. Second, those who have invested in the corporation by purchasing its securities are not liable for any legally compensable harm that may be inflicted using the assets purchased with their investments in the same way that an owner who controls the use of an asset is liable. Instead, the corporation is liable, and thus investors' liability is "limited" to the amount of their investment in the corporation. The managers who exercise control over the use of the assets are normally not personally liable for such harm either.

Applying the Concept of "Ownership" to the Governance of the Corporation

Adolph Berle and Gardiner Means have characterized the phenomena of managerial control of corporate property and the inability of the shareholders of widely held corporations to exercise the prerogatives of property ownership as the "separation of ownership and control" in their classic work.[4] They raise important issues of competence and responsibility with respect to the use of corporate assets, both with respect to investors and members of society affected by these uses.[5] Scholars have pointed out that one of the de-legitimating effects of the separation of ownership and control is that power relationships in economic production ceased to be bilateral. Relationships among those engaged in production of goods and services were subject to the indirect control exercised by the competitive market and refusal to contract. With the rise of the firm as a productive entity, however, relationships moved to direct control through hierarchical organizations of production of those relationships inside the firm. Firms also dominated production relationships outside the firm through superior economic power in supply and distribution markets.[6]

Berle and Means's analysis of the problems of competency and responsibility utilized the conceptual framework of property to illustrate the issues, possibly in reaction to the classic description of capital markets as the source of funds for entrepreneur-owners. However, the use of the property conceptual framework has been criticized because its foundational relationship, that of the owner of property, does not reflect the legal nature of the investor-manager relationship. One criticism is that the very abdication of proprietary controls that is the justification for investors' limited liability in corporate law is now treated as the source of the illegitimate exercise of power by management because that exercise is inconsistent with the status of investors as owners.[7] Assuming that the separation of ownership and control is a normal facet of a large publicly held corporation, this still leaves us with the problem of corporate social responsibility. The challenge is to design a corporate governance regime that is socially responsible and that provides coherent standards for managerial decision making.[8]

In addition, one question that can legitimately be raised concerning the attempts by institutional investors, including pension plans, to exert control over the corporations in which they have invested is whether an improvement will occur from a social responsibility viewpoint. Without accountability to and control of pension plan decisions in this area by participants, however, there is little reason to hope that an improvement will occur, given the passive response of many pension plans to the institutional investor movement during the last twenty years.[9]

Indeed, this passivity appears to predominate even where the plan's beneficiaries are unionized. Recently, a study of the social investing policies of those Canadian pension plans where trade unions represented the members of the plan was conducted using an index of twelve social investing activity criteria to measure responses to a survey. The authors reported that, of the 189 pension funds that agreed to participate, there was no social investing activity at 69 percent of the funds and that 19 percent had a positive response to only one of the items on the index.[10] Although there was a positive correlation between union representation on the board of trustees and its investment committee and the likelihood of positive response to items on the social index, the results did not achieve the level of significance, only approached it. The authors suggest that leadership, support and expertise, and trustee education are key factors in the likelihood of some form of social investing for a pension fund, while concerns about fiduciary responsibilities and inappropriate risk/return results were significant factors in the absence of social investing activity.[11] Nevertheless, recent developments in Canada indicate that a change may be occurring. In 2000, the Shareholder Association for Research and Education was created by the Canadian labour movement to provide leadership in responsible investment. It offers proxy voting and shareholder engagement services, as well as education in governance skills for pension trustees.[12] As noted earlier, there has been an increase from $65.46 billion in 2004 to $503.61 billion in 2006 in the Canadian assets under management that incorporate environmental, social, and governance (ESG) issues into their corporate governance activity, primarily as a result of the adoption of socially responsible investing by several large public sector pension funds.[13]

Before one can begin to undertake a rigorous analysis of any potential for improvement in the passive attitude of trustees towards direct accountability to plan participants, it is necessary to look at how the legal structure of corporate governance both empowers and limits plan fiduciaries' exercise of corporate governance.[14]

Formal Governance by Shareholders

Corporate law provides a number of avenues through which shareholders may exert some control over corporate policy or direction. These include electing the corporation's directors, submitting resolutions for a vote at the shareholders' meeting, either in writing or in person, commencing derivative litigation seeking to require directors and officers to act in the best interests of the corporation, and using the oppression remedy to obtain the intervention of the courts in circumstances in which corporate activity is highly prejudicial to their reasonable expectations.

One of the means by which shareholders participate in corporate governance is through the right to vote on certain matters. The right to vote can be granted either through ownership of a share that has a voting right or through a statutory right to vote on certain fundamental changes to corporate structure that affect non-voting shares as well as voting shares. The voting rights that will be the subject of most of the discussion in the rest of this book are those that attach to voting shares. A number of corporate law provisions deal with the voting and ancillary rights of such shares, including the rights to attend annual meetings, elect a board of directors, and confirm the choice of the outside auditors. In addition, voting shareholders have the right to make proposals to the other shareholders to be voted on at the annual meeting, nominate their own candidates for director, and raise any proper issue for discussion at the annual shareholders' meeting.

Until recently, however, the voting of their stockholdings by institutional investors required a fairly cumbersome process involving contractual agreements with their investment managers with respect to control of the proxy and with the Canadian Depositor for Securities Limited (CDS), which acts as the clearinghouse for many securities trades made by these investors. The need for the contractual arrangements arose because corporate law statutes entitled only the shareholder of record to vote, and often shares were held in the name of CDS or a registered broker. Thus, the means by which the actual beneficial owner of the shares was allowed to vote depended on the agreements between it, its investment managers, the brokers, and CDS to provide the service. The need to pay for such services and the fact that enforcement was available only through private law remedies for breach of contract certainly served as one disincentive for smaller pension funds to engage in active corporate governance by monitoring the voting of the shares they beneficially owned. As will be discussed later, recent amendments and additions in the corporate law and securities regimes may have reduced this disincentive.

Electing the Corporation's Directors

A corporation's directors are charged with either managing the corporation or supervising the management of the business and affairs of the corporation.[15] The model that has been adopted for most widely held corporations is that of part-time directors who assume a supervisory role over the activity of the corporation's management, with a number of those management employees also serving as directors. Corporate statutes typically limit the number of employees and officers who can serve on the board of directors, and corporations that offer their securities on some stock exchanges must meet more stringent numerical limits on the number of related directors on the board.[16] Directors are elected at the first shareholders' meeting following incorporation for terms of up to three years, and thereafter at the annual shareholders' meeting following the expiry of their term of office.[17] Thus far we have described a system that has a democratically elected body charged with the management or supervision of the management of the corporation's affairs. Why, then, don't pension funds or other institutional investors put forward candidates, elect them, and institute accountability to the pension plan's participants through the election of directors who are accountable to the plan?[18] Another possibility would be to have a responsible official of the pension fund appointed as a director at corporations in which the fund was heavily invested.

Three reasons are foremost among possible explanations for the absence of such strategies. The first is that there will be inevitable conflicts between the fiduciary duties owed by such directors to the corporation and any accountability to, or preference of, the interests of those who elected them. Second, in cases of direct appointments, besides the conflicts, there would be "insider" restrictions imposed on the ability of the pension fund to deal with its shareholdings.[19] Finally, the requirement of diversification of investments among different equities means that perhaps only the largest shareholders could amass the amount of stock needed to cross the "threshold" beyond which shareholders are permitted to nominate their own slate of directors without the requirement of a costly dissident information circular.[20] Until recently, in the United States, unlike in Canada, there has been no access to the management proxy circular for shareholders who wish to nominate their own candidates for the board of directors. The US Securities and Exchange Commission (SEC) staff would routinely advise corporations that it would take no enforcement action against them if they excluded shareholder proposals that would lead to contested elections for directors at the corporation. Instead, US shareholders could only suggest their nominees to the nominating committee of the board of directors, or nominate candidates from the floor of the annual meeting if they wished to avoid the expense of preparing and circulating a dissident proxy circular.[21]

Following receipt of a staff report suggesting that the SEC consider reforms that would provide access to the management proxy circular for shareholders who wish to propose their own candidates for director, the SEC issued a proposed rule on "Security Holder Director Nominations" providing for the inclusion of nominees for director nominated by shareholders in the management proxy circular in certain situations.[22] The proposed rule would allow shareholder nominations in the management circular if either of two "triggering events" occurred within two years of the election: (1) more than 35 percent of the votes cast had "withheld" their votes from one or more of the corporation's directors, or (2) a resolution to allow shareholder nominations pursuant to the proposed rule, submitted by security holders who had held more than 1 percent of the corporation's voting shares for more than one year, was supported by more than 50 percent of the votes at a meeting after January 1, 2004.

The SEC also announced that it was considering a third "triggering event" that would provide shareholders with direct access to the nominating process, namely, where a shareholder proposal had received a majority vote and it was not implemented by the board of directors. The SEC staff report viewed triggering events as a means of limiting the disruptive effects of a contest for a director's position to circumstances where the ordinary means of shareholder input are apparently having little or no effect.[23] Once the triggering event had occurred, any shareholder or group of shareholders who together had owned more than 5 percent of the voting securities for two or more years would be able to nominate one or two directors, depending on the size of the corporation's board. Before the proposed rule was published, several large institutional investors publicly denounced it as window dressing.[24] Moreover, the issue of enhanced access for shareholder nominations of directors had been before the SEC periodically since 1942 without the promulgation of any rules allowing such access.[25]

Following the publication of the proposed rule, the SEC indicated that it intended to move quickly to implement it. However, it has still not been implemented. The SEC extended the comment period, and the Commission chair, William Donaldson, resigned on 30 June 2005 with the rule still not in place. The SEC staff also reversed itself. After inviting shareholders to file "direct access" proposals, it reverted to its previous position that it would not undertake enforcement activities if a corporation excluded such proposals from the management proxy circular, since it did not seem that the Commission was going to implement the rule.[26]

In 2006, however, the United States Court of Appeal for New York breathed new life into the issue when it ruled that the SEC's interpretation of its rule was incorrect and that a proposed bylaw amendment for direct access to the nomination process could not be excluded from the management proxy circular under the existing rule.[27] The Court's decision has prompted two reactions by the SEC. First, the current SEC chair has announced a new consultation process aimed at resolving the issue of shareholder nomination of directors, as well as a re-examination of the role of the SEC in proxy regulation relating to matters governed by state corporation law.[28] Second,

SEC staff has begun expressing no view about whether or not it would take enforcement action if a corporation excludes a shareholder proposal for a bylaw amendment instituting direct access to the director nomination process from its management proxy circular.[29] In late 2007, after issuing two proposed rules leading to either a complete prohibition on the inclusion of proposals to change corporate bylaws to allow shareholder nominations for directors to be included in management proxy materials or to permitting such bylaw amendment proposals to be included in certain circumstances, the SEC acted by amending its rules. The amendment prohibited the use of the shareholder proposal rules to include proposals for bylaw amendments that would lead to a contested election in the management proxy circular.[30]

Although institutional investors could certainly pool their votes to nominate and elect directors, US and Canadian scholars have reviewed a number of other concerns that may arise from the confluence of securities regulation and attempts by groups of institutional shareholders to elect directors. In particular, securities regulation treats groups that wish to coordinate their votes and whose share ownership exceeds a particular threshold as if an individual owned all of their shares. This regulatory aggregation imposes additional reporting requirements or restrictions on the use of the shares that create certain legal obstacles to concerted action.[31] The effect of securities regulation on the nomination and election of directors, as well as on the circulation of shareholder proposals and solicitation of votes in support, will be discussed in more detail in Chapter 5.

Another problem for the exercise of corporate governance through the election of directors, exogenous to the process by which shareholders choose the directors, is that the ability of directors to conduct their supervisory duties is seriously hampered by their deep-rooted social and cultural links to corporate management, notwithstanding their ostensible independence from any formal ties to the corporation and its management.[32] These ties, coupled with the serious difficulties in electing directors who are not nominated by the corporation's management, explain why directors often do not feel particularly accountable to shareholders and why shareholders would want that situation to change by ousting incumbent directors in cases of egregious failures of supervision.

Conflicts and Fiduciary Duty

Corporate law requires that directors act in the best interests of the corporation in exercising their duties and powers.[33] Despite the often-cited equation between the best interests of the corporation and those of its shareholders, these interests do not always coincide, especially where the shareholders' interests are measured over the short term. Indeed, in the United States, various states have enacted corporate constituency provisions in their corporate law providing that directors may (or in some instances must) consider the interests of a number of "stakeholders" in the corporation in their decision making.[34] In Canada, although no such provisions have been enacted, the judiciary has not adopted a complete shareholder primacy view of directors' duties.[35] In *Peoples Department Stores Inc. (Trustee of) v. Wise,* the Supreme Court of Canada made the following points about directors' duties:[36]

- Directors of a corporation owe a statutory fiduciary duty of loyalty to act only in the best interests of the corporation, and those interests are not to be confused with the interests of other stakeholders.[37]
- In determining what is in the best interests of the corporation, "it may be legitimate, given all the circumstances of a given case, for the board of directors to consider, inter alia, the interests of shareholders, employees, suppliers, creditors, consumers, governments and the environment."[38]

Corporate statutes do not prohibit individuals whose duties may be in conflict from serving as directors, provided they declare the nature of the conflict with respect to any transaction or contract and refrain from voting to approve such a transaction.[39] The fiduciary standards in pension fund legislation are not as forgiving, however, and prohibit a trustee or agents of the trustee from allowing anything to conflict with their fiduciary obligations to the beneficiaries.[40]

Accordingly, institutional investors should not participate in the nomination and election of directors with a view to establishing an agency relationship with those directors they have supported. Rather, the better view of governance through active participation in the nomination and election of directors is that the goal is to upgrade the competence and diligence of the directors above the level exhibited by the incumbent directors. In addition, ousting incumbent directors provides incentives to both the board of directors and the management of the corporation to improve corporate governance and the economic performance of the corporation.[41]

Just Vote "No"

One tactic adopted by US institutional investors in corporate director elections commencing in the early 1990s is that of using their proxy votes to withhold their votes with respect to some or all of the directors nominated for election in the management information circular.[42] While such a vote could not result in the defeat of the target directors, the total "no" vote had to be publicly reported, thus giving directors and the corporate management incentives to avoid the public embarrassment that would result from a sizable vote of no confidence by the shareholders.[43] It also allowed institutional shareholders to register their disapproval without potential litigation over management's refusal to include a resolution in its information circular or the expense of circulating a dissident information circular with their own candidates for director.

The Rebirth of the "Independent Director"

Many institutional investors sought to improve corporate governance in the late 1980s and early 1990s by seeking the nomination and election of "outside" and/or "independent" directors. An outside director was one who was not part of the management team at the corporation. An independent director was an outside director who did not have any significant economic ties to the corporation (such as a supplier, member of the corporation's law firm, etc.) or had not been an employee for five years or more.[44] Recently, following the collapse of Enron and the revelations of accounting fraud at WorldCom, the importance of the independent director has increased in the US due to the requirement in listing standards that they make up a majority of the board of directors, and in legislation that they make up all of the board's audit committee.[45] The theory behind the use of outside or independent directors is that since they are not part of the management team, they will ally themselves with the shareholders' interests rather than those of management.

The problem remains, however, of why independent directors should effectively monitor management on behalf of the shareholders? For a number of years, scholars have criticized the use of independent directors as a substitute for regulation.[46] Ronald Gilson and Reinier Kraakman examine this issue and conclude that the two reasons offered for effective monitoring are not sufficient to overcome the counter-incentives that presently exist.[47] The two reasons offered are *noblesse oblige* (arising from the good character that forms the basis on which they are chosen to serve in the first instance) and concerns about their reputations in a market for directors. There are at least three counter-incentives to *noblesse oblige.* The first is the fact that a director's continued tenure on the board is dependent on his or her being renominated by management. The second is that there are strong social and cultural ties between management and directors, who are often senior executives at their own corporations. Third, there is an extreme imbalance between the financial compensation and the amount of work required to be diligent in discharging a director's duties. As for the market for directors, the authors point out that there is no evidence of the existence of such a market, let alone that it has perfect information about directors' behaviour to provide the appropriate incentives to be diligent.[48] After reviewing these counter-incentives, they conclude:

> This, then, is where the problem stands. On the one hand, the board of directors is the only existing device for monitoring managers. On the other, both more and less sympathetic observers of boards of directors have come

> to acknowledge what should have been obvious all along: The traditional corporate solution of introducing outside directors to bridge the separation between ownership and control has dramatic limitations.[49]

Gilson and Kraakman's proposed solution is to create a real market for outside or independent directors. The market is created by designing a position of professional outside director to be filled by individuals with the requisite qualifications who would make a career out of sitting as directors on the boards of half a dozen corporations in return for the remuneration generated by the combined director's compensation. As the authors point out, however, such a market could arise in the United States only through the cooperation of a number of institutional investors whose combined holdings would be sufficient to ensure the election of a professional director.[50] These professional directors would not be dependent on the management of just one corporation for their livelihood, but rather on those institutional investors whose satisfaction with their performance would determine their chances for re-election to all boards on which they served.

Other scholars have been more conservative in their conclusions about the potential for institutional shareholder cooperation and/or initiative on the scale envisioned by Gilson and Kraakman. Their caution is based upon the fact that institutional shareholders have their own internal agency problems that reduce the likelihood that these institutions will take full advantage of the opportunities for collective action arising from their potential for collective gain through joint corporate governance initiatives.[51] Edward Rock sets out the potential connections between greater concentrations of shareholding and the increasing rationality of expending institutional shareholder resources to discipline management. Yet he goes on to caution that just because concentration has potentially decreased collective action problems, this does not mean that the agency problems inherent in the institutional shareholders' beneficiary/fiduciary relationships have been overcome.[52] One of the most problematic of these agency problems is that of the potential conflicts of interests between the investment managers and the beneficiaries. There are two types of conflicts possible. The first is where the managers face certain costs (in the form of offending potential corporate customers) if they pursue the beneficiaries' interests in improved corporate governance. The second type allows the manager to reap private benefits that cost the beneficiaries (such as short-term political gain from a popular stand that generates long-term financial costs).[53]

Moreover, Rock points to a potentially even more troubling agency problem, namely, that the investment managers lack the incentives to engage in corporate governance activities. This is because the benefits of any such activity will be reflected in the performance of a fund's entire portfolio because funds are predominantly passively managed index funds. Therefore, since the entire portfolio benefits and it is impossible to discern the effects of corporate governance activity by a particular manager, that enhanced performance will not redound to the individual manager's credit. If managers are being evaluated against the performance of other managers or a market index, there are no selective incentives for individual investment managers to engage in corporate governance that increases the value of portfolios or of an index; rather, there are counter-incentives, based on competition among managers over the cost structure of passive investments.[54]

As a result of these factors, Rock is critical of Gilson and Kraakman's proposal that institutional investors collectively utilize professional independent directors, whom they would monitor to ensure proper performance of their duty to monitor corporate management. He points out that the lack of selective incentives among the large passively invested institutional investors and the presence of counter-incentives means that the increase in the size of institutional shareholdings cannot explain or support the degree of monitoring of the professional directors that is essential to their proposal. Thus, although he shares their critique of the independent or outside directors as insufficiently bound to advance the interests of shareholders, Rock remains unconvinced that investment managers will be able to sustain the effort required to implement Gilson and Kraakman's proposal solely because it would benefit the fund's beneficiaries.[55] In his view, either new incentives for investors to monitor professional directors must be created or those who do participate must be obtaining private benefits from the participation, benefits that increase the potential conflicts between their interests and those of the beneficiaries.

In Canada, MacIntosh has expressed serious reservations concerning Gilson and Kraakman's proposal for the selection and election of professional directors. His reservations centre on the likelihood that qualified individuals would be unwilling to serve as directors, given the lower compensation they would earn. He is also concerned about the practical problems of monitoring the directors' performance. In particular, he is concerned that a monitoring agency would be unable to separate out the performance of the minority, shareholder-nominated directors from the "noisy" performance of the entire team composed of the board of directors and senior management.[56] He reasons that the inability to accurately evaluate "independent directors" would lessen their dependency on the institutional shareholders, and thus their effectiveness.

Of course, the agency problems identified by Rock and Black are not unique to the use of the power to elect directors as a corporate governance tool. They are applicable to all types of corporate governance activity by institutional investors since the problems reside in the decision-making structure of almost all institutional investors in which fiduciaries, bound to act in the best interests of the fund's beneficiaries, are the decision makers in the fiduciary/beneficiary relationship. Although the corporate managers who control the investment and proxy voting activities of pension funds may also be participants in the pension plan, they face the same array of weak or absent positive selective incentives and more immediate counter-incentives when considering active corporate governance initiatives. That is, the benefits that may accrue to the pension fund's performance are generalized and distributed among numerous beneficiaries, whereas the pressure from other managers to refrain from active intervention is specifically directed towards them, as is the implicit threat of retaliation for any intervention. Therefore, another, more powerful positive or negative incentive is needed in order to overcome the agency problems within the institutional investor.[57] One possible form that such an incentive might take is direct accountability to the beneficiaries for the corporate governance activities of each fund. Utilizing a form of accountability as a means of overcoming the tendency of institutional shareholders to vote with management is not a new idea. Ralph Nader, Mark Green, and Joel Seligman presented a proposal in 1976 that all financial intermediaries be required to pass-through voting proxies to the beneficial owners of such shares.[58] The concept was even discussed at US Congressional hearings concerning pension funds in capital markets in 1986, although one scholar reports that support for the idea was mixed.[59]

Scholars in Canada have also advocated direct accountability to the beneficiaries of institutional investors. Following their review of a number of studies of the state of corporate governance activity in Canada,[60] Ronald Daniels and Randall Morck suggest that the beneficiaries of pension funds should elect senior managers of corporate and public pension funds. The suggestion was made in order to deal with concerns about the managers' commitment to the beneficiaries' interests arising from their employment by fund sponsors. They also recommended that any breach of their fiduciary duty to the beneficiaries should make them liable to class action lawsuits by the beneficiaries.[61] Recently, another US author has suggested that an appropriate response to problems of corporate governance following the Enron and WorldCom revelations is to combine Gilson and Kraakman's concept of independent directors recruited by associations of institutional investors with instructions on choice of director being provided directly by plan participants.[62] The proposal would see individuals with defined contribution plan accounts or self-directed retirement accounts providing voting instructions to the fund managers concerning their choice among candidates for director. These directorial candidates would be nominated by different institutional investor associations who would choose from a pool of such potential nominees who had been vetted by a commercial clearinghouse.

John Coffee Jr. has advanced another proposal to overcome these obstacles to active corporate governance. It involves creating a market for professional proxy advisors through regulatory initiative. The market would be created by unbundling the prices charged by investment managers for investment management from those charged for proxy voting services, regulation of the minimum contents of such services, and restriction of the number of different stocks held by a single pension plan to reduce "excess" diversification.[63] Finally, Coffee proposes that an incentive compensation system be created that would reward successful corporate governance initiatives by investment managers. He acknowledges, however, that designing such a compensation system would be very difficult for passively invested funds because the only performance benchmark, the returns on the market index, is also the benchmark that the fund's investments are designed to reproduce without any corporate governance activity by the manager.[64]

Shareholder Proposals

Corporate law statutes also provide shareholders with the power to make proposals to other shareholders about the conduct of the corporation's affairs. Proposals may be made in writing prior to the meeting in order to seek the support of other shareholders and obtain their favourable vote by proxy, or in person, at the annual shareholders' meeting. Unless the proposal is not eligible, pursuant to certain statutory criteria, management must circulate the shareholder proposal, plus a short written explanation to all the other shareholders, with the management's information circular.[65] Grounds for exclusion of proposals from management's circular vary from statute to statute and include a prior defeat within a prescribed time period, failure to present the proposal at the shareholders' meeting, seeking to pursue a personal grievance, or inability to demonstrate a significant relationship between the proposal and the corporation's business or affairs.[66] In addition, Canadian federal corporate law provisions concerning shareholder proposals have recently been amended to impose a "threshold" shareholding requirement before any proposal can be made by a shareholder.[67] However, other amendments to the federal statute have arguably made it easier for institutional investors to solicit support for proposals without requiring an onerously expensive dissident proxy campaign. No dissident information circular is required where the number of shareholders solicited is fifteen or less, or where the solicitation is contained in a public broadcast, speech, or publication.[68]

Before becoming too involved in the mechanics of the shareholder proposal mechanism in corporate governance, however, one point needs to be discussed in light of the purposes of corporate governance activities by institutional investors. For the most part, shareholder proposals that obtain the support of a majority of the shareholders voting at an annual meeting are merely advisory, rather than binding on the board of directors and management of the corporation. This advisory status arises in part from the language of the corporate law statutes that, in the federal statute, for example, states:

> 102. (1) Subject to any unanimous shareholder agreement, the directors shall manage, or supervise the management of, the business and affairs of a corporation.[69]

One explanation for this legal constraint, which was adopted by the Organisation for Economic Co-operation and Development (OECD) in its corporate governance guidelines, is that, as a practical matter, a shareholder referendum is an inappropriate decision-making process for a business environment in which change is rapid and opportunities are fleeting.[70] Michael Whincop offers an efficiency explanation that justifies the inability of the shareholders to dictate the ordinary management of the corporation on the grounds that shareholders' decision making on ongoing operations is vulnerable to "cycling" through various alternative results as a result of the social choice problems of voting by shareholders with differently ordered preferences, as illustrated in Kenneth Arrow's work.[71] He further points out that the rule also prevents shareholders from imposing inefficient hold-ups on corporate decision making while they seek their own private benefits. Whatever the theoretical explanation for the presence of this rule in our corporate law regime, it does pose some serious issues for one of the main themes of this work. The theme is that the effort and expense of exercising corporate governance rights by pension fund fiduciaries is justified both by the potential increase in the value of the investments and the collateral benefits generated for the beneficiaries of these funds.

As will be discussed in more detail below, however, this facet of the legal rules surrounding the corporate governance activities of shareholders may also answer some of the concerns about that theme. One concern is that unqualified shareholders (the pension fund's participants) are unduly "interfering" with the exercise of corporate management's expertise in the management of the corporation's affairs through their corporate governance activities. Another concern that may arise is whether a majoritarian adoption of an activist corporate governance policy may become oppressive to the minority of pension fund participants who do not want to interfere with the management of their investments for fear of risking lower returns on their plan's assets from such interference. The "advisory" status of shareholder proposals, however, diminishes the force of these concerns as the management of the corporation is not being usurped by shareholder proposals. Rather, shareholder support for a proposal marks the beginning of a dialogue or debate with a corporation's management concerning the issues raised by such a proposal, and thus injects valuable elements of the democratic system into the decision-making process. These elements include the free exchange of ideas and a requirement that decision makers provide their rationale and be prepared to defend it in a forum in which both the acceptability of the rationale and the effectiveness of any counter-rationale will be subject to periodic tests through shareholder votes.[72]

This leaves the issue of the relationship between the costs and benefits of institutional shareholder activism, however. Roberta Romano has taken issue with those who claim that institutional investor activism is value enhancing, on the grounds that empirical studies have not generated any evidence that shareholder proposals generate increased value. In her view, the problem is that the subject matter of the proposals – corporate governance issues – has no significant effect on the cash flow of the corporation, so success or failure will be irrelevant. The only consistent explanation of positive results is that the market perceived the willingness of management to negotiate with the proposals' sponsors (rather than have the proposal submitted to a vote) as a signal of management quality and priced the stock accordingly.[73] Notwithstanding her view that there is a lack of direct empirical evidence of value enhancement, Romano does not advocate abandonment of the strategy. Instead she proposes a two-pronged reform. First, institutional investors such as pension plans should produce annual public reviews of their corporate governance programs and provide them to their plan members or beneficiaries. These reviews ought to be accompanied by an internal justification to the plan's trustees of the costs of any corporate governance activity.[74] The second aspect of the strategy is legislative reform to remove what she characterizes as the "subsidy" of shareholder proposals by the corporation, by requiring that shareholders bear the cost of communicating their proposals in proportion to the degree of support the proposals receive.[75] It is interesting that Romano does not advocate the elimination of shareholder proposal activity by institutional investors, despite her claim that they have no significant impact on firm value. Rather, she would require these investors to focus only on proposals that generate increased firm performance (which remain unspecified, other than changes to takeover defences made on a firm-specific basis). One wonders, therefore, whether the lack of empirical evidence of improved performance is a function of the actual absence of any such evidence or of the inadequacy of the analytical tools available to measure the links between changes and value. It is also clear, however, that Romano's objection to activism is not one of principle, based on the advisory status of the successful proposal, but rather is based on what she views as the factual grounds that such a proposal is ineffective in enhancing firm value.

In addition, corporate law does not completely restrict shareholders' votes to an advisory role. Institutional investors have also begun to utilize their votes to pass amendments to the corporation's bylaws, and, unlike proposals, such bylaws are binding on the corporation's board of directors. Thus, to the extent that shareholders may amend the bylaws, the concern that activism may not accomplish changes in corporate policy directly through a majority vote is mitigated.

Bylaw Amendment

In the United States, the debate over shareholder-initiated bylaw amendments has been invigorated by recent institutional shareholder initiatives concerning takeover defences adopted by corporate boards of directors. The debate concerns the proper interpretation of state corporate law statutes that restrict the ability of shareholders to manage the corporation yet permit shareholders to amend the corporation's bylaws. The central issue is the relationship between these two provisions when a bylaw amendment appears to conflict with a managerial decision by the corporation's directors.[76]

In the United States, the issue has arisen as a result of the successful attempt by a union pension fund to have a bylaw amendment proposal circulated as a shareholder proposal over the corporate management's objections that it unlawfully interfered with its power to manage the corporation's affairs.[77] The proposed amendment would require the board of directors to redeem the existing shareholder rights plan and to get majority shareholder approval for any new plan. The shareholder rights plan (often called a "poison pill") is a takeover defence that allows the board of directors to issue new shares to existing shareholders upon the occurrence of a specific event, such as the acquisition of substantial shares by a potential acquirer. By issuing numerous new shares, the directors make acquisition a much more difficult and expensive operation. When the state Supreme Court dealt with the issue, it held that the fact that the board had the power to create poison pills did not mean that the power to deal with bylaws was exclusive. The Court pointed out that the state corporate law statute also permitted shareholders to pass bylaws. It authorized shareholders to pass bylaws that may "contain any provision, not inconsistent with law or with the certificate of incorporation, relating to the business of the corporation, the conduct of its affairs, and its rights or powers or the rights or powers of its shareholders, directors, officers or employees."[78]

In reaching its conclusion, the Court adopted reasoning similar to that used in academic writing on the subject, holding that takeover defences have two contradictory aspects. On the one hand, they may provide protection to shareholders by enabling corporate management to solicit more lucrative bids or create an auction, thus increasing the price paid to shareholders for control. On the other hand, they may also entrench management and make otherwise beneficial takeovers prohibitively expensive.[79] The Court held that the power to manage the corporation was not granted to the board of directors without limitation and was expressly subject to the corporate governance scheme of the statute, inclusive of the shareholders' power to enact and amend bylaws concerning the corporation's business.[80]

Jonathan Macey has analyzed the double-edged nature of takeover defences in the context of shareholder bylaw amendment powers by pointing out that shareholders are vulnerable to both the incumbent management and the acquiring company during a takeover bid.[81] He explains that the poison pill takeover defence protects shareholders from being subjected to a "prisoners' dilemma" two-tier bid by potential acquirers. This type of bid promises to pay a substantial premium for all shares tendered to the point that the acquirer has obtained majority control. Thereafter, the acquirer will obtain the rest of the shares at a much lower price. The concern is that shareholders will not have the benefit of any competing bids nor the time to assess whether the premium is sufficient in light of the company's potential earnings.[82] The poison pill allows a corporate board of directors to delay the acquirer's acquisition of a majority share by making the number of shares needed to get a majority a much larger number. In that time, another bidder may be found who will make a better offer.

This type of two-tier bid is prohibited under the Ontario *Securities Act,* which requires that identical consideration be offered to all security holders of the same class in a takeover bid and prohibits arrangements that would have the effect of giving greater consideration to some security holders in the same class.[83]

Takeover defences also increase the cost of a takeover and increase the risk that later bidders alerted by the initial bid will be successful in their bids without incurring the costs the initial bidder paid to acquire the information about the value of the target corporation's shares.[84] This "free riding" on another's investment is a phenomenon that arises where the benefits of costs incurred by one individual are distributed amongst all interested parties, irrespective of their investment in the benefit-generating activity. This ability to increase costs means that takeover defences are also potentially abused to entrench incumbent management. Jeffrey Gordon points out that this potential has been increased by recent court rulings supporting incumbent management's right to "just say no" to tender offers without having to justify the decision in any substantive manner.[85] He offers a justification of the shareholder bylaw amendment power rooted in the nexus of contracts theory of corporate law in which the appropriate rule attempts to reproduce the results of costless *ex ante* bargaining among the corporation's various stakeholders. Due to the difficulties and problems with thousands of shareholders running a business, such bargaining would result in the directors making the specific daily decisions concerning the business of the corporation. However, Gordon sees a role for shareholders in specifying rules about how power-redistributing changes are made in the corporation, either through general bylaw provisions or as a reaction to a specific change through a bylaw requiring shareholder approval.[86]

Corporate law provisions that also give the bylaw enactment and amendment power to the directors further complicate the issue of shareholder bylaw amendments. In the United States, the grant of such a power to the directors is often made in the certificate of incorporation. In two of the major Canadian corporate law statutes, the power is expressly granted to the directors; however, its exercise is subject to the subsequent ratification of a majority of shareholders.[87] In both countries, the question arises as to whether a corporation's board of directors may amend or repeal a bylaw that has just been enacted by a majority vote of the shareholders. John Coffee Jr. has carefully reviewed the issue in the context of the Delaware corporate law statute and the jurisprudence from the Delaware courts that deals with the relationships between the power of each body to enact, amend, or repeal bylaws enacted by the other body.[88] He points out that logically the directors' bylaw power, arising from the certificate of incorporation, has priority over the bylaw enacted by shareholders.

The Delaware statute provides, however, that where directors are given the bylaw power in the certificate, that grant of power does not either divest the shareholders of their bylaw power or limit it.[89] In addition, he reported that at least one Delaware case contained a dictum that seemed to approve a shareholder bylaw that contained a prohibition against its subsequent repeal or amendment by the board of directors.[90] Notwithstanding this dictum, Coffee concludes that the issue is still uncertain in Delaware law since there have been cases where Delaware courts have allowed shareholder initiatives to be frustrated by the board of directors.[91] In other US jurisdictions and in the Revised Model Business Law, the power of shareholders to restrict the ability of the directors to amend or repeal a shareholder-approved bylaw is expressly provided.[92] Nevertheless, Coffee suggests that even in Delaware, shareholders can place sufficiently strict procedural limitations on board amendments to their bylaws as to make repeal or amendment practically impossible.[93] One US scholar has summarized the situation as follows:

> Just as this nascent effort to shift the balance of corporate power from directors to stockholders through the use of stockholder-adopted by-law provisions is gaining momentum, however, it has exposed a critical dearth of precedent. For while stockholders have unquestioned power to adopt bylaws covering a broad range of subjects, it is also well established in corporate law that stockholders may not directly manage the business and affairs of the corporation, at least without specific authorization either by statute or in the certificate or articles of incorporation. There is an obvious zone of

conflict between these precepts: in at least some respects, attempts by stockholders to adopt by-laws limiting or influencing director authority inevitably offend the notion of management by the board of directors. However, neither the courts, the legislators, the SEC, nor legal scholars have clearly articulated the means of resolving this conflict and determining whether a stockholder-adopted by-law provision that constrains director managerial authority is legally effective.

Related to this gap in legal authority is a less substantive but nearly as important area of legal uncertainty. Even if the stockholders could validly initiate and adopt a by-law limiting the authority of the directors, such a by-law amendment would accomplish little or nothing if the board of directors could simply repeal it after the stockholders adopted it. In some jurisdictions, of course, there is no question that such repeal can be prevented. Under many statutory schemes, the board of directors may not repeal a stockholder-adopted by-law if that by-law expressly prohibits such repeal. In other jurisdictions, however, notably Delaware and New York, the corporation statutes allow the board of directors to amend the by-laws if the certificate or articles of incorporation so provide and place no express limits on the application of such director amendment authority to stockholder-adopted by-laws. The second significant legal uncertainty, therefore, is whether, in the absence of an explicitly controlling statute, a stockholder-adopted by-law can be made immune from repeal or modification by the board of directors.[94]

As noted above, major Canadian corporate law statutes provide much clearer guidance on the effect of shareholder-approved bylaws and their relationship with the vesting of the management of the firm in the board of directors.[95] Both the federal and Ontario corporate law statutes provide that while directors may enact, amend, or repeal the corporation's bylaws, that decision must be ratified by a majority of the shareholders at the next shareholders' meeting. The bylaw is effective from the date it is enacted by the directors.[96] However, if the bylaw or changes to it passed by the directors is rejected during the mandatory shareholder vote, it is no longer in effect from the day it is voted on and "no subsequent resolution of the directors to make, amend or repeal a by-law having substantially the same purpose or effect is effective until it is confirmed or confirmed as amended by the shareholders."[97] Thus, the procedural debate over whether or not the shareholders' bylaw could or should be amended or repealed by the directors is resolved in favour of the shareholders, since they have the last word in the bylaw amendment procedure.

The debate over bylaw amendments by shareholders does not end there, however. This is because Canadian law regulates the substance of such bylaws much more closely than comparable US regulation. The Oklahoma state corporation law at issue in *Teamsters v. Fleming* allows shareholders to pass bylaws that contain any provision concerning the business of the corporation, provided there is compliance with law and the certificate of incorporation;[98] Canadian corporate law statutes provide that shareholders may submit bylaws to a shareholder vote provided the bylaws conform to the requirements for the submission of proposals in those statutes.[99] The requirements for the submission of proposals have recently undergone substantial amendments in the federal corporate law statute.[100] For our purposes, however, we will concentrate on the criteria that are most relevant to the issue of the relationship between the directors being vested with the management of the corporation and the shareholders' power to enact bylaws.

The relevant statutory criteria are those that allow the corporation to refuse to circulate a proposal submitted by a qualifying shareholder where the refusal is based on the content of the proposal.[101] (A shareholder must also have a minimum level of shares and meet certain timing criteria in order to have a proposal circulated.)[102] The two exclusionary criteria shared by the Ontario and federal legislation are that the purpose of the proposal is to redress a personal grievance or enforce a personal claim by the shareholder, or that the proposal does not relate to the corporation's business in any significant way. The federal statute also allows exclusion on the grounds that the right to make proposals is being abused to obtain publicity. The limits of some of these exclusionary provisions were not subjected to judicial interpretation until 1997, in a case involving an individual shareholder and the National Bank of Canada.[103] In that case, the shareholder submitted a number of proposals dealing with limits on executive compensation, the makeup of the board of directors, and limits to the length of their tenure as directors, all of which were excluded by the Bank. The court ruled that the shareholder was entitled to have the proposals circulated and that the intent of the legislative provisions was to be interpreted as encouraging calm, civilized discussion of shareholder concerns, in a manner that fostered investor participation at general meetings.[104] Scholarly comment on the reasoning in the decision concluded that lawyers saw the case as precedent that would make it difficult to exclude such proposals.[105] Nevertheless, Brian Cheffins argues that bylaw amendments that concern the managerial responsibilities granted by the statute to the directors may well be ruled invalid for usurping the directors' power to manage.[106]

Thus, despite somewhat differing statutory language and schemes, Canadian and US courts may have to face the same issue – where is the appropriate line between the shareholders' power to enact, amend, and repeal bylaws and the managerial authority of the board of directors? The Canadian statutes do contain one important difference from the Delaware and Oklahoma statutes. They provide shareholders with an express power to veto directors' enactment, amendment, or repeal of the corporation's bylaws. A power to veto is not equivalent to a power to enact binding bylaws concerning the management of the affairs and business of the corporation, but the Ontario provisions granting shareholders the power to initiate bylaw proposals provide that, if approved by a majority of the shareholders, the shareholder-initiated bylaws require no further confirmation and are effective immediately.[107] The authors of a Canadian business law text conclude that such shareholder-initiated changes are effective when passed by a vote of the shareholders and are not just recommendations to the board of directors.[108]

Lawrence Hamermesh is critical of attempts by other scholars to define the border between the statutory grant of managerial power to directors and the legitimate sphere of shareholder bylaw initiation on grounds that valid bylaws deal only with general rather than specific matters, procedural rather than substantive matters, or ordinary rather than fundamental matters.[109] He argues that these distinctions are incoherent when applied to the practical functioning of a corporation, and that a rule should therefore be adopted that any bylaw that limits directors' managerial authority is invalid.

Clearly, the degree to which the formal mechanisms of shareholder democracy should be available to groups of institutional shareholders that wish to reform the governance of the corporation, as well as the effectiveness of these mechanisms, is the subject of considerable disagreement among US scholars. For the purposes of this book, it is important to note a significant area in which there is a potential for corporate governance activity through a proxy voting policy for shareholder proposals and/or bylaw amendments. As well, corporate law does not prohibit shareholder nomination and election of some or all directors, although significant securities law regulatory obstacles do exist. In fact, some recent corporate law reforms appear designed to encourage institutional investor activism, and Canadian investors appear to have responded positively to the changes.

Recent Developments in Canada

Despite this uncertainty about the appropriate border between directors' managerial authority and the use of shareholders' bylaw power, there have been developments that may lead to increased use of proxy voting by institutional investors in Canada. First, recent changes to the federal corporate law statute have reduced some of the obstacles faced by institutional investors in participating in the proxy voting process in the firms in which they have invested. In particular, amendments to the statute allow beneficial owners of the shares to control the voting of those shares.[110] Prior to these amendments, only the person in whose name the share was held on the date set by the corporation to establish status as a shareholder could exercise that share's vote.[111] For institutional investors, most if not all of their investments are held in the names of their investment managers or a third-party trust company, and therefore the right to vote those shares had to be negotiated with the investment managers.

In addition, there have been some new initiatives by Canada's securities regulators to enhance the ability of beneficial shareholders (those whose names do not appear in the shareholders' record book of the company, but who are the entities on whose behalf the record shareholder, such as CDS, is holding the share) such as pension funds to exercise their voting rights. They have constructed a rules-based regime requiring disclosure of beneficial owners to the corporation prior to the record date, and the circulation of proxy materials (including proxy voting cards) to those beneficial owners by the corporation in a manner that will entitle the beneficial owners to assert the same rights as a shareholder of record.[112]

Another amendment to the *Canada Business Corporations Act* (CBCA) permits a shareholder who is not acting on behalf of management to solicit fifteen or fewer shareholders to form an alliance on proxy voting strategies, without requiring that the shareholder circulate a dissident proxy circular.[113] In addition, a shareholder can now solicit proxies by public broadcast, speech, or publication without having to circulate a dissident proxy circular.[114] Taken together, these changes appear designed to encourage active participation in corporate governance by institutional investors.[115]

Concurrently with the enactment of the CBCA amendments, a number of pension funds and investment managers that collectively control over $1.4 trillion of investments have formed the Canadian Coalition for Good Corporate Governance. One interesting facet of this organization is that it includes both large public sector pension funds and large investment management firms, including those affiliated with major banks. They have agreed to share information and to "take the initiative to hold management accountable for growing long-term shareholder value."[116] As yet, the meaning assigned to "long-term shareholder value" has not been clarified.[117] It is worth noting, however, that the usual formula of "share price maximization" has not been used, and that two of the biggest pension funds in the Coalition have equal employee and employer representation on their boards of trustees.[118] The Coalition's website contains the following mission statement: "The mission of the Canadian Coalition for Good Governance is to represent Canadian institutional shareholders through the promotion of best corporate governance practices and to align the interests of boards and management with those of the shareholder."[119]

One of the fundamental goals of the Coalition is that shareholders exercise their proxy voting powers, and it intends to develop a proxy voting guideline for its members and other interested shareholders.[120] The creation of the Coalition will likely provide an opportunity to test the limits of the exercise of shareholders' power through their votes in the courts. In particular, it may test whether the structure of the bylaw amendment power in Canadian legislation is friendlier to shareholders than it appears to be in the US. At present, there is no reason to completely discount this avenue as one that may allow pension fund beneficiaries to influence corporate policy through the votes of the shares held by their funds.

An important aspect of the link between beneficiaries and their ability to influence corporate policy remains to be set out in detail, however. As Janis Sarra has observed, an important question is how these funds will approach the question of balancing the interests of their beneficiaries with those of other stakeholders.[121] At least it is possible to raise the issue of this balance in defining the content of long-term shareholder value in contrast with short-term share price maximization. What is required now is the mechanism or process by which those employee-beneficiaries who are affected by this initiative can have meaningful and effective input into creating the definition. Before embarking on a discussion of some potential mechanisms, it is necessary to explore some of the remaining avenues in corporate and securities law by which shareholders (including institutional investors) may influence corporate policy.

Shareholder Litigation

This section will deal with those legal rules that permit shareholders to initiate legal proceedings against a corporation's officers and/or directors for actions or failures to act in their official capacities. One important distinguishing feature of this avenue is that it is almost entirely retrospective in its outlook. With the exception of proceedings seeking injunctive relief, the basis for the proceeding will be some event or failure to act in the past for which the shareholder is seeking a remedy. This can be contrasted with shareholder votes, which are focused on prospective changes in the corporation's governance based on claims that potential improvements beneficial to shareholders will result from such changes. The retrospective and fact-specific nature of the shareholder litigation governance tool makes it somewhat more difficult to design a means by which pension fund trustees making decisions concerning potential litigation can be accountable to plan participants for these decisions. It may be that a combination of guidelines and procedural rules requiring consultation with the participants may be essential in order to provide the necessary degree of accountability.

The Relationship between Shareholder Litigation and Corporate Governance by Institutional Investors

Shareholder litigation has two effects. First, it acts as a deterrent to those who might otherwise follow in the footsteps of those who were found to be in the wrong during the litigation,[122] and second, it compensates those harmed by the wrongdoing. In both the United States and Canada, a shareholder may bring a derivative action in the name of the corporation against the corporation's directors and officers alleging that their breaches of their duty to the corporation have caused harm to that corporation. In Canada, corporate statutes also provide a statutory "oppression remedy" that grants certain complainants (which include shareholders) the right to seek a remedy for conduct by corporate officers, directors, or other shareholders that is oppressive or unfairly prejudicial to the shareholders' interests.

While the subject of shareholder litigation may initially seem somewhat remote from the issues in this book, corporate governance changes are now being included in settlements reached in shareholder litigation initiated by institutional investors in the United States.[123] In addition, settlements have also included steps to remedy some social responsibility issues (such as sexual harassment) in cases where the failure to have adequate policies on those issues has been identified as one of the sources of the losses to shareholders.[124] The California Public Employees' Retirement System (CalPERS) has developed a formal screening process to determine whether it will become active in litigation based on the extent of its stockholdings, the amount of potential damages, and whether or not CalPERS involvement could add value to any potential settlement.[125] Thus, at least one large public sector pension fund has publicly taken the position that it will pursue corporate governance through shareholder litigation as well as through the exercise of shareholder votes.

As a number of scholars have pointed out, certain types of shareholder litigation have been the subject of much criticism in the US on the grounds that they are used by class action attorneys to obtain unjustifiable settlements that benefit them but not their ostensible "client-shareholders."[126] Two types of litigation are involved in this criticism. The first type, a derivative claim, is one in which a shareholder files in the name of the corporation, claiming that some action of its directors or officers has resulted in a loss to the corporation (and indirectly to the value of the shareholder's shares).[127] If the corporation will not sue the responsible officials, the shareholder may do so in the corporation's name, with all financial recovery to the corporation if the shareholder is successful.[128] On the other hand, where a shareholder's individual rights are violated, the shareholder can bring a direct action for damages in the shareholder's own name, and is entitled to receive the damages awarded as compensation.[129]

Another class of shareholder litigation, securities law litigation, is much more common in the US than in Canada, although recent legislative amendments may increase its incidence in Canada.[130] This litigation involves claims for loss of the value of shares and/or loss of opportunity to sell the shares as a result of a failure to disclose accurate and/or complete information about the corporation that was material to its market value. Although this is a form of individual shareholder litigation, it does have implications that are more easily fully discussed in the section dealing with securities regulation, below. Accordingly, we will concentrate on derivative and oppression remedy litigation in this section.

Canadian Derivative and Oppression Remedy Litigation

In Canada, a statutory derivative action right is found in corporation legislation. The provision authorizes a shareholder to commence a derivative action in the corporation's name if certain prerequisites have been met and leave of the court has been obtained.[131] Brian Cheffins summarizes the history of the statutory derivative action in Canada. He points out that the statutory derivative action was a reaction to the inadequacy of the common law.[132] Prior to the statutory amendments, the rule in *Foss v. Harbottle*[133] required a majority of shareholders to approve any suit by the corporation to recover damages for a wrong done to the corporation.[134] The application of this rule often meant that shareholders who became aware of a breach of fiduciary duties were unable to enforce them, especially if the directors who were implicated in the breach were also the majority shareholders, as was often the case in Canadian corporations.[135] As a result, one Canadian scholar concluded that the "shareholders' derivative action was available only in very exceptional circumstances."[136]

Stanley Beck highlighted the crucial nature of the derivative action and other company law rights for minority shareholders in private companies (whose shares were not traded publicly). Company law rights are crucial to these shareholders because they lack both the "exit" option of selling their shares at a price set in a competitive market and the protection of securities regulation available to minority shareholders in publicly traded companies.[137] Pension fund investments are primarily in securities traded in the market and thus the funds receive the protection offered by securities regulation. Yet, the pension funds' ability to "exit" by selling their entire stake in a corporation is restrained. The restraint arises from the depressing effect such a large-volume sale (in relation to total market capitalization) might have on the price they could obtain.[138]

In addition, until recently, any such restraints would be exacerbated in Canada by the restrictions imposed on the percentage of foreign securities that could be held in a pension plan's investment portfolio.[139] These restrictions were removed in 2005, so pension funds are now free to invest any proportion of their assets in foreign securities. Thus, "exit" from a Canadian corporation no longer requires "entrance," through the purchase of its securities, into another Canadian corporation. Since most Canadian corporations' capital structures have a majority owner/controlling stockholder, once pension funds exercise the "exit" option, they must assess the potential for majority/minority conflict if they decide to invest in another Canadian corporation. One factor they will have to consider is that majority/minority conflict requires effective corporate law (rather than securities law) to address its problems.[140]

One means of redress offered by Canadian corporate law is the statutory oppression remedy. A "complainant" may bring an application in court for remedial and compensatory relief.[141] If the court finds that the complainant's interests are oppressed, unfairly prejudiced, or unfairly disregarded through an act or omission of the corporation, the conduct of its affairs, or the use of the powers of the directors, the court may grant relief under the provision.[142] The court has the power to grant a number of specific remedies, as well as a general power to grant "any interim or final order it thinks fit."[143] As the authors of a recent article have pointed out, in addition to the general power to grant any order it thinks fit, the court has also been given the power to grant relief on behalf of the corporation in two of the specified remedies.[144] The court may vary or set aside a contract to which the corporation is a party, and it may order compensation to an aggrieved party, which can include a corporation.[145]

The overlapping relief and different procedural requirements of derivative litigation and the oppression application have led to a concern that claims that are essentially derivative claims will be pursued under the oppression provisions, where the initial procedural hurdles are less onerous.[146] There is no requirement in the oppression provisions that the complainant either provides notice to the corporation's board of directors or obtains leave of the court in order to pursue an oppression remedy claim.[147] Edward Iacobucci and Kevin Davis argue that the suggestions by some courts and commentators that the procedural requirements for derivative actions ought to be imposed under both the derivative action and oppression remedy provisions focus on the wrong explanation for the presence of those procedural requirements.[148] In their view, the requirements are present in derivative actions in order to counter the incentive to bring non-meritorious actions created by the potential indemnity for the complainant's legal costs provided under the derivative action provision.[149] The indemnity was introduced to overcome the free-rider problem that would otherwise inhibit meritorious derivative actions. Since the derivative action is brought by the shareholder but in the name of the corporation, any compensation is normally awarded to the corporation rather than the complainant shareholder. This means that, at best, the shareholder will gain only that proportion of the increase in the corporation's residual value represented by his or her individual shareholding. Although successful plaintiffs in Canada are awarded their "costs," these awards typically compensate only up to 60 percent of the shareholder's actual legal costs. Therefore, while the complaining shareholder may see a positive recovery net of costs, non-complaining shareholders will realize a greater proportional benefit, since they will not bear any of the litigation costs expended to realize the total compensation to the corporation.[150] As result, no shareholder wants to be first when that means that the shareholder gains a lesser proportional benefit than the other shareholders.

The statutory derivative action overcomes the free-rider problem by offering to recompense the shareholder complainant's legal costs, thus removing the disincentive for first movers. It then imposes a leave requirement to allow a mandatory screening for merit to be conducted by the court before it requires the corporation to indemnify the complainant's costs. This leave requirement is similar to the disincentives to non-meritorious complaints provided in ordinary litigation (including the oppression application). The disincentives are provided through the imposition of both the complainant's and the defendant's legal costs on losing complainants and the ability of the defendant to seek summary judgment in its favour at an early stage in the proceedings.[151] Thus, as one early commentator noted, the subsequent amendment of the corporate law statutes to include the statutory oppression remedy, together with the willingness of the Canadian judiciary to allow derivative claims to proceed under the oppression remedy, have lessened the importance of the statutory derivative action.[152]

Canadian corporate law thus appears to provide a mechanism by which the institutional investor may seek to remedy some of the structural weaknesses in a particular corporation's corporate governance. Among the specified remedies available are the court's power to regulate the corporation's affairs by creating or amending its bylaws or a unanimous shareholders' agreement, and the power to remove existing directors and appoint new ones in their place.[153] The ability to obtain a remedy is constrained by a number of factors, however. One is the requirement that the action or inaction complained of constitute oppression, unfair prejudice, or unfair disregard of the interests of the complainant. In the presence of a majority/minority capital structure, the courts have said that they will not intervene merely to overcome the problems that arise for minorities in such structures.[154]

In addition, the breach of fiduciary obligations or principles of fairness that constitutes the threshold for entitlement to a remedy is not yet equivalent to a failure to opt for corporate social responsibility. The latter is not the type of obligation that can ordinarily be enforced through the statutory derivative action or oppression remedy. Institutional investors can use shareholder litigation to create corporate governance structures in which the possibility of debating the need for and place of corporate social responsibility may occur. Before that can occur, however, other constraints on the use of shareholder litigation to reform corporate governance must be relaxed.

One of the main constraints is the perception that shareholder litigation is more susceptible to the initiation of strategic lawsuits (sometimes called "strike suits") whose main beneficiaries are the lawyers who settle them in order to obtain lucrative fees. This perception has many adherents in the US, where the perception is applied to both derivative actions and securities law litigation. I believe that different considerations apply to each of these types of litigation and propose to deal with securities litigation in Chapter 5. Many US academics have not differentiated between the two when dealing with the "strike suit" issue. As one US scholar noted, however, derivative litigation in the United States can be based on violations of federal securities law as well as state corporate law.[155] Writing in the 1960s, this scholar argued that the increase in the volume of derivative litigation at that time was a function of the separation of ownership and control, and the amendment of state corporate law to increase managerial discretion. Thus, the derivative suit was one of the last remaining avenues of accountability.[156] By the 1990s, however, many scholars and courts were viewing the derivative suit as suspect.

One important factor that distinguishes the US litigation regime from that in Canada is its cost structure. In Canada, losing parties pay the winning parties' costs. There is no such costs rule in the US. Thus, in the case of a US derivative suit, the plaintiff and defendant are each responsible for their own costs, win or lose. This factor helps explain the strike suit phenomenon in which a plaintiff (who could also be an attorney) would buy a few shares in a corporation and then initiate a derivative action on flimsy grounds. The plaintiff would then settle (thus incurring minimal costs) for less than the legal costs that would be incurred by the corporation to reach the point at which summary judgment would be available to it. Concern about such suits has already spawned a series of state corporate law reforms. These reforms allow the corporation to obtain "security for costs" orders in any derivative litigation initiated by a shareholder holding less than 5 percent of the shares, unless the shares held by the plaintiff were valued above a certain monetary threshold.[157] Federal courts, however, were reluctant to apply this state corporate law requirement to derivative litigation based upon alleged violations of federal securities legislation.

By 1995, the US Congress had passed the *Private Securities Litigation Reform Act* (PSLRA), which imposed greater procedural restraints on securities litigation. Critics of shareholder litigation have undertaken studies showing that recovery in shareholder class actions per share is relatively small and that in derivative actions even smaller, and that no significant positive effects on share prices were observed as a result of events in the litigation.[158] James Cox argued that the impetus for imposing the PSLRA's procedural restraints arose out of the confusion of two goals of shareholder litigation. The first goal was private compensation of those who suffered losses, and the second was the validation of social norms, including confirmation of the fiduciary and fairness obligations of corporate officers, and deterrence. In the discussion of the goals leading to the enactment of the PSLRA, the first goal was given primacy over the second. In Cox's view, this led to a discounting of the social norms validation role of the litigation when the first goal did not seem to be fulfilled by shareholder litigation.[159]

Cox argues that the legislators' reactions to the compensatory shortfalls may enhance the potential for enforcement of the social norms of corporate governance by giving shareholder suit procedures the kinds of effects that increase their potential to validate social norms. These validating effects are enhanced because of the PSLRA's heightened pleading requirements and the requirement that a "lead plaintiff" with a significant shareholding choose class counsel. These requirements allow the suit to be viewed as raising legitimate questions and as being directed by someone who has a sufficient interest in the result to remain independent of the class counsel, and thus curb the prosecution of non-meritorious suits since they also harm the lead plaintiff's interests.[160] However, these requirements are absent in the case of the derivative suit based solely on state corporate law, and Cox concludes that the derivative suit lacks social legitimacy as a result. As well, he concludes that the settlement process in shareholder suits based upon securities legislation robs such suits of much of their PSLRA-enhanced legitimacy, as such settlements appear to be driven more by the amount of insurance coverage than the merits of the case.[161] He recommends reforms that would include a requirement that plaintiffs in derivative actions be adequate representatives of the shareholders, and a requirement that the individual corporate officers make a personal contribution to any settlement of securities class actions. Cox views such steps as affirming the public nature of shareholder litigation by ensuring that it is not primarily a lawyer-driven attack on the corporate treasury.[162]

Some Canadian jurisdictions have recently amended their securities legislation to introduce a statutory civil liability regime for secondary market participants. Securities issuers and their officers and directors will be liable to security holders for misrepresentations and omissions from their securities disclosure documents and public statements, without the security holders having to prove reliance on the misleading information.[163] These provisions contain two features that affirm the public nature of the remedy and restrain the ability of entrepreneurial lawyers to turn them into raids on the corporate treasury. First, the legislation caps damages payable to security holders by the corporation and its officers and directors.[164] Second, no action seeking statutory civil liability may be commenced until leave of the court has been obtained, and once commenced, no action may be discontinued or settled without the court's leave.[165] The court will grant leave only if it is satisfied that the action is being brought in good faith, and that there is a reasonable possibility that it will be resolved in the plaintiff's favour. The parallels with the corporate law requirements for leave in derivative actions are obvious; arguably, these provisions serve the same purpose of deterring non-meritorious suits. They also enhance the legitimacy of any action that successfully obtains the court's leave to proceed. It remains to be seen whether pension funds and institutional investors, impelled by fiduciary duty, use these new liability provisions to deter poor disclosure practices by directors and officers and to obtain some compensation for the losses to the beneficiaries.[166]

In the area of derivative actions that are based on US state corporate law, two doctrines have restricted the use of such actions to situations in which self-dealing, rather than negligent performance, is the basis for the claim. The first doctrine is the requirement that the plaintiff submit a demand to the board of directors that the corporation initiate the litigation before filing a derivative suit in the courts. If the board (or a special litigation committee of the board) decides not to pursue the litigation, the individual shareholder-plaintiff will not be allowed to do so. The court treats the decision on whether or not to pursue litigation that may result in compensation to the corporation as an exercise in the board members' "business judgment," to which it will defer except in certain circumstances.[167] One circumstance where the court will not defer is when those members of the board who made the decision were somehow involved or implicated in the decisions that are the subject of the proposed litigation. If all of the members of the board are so implicated, the need for a demand will be "excused." Thus, the court does not examine the merits of the proposed derivative action but rather the independence of the board members who decided not to pursue it.[168] Even where the board members are implicated in the decision, however, they may appoint new "independent" directors to serve as a special litigation committee, which can then determine that the derivative action should not be pursued.[169] In some states, courts will inquire only into the committee's good faith and independence, and the adequacy of the committee's investigation. They will normally defer to the business judgment of the committee.[170] In Delaware, however, the courts have articulated the need to exercise their own judgment as to whether the litigation is in the corporation's best interests when reviewing the decision of a special litigation committee to terminate a lawsuit in which demand was excused.[171]

The rationale often offered for these procedures is that, due to the separation of ownership and control, control over the corporation's decision to litigate is in the hands of the corporate managers, whose actions are often the basis for the harm to the corporation. Since their interests conflict with the best interests of the corporation in these circumstances, they cannot be allowed to have total control over the litigation decision. In derivative actions in the US, plaintiff's counsel is in actual control of the decision to litigate and of the terms of any settlement, but there are divergences between the interests of plaintiff's counsel and the best interests of the corporation as well. Thus, the rationale is that the business judgment of the directors ought to prevail where there is no conflict, whereas the court should exercise its best judgment where such a conflict exists. Much of the commentary concentrates on the issue of when and in what manner the court ought to exercise its judgment concerning proposed derivative actions.

A number of scholars have made suggestions for reform in the area of derivative litigation in the US.[172] For the purposes of this book, it is sufficient to note the continuing dissatisfaction with the balance struck between the interests of the corporation, its managers, and plaintiffs' attorneys in the courts' interpretation of the demand requirement. This has led some to conclude that the development in the demand requirements has cast a chill on derivative litigation in that country.[173] At least one commentator believes, however, that the Delaware courts have recently commenced a reconsideration of their use of the business judgment rule in shareholder litigation following the events in Enron, WorldCom, and others. In a recent meeting of the International Corporate Governance Network, he argued that corporate directors have been more open to requests from institutional investors to be allowed to nominate a minority of the board of directors included in a management proxy as a result of recent pronouncements of members of the Delaware judiciary.[174]

In Canada, the somewhat confusing US procedural regime has been dispensed with in favour of a statutory regime that arguably applies the substantive review of the merits of the litigation sought by many US scholars to all types of derivative claims. Thus, any constraints arising from the perception that shareholder litigation is fundamentally beneficial only to the plaintiff's lawyers because they can settle non-meritorious claims ("strike suits") on terms that are advantageous to them but not the shareholders seem unjustified and inconsistent with the actual regime for such suits in Canada. The regime has avoided the trap of using either director or shareholder approval as an absolute bar to the court's review of the derivative claim. The relevant statutes provide that such approvals shall constitute evidence that a court may consider in deciding what order to grant.[175]

In addition, there is recent evidence that the courts are willing to entertain issues primarily thought of as corporate governance issues in the context of a statutory oppression claim. Thus, the court entertained an oppression remedy case involving executive compensation. The case involved the failure of the board of directors to adequately analyze an employment contract provided to a controlling shareholder, which allowed the shareholder to obtain compensation without performing any cognizable services for the corporation. The court held that the directors had breached their fiduciary duty to diligently assess the contract and had acted to unfairly prejudice the shareholders' interests, and it set aside the contractual terms that it found oppressive.[176]

Institutional investors have brought other oppression applications involving corporate governance matters, most notably Catalyst Fund General Partner I Inc. (Catalyst) in the ongoing problems at Hollinger Inc. concerning various payments to its controlling shareholder and loans made to related parties without approval by independent directors. Catalyst successfully applied under the oppression remedy to have certain directors who were representing the controlling shareholder removed from the board of Hollinger Inc. because of their failure to control related-party transactions and the impediment they posed to a settlement of US regulatory proceedings against Hollinger Inc.[177]

Another institutional investor, Greenlight Capital Inc., a hedge fund, brought an oppression remedy application complaining that the controlling shareholder of MI Developments Inc. had used a real estate holding corporation's assets to fund a personal project to create a horse-racing and gambling conglomerate.[178] It complained that a special committee of independent directors lacked real independence and that some of its advisors also lacked independence. The court dismissed the application because the relationship between MI Developments and the gambling subsidiary had been disclosed and the controlling shareholder's influence was not beyond the reasonable expectations of other shareholders.

The Ontario Municipal Employees Retirement System (OMERS) brought a successful oppression remedy application against Ford Motor Company of Canada.[179] The court held that OMERS was entitled to a remedy as a Ford shareholder because the inter-corporate transfer pricing agreement between Ford Canada and its parent, Ford US, was unfairly prejudicial to the interests of the minority shareholders of Ford Canada. The court held that the agreement allowed Ford US, which owned 96 percent of Ford Canada's shares, to profit at the expense of Ford Canada and that the agreement was not one that could have been the result of arm's-length bargaining, contrary to the public representations about it in Ford Canada's public disclosures. There are also a number of reported cases of oppression remedy claims where the applicants included institutional investors, where the applicants met with varying degrees of success.[180]

The potential for the development and use of the oppression remedy by pension funds to seek corporate governance remedies was canvassed by Poonam Puri and Stephanie Ben-Ishai in their study of oppression remedy cases filed between 1995 and 2001.[181] Although they saw some potential for the courts to accept oppression claims based on interests other than wealth maximization, any change would require a change in the current perspective of practitioners and the courts.[182] The courts have consistently held that the remedy is available only to protect the interests of security holders, directors, officers, and creditors "as such," and that it cannot be used to protect the other interests of those individuals.[183] The ability of pension funds to use the oppression remedy as a means to further beneficiaries' interests in social responsibility will thus depend on the willingness of courts and practitioners to expand the scope of issues that are legitimately considered to be the interests of security holders, directors, officers, and creditors.

In summary, there is a statutory regime for shareholder litigation in Canada that offers an alternative to the often-unsatisfactory exit option, as well as an opportunity for institutional investors to seek structural changes in corporations as part of their remedial relief from the courts. It appears to be free from some of the more problematic aspects of shareholder litigation procedures that plague the US for two reasons. First, the Canadian regime regarding the shifting of legal costs serves as an important check on the commencement of strike suits. Second, where a cost indemnity is provided, it is conditional on a court's approval of the merits of a derivative action. However, although some corporate governance concerns (such as executive compensation, or excessive dilution from stock options) may serve as the grounds for such litigation, failures in the area of corporate social responsibility may not be recognized by the courts as grounds for commencing derivative actions. In such circumstances, institutional investors may wish to concentrate on remedial structural changes that may make the corporation more responsive to these concerns in the future.

5
The Enhancing and Constraining Effects of Securities Regulation on Corporate Governance by Pension Funds

At first glance, the connection between the regulations applicable to the sale of a corporation's securities and the corporate governance activities of those shareholders who are utilizing the rights attached to those shares is not obvious. Yet concerns over the effects of securities regulations are often cited as the source of substantial constraints on institutional investors' corporate governance activity. The concerns are of two types. First, there are concerns about the positive obligations that securities regulations may impose on activist institutional investors. Second, there are concerns that arise from what are viewed as gaps in the regulatory regime that either give corporate managers important strategic advantages or impose significant costs on those investors who wish to become active in corporate governance.

Securities regulation, however, also provides potential for institutional investors and other shareholders to create a climate more conducive to effective corporate governance through its attempts to create more efficient capital markets. Scholars have pointed out the potential of securities regulation's requirement to disclose "material" information as a means of creating markets for socially responsible corporate governance. One question that arises in this context is the relationship between the disclosure requirement and a cost-effective and reliable means of providing the type of nonfinancial information that would permit institutional investors to undertake corporate governance through a market mechanism. This chapter will review both the concerns and the potential for a market mechanism with a view to analyzing those regulatory features that appear to be most likely to require change. The changes discussed may be necessary, but not sufficient to create accountable corporate governance activity by pension fund fiduciaries. Accountability will require additional changes to the internal governance structure of the funds themselves, changes that will require certain regulatory steps by public authorities and governments.

Securities Regulation as Constraint: Are the Concerns Justified?

As outlined above, the constraints imposed by securities regulation are both positive and negative. The positive constraints are those that are viewed as accompanying any effective steps taken by institutional investors to assert direct control over the corporate governance of a particular corporation. They range from restrictions on trading attaching to the exercise of control, to incurring costly reporting requirements as a significant shareholder, to triggering takeover defences by making alliances with other institutional investor shareholders in order to elect directors or change corporate policy, to requiring dissident proxy solicitation in certain circumstances. Although some recent reforms in Canadian law have addressed some of these concerns, others remain outstanding. Some of the negative constraints include minimum shareholdings requirements for the exercise of corporate governance rights, and the absence in Canada of the "fraud on the market" right of shareholders to sue corporate managers for material misrepresentation.

Positive Constraints: A Failure to Distinguish?

At its heart, securities regulation has two purposes. These are protection of investors and support of the fair and efficient operation of capital markets as well as confidence in those markets.[1] The problem for institutional investors arises because, unlike the retail investor, when they take certain steps to exercise the corporate governance tools at their disposal, they exhibit certain characteristics of the types of shareholders that securities regulators are anxious to constrain – shareholders who are often called "control persons" or "insiders."

These constraints have been discussed by US scholars in the context of the increasing concentration of shareholding in institutional investors in the second half of the twentieth century and with respect to the election of independent directors to corporate boards of directors by institutional investors.[2] Canadian scholars have also cited the legal regime as a significant constraint on institutional shareholder activity in Canada.[3]

"Control" and the Rationales for Regulation

One of the major concerns for institutional investors that arise from securities regulation is the danger of being labelled a "control person" for the purposes of securities regulation. As Jeffrey MacIntosh explains, this designation can lead to the investor's having to comply with restrictions on the sales of a company's securities that impair the liquidity of the investor's holdings, including having to hold the securities for a specific period and having to file an intention to sell, a declaration that one has no undisclosed material information, and an insider trading report.[4] Similar concerns have been expressed by US scholars investigating the puzzle of the seeming disjuncture between institutional shareholders' collectively high levels of shareholdings and their low level of corporate governance activity.[5] Under Canadian law, anyone who has a sufficient number of securities to "materially affect the control of that issuer" is liable to have any sale of their securities deemed to be a "distribution" under securities legislation.[6] In addition, securities legislation provides that any combination of shareholdings equal to or greater than 20 percent of the voting shares will be deemed to be able to materially affect control unless evidence to the contrary is provided.[7]

The combined effects of a lack of definition of "materially affect the control" and the 20 percent deemed ability to affect control impose serious constraints on certain kinds of corporate governance activity. MacIntosh sets out two types of activities that may subject institutional investors to the control person provisions in securities regulation. The first involves coordinated activity aimed at corporate governance of a particular corporation. The second is the problem of aggregation, in which fund managers who work for different pension plans or individual RRSP beneficiaries purchase securities in a single corporation above the 20 percent limit when all of their holdings are aggregated. If the fund managers also vote the securities, they may be considered control persons.

The problem of coordination is crucial to the increase in institutional corporate governance activity by institutional investors, particularly pension funds. Their ability to directly acquire a large shareholding in a corporation is constrained by the pension investment rules that prohibit owning more than 10 percent of a particular corporation's equities.[8] Collectively, however, institutional investors own a significant portion of the voting shares in many publicly traded companies in Canada. They can thus increase their impact in corporate governance by coordinating their corporate governance activity, including nominating directors, voting on management proposals, proposing shareholder resolutions, and/or using voting agreements. These activities also expose them to increased risk of being labelled a control person.[9]

It is important to recognize that the rationale behind the regulation is to prevent those who have gained inside information through their ability to control the corporation from using that information in a manner that disadvantages other market participants who lack the information.[10] Accordingly, since the institutional investors are only coordinating their corporate governance activity on an episodic and ad hoc basis, there are no grounds for concern about the misuse of inside information. In fact, where they are acting in opposition to management (the likely source of any undisclosed information), this may confirm that concerns about insider advantage are misplaced in such circumstances.

Aggregation of shares above the 20 percent threshold for institutional investors can happen in a number of ways that do not involve intentional acquisition.[11] An investment manager acting for a number of different funds can acquire more than 20 percent, leading to the risk that either the manager or the clients will be considered a control person. Another possible aggregation would result if a larger pension fund split its investments among a number of different managers, both internal and external, and collectively these managers acquired more than 20 percent of the voting stock for the fund. Other aggregations involve institutions where investment decisions are made by different branches or departments, or where different investment products (such as mutual funds) are offered to the public and separately managed. While some of the concerns about unintended aggregation of an institutional investor's holdings exceeding 20 percent will not affect the individual pension plan, they may affect their fund managers' ability to trade in the securities of the corporation that are held for the benefit of the plan. Any such restrictions on the investment managers would indirectly reduce the liquidity of that particular plan's investment.

In his 1993 article, MacIntosh argued that these provisions and the uncertainty surrounding their applicability to episodic coordination and unintended aggregation create a serious disincentive for institutional investors. It discourages them from acting jointly in corporate governance initiatives and from acquiring larger blocks of shares. He suggested that the presumption of inside information that justified the control person provisions could be "safely dispensed with" in the case of institutional investors where investors clearly did not have access to confidential information. He reviewed the literature that found that institutional investors rarely "beat the market" in their return on investment, and even where there was some evidence of slightly larger returns, suggested that the increased returns might just cover the cost of research necessary to obtain them. Thus, in his view, a complete exemption from control person regulation was justified for institutional investors, or at least a safe harbour for both ad hoc coordination and aggregation where there was either split management and common ownership, or split ownership and common management.[12] Although it took some time, securities regulators responded to some of these concerns and promulgated rules in 2000 that exempted trades by qualified institutional investors from the prospectus requirement and other restrictions on liquidity, provided the conditions that might raise issues of access to confidential information were not present.[13] Thus, at the point that Canadian institutional investors are considering coordination of corporate governance activity, they ought not to be concerned that doing so will subject them to the restrictions on liquidity that attach when a shareholder becomes a control person. However, one of the requirements for exemption as an "eligible institutional investor"[14] from the restrictions on trades by a control person does directly affect one of the strategies for corporate governance that some scholars have suggested might be pursued by institutional investors. This strategy is the election of outside directors accountable to the institutional investors.[15] Among the conditions that will disentitle an otherwise eligible institutional investor from exemption from the control person restrictions is that "there are no directors or officers of the reporting issuer who were, or could reasonably be seen to have been, selected, nominated or designated by the eligible institutional investor or any joint actor."[16] Thus, institutional investors who coordinate their actions to nominate a director must be prepared to have their trading activity in that corporation's securities be subject to the restrictions on liquidity that accompany treatment as a control person under applicable securities regulation. Although MacIntosh points out that some institutional investors, including pension funds, may not see temporary illiquidity as an important cost due to their long-term investment horizons, he warns that nominating or electing a director may also open an institutional investor to treatment as an "insider."[17]

What Makes an "Insider"?

An insider is someone, such as a corporate officer or director, who is in a position to obtain material information about the corporation that if known would affect the trading in its securities. Securities regulation both defines those who will be considered insiders and prohibits trading in securities by those insiders when they have confidential information about the corporation. In addition, the regulators require that insiders report all of their trades of the corporation's securities.[18] The problem with being treated as an insider is that liability risk increases dramatically. Insider trading can subject one to criminal conviction and fines under securities law, civil liability to both the issuing company and the party on the other side of the trade, and administrative penalties that amount to exclusion from the securities market.[19]

As one securities text notes, a number of rationales have been offered for the regulation of insider trading. These rationales include: unfairness to other market participants; the use of the information as appropriation of a corporate asset; and the adverse effects on market participation and/or the cost of capital from the perception of widespread insider trading.[20] In order to assess these rationales, one needs to look at the definition of insider that encompasses both defined classes of individuals and companies and those who are in a special relationship with the company.[21] One of the most important parts of the definition of insider for larger pension funds is that which applies the definition to any person or company that beneficially owns or exercises control and direction over more than 10 percent of the voting securities of a reporting issuer. The other aspect of the definition is that which attaches the "special relationship" prohibitions on trading to anyone who receives material information about a company from someone who is an insider or in a "special relationship."[22]

Since directors of the company are by definition insiders and in a special relationship with a company, any material information they communicate would result in a prohibition on trading in the company's securities until the company makes the information public. There is also a risk that a company will not consider certain information material and will therefore not disclose it, but that a court may find that the information was material. Anyone who traded while in possession of that undisclosed information would then be subject to insider trading liability. Thus, concerns about the actual and potential liability for insider trading would mean that institutional investors, even if not concerned about constraints on liquidity from the control person provisions, would still be concerned about insider trading liability in selecting or electing a director in a publicly traded company. As MacIntosh points out, the only effective means to prevent the communication of non-public material information, and thus escape any potential insider trading liability, is to forbid any communications with the representative director by employees of the institutional investor. This inability to communicate, however, greatly diminishes the ability of institutional investors to use the director to monitor management.[23]

Ronald Gilson and Reinier Kraakman's proposals raise similar concerns in the US securities regulation context, given their express intent to make the directors nominated and selected by institutional investors "dependent" on those investors rather than independent.[24] Nevertheless, these authors are skeptical that regulators would view the episodic attempt to elect a director by a group of institutional shareholders as grounds that would require them to forgo any profits from "short-swing" trades.[25] They offer several grounds for their skepticism. In particular, they argued that the lack of a connection to the investor organization and the use of an intermediary organization to select the directors mean that regulators would not treat them as a deputy of the institutional investors.[26] According to the authors, to be treated as a deputy, the director would have had to have authority over the investments of the institutional investor.[27] In addition, they argue that the rationale for prohibiting short-swing profit for those whose shareholdings exceeded the 10 percent threshold (a concern that the large shareholder had inside information) did not apply to a dissident group of institutional investors. Therefore, they believe it is unlikely that regulators would aggregate the groups' holdings so as to reach the 10 percent threshold.[28]

Whatever the outcome of the concerns regarding insider trading in the US, MacIntosh argues that similar concerns would inhibit the strategy of director selection in Canada. In addition, he is concerned that the same potential for aggregation of holdings exists as with respect to the control person regulations. Even where no intentional coordination was occurring, he sees a potential for aggregation because the definition of the 10 percent threshold includes a reference to having control of voting securities.[29] Recent changes to securities regulation in Canada, however, have addressed some of these aggregation problems by providing aggregation relief for "eligible institutional investors." National Instrument 62-103 contains provisions allowing such investors to "treat securities that are owned or controlled through a business unit ... separately from securities owned or controlled through any other of its business units" for the purposes of securities regulation. The provision for separate treatment requires compliance with a number of conditions, including the following:

(a) decisions on each of the acquisition, disposition, holding or voting of the securities owned or controlled by a business unit are made in all circumstances by that business unit;
(b) the business unit is not a joint actor with any other business unit with respect to the securities, determined without regard to the presumption in securities legislation that an associate or affiliate of an offeror is presumed to be acting jointly or in concert with the offeror;
(c) no entity that makes, advises on, participates in the formulation of, or exercises influence over, decisions on the acquisition, disposition, holding or voting of securities owned or controlled by or on behalf of a business unit also makes, advises on, participates in the formulation of or exercises influence over, decisions on the acquisition, disposition, holding or voting of securities owned or controlled by or on behalf of any other business unit, except for the purposes of
  (i) preparing research reports,
  (ii) monitoring or ensuring compliance with regulatory requirements, or
  (iii) setting, monitoring or ensuring compliance with general investment policies, guidelines, objectives or restrictions.[30]

Eligible institutional investors must also ensure compliance with securities legislation and the provisions of applicable rules by their business units in order to qualify for aggregation relief. There is also aggregation relief available for eligible institutional investors where the securities are held in an investment fund, provided the following conditions are met:

(a) the investment fund is not a private mutual fund;
(b) a portfolio adviser manages the investment fund on behalf of the eligible institutional investor under a written agreement;

(c) the portfolio adviser has been identified as managing the investment fund in a document provided to an investor;

(d) none of the eligible institutional investor, its affiliates or associates, or a director, officer, partner, employee or agent of the eligible institutional investor or its affiliates or associates, makes, advises on, participates in the formulation of, or exercises influence over, decisions made by the portfolio adviser on the acquisition, disposition, holding or voting of securities, except for the purposes of

  (i) preparing research reports,

  (ii) monitoring or ensuring compliance with regulatory requirements, or

  (iii) setting, monitoring or ensuring compliance with general investment policies, guidelines, objectives or restrictions;

(e) the eligible institutional investor or affiliate or associate has reasonable grounds for believing that the portfolio adviser complies with the applicable provisions and securities legislation related to the applicable definitions in connection with securities owned or controlled by the investment fund;

(f) the portfolio adviser neither controls nor is controlled by the eligible institutional investor or an affiliate or associate of the eligible institutional investor.[31]

In order to take advantage of these types of aggregation relief, an eligible institutional investor must also comply with certain disclosure and record-keeping requirements. These requirements allow other investors to know that an institutional investor it is relying on these provisions, and regulators to know which funds the institutional investor is claiming are eligible for aggregation relief.[32]

Two concerns arise from these provisions. First, to what extent do they constrain the coordination of corporate governance activity by groups of institutional investors? Second, can they act as an impediment to the direction of funds' corporate governance activities by the funds' beneficiaries? The concerns with respect to the first issue arise from the references to "joint actors" in the aggregation relief provisions. "Joint actor" is defined as follows: "in relation to an entity and a security, another entity acting jointly or in concert with the entity in connection with the ownership of, or control over, the security."[33] Would ad hoc cooperation with respect to shareholder resolutions, director nominations, or bylaw amendment qualify as acting jointly or in concert with another entity? Undoubtedly such activity would fit within this part of the definition. But would such activity also constitute "acting ... in connection with the ownership of, or control over, the security"? There seems to be a reasonable risk that they might be treated in this fashion. Much will depend on the issues on which the investors are cooperating. As MacIntosh has pointed out, the rationales for the prospectus requirements and insider trading restrictions (concerns about privileged access to material information arising from the size of one's holdings or the ability to control the corporation) are not easily applicable to situations where one is aggregating the holdings of investors because they are cooperating on an ad hoc basis.[34] These rationales may be more applicable where the cooperation involves the nomination and election of members of the board of directors, unless there is some form of acceptable mechanism to maintain some accountability to the nominating organizations yet prevent the communication of material information that has not yet been disclosed by the directors to those same organizations.

With respect to the second concern, the conditions imposed to obtain aggregation relief could certainly act as constraints on the ability of the beneficiaries of pension funds and other institutional investors to direct the corporate governance activities of the funds' fiduciaries. Much will turn on the meaning of the exception to the prohibition on common control of decision making that allows for the "setting, monitoring or ensuring compliance with general investment policies, guidelines, objectives or restrictions" by eligible institutional investors.[35] The level of specificity that will trigger the aggregation of a particular fund's securities is not clear from the wording, but certainly the exception would include general issues of corporate social responsibility and corporate governance structures, especially if they can be expressed as a policy. The problem will arise, if one does, with respect to ensuring the compliance aspect of the exception, since that will involve comparing the voting decision of the investment fund or business unit manager with the policy of the institutional investor and seeking to direct the manager as to what constitutes compliance in a particular case. If compliance assurance is done on an *ex ante* basis, by requiring managers to report their decisions on particular proxy solicitations to the institutional investor and then advising managers as to whether or not the decisions are in compliance with the guidelines, it may start to look considerably more like common direction. Nevertheless, the exception appears to provide sufficient room for the operation of the type of beneficiary control envisioned in the proposal in this book, in which the beneficiaries will set corporate governance policy for a fund's fiduciaries, rather than make each decision as it arises. Fiduciary accountability will be ensured through an *ex post* process involving the election of the fiduciaries on a regular basis, at which time their ability to achieve compliance with the fund's corporate governance policies may be one of the issues.

MacIntosh identified two other securities regulation requirements as significant inhibitions on both the acquisition of relatively large blocks of stock and on coordination of corporate governance activity due to the onerous nature of the requirements. The first requirement is the "insider reporting" regime in which anyone who acquires 10 percent of the voting stock must file monthly reports on all of his trading activity in that stock. The second requirement is the "early warning system," in which anyone who acquires 10 percent of the voting stock must issue a press release and file a report with the securities regulator and cannot acquire additional voting stock for one business day thereafter. Thereafter, each time an additional 2 percent of the voting stock is acquired, the same requirements and restrictions will apply.[36] MacIntosh is critical of the application of these requirements to institutional investors, noting that the rationales for these requirements have little applicability to their circumstances. Institutional investors rarely have inside information; thus, there is no justification for requiring them to incur the costs of reporting monthly. With respect to the early warning requirements, he notes that institutional investors rarely participate in takeovers as acquirers, and many are prohibited from holding a substantial fraction of a single corporation's stock in their portfolios. Thus, requiring them to report would not further the regulatory purpose of obtaining early warning of possible takeover bids.[37] The concern about aggregation, as set out earlier, either through taking all the institutional investors' separately managed accounts as one or by aggregating an investment manager's separate client accounts into one, has been dealt with by the recent introduction of aggregation relief in securities regulation for eligible institutional investors. Where aggregation is not an issue, relief is provided to eligible institutional investors through a simplified monthly reporting system for both the insider reporting and early warning system requirements.[38]

There remains, however, the concern about coordination of institutional corporate governance efforts resulting in the aggregation of different investors' holdings. This concern is heightened by the "deemed effective control" provisions of securities regulation that deem a shareholder and any "joint actors" with that shareholder whose voting shares equal at least 30 percent of the outstanding voting shares to have effective control.[39] Having "effective control" disentitles eligible institutional investors from the exemption from the insider trading reporting requirements, as does having selected, nominated, or designated a director or officer of the corporation.[40] Thus, the amount and type of coordinated corporate governance activity institutional investors can take part in before securities regulators begin to treat them as joint actors remains an open question. The uncertainty over these issues can act as a serious constraint on those institutional investors who wish to become more active, as well as a plausible excuse for inaction for those investors who do not. While a purposive interpretation of securities regulation would seem to indicate that inhibiting such activity would be contrary to the intent of the legislation in almost all cases, such an interpretation cannot be guaranteed *ex ante.* In addition, there is a legitimate concern that a blanket exemption for all joint activity by institutional investors may lead to oppressive actions against small retail shareholders by relatively large institutional shareholders.[41] However, remedies provided in the corporate law statutes, such as the appraisal right, special voting regimes, and the oppression remedy, may address much of this concern.[42] It is therefore important to determine what additional role for securities regulation is a necessary feature of securities regulation situated in the context of all of the other protections offered to minority shareholders. Only then would one be justified in deciding that joint action by institutional shareholders that is not a takeover bid or fundamental change to the corporate capital structure represents a threat to other shareholders' legitimate interests. At one point some signs that a securities regulation regime more favourable to institutional investor activism may be in the offing in the US.

Recent Developments in the US regarding Securities Regulation and Director Nomination

Some recent US developments had the potential to affect the constraints on a strategy of director nomination arising from securities regulation in the US. However, as outlined in Chapter 4, the Securities and Exchange Commission (SEC) has withdrawn its proposed rule, "Security Holder Director Nominations," which would have provided limited direct access to management proxy circulars for shareholder nominees for director when certain triggering events had occurred.[43] Instead, it has embarked on the opposite course by amending its rules to prevent shareholder proposals that amend the corporation's bylaws to permit shareholder nominations of directors from being included in management proxy circulars.[44] The SEC's decisions do perpetuate some of the plausible excuses currently available to those passive institutional investors for their inaction. As a result, an inquiry into their passivity must focus on two issues, the impact of securities regulation and the effects of conflicts between their interests and those of their beneficiaries.

Besides the effects of positive constraints in securities regulation, it is important to look for gaps in existing policy instruments, the filling of which would encourage accountable corporate governance activity by institutional investors.

Negative Constraints: Should the Law Fill the Gap?

In contrast to the concerns set out above, the concern in this section is that the law or regulator has not gone far enough to overcome the constraints that inhibit effective corporate governance activity by institutional investors. MacIntosh has identified a number of reforms that would enhance the ability of institutional investors to monitor and influence the corporate governance of their portfolio companies.[45] Ronald Daniels and Randall Morck have recommended a comprehensive review of the legal regime in order to overcome any obstacles to this activity by institutional investors.[46]

Using Securities Regulation to Mitigate Fiduciaries' Conflicts in Proxy Voting

One of the most important gaps identified by MacIntosh is that, as presently constructed, the shareholder voting regime does nothing to counter the pressure that can be exerted by corporate management on fund managers or on corporate officers serving as fiduciaries. The pressure arises from management's threat to deny fund managers access to their investment business or to use their own control of corporate pension funds to retaliate against corporate management that becomes an active investor.[47] MacIntosh recommends that a regime of confidential voting for shareholders, supervised by independent scrutineers, be implemented to alleviate the potential and actual pressure on fiduciaries by corporate management, who at present can identify each institutional investor's votes as they receive their proxy cards.[48] Other scholars concerned about the conflicts have advocated "liberating" the funds from their sponsors by permitting beneficiary control over the tenure and replacement of fund managers.[49] Others suggest enhancing legal enforcement of the fiduciary obligation to vote a fund's shares in the beneficiaries' interests through the creation of a regulatory supervisor, while creating commercial share-voting trust companies that would exercise that fiduciary duty in return for compensation. Presumably the advocates of the latter option believe that such companies would exercise the votes free from managerial pressure.[50]

Mandating the Disclosure of Voting Records

Another gap, which fits neatly into the regime of disclosure mandated by securities regulation, is that of the disclosure of vote results. Canadian corporations, unlike their US counterparts, are not required to make public the results of shareholder votes. Thus, unless one is a shareholder, one is not entitled to know the percentage of those voting who supported a shareholder resolution that was opposed by management, or who opposed a management resolution. If a corporation is publicly traded, the extent of shareholder dissatisfaction as evidenced by vote results may be material information in determining whether to discount the share price due to the potential for mismanagement or to require further investigation to determine the cause of the dissatisfaction.

For beneficiaries of pension funds, the funds' trustees are not required to disclose their proxy votes as well. In the US, the SEC recently promulgated a rule requiring mutual funds to disclose to their beneficiaries their voting records as well as the policies they have adopted concerning proxy voting issues.[51] Canadian securities regulators implemented their own rule requiring similar disclosure by mutual funds in 2005.[52] There has been some movement to impose similar requirements on pension funds.

At the request of Senator Edward Kennedy, the US Government Accountability Office produced a report recommending that the *Employee Retirement Income Security Act* (ERISA) be amended to require that proxy voting guidelines and proxy votes of pension funds be disclosed. No amendments requiring such disclosure have been enacted.[53] The United Kingdom incorporated provisions in its recent *Companies Act 2006* that give regulators the power to implement regulations requiring institutional investors, including pension plans, to disclose proxy voting policies and votes.[54] However, the government has said that it will wait to determine whether an acceptable market practice evolves before exercising its regulatory powers.[55] Klaus Schmolke reports that the European Commission (EC) proposed an action plan in 2003 that in the medium term would require pension plans and other institutional investors to disclose their proxy voting policies and votes.[56] After proposing the action plan, however, the responsible officials at the EC held another consultation in 2006 on this and other provisions of the plan. As Schmolke reports, the results of the consultation concerning disclosure of institutional investor voting were mixed, with a significant proportion supporting transparency; however, the need for regulation at the European Union (EU) level was supported and opposed by a similar proportion of respondents. The EC has not made any public announcement concerning its intentions with respect to the voting disclosure proposals in the action plan. Whether through securities regulation or pension legislation, it would seem that the same disclosure obligations should apply to the proxy voting policies and voting record of all types of institutional investors.

One fact that is often overlooked in analyzing the complexities of securities regulation is that one of its purposes is to support a "market" for the securities that are subject to these regulations. The next section reviews the potential for corporate governance activity by institutional investors through the markets in which corporations produce and trade, particularly the effects of regulatory activity on the creation and effectiveness of these markets.

Informal Avenues of Governance

Scholars have suggested that, in addition to the corporate law provisions through which corporate management is formally accountable to shareholders through the exercise of their vote or through the shareholders' rights to initiate court proceedings, there are other avenues of accountability. One such avenue, often cited by scholars, is that of the market, in which various markets are said to exercise constraints on management's discretion by imposing sanctions on any managerial behaviour that is harmful to shareholder interests. The markets often cited include the markets for corporate control, managerial employment, products, corporate securities, and credit.

Another means by which, scholars have argued, managers are constrained is through the influence of corporate governance norms on their behaviour. The norms literature looks at the extra-legal sanctions imposed on managers who behave contrary to the accepted norms of their peer group and proposes that the deterrent effect of these sanctions is sufficient to keep unacceptable behaviour in check. These two avenues are not completely unconnected, as there are clear intersections between these norms and many of these markets in the form of a discount caused by the presence of management whose behaviour conflicts with accepted norms.

These informal avenues intersect with the accountability concerning corporate governance to a pension plan's beneficiaries in the plan's policies concerning screening of investments for those that advance the collateral interests of the beneficiaries. This type of screening, sometimes called "socially responsible investing," is used by a number of relatively large mutual funds in North America, as well as some pension funds in North America and Europe. It differs from the previously discussed methods that can be used by pension plan trustees because it uses the market, rather than the corporate governance machinery provided by corporate law, to engage the corporation's management on the issue of the appropriate use of the corporation's resources and productive power.

Theories of Governance through Market Mechanisms

William J. Carney credits the work of Henry Manne for developing the concepts at the foundation of the theories of corporate governance through market mechanisms that have dominated much of corporate scholarship and law throughout the latter half of the twentieth century.[57] Manne rejected the concept of shareholder control through corporate democracy because widely dispersed shareholders faced daunting information costs in assessing competing claims about particular corporate management, and were also rationally apathetic because they could use information obtained by other shareholders to realize gains without having to incur the information costs.[58]

However, he also rejected Adolph Berle and Gardiner Means's description of the corporation as a forum for managerial exercise of power virtually unconstrained by shareholders, on the grounds that managers were subject to the constraints of competition in product markets, the market for managerial employment, and the market for corporate control. These constraints limit the agency costs arising from the separation of ownership and control. In particular, the market for corporate control sets limits on managerial incompetence or self-dealing based on the incumbent management's adverse reaction to potential loss of control. In Manne's view, a decline in share prices caused by such destructive managerial behaviour would cause another firm to offer shareholders a control premium for their voting shares based on the offering firm's belief that it could increase cash flows and raise the price of the shares they had purchased.[59]

Manne recognized that the information costs that fuelled rational apathy among dispersed individual shareholders were issues of economies of scale, which could be overcome if a sufficiently large market for this information could be created. Carney notes, however, that it was not the individual shareholders who became the customers in the market for information, but rather large institutional investors, including pension funds, who utilize intermediaries to perform cost sharing on research. He concludes that Manne was right that scale economies were needed to make the proxy more vigorous, but he did not anticipate the impetus that indexing investment strategies would give to increased corporate governance activity by institutional investors.[60]

It is this increased corporate governance activity by institutional investors that Robert Monks sought to encourage and promote in his most recent publication, in which he advocated that this activity should expand into global investment markets, urging governments to "remove the obstacles they have created to the working of a free market in corporate governance."[61] In an earlier article, I sought to analyze how such a market would function in the context of the operations of large multinational enterprises (MNEs) and their effects on the human, social, and political rights of citizens in developing nations.[62] It is in the context of international capital flows and national regulatory regimes that the necessary connection between the market for responsible corporate activity and the presence of effective enforcement of legal obligations – whether of human, political, or social rights or the protection of the environment – becomes clearest. Clearly, the most direct means of encouraging responsible corporate activity in this area is to impose substantial costs on the corporation for any violations of their obligations in these areas.

As I sought to demonstrate in the article, however, this option not readily available as a result of two factors. The first is the present state of international law, which generally concerns itself with relations between nations, and not the regulation of MNEs. Some nations are either incapable or unwilling to effectively regulate the MNEs' activity within their borders. The second factor is the limited liability attached to the corporate form and the ability to run subsidiary operations in a fashion such that the subsidiary's surplus assets are transferred out of the jurisdiction of the nation in which the operations are being carried out. Even a capable or willing host state would thus be faced with a corporation whose liability is limited to its assets and whose liquid assets have been transferred to the parent MNE, an entity beyond the jurisdiction of the host nation. Thus, pension fund trustees who wished to invest in MNEs and were concerned about the adverse effects of corporate activity that violates international law norms would have to either buy the securities of a responsible MNE in the market or expect to influence the MNE's policies towards compliance with these norms.

In order for the trustees to impose limits on a corporation's management, however, they first need to know what its management is doing with respect to the environment and human, social, and political rights in host countries. Second, they need to be able to provide MNEs with clear guidelines for permissible and impermissible activity in these areas. For pension fund trustees, a cost/benefit "arbitrage" would not be possible without some reliable method of determining the costs, including the harm to environmental, social, civil, and political rights, of particular investments in the absence of clearly enforced laws as a benchmark for assessing these costs. Investors need both appropriate standards and a reliable source of information if the "arbitrage" is going to lead to anything but further harmful exploitation in the name of profitable returns for the MNE.[63]

This same lack of standards and reliable information about compliance with those standards also undermines the second source of control of the MNE envisioned by Monks – a free market in corporate governance.[64] Monks assumes that pension fund trustees or their investment managers will have access to the kind of information about the international activities of subsidiary corporations of the parent MNE that will enable them to make judgments about these activities' effects on the environment and the social, civil, and political rights of the host country's citizens. He also assumes that there is agreement on the appropriate standards of compliance to be applied, as well as on the effects of MNEs' activities on these rights. Pension fund trustees would invest in those MNEs that respected these rights and divest their holdings in MNEs that did not, and/or seek changes in corporate activity through the exercise of their power as shareholders.

As has been pointed out with respect to the attempts to control MNEs through the consumer market, however, meaningful standards of behaviour and reliable information about the compliance of the MNE with those standards in all aspects of its operations are extremely scarce.[65] Without such information, pension funds will not be able to either effectively control management of the MNE and/or determine which corporations are engaged in activities that harm their interests as global investors. It is highly unlikely that the funds will be able to justify the costs of doing the on-site research necessary in the absence of verifiable audits of corporate activities overseas, in view of the diversified investment portfolios each fund is legally required to maintain. Diversification limits the amount of resources a pension fund can justify expending with respect to a single investment.[66] In such circumstances, pension funds will have to rely on information produced by third parties. Thus, merely having the pension fund trustees committed to trying to control the management of a MNE will not necessarily generate either clear guidelines or reliable information about the compliance of the MNE and its subsidiary corporations with such guidelines.

In addition, some of the lessons from the financial markets would indicate the need for international standards and credible, consistent reporting on compliance in order for a corporate governance market to work. As Stéphane Rousseau points out, a regime of voluntary disclosure of corporate governance information makes it difficult to distinguish between accurate reporting and window dressing, and this may lead to an adverse selection problem.[67] That is, if the information that the investors have about the quality of corporate governance does not enable them to distinguish between the corporations with good corporate governance and those with problematic governance, this difference will not be reflected in their prices.[68] Corporate and securities law tries to mitigate the problems for financial markets caused by asymmetric information by mandating regular disclosure of relevant financial information and regulating insider trading. In the area of corporate governance, however, and especially with respect to compliance with international norms of human rights and environmental, political, and social rights, there is no highly developed regulatory scheme of disclosure and verification to mitigate the inability of investors to judge corporate quality.

The Place of the Securities Law Disclosure Regime in Regulating Corporate Activity

One of the foundational building blocks of securities regulation regimes is mandatory disclosure. Securities may not be traded publicly without complying with the disclosure requirements of securities regulation. These consist of the preliminary disclosure that accompanies the first issue of securities by a company (the "prospectus"); periodic disclosure of ongoing financial information; and continuous disclosure of other material information about the company's operations.[69] In the US, registration of securities under the *Securities Act of 1933* (the "33 Act") is required if the securities or communications concerning them are part of any interstate commerce, transportation, or use of the mails.[70] The procedure for registration of securities imposes certain restrictions on the activities of the issuer and those securities dealers ("the underwriters") who are involved in the issue of the securities. Broadly speaking, these restrictions are as follows:

1 No publicity concerning the issue[71] and no solicitation or receipt of offers to purchase the securities are permitted prior to "filing."[72]

2 Oral communications and written offers in the form of a preliminary prospectus containing substantially complete disclosure about the issuer and the securities offered are permitted to be circulated after filing, and prior to the effective date of registration.
3 Commencing on the effective date, sales of the securities may be made, provided that purchasers[73] receive a final prospectus containing complete disclosure concerning the securities at or before the point in time that the sale is finalized during a prescribed period following the effective date.[74]
4 Once the prescribed period for prospectus delivery has elapsed, normal trading in the securities, including their purchase and resale by dealers, may take place without a delivery of the final prospectus as part of the sale.

The content of both the preliminary and final prospectus is specified in some detail in the prescribed registration forms.[75] In addition, it is subject to the requirement that it not be misleading through either a positive misstatement or omission of a material fact. Both criminal[76] and civil liability[77] may be imposed if the information in the prospectus or in any oral communications concerning the securities is misleading. Thus, the procedures provided under the 33 Act emphasize the complete disclosure of information in a manner that would not mislead a reasonable investor.

Under the *Securities Exchange Act of 1934* (the "34 Act"), the Securities and Exchange Commission was given the power to regulate the content of the annual proxy statement sent out by management to a corporation's shareholders. The proxy statement is sent out with a proxy card to seek shareholders' support for management's slate of directors, the appointment of the auditors, and any other resolutions that are properly subject to shareholder votes. In order to solicit these votes, management must send out the proxy statement and it must conform to the SEC's requirements.

In Canada, the prospectus process is subject to provisions similar to those in the US. Trading in the securities is prohibited until the receipt for the final prospectus is issued.[78] Once the preliminary prospectus has been released, limited communication regarding the offer is permitted, but advertising amounting to selling is not permitted.[79] Canadian securities regulation also regulates the annual proxy statement by management, but (since there is no federal securities law or regulator) has taken a somewhat different approach to the relationship between corporate law and securities regulation. In particular, securities legislation in Ontario deems compliance with equivalent corporate law proxy requirements to be compliance with the securities law requirements.[80] Management must solicit shareholders' proxies for all publicly traded companies and must circulate an information circular containing prescribed information that is current as of thirty days prior to the date it is sent to the shareholders.[81] The Ontario Securities Commission is given the power to make rules prescribing the requirements for the validity and solicitation of proxies.[82] In contrast to the regime in the US, however, there was no statutory civil liability in Canadian securities legislation until recently, and, absent outright fraud, common law liability for misleading statements faced barriers that were "almost insurmountable."[83] Securities legislation has now been enacted that imposes statutory civil liability for misrepresentation in prescribed disclosure.[84] The potential effect of this new regime on corporate governance will be discussed later as part of the discussion of securities litigation as a corporate governance tool.

There has been considerable academic debate as to whether or not the requirement of mandatory disclosure is efficient and in what sense it may be efficient. There is disagreement as to whether or not the 33 and 34 Acts' provisions have had any affect on the prices of securities.[85] There is also disagreement about whether or not the mandatory disclosure requirements have enhanced efficiency; in particular, there are claims that the price of the security already reflects the information at the time the disclosure of that information is mandated by these statutes.[86] There is also disagreement in the academic literature as to whether or not the mandatory disclosure required by securities regulation can overcome informational inefficiencies that lead to either overproduction or underproduction of information concerning securities by investors. Various authors contest both the ability of a market to be informationally efficient[87] and the ability of the present regulatory regime to overcome this inefficiency.[88]

John C. Coffee Jr. has advanced alternative explanations of the economic basis of requiring mandatory disclosure that do not rely on the validity of the efficient capital market hypothesis. He offers four justifications for disclosure: preventing underprovision of socially useful securities research; preventing overallocation of resources to the pursuit of trading gains; the continuing problem of the imperfect alignment of managerial and shareholder interests; and provision of information that efficient markets will not generate.[89] He points out that information about a number of factors, from both inside and outside the corporation, will have an effect on a corporation's future earnings, and that such information has the characteristics of a public good. A public good is one from which the public cannot be excluded, and its use by one person does not diminish its availability to another. As a result, the production of such information is subject to the free-rider problem. In the free-rider problem, if the production of such information is left to the private market, the ability of anyone to obtain free access to any such information leads to a refusal to fund the research necessary to produce it.[90] This problem means that without mandatory disclosure, a less than socially optimal amount of research will be produced. However, by mandating detailed financial disclosure as well as disclosure of "soft information" such as management discussion and analysis, securities regulation subsidizes the research and thus encourages the production of additional information.

A related efficiency factor is that mandatory disclosure of material information may inhibit the overproduction of research by denying investors the private benefits of being the first to discover information. If the first mover can gain an advantage through trading on information that is not yet public, then too many resources may be invested in trying to be the first to discover the information in relation to the total amount of social benefit generated from the duplication of research efforts. As Coffee points out, in the secondary market, the trades are a zero-sum game, since one party's loss is the other party's gain and no social wealth is created through such trades.[91] These rationales are not without their critics, who note that the mandatory disclosure regime does not eliminate the advantage to the discoverer of material information that is not yet public, and doubt that the regime affects the overproduction of research in any significant manner.[92] Nevertheless, to the extent that relevant information is disclosed under the mandatory disclosure regime, both the potential that there will be a failure to expend sufficient resources to obtain information and the potential that there will be a duplication of expenditures to obtain this information will be avoided.

Another problem that mandatory disclosure may address is the question of the allocative efficiency of capital markets. Even if trading in the secondary market is a zero-sum game or a costly casino, the price of a corporation's shares in that market affects the cost of capital for that corporation. If these prices depart too far from those that would prevail in an efficient market, then capital allocation in the society will become inefficient and reduce overall social welfare. This reduction in welfare will occur even if the trades between buyers and sellers in the market are efficient in the sense that they utilize all of the information available to them. Coffee cites evidence that the price dispersion on new issues (which he treats as a measure of the ignorance in the market) had been reduced in the US market following the introduction of federal securities legislation as possible proof that disclosure had increased allocative efficiency.[93] Lynn Stout points out, however, that the heterogeneous expectations that lead to allocatively inefficient trading are a function of both ignorance of material information and disagreement over the meaning of that information.[94] Thus, although mandatory disclosure may reduce the inefficiency associated with ignorance, it will not affect that related to disagreement.

The third efficiency argument for mandatory disclosure is its constraining effect on the agency costs associated with the corporate form arising from the separation of ownership and control. M. Jensen and W. Meckling have developed a theoretical model of the agency costs of "outside" equity and debt to demonstrate that a sole shareholder/manager of a corporation that issues either equity or debt would incur agency costs that would decrease the market value of the firm.[95] When equity is issued to an outside shareholder, the manager is subject to increased incentives to consume more corporate resources (in the form of perquisites or increased compensation) or perform less work after the sale than prior to the sale. These increased incentives arise because the cost of this self-interested behaviour is now divided between the manager and the outside shareholders, while the manager continues to enjoy the exclusive benefits. The outside investors will therefore discount the price of the shares in order to account for the risk of increased consumption arising from the principal and agent relationship where shareholders and management are different.[96] In addition to the perquisite consumption problems highlighted by Jensen and Meckling, "empire building" through the use of corporate resources to fund growth by investing in negative present value projects has also been the subject of academic analysis.[97] It is these self-interested transactions by managers, together with what they term "lapses in managerial competence and effort," that George Triantis and Ronald Daniels refer to collectively as "managerial slack."[98]

Of course, in the model created by Jensen and Meckling, the agency costs of the perceived potential for managerial slack fell on the original owner, who had to accept discounted prices for the stock sold to outsiders. Managers therefore had strong incentives to reduce these costs in order to reduce or eliminate the discount, by ensuring that potential buyers believed that all relevant information had been disclosed through signals that the managers' interests and those of the buyers were closely aligned.[99] Coffee summarizes these techniques and argues that those scholars who rely on these mechanisms to serve as a sufficient constraint on managerial slack are overestimating managers' commitment to acting as repeat players in this market. He also believes that they are underestimating the potential for large one-time transfers of wealth from shareholders in a regime without mandatory disclosure.[100] He argues that the market for corporate control has undermined any realistic prospect for managers' long-term employment, and thus undermined any constraints on them that might be exercised through the market for managerial employment. Thus, one of the justifications advanced by scholars is that mandatory disclosure assists in the reduction of the "agency costs" that arise when ownership and control of the corporation are split.[101]

Cynthia Williams has undertaken an in-depth analysis of the securities regulation regime in the US and its ability to require what she characterizes as "social disclosure."[102] She suggests that the purposes of the US regulatory regime and the broad language used in granting the regulator rule-making power provide the power to require disclosure of corporate social accountability through the mandatory disclosure regime used for securities regulation. In particular, she proposes that the provisions of the 34 Act granting the SEC authority to regulate the content of proxy disclosure by a corporation's management had two related purposes. The provisions were intended both to control the classic agency costs of self-dealing managers and to provide shareholders in publicly traded companies with the information about management policies necessary for them to act as responsible owners of those corporations.[103]

In her review of prior SEC action in this area, Williams reports on two prior rejections of expanded social disclosure by the SEC, but claims that rejection was based on factual grounds that no longer apply, not on jurisdictional grounds. In 1974, some socially active shareholder organizations sought rules requiring increased disclosure of environmental harms and civil rights policies. By the time the judicial review of the SEC's refusal to issue additional rules had reached the relevant federal court of appeal in 1979, the SEC was undertaking further study of its entire corporate disclosure regime. In addition, it argued that it intended to pursue failure to disclose civil rights litigation that was material through enforcement litigation. The court of appeal held that these actions were reasonable and refused to require additional rule making from the SEC.[104]

The second rejection of expanded social disclosure occurred during the study of the SEC's corporate disclosure regime that took place in 1979-80. The study was prompted by revelations of illegal corporate campaign contributions commencing with the Watergate investigation and expanding to revelations of bribery of foreign government officials and other abuses of managerial power. These abuses included significant "off-the-books" accounts and failures to accurately portray the company's financial position in the financial reports disclosed under securities regulation. During the study, the SEC's Advisory Committee sought submissions about the definition of materiality and whether filing should disclose information on environmental and other socially significant information not normally required to be disclosed.[105] In the end, the SEC decided not to require such disclosure.

The SEC advanced a number of reasons for this refusal. First, it claimed that to the extent that expanded social disclosure and economic materiality overlapped (in that the effects of the civil rights violations would include the costs of civil rights litigation compensation orders), the corporation was already obligated to disclose those facts. However, Williams claims that materiality on its own is not sufficient, noting that there must be an independent duty to disclose.[106] In addition, she points out that the SEC's position on disclosure of bribery convictions is not based on economic materiality but rather on the materiality of management's integrity to the shareholders' decision about whether to vote for their candidates for director in the annual proxy solicitation. Similarly, the requirement to disclose executive compensation is not connected to any requirement that the compensation have an economically material element.[107] In addition to the argument that there was overlap with existing disclosure requirements, the SEC argued that the interest among investors in socially responsible investing was so low (socially responsible mutual funds represented 0.005 percent of the market in the early 1970s) that such information was not relevant to a significant proportion of investors. By the end of 2001, according to an organization of social investing organizations, approximately 12 percent ($2.32 trillion) of funds under professional management in the US were using one or more social "screens" to choose investments and/or conduct shareholder advocacy.[108] Williams concluded that the statistics provided evidence that a rapidly growing sector of investors found such information relevant.[109]

Another reason the SEC offered for its refusal to order such disclosure was that it was intended solely to affect the corporate governance of the corporation, something that only states had the jurisdiction to regulate. This rationale would not hold up today, however, as the SEC has clearly used disclosure to affect corporate governance through its expanded requirement to disclose committee structure and the composition of the board of directors. Williams notes that in defending its rules requiring this disclosure, the SEC expressly claimed that it had the power to require disclosure for the purpose of influencing corporate conduct through the proxy voting process.[110] The final reason that the SEC proffered was that the power to order disclosure in the public interest was implicitly limited to that disclosure that was related to the goals underlying the securities legislation in the US. As Williams points out, however, even from a relatively restricted investor point of view, much of what has been described as social disclosure seems relevant to a decision to invest, and about how to cast one's vote at the annual meeting. From the investor point of view, it is relevant in terms of assessing both the quality of management and potential costs from irresponsible management actions.[111]

In her article, Williams divides social disclosure into two categories: disclosure about compliance with the law (including international treaties signed by the US) and disclosure beyond compliance with the law (such as compliance with best practices in employment, environmental management, and social responsibility). It is with respect to the latter category that any controversy about the need for disclosure may remain, since the potential costs of illegal acts and the requirement that corporations disclose information bearing on management's integrity should be sufficient to require disclosure regarding compliance with the law. The economic arguments for disclosure of actions beyond compliance with the law centres on the potential for losses in the consumer markets resulting from adverse publicity or from competition from producers who are "labelled" as companies that meet internationally recognized standards for socially responsible companies. Indeed, some of the corporate social responsibility reporting initiatives in the European Union, discussed below, represent important challenges to companies from other jurisdictions in global consumer markets. The other argument advanced is that the number of investors utilizing social criteria in their investment decision making has become a large enough segment of the investing public to justify mandatory disclosure of such information.[112]

Recently, the SEC has indicated that it will require that certain information about the activities of foreign multinational enterprises (MNEs) in host countries be disclosed, including:

- the ceasing of purchasing, or divestment, of securities of a company by an investor because of the company's actions in a particular country, since such actions could have a foreseeable material impact on the company's ability to raise cash through the sale of its securities
- a consumer boycott of a company if it were viewed as having a potentially material impact on the company's revenues
- business risks imposed by political instability or the imposition of economic sanctions; for example, those companies operating in countries under economic sanctions, such as the Sudan, by the US Treasury Department's Office of Foreign Assets Control (see text of article entitled "US House Condemns Sudan, Tells Companies to Disclose Business," by Paul Basken, dated 13 June 2001, as reported on Bloomberg's)
- public opposition to the company's activities.[113]

As set out above, however, provision of information about the global corporate activity of MNEs suffers from the problems of inadequate means of verification and non-comparability with respect to global activity, and this also applies to domestic information about activity beyond compliance with the law.[114] The questions that remain open with respect to the proposal for increased social disclosure are the degree to which the mandatory disclosure regime is able to achieve the necessary degree of comparability, and verifiability of such information. How suitable to this end is the securities law regime's policy mechanism of personal and/or corporate liability for misrepresentation in mandated disclosure? Will it resolve inefficient under- or overproduction of social disclosure information? An additional question is whether it is sufficient to merely mandate disclosure where there is no reliable means of enforcing existing law (as is the case with international treaties and MNEs) or verifying information about adherence to best practices beyond compliance with the law. A number of international initiatives have been undertaken by various bodies, both governmental and non-governmental, to try and address this issue.

Disclosure and Measurement Initiatives in International Markets

There are some recent initiatives that may improve the quality and comparability of information available about an MNE's operations. The Coalition of Environmentally Responsible Economies (CERES) and the United Nations Environment Programme (UNEP) have jointly initiated an ambitious project, funded by UNEP, called the Global Reporting Initiative (GRI). The GRI has developed a "Sustainability Reporting Framework" to be used by MNEs to provide information with respect to their economic, environmental, and social performance globally. The purpose of the framework is summarized as follows:

> The GRI's vision is that reporting on economic, environmental, and social performance by all organizations is as routine and comparable as financial reporting.
>
> The Sustainability Reporting Framework – of which the Sustainability Reporting Guidelines are the cornerstone – provides guidance for organizations to use as the basis for disclosure about their sustainability performance, and also provides stakeholders a universally-applicable, comparable framework in which to understand disclosed information.[115]

The GRI has created a permanent organization to promote and develop the guidelines. The members of the permanent organization include the reporting corporations themselves, UNEP, non-governmental organizations, and some national government agencies. Although the present framework provides for self-reporting, the GRI is now providing a means of addressing independent "verification" or "assurance" concerning any reports generated using the GRI G3 Framework. Under the G3 Framework, reports are given A, B, or C Application Levels, depending on the range of the framework criteria used in the report. Reporting organizations can indicate that their report has been externally assured by an independent competent body by using the "+" sign (e.g., B+) on the report. More importantly, the GRI is offering a "GRI-Checked" logo for those reporting organizations that submit their report to the GRI for review. The GRI has indicated that it will not provide the logo unless all items in the appropriate Application Level have been appropriately disclosed in the report.[116]

Reporting under the GRI G3 Framework, as with many other such initiatives, is entirely voluntary, however. In addition, the reports themselves do not provide any standards against which to judge the types and levels of activities reported. They provide information about the trends in the various activities reported, and leave it to the individual investor to determine whether sufficient progress is being made and whether or not the level of activity reported is acceptable. For example, the engineering reports concerning the state of environmental controls may be reported as an investment in environmental engineering by the parent corporation. There does not appear to be any mechanism that would require the corporation to link the commissioning of the report to its willingness to follow the report's recommendations.

Similarly, a European Parliament proposal that a committee of the European Parliament could serve as a temporary European Monitoring Platform is based on voluntary participation. All interested parties could both praise companies that are acting in accordance with international standards and criticize companies that fail to comply, and this praise and criticism would also provide increased information to activist investors.[117] The proposed participation and reporting by companies would be voluntary and motivated by a desire to "show their stakeholders that they are conforming with best practice."[118] The European Parliament saw this platform as merely a temporary measure while the European Commission and Council developed the legal basis for a binding code and monitoring system in the EU in accordance with its resolution.[119]

In 2001, the Commission of the European Union issued two communications dealing with corporate social responsibility. The first one ("Core Labour Standards Communication") set out its approach to the issue of social governance and promotion of core labour standards in its trading relations with other states.[120] In the communication, the Commission rejects sanctions as the appropriate method for promoting such standards. Instead, it prefers strengthening the role of the International Labor Organization (ILO) and its complaint mechanisms by providing technical assistance to the ILO.[121] The communication also approves of denying preferential access to EU markets to products from countries that permit violations of the ILO's core conventions.[122]

The Commission also published a "Green Paper" on corporate social responsibility (CSR).[123] The Green Paper envisions the role of the European Union as that of "promoting" CSR through provision of a "framework" that provides transparency, coherence, and best practices, and by assisting in development of the appropriate evaluation and verification tools. The Green Paper does not discuss the European Parliament's 1998 resolution concerning a model code of conduct for MNEs and the creation of a monitoring platform. The potential for creation of such a model code is present in the proposed "framework," and it could arguably result from the consultation process following the issuance of the Green Paper.[124] However, the Commission expressly refrained from making any concrete proposals in the Green Paper because the discussions concerning the role of the EU in corporate social responsibility were only at the preliminary stage.[125]

Following the consultation, the Commission issued a "Communication to European Institutions and Member States" setting out a proposed strategy on CSR for the Commission.[126] The EU Communication presented a definition of corporate social responsibility that emphasized its voluntary nature, its intimate links with sustainable development, and its dimension of exceeding minimum legal standards.[127] It also recognized the global dimensions of CSR by referring to the need to develop an effective system of "global governance," including social and environmental dimensions. The EU Communication then went on to refer to globalization's bringing "increased exposure to transboundary economic criminality, requiring an international response."[128] However, the international response envisioned by the Commission is to follow the strategies of encouraging compliance with international standards, and using trade preferences to encourage compliance outlined in the Core Labour Standards Communication and extending it to all areas of corporate social responsibility.[129] The Commission also identified problems with transparency and comparability of standards for measuring CSR; in response to this, a resolution of the European Parliament urging it to do so, and other problems, it created an EU Multi-Stakeholder Forum on CSR that was to report in 2004 on a number of topics, including:

- effectiveness and credibility of codes of conducts, to be based on internationally agreed principles, in particular the Organisation for Economic Co-operation and Development (OECD) guidelines for multinational enterprises
- development of commonly agreed guidelines and criteria for CSR measurement, reporting, and assurance
- definition of commonly agreed guidelines for labelling schemes, supporting the ILO core conventions, and environmental standards
- disclosure of pension and retail funds' socially responsible investment (SRI) policies.[130]

The Multi-Stakeholder Forum Report was able to deliver only very general recommendations, however. The Commission acknowledged this in its 2006 communication "Implementing the Partnership for Jobs and Growth: Making a Pole of Excellence on Corporate Social Responsibility." The Commission reported: "The Forum also reached consensus on the need for further awareness-raising and competency-building activities. There was no consensus, however, on topics such as company reporting requirements or the need for European standards on CSR."[131] Specifically, there were no recommendations that institutional investors disclose their SRI policies or that they report on how they were implemented. In addition, no recommendations on standards for measuring and accounting for CSR performance by businesses were presented. The Commission is now pursuing a new initiative, a European Alliance for CSR, in which it will support initiatives by EU businesses to promote CSR.

Since July 2000, the United Kingdom has required pension plans to disclose the extent to which social, environmental, or ethical considerations are taken into account in the selection, retention, and realization of investments, and their policy in relation to the exercise of rights attached to their investments.[132] Several other European countries (including Belgium, France, and Germany) and Australia have required pension funds to disclose social, environmental, or ethical considerations in their investment activities.[133]

The United Kingdom Social Investment Forum's "Just Pensions" project carried out surveys between 2002 and 2006 of pension trustee beliefs about the considerations that would have a substantial impact on the long-term value of the pension fund's investments. Comparing results from 2003 and 2006, it found increases of between 5 and 8 percent in trustees' perceptions that issues such as effective environmental management, good employment practices, and respect for local needs in the developing world had a substantial impact on the long-term value of their investments.[134] About 66 percent of trustees surveyed also agreed that further government regulation was required to require pension plans to report on the implementation of their investment and voting policies.[135]

Thus, despite this encouraging attitude towards CSR in the European Union, one is left wondering how pension fund trustees are to exercise either their investment choice or their corporate governance "voice" in a manner that will actually encourage socially responsible action by the corporations whose activity is being reviewed. How will they be able to verify claims by MNEs about their degree of compliance with their international legal obligations and/or international standards for socially responsible conduct? To the extent that the production of such information is subject to the same "public goods" problem as that described by Coffee, will a securities law regulation requiring social disclosure be sufficient to overcome these problems? Will it be possible to generate the type of information that will enable trustees to monitor the social responsibility of the corporations in which they are invested at a cost that is justifiable in terms of the benefits to the fund's portfolio?[136]

What about the "Gatekeepers" in a Corporate Governance Market?

Some of the answers to the questions posed above will have to await the outcome of processes like the GRI or the EU's CSR study. If a common code of conduct or responsibility covering a sizable market is created without government intervention, then commercial enterprise will be the only possible source of information on social responsibility ratings available at a cost that trustees may be able to justify expending. Such enterprises now provide proxy voting advice and corporate governance ratings to major institutional investors.[137] Still, one of the questions that lingers after Enron and other recent corporate failures is the role of other commercial rating agencies and their failure to provide any warning of various corporate meltdowns. Will the corporate governance ratings industry follow the same route?

One scholar argues that the facts surrounding Enron show a systemic failure, not only in the corporate governance structure but also in the structure of "gatekeepers," on which depends much of the regulatory regime for publicly traded companies in the US.[138] After documenting what he described as a pattern of "increased deference" to the audit client by auditors or a reduction of "independence and objectivity" by securities analysts, Coffee offers some possible explanations for this systemic breakdown. They include a combination of legal decisions and legislative changes during the 1990s that limited or eliminated certain liability risks, together with the growth in the sale of consultancy services by audit firms and investment banking services by securities analysts' firms. The effect of the combination of these changes was to make it possible for corporate management to discipline the audit firm by denying it much more lucrative work as a consultant without firing it as an auditor (a move that might alarm investors or the regulator). As well, the securities analysts' income from investment banking business far exceeded the income from providing securities analysis. Coffee concludes that these factors, combined with a "bubble" mentality among investors, drove down the constraint that preservation of reputational capital might otherwise have exerted on these gatekeepers. The lessening of these gatekeeper constraints was combined with the removal of the requirement that corporate management hold the stock it received from exercising options for at least six months. The removal of the hold requirement meant that managers could now profit by increasing the short-term price of the stock through various financial manipulations that would inevitably erode its price over the long term, but well after the managers had cashed in their stock. Thus gatekeepers were also subjected to increased pressure by corporate management to be aggressive in their accounting strategies in order to increase the managers' personal wealth.[139]

These failures among gatekeepers in a regulated sector of the securities market raise significant concerns about the use of commercial corporate governance rating agencies in order to overcome the costs of monitoring by institutional investors. They are largely unregulated and have no industry standards, yet they are trying to make value judgments about factors that have never been measured before and in which, in the words of one practitioner, there are "validation issues in all areas of governance."[140] In addition, since much of their ratings-generating activity must necessarily take place in a "black box" in order to preserve the commercial value of the ratings and prevent free riding, they are prone to classic agency problems, problems that may be mitigated only by their reputational capital. Should these enterprises begin to provide corporate governance improvement consulting services in addition to their rating services, the level of concern about capture would justifiably increase.

Thus, the market for good corporate governance can play a role in permitting fiduciaries such as pension fund trustees to obtain relevant and useful information about their portfolio companies' corporate governance at a relatively modest cost. Recent amendments to securities regulation require increased disclosure concerning important corporate governance factors such as director independence, nominating and audit committees' charters and the role of independent directors on such committees, and the presence and degree of financial literacy on the audit committee.[141] If a corporation adopts social or environmental policies that are fundamental to its operations, they must be disclosed on its Annual Information Form filed pursuant to Canadian securities regulation.[142] In addition, corporations must include disclosure on corporate governance matters whenever they solicit proxies for the election of directors. The disclosure covers director independence, codes of conduct, training and orientation of directors, the process for determining compensation and nominating directors.[143] Corporations are free to adopt any corporate governance form they wish, although the securities regulators have adopted a policy setting out best practices in corporate governance.[144] Mandatory "social disclosure" of the type envisioned by Cynthia Williams has not yet been required, however. To the extent that either increased corporate governance disclosure or social disclosure relies on market forces to generate the information, it is subject to the problems of a "public good" and the dangers of having its providers captured by corporate management should they become effective gatekeepers. In addition, there are reliability and comparability problems that are more complex than those attached to more traditional financial information.

Nevertheless, the existence of a corporate governance rating industry, however unregulated, demonstrates that there is a demand for this information and thus the potential that it could form the basis for an accountability regime between trustees and beneficiaries. One possibility is a regime in which the beneficiaries would specify a range of corporate governance ratings towards which the fund would seek to move the portfolio companies whose rating fell below that range. In addition, those portfolio companies whose ratings were low would be subjected to particular attention by their institutional investors. The existence of this industry and the social investment mutual fund industry also demonstrate the potential for the assembly and dissemination of corporate social responsibility information as part of a corporate governance rating system. Its growth and potential for success would be enhanced by the adoption of a single standard by a substantial part of the market, and by securities regulation mandating social disclosure.

Investor-Driven Initiatives

Lately, the international institutional investor community has begun to show increased interest in some environmental issues through the Carbon Disclosure Project and in "responsible investment" through the United Nations' Principles for Responsible Investment (PRI). The Carbon Disclosure Project describes itself as follows: "The Carbon Disclosure Project provides a secretariat for the world's largest institutional investor collaboration on the business implications of climate change. CDP represents an efficient process whereby many institutional investors collectively sign a single global request for disclosure of information on Greenhouse Gas Emissions."[145] In 2007, over 280 institutional investors, who collectively invested assets worth more than $41 trillion, signed the request for disclosure. More than 940 large companies responded to the request sent in 2006. All responses are posted on the CDP website and are available for free to anyone who wishes to download them.[146]

A second initiative, the Principles for Responsible Investment, was developed under the auspices of the United Nations Secretary-General. PRI is a framework of principles for institutional investors to give appropriate consideration to environmental, social, and corporate governance issues in the management of their investments. The principles were developed by some of the world's largest institutional investors and have been adopted by over 180 leading institutional investors with over $8 trillion in assets.[147] The principles begin with the following statement of intention:

> As institutional investors, we have a duty to act in the best long-term interests of our beneficiaries. In this fiduciary role, we believe that environmental, social, and corporate governance (ESG) issues can affect the performance of investment portfolios (to varying degrees across companies, sectors, regions, asset classes and through time). We also recognise that applying these Principles may better align investors with broader objectives of society. Therefore, where consistent with our fiduciary responsibilities, we commit to the following: ...[148]

The six principles that follow commit these institutional investors to: (1) incorporating ESG issues into their analysis and decision making; (2) actively engaging on ESG issues with the companies in which they are invested; (3) seeking disclosure of ESG matters from these companies; (4) promoting the acceptance of the principles in the investment industry; (5) working together to enhance the effectiveness of the principles; and (6) reporting on their progress in implementing them. The latter two principles are aimed at the collective action problems that might arise if everyone waited for other institutional investors to make the first move so that they could reap the benefits free of costs (the free-rider problem), or had to decide whether to expend resources without knowing whether others were also doing their "fair share" (the prisoner's dilemma).

One of the initiatives implemented in the first year of the PRI is the Engagement Clearinghouse, where investors can exchange information about their ESG activities and coordinate action internationally on ESG issues. The signatories to the PRI have just completed their Reporting and Assessment Questionnaire and the results were released in July 2007.[149] After noting that the number of signatories had grown to more than two hundred and the assets managed by the signatories had increased to US$9 trillion, the PRI's Report on Progress showed that 88 percent of asset manager signatories and 82 percent of asset owners are "conducting at least some shareholder engagement on ESG issues." Integrating ESG issues into investment decisions and policy and into proxy voting policy were the principles the PRI signatories were most likely to have implemented in their first year as signatories. Suprisingly, 40 percent of signatories said they had used the Engagement Clearinghouse, despite the fact that the Clearinghouse had only been in place since late 2006.[150]

These developments represent a fundamental shift in the perceptions and beliefs of a significant sector of the financial investment industry that had, not long ago, defined ESG issues as non-financial information that was at best irrelevant and at worst harmful to the return earned on investments. While recognition of the importance of ESG issues to the long-term return on investments is admirable, it may also be short-lived in view of the difficulty of measuring the beneficial effects of improved ESG performance on financial returns. This difficulty is reflected in the PRI Report on Progress 2007's results concerning the relatively low levels of signatories that are undertaking evaluations of the impact of their ESG activities on corporate behaviour and on their investment portfolio performance. Approximately, 28 percent of asset owners and 49 percent of investment managers have gathered evidence of impact on corporate behaviour, and less than a third of asset owners, in contrast with two-thirds of asset managers, have tried to assess the impact on their portfolio of investments.[151] Increasing the frequency and reliability of these measurements will be crucial to sustaining the engagement of signatories in initiatives such as the PRI.

A Summary of the Impact of Securities Regulation

Securities regulation has both a positive and a negative impact on the ability of institutional investors, such as pension funds, to exercise all of their potential corporate governance tools. It assists them through its requirements that publicly traded companies issue a management proxy circular and solicit shareholders' proxies, by providing a regulated forum in which shareholders can exercise their right to vote granted by corporate law, without requiring that they personally attend each shareholder meeting of each corporation in their portfolio. In addition, securities regulators have developed a system by which beneficial owners, such as pension funds, can actually control the exercise of the proxy vote of their shares, even though those shares may be registered in the name of their broker, investment manager, or the Canadian Depositor for Securities Limited. The securities regulatory scheme also mandates continuous disclosure of material information about a corporation's operation, and increasingly about its corporate governance structure and program.

Securities regulation also constrains institutional investors' corporate governance activity, however, particularly their attempts to coordinate actions with respect to a particular corporation, through its protective provisions dealing with control persons and insiders. There have been some recent reforms of these provisions to allow institutional investors to escape some of the more onerous provisions, particularly to escape aggregation of shareholdings that are effectively independently managed, but these reforms have not exempted institutional investors from the restrictions when they coordinate their votes to nominate or select directors. Before restrictions are eased, however, regulators would need to be satisfied that the degree of accountability of these directors to their institutional shareholder sponsors could not result in the receipt of insider information or the control of the corporation's actions towards other shareholders by institutional investors that these restrictions are designed to govern.

Finally, securities regulation, particularly the disclosure regime, provides a base on which a market for corporate governance and, potentially, socially responsible corporate behaviour may be built. This market is not one in which one trades a badly governed or socially irresponsible corporation's securities for those of a well-governed and socially responsible corporation. Such trading is likely to have little net effect on the quality of corporate governance and socially beneficial activity in the market as a whole, since the secondary trades are themselves zero-sum exchanges. For diversified investors (especially those who use indexing), it is improvement in these areas across the entire market that is likely to bring long-term improvement on overall returns. Thus, the market would be involved in the identification and comparison of the factors that demonstrate good corporate governance and socially responsible corporate activity. The commercial aspect would involve the selling of these informational syntheses in the form of corporate governance ratings, and perhaps in the form of recommendations for potential improvements that the investors can pursue in their corporate governance activity. However, the current disclosure regime suffers from a failure to explicitly acknowledge that such information is material to the shareholders' decision about how to exercise their corporate governance rights. It is also material to an assessment of the quality of management and the risk/return ratio (and thus the appropriate price) represented by that investment.[152] With respect to multinational enterprises, it also suffers from the inability of our present system of international law to provide reliable and comparable information about MNEs' compliance with international law, let alone being capable of providing such information about responsible activity beyond compliance.

Overall, securities regulation no longer imposes the potential costs and liabilities on most forms of coordinated activity in corporate governance by institutional investors that it once did. Therefore, to the extent that these potential costs and liabilities represented legitimate reasons for pension fund trustees to refrain from active corporate governance, they can no longer excuse passivity. So long as the corporate governance issues on which the beneficiaries are directing the trustees are confined to matters of "general investment policies, guidelines, objectives or restrictions," there should be no issue of aggregation for various investment managers that are subject to such directions. Beneficiaries should therefore be able to pursue accountability for corporate governance activity from the trustees of pension funds, since the reasons for restraint stemming from securities regulation are no longer in place.

Thus, although there are problems and areas where reform is important, trust, pension, corporate, and securities law are not a complete bar to either corporate governance activity by institutional shareholders or the accountability for such activity to the beneficiaries of pension funds, mutual funds, or retirement savings funds. The time has come to examine the proposal made in this book for accountability to beneficiaries more closely.

6
Designing Democratic Corporate Governance Accountability Options

Why Should Trustees Be Accountable to the Beneficiaries for Corporate Governance?

The reasons for accountability can be divided into two types. First, there are those that are internal to the pension fund and its relationship as an investor with the corporation. Second, there are those that are based on the belief that the process itself may be valuable both to the participants and to society.

Internal Reasons for Accountability to Beneficiaries

The internal reasons are that agency problems pervade the pension fund investment realm and that the evidence is that a combination of these agency problems and actual conflicts of interest inhibit value-enhancing corporate governance moves that are easily within the power of pension fund trustees. In addition, there are problems of a conflict between the incentives of investment managers and the investment time horizons that must inform prudent pension investment. This conflict plays out in what might seem to be a less controversial arena of shareholder value maximization. The controversy is over how that maximization is to be achieved over the investment time horizons of pension funds and how those time horizons are correlated with the reviews of investment manager performance, which are based on quarterly reports. For example, in one article, the authors describe the practice of "window dressing" by pension fund managers who sell stocks that have declined in value from their portfolio just before their annual performance report is due to be given to the pension fund. After reviewing the trades of 769 pension funds, the authors find significant evidence of window dressing, especially in smaller pension funds.[1] Finally, to the extent that corporate governance activity represents an opportunity to generate collateral benefits for the beneficiaries (such as quality of life, stable economic growth, and reduced environmental harm) as well as return on investment, it is the beneficiaries who have the most interest in achieving these benefits. To the extent that the already conflicted pension fund managers consider this potential, they feel constrained by the one-dimensional abstraction of the shareholder that pervades the corporate law understanding of what it means to be loyal to the shareholders' interests.

External Reasons for Accountability to Beneficiaries

These reasons are grounded in the transition from thinking of the beneficiaries as abstract "shareholders" whose sole preference is profit maximization to seeing them as "citizens" in their concrete embodied selves with heterogeneous preferences.[2] In making this transition, the question arises as to whether it is legitimate to restrict the exercise of the corporate franchise only to economic rather than social matters in connection with the policies of the corporation in which the shareholders have invested. As well, there is the value of citizen participation in self-governance, which affirms the respect for individual equality that is embodied in our notion of democratic governance. This means that active participation and debate concerning the way forward has some intrinsic value, in addition to its potential to generate better solutions to social or economic problems. Amartya Sen suggests that the same result achieved through democratic decision making has more value than if it were achieved through sovereign command, because the first process enhances important human capabilities that are necessary for continued development of society.[3] Finally, there is the concern that the separation of corporate ownership and control, when accompanied by the limited liability that accompanies the corporate form, has unleashed power in society for which "no one" is accountable. As one scholar put it:

> Corporations are technology's bureaucratic face. Like machines, bureaucracies amplify each individual's power. That in itself is good. But when something goes wrong, when there is a fatal gas leak in Bhopal, or a contraceptive shield turns into a user's peril, the outside world may be unable to place responsibility. Indeed, even the participants, including those nominally "in charge," may, like Tolstoy's generals, have only limited appreciation of what their whole enterprise is up to.
>
> This is a troublesome prospect, for social activity of all sorts, from manufacturing to services to charities and education, is increasingly being conducted through corporations. Beyond question, the corporate form is a positive force for getting things done. But the age-old techniques of social control, designed before giant organizations evolved, must be reconsidered in the new context. Today, when dangerous products are produced or politicians are bribed or the workplace is poisoned, the bureaucratic labyrinth and the corporate form are likely to be implicated. How are we to adjust?[4]

However, the same author rejects "shareholder democracy" as a solution to the problem of creating social responsibility among corporations:

> It strikes me as stupendously naive to expect that the common shareholders, if only we would restore them to a position of electoral control over management, would exorcise whatever shady practices have been lining their pocketbooks. Perhaps I take too jaundiced a view of human nature. But I see no reason to suppose that the equity interest-holders would pursue profits any less singlemindedly than the professional managers now at the helm. On the contrary, it seems to me that professional managers whose compensation is not altogether correlated to corporate profits are at least as likely to subordinate profits to worker health and safety, for example, than would the average investor.[5]

Another scholar points to what he characterizes as an unjustified confusion of the topic of making management more sensitive to shareholders and the desirability of corporations' being socially responsible. David Engel argues that where social responsibility intersects with profit maximization, these two areas generate conflict, rather than being logically complementary. While he concedes that there is some overlap in the concerns in both areas, he suggests that many of the concerns in the social responsibility area are unique and therefore it ought to be considered separately from management accountability to shareholders.[6] He also concedes, however, that his definition of social responsibility requires a case in which there is no ambiguity or uncertainty about the fact that profit maximization (including long-term maximization) is being sacrificed for some worthy goal without any legal coercion.[7] In making this concession, he has left a rather large field of actions where there is uncertainty as to the effect on profit and no uncertainty about their social benefit. Thus, there are areas of corporate activity where corporate governance by institutional investors may enhance corporate social responsibility without encountering the inherent conflict that Engel posits is attached to shareholders' assumed preference for profit over socially responsible behaviour.[8] In addition, the preference for profit over responsibility is assumed instead of being determined through institutional investors' accountability to the beneficiaries.

We will next examine how the present regime governing pension plans provides for accountability to the pension funds' beneficiaries and whether that regime is sufficient for that purpose.

An Overview of the Accountability Regime

At present, many fiduciaries would argue that there already exists an effective regime of fiduciary accountability to beneficiaries of pension funds for the funds' corporate governance activities. In their view, accountability is provided by both the common law and pension legislation. The core accountability mechanism is the fiduciary obligation of the funds' trustees under both the common law and pension legislation to manage the funds in the beneficiaries' best interests.[9] These obligations are enforceable through court proceedings or through proceedings before the pension regulator.[10]

The Present Regime

The argument concerning the effectiveness of the present regime becomes weaker when one looks at the information provided to the beneficiaries concerning their funds' corporate governance activity (or lack thereof). Once individuals become eligible for benefits under a pension plan, the plan's administrator is required to provide them with certain information about the plan and how they will accumulate benefits under the plan.[11] Thereafter, the administrator must provide them with a statement of their benefits and other required information on an annual basis.[12] In addition, plan members may inspect on request certain plan documents at the employer's premises, and make copies of the inspected documents.[13] None of the mandatory information relates to the investment and corporate governance policies of the fund.[14] In order to review those policies, plan beneficiaries must request an opportunity to review them at the employer's premises, and may then request to be provided with a copy of the policy.[15] The requirement to create a document concerning the plan's investment policies and goals set out in the Ontario legislation requires that the contents of the "statement of investment policies and procedures" (SIPP) conform to the requirements of the federal regulation with respect to such policies.[16] The federal legislation requires only that the SIPP disclose "the retention or delegation of voting rights acquired through plan investments," in relation to corporate governance activity.[17]

Thus, the first constraint on the use of the present regime to create accountability is that a beneficiary must ask his or her employer (who is usually the administrator of the company's pension plan) to see the SIPP and pay a fee to the plan administrator for a copy of the SIPP.[18] The information that must be included in the SIPP relates only to whether or not the plan administrator has delegated the voting rights to someone else. In particular, there is no requirement to have a corporate governance policy or to provide investment managers to whom the voting rights have been delegated with general corporate governance policy instructions, and no requirement that votes cast on behalf of the fund be disclosed to the beneficiaries.[19]

The Free-Rider Problem and the Regime's Costs of Disclosure

Adding to this failure to require disclosure, which will impose research costs on any beneficiaries who wish to pursue some type of accountability, is the fact that the financial structure of pension plans creates a classic "free-rider" problem for individual beneficiaries' attempts to embark on this course. The individual beneficiary's efforts and expense expended in the courts or before the pension regulator result in improved and accountable corporate governance activity by the beneficiary's fund. This, in turn, results in increased earnings for the fund's investments. The benefits of these improved earnings will be spread across all of the beneficiaries, but the costs will have been expended only by an individual. This is the classic problem of widely dispersed shareholders being reproduced in the beneficiaries of pension funds. Everyone will therefore rationally wait for someone else to make the investment in increasing accountability in order to earn a larger net return than they would if they took on the task themselves.

There are some differences from the dispersed shareholder analogy, because many of the fund beneficiaries are also connected through a common employer. Unlike the classic widely dispersed shareholders, they will have other things in common, such as living in the same communities and having children in the same schools. In addition, the active employees may have overcome the free-rider problem in other fields through unionization, with its statutorily mandated exclusive representation of employees by a certified bargaining agent, or through an employer-mandated employee association. Nevertheless, we should be cautious about assuming the free-rider problem away, since its partial solution is dependent on activity (unionization) that is not present in the majority of employees' workplaces. There is also the problem that there will undoubtedly be a delay between the expenditure of the funds necessary to achieve accountable corporate governance activity and the direct receipt of any benefits from increased earnings by the individual beneficiaries. Indirectly, beneficiaries may notice that the funding position of their pension plan has improved or that their pension may have received some inflation protection. However, the enjoyment of this form of benefit must be delayed until one retires or the plan is terminated and surplus funds (if any) are distributed to the beneficiaries. These aspects of the relationship between employees and their pension plans are examples of the ways a temporal disconnect between employees' investment of the personal resources necessary to hold pension fund managers accountable and the generation of indirect benefits to the funding of pension plans may reinforce human cognitive and behavioural biases that tend to disregard or devalue these indirect benefits.

Some Aspects of Pension Plans Contributing to Accountability Concerns

Earlier in this book, the facts surrounding the destruction of the retirement savings of Enron employees were outlined.[20] One of these retirement savings vehicles was an "employee-directed" 401(k) plan. Under US law, fiduciary obligations are treated differently for employer-directed and employee-directed 401(k) plans. Employer-directed 401(k) plans and defined benefit plans are prohibited from having more than 10 percent of the plan's assets in employer stock, and the *Employee Retirement Income Security Act* of 1974 (ERISA) also imposes a fiduciary duty of prudent investment and diversification on the fund's administrators or trustees.[21] For those employee-directed plans that have individual accounts and meet the regulatory definition of participant control over the assets in the account, however, ERISA provides an exemption from fiduciary liability for any person "who is otherwise a fiduciary," and declares that the employee is not a fiduciary.[22]

Susan Stabile has written extensively on the problems that arise for participants in 401(k) retirement savings plans to whom the risks have been transferred under US law.[23] She points out that the rationale for exempting other fiduciaries (e.g., the employer who designs the plan, the investment manager who receives the employee's instructions on investment) from liability under ERISA, that of participant control of the assets, rests on shaky foundations, given the vulnerability of participants to intended or unintended employer influence through changes in the context in which options are presented.[24] Stabile observes that research in behavioural theory indicates that participant choices are influenced by context dependence; that is, both the options presented and the manner of their presentation affect their choices.[25]

Stabile's research also indicates that in addition to this vulnerability, employees generally do not make rational choices when faced with crucial decisions concerning participation in and levels of contribution to retirement savings plans. In addition, they make irrational choices of investment options, and whether or not to "roll over" their plans when changing employers.[26] She notes that, in addition to heavily investing in employer stock when it is offered as one of the choices, participants tend to be too conservative in their investment decisions. They also exhibit passive investment behaviour (sticking with the first choice they made when they joined the plan). As a result of these biases, participants' investments underperform by 2 percent compared with returns earned by institutional investors.[27] Jayne Zanglein reports that women and minority employees bear a disproportionate risk of earning lower returns because they choose more conservative investments than men.[28] Stabile concludes that these decisions result from a poor fit between the incentives provided by the legal regime and the biases of individual employees with respect to these issues, once one accepts as legitimate the statutory goal of encouraging saving for retirement as a justification for the regulation and tax subsidization of these decisions.[29]

These concerns are not merely theoretical. A recent study of US retirement wealth concluded that for those aged forty-seven and over, retirement wealth had actually declined between 1983 and 1998 for all whose net worth was less than half a million dollars. Retirement wealth had grown only for those with a net worth of over $1 million in 1998.[30] Since these figures represented the state of retirement wealth following fifteen years of increase in stock market prices to 1998, the subsequent decline in stock market prices has certainly eroded retirement wealth much more for these groups.[31]

Besides justifying regulatory intervention with respect to self-directed retirement savings plans, the research into the effects of these cognitive and behavioural biases with respect to retirement savings ought to inform both a critique of the present system of accountability and choices about future policy directions.[32] The present accountability regime for pension fund fiduciaries imposes non-trivial research and enforcement costs in the context of significant free-rider problems, and in the presence of demonstrated problems of cognitive and behavioural biases towards passivity about benefits that will be reaped only in the future. One would therefore be justified in concluding that, with respect to corporate governance activity, the present regime provides only formal, not practical, accountability. In the US, where the obligation to vote a pension fund's proxies in the best interests of the beneficiaries has been clearly identified as a requirement under ERISA, no enforcement proceedings have been taken against a pension plan for a failure to vote.[33] A US Government Accountability Office 2004 report said that US Department of Labor (DOL) enforcement activities had been limited because participant complaints about proxy votes were infrequent, at least in part because proxy votes were not disclosed.[34] Other limitations identified in the report included: the difficulty of identifying breaches of fiduciary duty in subjective decisions about how to vote; the difficulty of quantifying damages, a precondition to imposing a penalty for breaches of fiduciary duty; and limited resources for enforcement in the DOL. In Canada, where the obligation is only implicit in the fiduciary duty to administer the funds' assets in the best interests of the beneficiaries, there has also been no enforcement activity.

Irrationality, Rational Apathy, and Corporate Governance Accountability

While there is a problem regarding the individual investment decisions of employees, as Stabile notes, it is a function of the context in which options are presented and the failure to provide information about investment strategies while demanding a choice. Thus, while the ultimate decision may be considered "irrational" from a financial point of view, it is a completely understandable result of a flawed process. Asking employees without any financial training or advice to make a choice among options whose consequences are not explained must inevitably lead to overreliance on the "default" choice in the menu. This research does not suggest that plan members' choices regarding corporate governance policies for their pension plan investments will be irrational, but rather that the conditions under which they are made must include the provision of sufficient information about potential consequences and risks of alternatives to enable them to make an informed decision. In the following sections, I discuss some of the changes in the legal regime necessary to achieve these conditions.

The earlier discussion of rational apathy and the free-rider problem does not mean that there is no appetite among participants for making their pension plans accountable to them for their corporate governance activity. The best evidence of this is the growth in the involvement of trade union organizations in this activity. Trade unions are a means by which employees can overcome collective action problems such as rational apathy and free-riding by creating a mandatory membership organization that ensures that resources invested in improving conditions are contributed by everyone who benefits from the expenditure of resources. Tom Croft and Tessa Hebb document the rise of the Heartland Network, a union-sponsored initiative that began to investigate and critique the investment practices of pension plan funds in the context of the massive industrial restructuring in the US during the 1990s.[35] The AFL-CIO, the major US national trade union organization, became involved and it has created the AFL-CIO Office of Investment, which leads the AFL-CIO Capital Stewardship Program. This program encourages worker trustees and plan members to demand active corporate governance from their pension plans, and to require that the plans seek to advance sound corporate governance practices at the investee companies.[36] The Office of Investment has also developed proxy voting guidelines and conducts a "Key Votes Survey" of investment managers. The voting guidelines provide detailed guidance on corporate governance issues as well as environmental and social matters.[37]

In the United Kingdom, the Trades Union Congress (TUC) issued a strategy report in 2003 detailing how union trustees can pursue active corporate governance by their pension funds, and setting out plans for the Congress to provide support for these efforts.[38] The TUC website now provides voting profiles of UK fund managers in a searchable database, and provides trustee training in anticipation of the 2009 implementation of 50 percent member-nominated trustees for pension plans. Finally, on a global scale, the Global Unions Committee on Working Capital is a committee formed by large international trade unions that facilitates the sharing of information and development of strategies around matters such as trustee education, corporate and financial market governance, and shareholder activism.[39]

These initiatives demonstrate that plan member involvement and accountability to plan members for pension plan corporate governance activities are important matters on the agendas of organizations representing millions of employees. They view these activities as essential to the twin goals of ensuring that the financial returns of pension plans are adequate and using the financial influence of their investments to ensure that corporations act responsibly in creating long-term value for their shareholders. This involves two activities: educating their members about the issues and encouraging the financial management industry to focus on corporate governance and on social and environmental management as generators of value.

Constraints, Barriers, and Opportunities: A Summary of Changes to Regulatory Regimes

The starting point for a discussion of the required changes is the trust and pension law regime. Some trust law doctrines must be modified through changes in the pension regulation statute, while some of the statutory pension regulation obligations require modification as well. These changes must encompass the issues of providing sufficient information to allow informed decision making, choosing between direct and representative democracy, defining a voting constituency, and a decision rule.

Pension and Trust Law: Disclosure

The first barrier to effective beneficiary control is in the trust law doctrine governing the disclosure obligation to beneficiaries. As stated above, the common law of trusts requires only that trustees "account" for their administration of the trust by rendering a financial accounting of their investment and disposition of the trust property. Under trust law, beneficiaries cannot require the trustees to disclose the grounds for any exercise of the discretion granted to them under the terms of the trust. Pension regulation modifies this regime by requiring the disclosure of a number of documents and reports about the pension fund and its administration. However, neither the funds' policy on corporate governance issues nor the way in which the funds vote their proxies is subject to this disclosure regime.[40] Thus, beneficiaries are unable to take even the first step in holding trustees accountable by conducting an evaluation of the corporate governance activity of their fund. Accordingly, there are three preliminary changes required in the trust and pension law regulatory regime:

- Require each pension fund whose assets are invested in voting securities to develop a corporate governance and proxy voting policy.
- Amend the contents of the SIPP to require that it include the fund's corporate governance and proxy voting policy, and that it be disclosed to the shareholders.
- Require each pension fund to provide an accounting of how it voted, an explanation of any vote that did not comply with the voting policy, and a summary of any other corporate governance activity conducted on behalf of the beneficiaries (membership in shareholder coalitions, meetings with directors, submissions to regulators concerning the topic).[41]

What are the arguments against disclosure? When mutual funds were subject to a potential disclosure obligation by the Securities and Exchange Commission (SEC), they offered a number of arguments against mandatory disclosure. Although the mutual fund industry organization supported the disclosure of proxy voting policies and procedures, it opposed the disclosure of the votes themselves. Opponents of disclosure argued that their investors were not interested in voting, that it would interfere with the funds' ability to use confidential voting to avoid conflicts of interest/pressure from management, that it would improperly "politicize" the proxy voting process by making the funds' positions on social responsibility issues the subject of pressure tactics from special interest groups, and that the costs outweighed the benefits.[42] They also complained that they would be disadvantaged in relation to other institutional investors, who were not required to disclose their votes.

Alan Palmiter points out that, while one could argue that if disclosure of votes was important investors would demand that disclosure, there is evidence that mutual fund investors are not sufficiently sensitive to market forces and, therefore, the absence of demand is not a very compelling argument against vote disclosure. Thus, he suggests that the apparent lack of demand for disclosure may also be an artifact of this investor insensitivity.[43] In addition, the provision of such information may prove to be the foundation of a market for corporate governance activity among mutual funds, with mandatory disclosure serving to enhance the credibility of such information over that of information that is subject to episodic voluntary disclosure by fund managers.[44] This market may be enhanced by recent economic research that finds a positive correlation between governance structures that were more shareholder rights–oriented and relative performance.[45]

With respect to the concern that loss of confidentiality will lead to funds becoming more passive in order to attract and keep pension investment business from corporate managers, Palmiter suggests that this is a somewhat counterfactual argument. Those funds that are presently taking public activist corporate governance stands are also capturing larger portions of the investment market, which may point towards a potential market for funds whose better returns are driven by superior corporate governance strategies.[46] Palmiter also points out that concerns about politicization of mutual fund voting seems remote from the culture of the fund managers, and that disclosure itself will not cause politicization but rather permit investors to compare returns and corporate governance strategies in a more informed manner.[47]

Assuming that the costs of disclosure are reasonable, the amount of resistance from the industry seems puzzling. Disclosure would give them another opportunity to develop a unique product to sell to the investing public.

It may be that the implication of accountability that accompanies mandatory disclosure made the funds' management uncomfortable. One important difference from the situation in pension funds is that the debate over the disclosure of mutual funds' proxy voting policies and voting records took place in the context in which the mutual fund investors could use exit as a means of choosing their preferred corporate governance policy. Pension plan members do not have an exit option as a means of making that choice.

Putting Accountability in Place

The next step is one that engages the issue of the interests of various parties in the assets of pension funds. That step is establishing the exclusive right of the pension plan's beneficiaries to create and control the plan's corporate governance policy. It is interesting to note here that the policy recommendations of two Canadian scholars for corporate governance reform include turning all of the private pension plans into what effectively would be mutual funds. They recommend that all pension plans become defined contribution plans, with employees being given the freedom to invest the contributions in the plan of any employer, not just their own.[48] One of their reasons for making this recommendation was to enhance and clarify the beneficiaries' property rights so that the duty owed to them would be clearer than it might be in a defined benefit plan. I have argued, however, that there is no need for such a change, since the property rights and legal obligation to the plan's beneficiaries are clearly established for the vast bulk of the assets – those required to fund the accrued benefits. The only area of potential dispute over property rights in such a plan is the "surplus," and that surplus does not crystallize until the plan is terminated.[49] Thus, accountability to and control by beneficiaries of defined benefit plans is consistent with their funding arrangements, trust law, and the nature of the relationship of the beneficiaries' interests to the investment and corporate governance decisions of their pension plans.

A number of policy options can be exercised to obtain accountability. These can be divided into *ex ante* and *ex post* options. The *ex ante* options include amending legislation to clarify that a failure to vote a proxy in the best interests of the beneficiaries is a breach of fiduciary duty, "pass-through voting," ratification of corporate governance policies and procedures, and election of plan managers and executives. *Ex post* options encompass class action lawsuits for breach of fiduciary duty, using market incentives by permitting beneficiaries to transfer their investments to another pension plan, and permitting the recall of plan managers and executives. Ronald Daniels and Randall Morck advocate a combination of *ex ante* and *ex post* options to accompany the transformation of pension plans into defined contribution plans operating like open-end mutual funds.[50] The *ex ante* options include statutory clarification of fiduciary duty and election of the pension plan's managers and executives by the beneficiaries. Class action lawsuits and market incentives (generated by the ability of plan beneficiaries to exit a fund) are the *ex post* options.[51] Although it is implicit in their discussion of the recommendation for market incentives, Daniels and Morck do not expressly recommend mandatory disclosure of corporate governance policies and proxy voting records to the beneficiaries.[52]

Disclosure of these matters is a key component of any form of accountability, and is vital to the concept of beneficiaries taking an active role in setting and monitoring corporate governance policy. It overcomes the collective action problems that accompany the imbalance between the costs of obtaining disclosure and the benefits from that disclosure that accrue to the individual beneficiary. However, the total benefits of disclosure will accrue to the other beneficiaries, once disclosure is obtained, and those benefits justify the cost to them of a mandatory disclosure regime.[53] Mandatory disclosure is also viewed as an effective means of controlling the behaviour of agents whose interests can conflict with those of their principals.[54] One will recall the discussion earlier in this book of the generally accepted explanations for passivity of institutional investors (including private sector pension funds). One of those explanations is the conflict between their interests and those of their beneficiaries with respect to active corporate governance initiatives. Thus, mandatory disclosure must be part of any regime of accountability in order to begin to overcome this passivity by disclosing their corporate governance votes and voting policy to the beneficiaries and thus increasing the potential for control through the courts or regulator. No pension fund trustee or manager is going to be willing to say that their corporate governance policy is "I always vote for management."[55]

Once disclosure is in place, an issue arises about the need to involve beneficiaries in the design of proxy voting and other corporate governance policies. It is in this area that several factors need to be analyzed with a view to both pragmatic and theoretical concerns about beneficiary involvement. These factors include the problems of collective ownership, the desire to avoid a "dispersed shareholders" effect, the contest between relative expertise and rights of ownership as the grounds for assigning decision-making power, and the appropriate balance between specificity and generality in statements of corporate governance policy. One will also want to discuss the grounds for choosing between direct democracy (on the voter legislation model used in California, for example), representative democracy (such as that advocated by Daniels and Morck), and requiring adherence to legislative standards through either proactive supervision by a regulatory agency or an *ex post* complaints-based enforcement regime.

Accountability to Whom: The Issue of Majority Rule and Property Rights

One issue that arises in the context of defined benefit pension plans is the collective ownership of the plan's assets – that is, until the pension plan is terminated, the assets are held in trust for the benefit of all the plan's beneficiaries in order to fund their promised benefits. The collective aspects of the property interests of a beneficiary in the plan's assets are somewhat analogous to the interests of an individual shareholder in a corporation's assets. They both have a claim to the assets, but it is a contingent claim and one that is part of a collective claim to those same assets. One difference is that, unlike shareholders, beneficiaries cannot exit with their share of the assets until they retire or terminate their employment.[56] Another important difference is that, unlike shareholders, plan members do have a specific enforceable claim to a specific share of the plan's assets on retirement in the form of the benefits promised on retirement, in the case of a defined benefit plan, or the amount of contributions plus earnings in their account on retirement in a defined contribution plan. The undifferentiated interests of individual employees raise problems of the appropriate decision rule, that is, whether majority rule, unanimity, or some form of special majority is required in order to create or amend a fund's corporate governance policy. Corporate law has opted for several types of decision rules, with majority rule being the default rule. There is always the possibility of exit for a dissatisfied shareholder, however, and if the conduct of the majority is oppressive or unfairly prejudicial to the reasonable expectations of the shareholder, relief is available from the courts pursuant to the oppression remedy.[57] Even where it is not oppressive, in certain transactions a minority shareholder may force the corporation to buy him or her out.[58] In addition, corporate law provides the right to a super-majority vote where fundamental changes to the corporation or its capital structure are proposed.[59]

Unanimity is not an attractive option for a regime that sets corporate governance policy because such a regime encourages unjustifiable holdout behaviour, in which individuals can seek increased payments in order to withdraw their objection to the majority's wishes.[60] Yet majority rule may also have its problems. The first concern is that if "majority" is defined as a majority of the votes cast, then due to voter apathy it may be possible for the policy to be set by a minority of the total number of beneficiaries. This may become even more problematic if this minority is primarily made up of individuals with a political or social agenda that is divorced from, or even inimical to, using corporate governance activity in order to enhance the earnings of the pension fund.[61] This concern may be overstated, however. There are two regulatory constraints on such a political or social agenda. First, there is the fiduciary duty of the trustees to administer the fund in the beneficiaries' best interests. Anyone may seek to have such a policy declared a breach of trust in the courts and have the trustees enjoined from implementing it. Second, there is the requirement in corporate law that any shareholder proxy proposal must "relate in a significant way to the business or affairs of the corporation."[62] A minority whose corporate governance strategy consisted of submitting resolutions that were rejected by the courts on the grounds that there was no significant relationship to the corporation's business would not remain in control of corporate governance policy for very long.

In addition, the corporate governance policy design could be split into two types of decisions, one of which could be subject to a super-majority requirement. The first type of decision would encompass the policy concerning corporate governance activity, including proxy voting, director nomination and election, and other types of activities, such as shareholder litigation or meetings with corporate boards of directors. A simple majority rule would be sufficient in this area, as the influence on the potential earnings of the fund is relatively indirect, resulting from improvements in corporate performance over the long term. The second area would cover screening of investments, both for future investment and for potential divestment. Such activity has the potential to have a direct impact on the fund's earnings through improper exclusion or inclusion of a particular investment or class of investments, and perhaps a super-majority of the total number of beneficiaries should be required in order to vote for a particular policy or to amend it. Although majority rule does not fit comfortably with our notions of individual rights to the enjoyment of property, we should recall that the property rights of beneficiaries of pension plans are not absolute. They are regulated with respect to the timing and amount of the enjoyment that is permitted, pursuant to our tax laws and pension regulation. This regulation is in part protective of their future incomes as retirees, and in part protective of society's interests in ensuring that its older members are able to retain their independence and a reasonable standard of living without drawing on the finances of future generations to support them. Thus, the use of majority rule as a decision rule is justifiable, in light of the regulatory limits to the scope of the majority rule and the already limited nature of beneficiaries' property rights in the fund.

Direct versus Representative Democracy

The foregoing discussion of the place of majority rule leads to the discussion of whether direct or representative democracy is the most appropriate form of decision making for pension plan corporate governance policy. One form of direct democracy that has been discussed in this context is that of "pass-through" proxy voting, where the right to vote the proxy is passed-through to the individual beneficiary by the pension fund trustee or the fund's investment managers. This type of system would be a sort of passive direct democracy, as all that is required is that the trustee pass-through the right to vote on a proposal initiated by corporate management or a dissident shareholder. There is no provision in such systems for the beneficiary to initiate a shareholder proposal and have it taken up by the pension fund's trustees. The reader may recall from the review of securities regulation that there is already a regime to pass-through the proxy votes from the registered shareholders (either the Canadian Depositor for Securities [CDS], a broker, or the funds' investment managers) to the funds themselves.[63] Pass-through voting could be grafted onto this regime by treating the pension fund's trustees as just another layer of agents (just like the CDS, broker, or investment manager). Once the trustees have received the proxy circulars and proxy voting cards from their agents, they would have an obligation to forward copies of these documents to the pension fund's beneficiaries. In addition, once they have received the proxy voting cards back from the beneficiaries, they would have to fill out their proxy voting cards in accordance with those instructions. There are problems with such a regime, however, both pragmatic and theoretical.

Pragmatically, the exercise would require that the costs of reproducing millions of copies of proxy circulars and voting cards and of tabulating the returned cards be assumed by the pension fund. The proxy-voting season would have to be extended in order to provide time for delivery and return of the materials. This type of democratic decision making was considered and rejected by "Campaign GM" in the US, an attempt in the early 1970s to use the shareholder proposal process to put social responsibility issues on the management proxy circular.[64] Although some of these costs might be mitigated in today's Internet environment, there would still be the costs of tabulation and of communication with beneficiaries who do not use the Internet.[65] Even if these costs were not substantial, other considerations may militate against adoption of pass-through voting.

These considerations are founded on the insights of Adolph Berle and Gardiner Means into the dynamics of corporate governance of a corporation with a large number of dispersed shareholders.[66] They noted that the inability of the shareholders to control corporate management was a function of the inability to coordinate their efforts, with the costs of monitoring for each shareholder exceeding the benefits the shareholder might expect to receive from exercising that control. When combined with a liquid capital market in which these individual shareholders could sell their shares easily, the shareholders chose liquidity rather than control.[67] Thus, the ownership of the corporation was separated from its control. These insights into the problems of control with widely dispersed "owners" have informed opposition to pass-through proposals. Jeffrey MacIntosh opposes it because the result of a beneficiary's failure to provide instructions is that the stock is not voted at all. He recognizes the concern about the intermediary bowing to commercial pressures from the corporation that might justify disenfranchising the intermediary. However, he considers it better for the vote to be exercised than for it to be "sterilized" by a failure of the beneficiary to respond, since this would destroy the benefits of concentrated institutional share ownership by reproducing the Berle and Means universe of dispersed voters.[68] Therefore, in designing a means by which to create accountability to beneficiaries, one needs to be careful not to reproduce the problem of dispersed ownership and concentrated control.

The effects of dispersal and the problem of "rational apathy" with respect to the creation and amendment of the pension plan's corporate governance guidelines by beneficiary vote require that certain precautions be taken. In particular, it may be necessary to incorporate a voting threshold requiring a minimum number of beneficiary votes before any guideline will be considered binding by the plan's trustees or administrators. Such a threshold may prevent any capture of the fund's corporate governance activities by a minority of beneficiaries who might otherwise control decision making without the sanction of majority support.[69] If direct democracy is the means chosen to implement accountability to the beneficiaries, the adoption of a corporate governance policy or its amendment may have to be subject to a positive vote of at least a majority of the beneficiaries.

Another issue for a direct democracy regime is the mechanism by which policies are presented to the beneficiaries for consideration and then subjected to a vote. With a large number of beneficiaries, cost may become an important factor. If every beneficiary can require the trustees to submit a proposal to a vote, the costs of distributing the proposal and explanation, together with the trustees' recommendation, may become significant. Some political jurisdictions control the costs by requiring proponents to fund a preliminary petition campaign to gather a minimum level of voter support in order to include their proposal on the ballot. Consideration would have to be given to a similar requirement for beneficiary-initiated proposals or amendments in order to justify the expenditure of conducting a ballot among all of the beneficiaries.

Another issue that arises with a direct democracy regime is that of competence and expertise. A committee of the Senate of Canada, in its report on the governance practices of institutional investors, raised the issue of lack of expertise as follows:

> In general, business-oriented individuals, people accustomed to the nature of decisions that those running a pension plan deal with, are involved in the oversight of private pension plans. Members of the boards of public sector plans, on the other hand, are frequently individuals with insufficient experience in business-related matters. Qualities necessary to oversee an

institutional investor, such as a large pension fund, include an understanding of the principles of organisational behaviour, of investment in modern financial markets, of dealing with risk, and so forth. Such experience is usually acquired through some combination of formal training and hands-on experience. It is unlikely that an individual can acquire this foundation through general reading.

The Committee was told that it is very important to have as members of the boards of any financial institution, and of public sector pension plans, in particular, persons comfortable dealing with complex financial issues. Boards must ensure that a significant number of their members have the necessary scope, experience, knowledge and time to oversee the complex operations involved, which would include investment management, information systems, administration, communications, and risk management, among other things.

Can a lay board meet these expectations? The Ontario Municipal Employees Retirement System is probably the largest pension fund with a lay board, an approach which it defended vigorously before the Committee. Witnesses from OMERS put forward five points:

- because OMERS' board members are members of the pension plan, they are strongly motivated to monitor the operations of the fund;
- the clear separation of management and representatives of pension beneficiaries (current and future) acts as a powerful deterrent to conflicts of interest;
- investment decisions are left in the hands of professionals while those monitoring have experience relevant to running a pension plan;
- lay boards, more than expert boards, are committed to educating members of the board on their responsibilities;
- the OMERS board is more democratic than most executive boards, with executives elected for a single term of one year only.

The Senate committee concluded: "The Committee agrees that an educated lay board may bring fresh insight to professional staff who may take a more narrow focus in their decision-making processes."[70]

Roberta Romano, however, evinces less concern about the apparent absence of expertise in those trustees elected by the beneficiaries. She reasons that it is not a serious concern because there is no evidence of a correlation between a relative lack of financial expertise and a pension plan's returns; if adverse effects occur, beneficiaries would respond by choosing trustees with expertise, and education could be provided where required.[71] It is important to recall that the types of decision making that are involved in designing corporate governance policies for a pension fund are not primarily a question of financial expertise. Rather, they involve assessing the incentives created for management by a certain governance structure or the hazards to long-term shareholder value from certain initiatives proposed by the management of portfolio companies or by beneficiaries. Is this assessment within the expertise of investment managers, or should it be made by those whose returns on investment will be adversely affected if the assessment is wrong? In any event, unlike the circumstances discussed in the Senate report or by Romano, corporate governance policy design is not the same as the day-to-day management of the activities of the fund's investment managers by its trustees. Decisions do not have to be made about time-sensitive investment opportunities; rather, the beneficiaries will have the benefit of whatever expert advice the trustees determine is necessary to enable them to make an informed decision on their vote.

Financial expertise is implicated much more heavily in decisions about investment policies, due to the need to maintain adequate diversification both among asset classes and within each class. This greater need for expert advice explains why I suggested earlier that such decisions may require a super-majority vote of the beneficiaries before they are implemented by the trustees. Of course, the beneficiaries will also have the benefit of the expert advice that the trustees obtain for them before they cast their ballots. Therefore, an additional legislative change would impose a duty on the trustees to provide expert advice, where they deem it necessary, whenever the beneficiaries are voting on a corporate governance policy proposal. Of course, this requirement would also add force to the earlier recommendation that any beneficiary proponent of a new or amended corporate governance policy must gather a threshold level of support for the proposition from beneficiaries before any vote would be conducted among the beneficiaries. The cost of providing mandatory advice would be added to that of conducting the vote and tabulating the results, and would be justified by the demonstration of significant support

Given these problems with direct democracy, the question arises as to whether a republican model of accountability is likely to ameliorate some of them while maintaining an acceptable level of accountability to the beneficiaries. Under such a system, the beneficiaries would select the trustees by voting for those they wished to support from a slate of candidates.[72] Other scholars have also suggested that this would be a practical means of addressing the conflicts of interest and accountability issues.[73] The United Kingdom has recently amended its pension legislation to require at least one-third of pension trustees to be nominated in a process in which both active and retired members participate.[74] The legislation provides that this number can be increased to one-half by order of the responsible Secretary of State, and the Secretary has announced that it will be increased to one-half by 2009.[75]

How would such a regime ameliorate the problems of direct democracy? Elected representation is a system that is more familiar to most North Americans than is direct democracy. Its mechanism assumes that the voters are being offered coherent choices of policy or policy direction, and, after time to consider the alternatives, choose the one that they most prefer. Once elected, the representatives are accountable only to those who voted for them, through their vulnerability to defeat if they stand for re-election at the next scheduled time for election. Voters must otherwise trust in the representatives' commitments to them during the electoral process. To the extent that corporate governance policy is an issue in any trustee election, one would expect that candidates would commit to implementing a particular policy or set of policies. Unlike some political promises, it will be easy for the beneficiaries to monitor compliance with the commitment since implementation of the policy is within the trustees' power to achieve.[76] Another aspect of monitoring is assessing the degree of match between the requirements of the plan's corporate governance policy and any particular proxy vote or other corporate governance activity. The choice between direct and representative accountability mechanisms will probably not change the effort required to monitor this aspect of accountability. Whether the corporate governance policy is put in place by direct vote or by the elected representatives, the beneficiaries will still need to monitor the performance of their investment managers with respect to compliance with the fund's policy. On balance, the system of representative election of trustees appears to offer the best benefits in terms of accountability. Although one would want some form of direct beneficiary vote on the corporate governance policy when it is first implemented, the organs of representative democracy appear best suited to deal with implementation in a context where at least some of the decisions require expertise and continuity and monitoring will be most efficiently accomplished by a delegated few.

Who Are Eligible to Vote and How Much Should Their Vote Be Worth?

The peculiarities of pension funds raise some interesting issues for democratic decision making with respect to their corporate governance policies. Some scholars in differentiating between defined benefit and defined contribution plans have indirectly mentioned them.[77] The first issue is whether employees whose pension benefits have not yet vested may vote on corporate governance policy. The second issue is whether or not the votes of employees who have larger pension benefits (and thus a larger claim on a fund's assets) should count proportionately more than those of employees whose benefits are smaller.

With respect to the first issue, vesting of benefits means that a particular employee becomes eligible to receive a pension benefit from the fund when the employee reaches retirement age. It also means that the funds required to provide that amount of benefit are not available to the employee except in the form of a retirement benefit. Prior to vesting, even though the employer may have been contributing a certain amount annually to fund the non-vested employee's pension benefit in anticipation of vesting, the employee is not eligible to receive any part of those contributions. In Canada, under applicable pension legislation, the minimum standard for vesting of benefits is two years of service.[78] The argument against allowing such employees to vote is that they are not beneficiaries of the fund and may never become such. It would be contrary to the basis for requiring accountability from the trustees – their fiduciary duty to act in the best interests of the beneficiaries – to require them to be accountable to those to whom no such duty is owed. On the other hand, the policy decisions made by today's beneficiaries will affect the returns on the plan's assets in the future, including those that will fund the non-vested employee's benefits upon vesting. However, the argument about the potential adverse effects in the future has not led legislators to require that an employer give non-vested employees a vote with respect to surplus withdrawals from a pension plan. An employer need only seek support for the withdrawal from those employees who are "members" of the plan, a term that is restricted to employees who have been employed long enough to be entitled to vesting.[79] In light of the relatively short vesting periods in Canada, the requirement to wait for vesting before being eligible to vote seems reasonable. For jurisdictions with longer vesting periods, the arguments for voter eligibility will become more compelling the longer the period prior to vesting, and the larger the amount of the employer's contribution accumulated for that individual in the fund.

Once the employee's benefits are vested, another issue arises. Should those employees who have larger benefits get a larger say than the employees with smaller benefits? The argument for making voting proportional to the size of one's claim to the fund's assets is that the larger one's claim, the greater are one's losses and gains from corporate governance in absolute dollar terms. However, since the fund's rate of return is the mechanism by which the effects of corporate governance initiatives will be transmitted to the individual beneficiary, the effects will be felt proportionately to the ability of the individual's claim to absorb it. There may even be an argument that those beneficiaries with the largest claims (who will likely be long-service employees close to retirement) will not be as likely to be affected as those employees that have smaller claims (newer employees who have years before retirement eligibility). This difference in probable effect results from the likelihood that large-claim employees will have retired before any adverse effects manifest themselves. In any event, pension regulators have not seen fit to require proportional voting when assessing the support for employer surplus withdrawals from the plan's beneficiaries. The required level of consent is measured in relation to the number of beneficiaries, not in relation to the assets required to fund each beneficiary's benefits. Thus, it is reasonable to proceed on the basis of the number of beneficiaries rather than their relative claims to the fund's assets. Although beneficiaries' claims to those assets will vary, the distribution of the adverse or positive effects will vary in the same manner as well. Therefore, "one beneficiary, one vote" ought to be the standard for initiating or amending the fund's corporate governance policies.

Summary of the Issues with Respect to Accountability through Forms of Democratic Control

One factor that serves as a foundation for all forms of accountability for a pension plan's corporate governance activities is appropriate disclosure. Pension plans must be required to disclose whether or not they have a policy for corporate governance activity, the contents of that policy, the degree to which they have bound their investment managers to follow that policy, and the monitoring systems they have in place. In addition, plans should be required to disclose their proxy votes (and those of their investment managers) and explain any apparent deviations from the plan's policies within a reasonable time after the votes. The present pension regulatory regime does not require such disclosure, however.

The next issue for democratic accountability is the degree to which beneficiaries ought to be granted the power to initiate and amend corporate governance policies. Here, the debate is between systems of direct democracy, in which beneficiaries may require the trustees to conduct a vote among the beneficiaries on corporate governance policy proposals or amendments, and those in which they would have the power to ratify policies and amendments presented to them by the trustees. Coupled with this is the related issue of whether the beneficiaries should be permitted to vote on the policies at all, or whether it is sufficient to allow them to elect the trustees for a fixed term. Under such a system, the re-election requirement would impose accountability on the trustees for compliance with the existing policy and could serve as a means of obtaining changes to the existing corporate governance policy. These systems are not mutually exclusive and ratification could be easily combined with trustee election, with the latter serving as a means of holding trustees accountable for compliance with the policy. It seems reasonable, at least as a first step, to provide a system of ratification and trustee election as a means of achieving accountability. It is reasonable because such a system appears to be capable of dealing with a number of factors, including: the beneficiaries' rational apathy in the face of the individual cost/collective benefit profile of value-enhancing changes in a pension fund; the need for an elaborate system of plebiscite thresholds to control the costs of that mechanism; and concerns about the beneficiaries' knowledge and expertise in the field of corporate governance.

This last factor, together with the potential for rational apathy, also requires an assessment of what decision rule will be used for corporate governance policy ratification and amendment. The concern with respect to the decision rule is the extent to which there ought to be protection against the possibility that a politically motivated minority of beneficiaries will somehow hijack the fund's policy for their own ends, thus wasting the fund's corporate governance resources. There is also the concern about how much protection for minorities is required in corporate governance policy decision making. Regarding the first concern, the potential for hijacking stems from the normal rule that a majority of the votes cast is sufficient to decide an issue. In order to reduce the danger of hijacking, an additional requirement could be imposed that no decision would be made unless a threshold minimum percentage of the beneficiaries cast their ballots. Such a requirement would not deal with the second concern, which is that a minority of beneficiaries who feel that the return on their assets is being put at substantial risk by a corporate governance policy would have no recourse if the majority favours that policy. Requiring a super-majority vote to make any beneficiary-initiated changes to the fund's investment policies may alleviate this concern. In addition, beneficiaries who feel that a majority decision is seriously threatening the return on investments may also seek redress in the courts by alleging that the trustees' decision to implement the majority's policy is a breach of their fiduciary duty. Thus, there are limits to majority rule, defined by the doctrines of the law of trusts and fiduciary duties as well as by the duties imposed under pension legislation, and these limits appear sufficient to deal with concerns about minority oppression in this area of plan governance.

The final issue is eligibility to vote, and whether voting ought to be proportional to the size of one's claim on the fund's assets. Although there are arguments in favour of allowing employees who are not yet vested members of the plan to vote based on their contingent future interest, they are not compelling in view of the short two-year vesting rule in Canada. Similarly, the arguments for proportional voting would be more compelling if our political system also assigned votes based on an individual's taxable income. The impact of bad decisions may be greater in absolute terms, but every beneficiary will have the return on his or her investments reduced by the same percentage, and thus ought to have an equal voice in the selection of the policies that can affect this return.

Accountability through a Market for Corporate Governance Policy?

Daniels and Morck suggest that radical reforms to the system of pension regulation be considered in order to create a form of market for individual beneficiaries' pension assets among various pension plans. They advocate a complete conversion of all pension plans to pure defined contribution plans, in which each employee's pension benefit would be composed of all funds contributed on the employee's behalf, plus the earnings on those funds. Competition for beneficiaries' dollars would be introduced by allowing the beneficiary to choose to have his or her pension assets invested in any certified pension plan.[80] At present, the link between pension assets and the employer is undisputed. The Canadian income tax provisions permit employers to deduct contributions to a pension plan and the earnings on the plan's investments only when the plan is exclusively for the employers' employees. It would take a major revamping of these provisions before any competition for beneficiary dollars could occur.

There are two troubling aspects to this proposed market, however. The first is that it is designed to replicate the stock market by providing beneficiaries with a form of exit, similar to that available to shareholders who are dissatisfied with the performance of the corporation in which they have invested. In a way, such a market provides beneficiaries with liquidity with respect to the investment managers in charge of their pension assets. This raises the issue of whether such a market would increase the corporate governance activity of the pension funds or whether they would compete on other grounds. Berle and Means saw the availability of liquid markets for their shares as undercutting any desire of widely dispersed small shareholders to invest in costly corporate governance activity, rather than selling their shares at a much lower cost.[81] Will providing pension beneficiaries with liquidity have the same effect? In one sense, it may not, because unlike in the case of shareholders, this liquidity would not enable them to exit the market completely by exchanging their shares for cash. It may, however, lead beneficiaries to pursue higher returns through strategies other than improved corporate governance.

The second troubling aspect to the proposal is that a competitive market may also lead individual beneficiaries to incur unjustified costs in the transfer from one fund to another, and thus transfer wealth from the retirement sector to the investment management sector. In effect, the proposed changes would turn the pension system into one analogous to open-end mutual funds. The only difference with respect to dissatisfaction with the fund's management would be that beneficiaries would have to transfer the funds to another pension plan, rather than receiving their share in cash. Open-ended mutual funds are not known as corporate governance activists, unlike public sector pension plans. Therefore, the changes proposed by Daniels and Morck may not lead to the type of competition over which corporate governance policy provides both increased returns and collateral benefits to beneficiaries. Rather, plans may compete on their ability to keep administration costs lower than other plans, and those costs would include the costs of monitoring portfolio companies and conducting the necessary research to vote proxies so as to improve corporate governance at these companies. This was one US scholar's conclusion after surveying the present state of corporate governance in the mutual fund industry and the prospects for a corporate governance market in that industry.[82]

A third problematic aspect of this proposal is the conversion of pension plans from defined benefit to defined contribution plans. This conversion would have major public policy implications for pension policy because it would shift risk to the individual beneficiary from the collective assets of a defined benefit plan. This shift increases the sensitivity to market volatility of an individual's retirement income since the timing of one's retirement is relatively fixed.[83] In comparison, a defined benefit pension plan has a relatively higher tolerance for volatility given its ability to spread out liquidity requirements over a longer timespan and its continued renewal of its funding base.[84] One need only read a few of the stories about individuals' defined contribution plans being destroyed in the market since 2001 to become cautious about a shift in the pension system to a defined contribution model.[85]

In light of these issues, one would want to seriously review the structure of such a market before embarking on this type of venture. Given the similarities between Daniels and Morck's proposal and the present structure of the mutual fund industry, it seems that competition alone is not sufficient to motivate investment managers to overcome any conflicts of interest and engage in substantive corporate governance activity on behalf of pension fund beneficiaries. To be fair, this critique has treated this policy option in isolation from the other options that Daniels and Morck also proposed, such as beneficiary election of fund managers and disclosure of the fund's corporate governance policies and record of activities to beneficiaries. It may be that all of these reforms, taken together, would be sufficient to support a competitive market for the investment of beneficiary assets in which corporate governance would be a major component of the competition.[86] The critique does, however, signal the need for caution and a careful review of the alternatives before adopting the suggestion.

The Regulators: The Case for Command and Control

In theory, pension and mutual fund regulators already possess the tools and jurisdiction to insist that pension fund trustees, their investment managers, and the managers of mutual funds conduct corporate governance activity in the best interests of the fund's beneficiaries. The legal duty of pension fund managers to do this is most clearly spelled out in the US federal pension regulations.[87] Such a duty can be easily construed from the general fiduciary duties of trustees and mutual fund managers towards their beneficiaries. The difficulty with the use of the regulatory structure to enforce this duty is that effective enforcement is beyond the resources presently allocated to these regulators, and the remedial tools with which they must address the problem are an awkward fit with an effective remedy.

Robert Monks, a former US Assistant Secretary of Labor with responsibility for ERISA, makes the point about the lack of resources most clearly and authoritatively.[88] It is not just monetary resources that are insufficient, however; regulatory leverage is also absent. After all, unless the regulators wish to go into the business of designing model corporate governance policies and requiring adherence to those policies from all pension funds, they must find a cost-effective way to regulate a mass refusal to comply with legal duties by pension plan trustees. Individual prosecutions face an almost insurmountable defence by the particular fund's trustees. That defence was summarized by Monks and Allen Sykes as follows:

> Activism is only required when the benefits to an individual institution outweigh its costs. Few such benefits are certain because of the heavy costs and risks which fall on the individual pioneers. Hence individual fund managers will always be able to justify inaction as they have done in America. The only solution which can work is one that compels sufficient investment institutions and fund managers to act in consort, i.e. a generally enforced requirement. It is essential to mobilise the latent power of the combined institutions. Conscientious individual pioneers cannot and will not succeed.[89]

However, even if regulators were to commit to mass prosecutions of passive pension fund trustees, they would face the inevitable challenge of defining an acceptable standard of corporate governance activity, a task that we have already assumed (from their inactivity thus far) regulators do not want to take responsibility for completing. They would have to do so in a prosecution under their power to seek punishment for trustees who beach their statutory responsibilities in order to establish beyond a reasonable doubt that the trustees committed the offence.[90] Should the regulator decide to proceed by way of issuing a remedial order, such an order would have to contain the directions as to what the trustees must do in order to bring themselves into compliance with the pension legislation.[91] Thus, on the one hand, we have a situation of mass non-compliance, and on the other hand, the reluctance of pension regulators to impose a policy. One solution to this dilemma is to download the task of designing and/or approving a pension plan's corporate governance activity to the beneficiaries as those who are intended to receive the benefits of such activity. Regulatory action could thus be confined to ensuring that the plan had a corporate governance policy and that it had received the required level of support from the beneficiaries. Although this regulatory downloading might require increased monetary resources for compliance monitoring and adjudication of complaints from beneficiaries, it would be a more comfortable fit with the regulators' traditional role. It would be more comfortable because it would not require regulatory responsibility for internal plan governance, or the acquisition of a new type of expertise in the design of such plans.

Is Beneficiary Complaint to the Courts a Viable Alternative to Democratic Accountability?

Another option for increasing corporate governance activity among pension fund trustees might be to rely on beneficiary complaints to the courts regarding the failure of the trustees to carry out their fiduciary duty to conduct corporate governance activity in the exclusive interest of the beneficiaries. The procedural structure for such complaints is in place in many jurisdictions.[92] In addition, the courts have not taken the position that the jurisdiction of pension regulators over such complaints has superseded their jurisdiction to entertain them. However, a number of factors make heavy reliance on a complaint-based court proceeding as a means to increase corporate governance activity unwise. They include the following:

- Pension plans are not legally obliged to disclose their corporate governance policy and record.
- The potential legal costs far outweigh any financial benefits to the individual beneficiary from a successful complaint.
- Court proceedings are expensive and that expense will be funded using the beneficiaries' assets in the pension fund.
- Courts are more comfortable righting past wrongs than imposing forward-looking injunctive remedies, especially when that remedy is beyond their traditional expertise.

The impact of the first factor (the lack of disclosure of policy and voting record) has already been discussed in the other contexts, and in the context of beneficiary-initiated proceedings, it is fatal to any systematic change to funds' corporate governance activity. Individual beneficiaries will lack the basic information they need to assess whether the time and expense of a court proceeding is worthwhile. In class proceedings, where the real decision makers on the plaintiff's side are often the legal counsel, the cost of obtaining even enough information to make an educated assessment of the chances of winning will likely discourage such counsel from even entertaining a request to act for a representative beneficiary. Typically, class proceeding firms fund both their own legal fees and the costs for disbursements, filing fees, and so on. In return, they receive much larger fees if they are successful. A number of US scholars have suggested, in the context of US securities litigation, that the representative plaintiff, rather than being the counsel's principal, is in fact the agent of the class proceeding counsel, having been recruited by counsel and having a much smaller financial reward than does counsel in the event of a successful proceeding.[93]

A much more serious problem faces beneficiaries contemplating a proceeding, even with the disclosure of the pension plan's policy and record. That problem is the risk of litigation. Although most class proceeding counsel will agree to take the risk of their own costs, contingent fee arrangements do not obligate them to also take on the risk of having to pay the opposing side's legal costs. In Canada, the general rule is that the loser pays the winner's legal costs. These costs can be quite high and will outweigh the potential financial gain an individual beneficiary can expect if a pension fund's corporate governance policy is improved.[94]

The courts are in much the same situation as the pension regulators with respect to expertise, and this has been recognized in the corporate law context in the "business judgment rule," which sees the courts deferring to the judgment of corporate management except in cases of egregious negligence or conflict of interest. One article has described its origins as follows:

> This limitation of scope, embodied in the business judgment rule, stems from a recognition of informational constraints on the process of judicial enforcement. The risk-return calculations prevailing at the time of initial investment cannot be reconstructed ex post; the fact of failure invites the ascription of incompetence to conduct better described as considered risk-taking.[95]

A similar description encompasses the exercise that a court would have to undertake with respect to a claim that a particular policy or proxy vote was a breach of the trustees' fiduciary duty. The court would have to reconstruct the trustees' risk-return estimate at the time of the decision at issue in order to assess the trustees' defence that their best estimate indicated that the benefits of a particular corporate governance activity did not outweigh the costs or potential losses to the fund. It is likely that the courts might also develop a form of business judgment rule in cases involving corporate governance policy and alleged breaches of fiduciary duty. Such a rule would remove any potential for accountability through court proceedings without setting any substantial standard for an acceptable corporate governance program. Thus, accountability through court proceedings does not appear to have any potential to create a change in the behaviour of pension fund trustees and investment managers with respect to their corporate governance activity. This does not mean that regulatory activity or judicial initiatives have no role to play, but rather that they should form part of a comprehensive package of reforms and policy changes aimed at providing accountability to the pension fund's beneficiaries for their corporate governance activity.

The Outlines of the Internal Pension Fund Accountability Reform "Package"

To summarize and distill the essence of the reforms necessary to increase accountability that have been discussed in this chapter, one begins with mandatory disclosure by pension fund trustees of their present corporate governance policy, and the record of the fund's proxy votes is the foundation of any accountability system. Next, it will be necessary to amend applicable pension legislation to require that every fund have a corporate governance policy with a comply-or-explain requirement. An important part of this particular policy initiative is that the policy must impose a duty on the trustees to exercise the corporate governance tools available to them in the best interests of the beneficiaries.[96]

In order to complete the accountability circle, the trustees would have to submit the corporate governance policy for ratification by the beneficiaries. In addition, the beneficiaries would have the right to elect the pension plan's trustees at regular intervals. Between elections, beneficiaries would have the right to propose changes to the plan's policy, subject to obtaining a substantial number of beneficiary signatures supporting the submission. Any proposed change to the asset classes available for investment or to the discretion of the trustees with respect to choice of investment would require a super-majority of the beneficiaries in the plan (not just the votes cast) before it could be implemented. Any beneficiary affected by a change requiring a super-majority would have the right to bring an application to court seeking a permanent injunction on grounds that to implement the change would be a breach of fiduciary duty. Upon receipt of such an application, the court would issue a temporary injunction, pending a hearing to be held within ten days of the application on whether such an injunction should remain in effect until the hearing of the application.

Finally, applicable pension legislation should be amended to provide that it is a breach of the legislation for a trustee or pension fund manager to fail to follow the plan's policy without a reasonable explanation. Beneficiaries would have the right to complain to the pension regulator about a failure to follow the fund's corporate governance policy, and the regulator should have the jurisdiction to order the trustees to follow the policy. This regime would provide sufficient monitoring and accountability to overcome the conflict-induced passivity of most pension trustees, without the beneficiaries' trespassing onto the expertise of the trustees and their professional advisors. Any further reassignment of decision-making power to the beneficiaries will require a baseline of experience with this proposed regime in order to provide the basis for a substantive discussion about the necessity of changing the fundamental relationship between beneficiaries and trustees in a pension plan even further in order to achieve the appropriate amount of corporate governance activity in the plan.

Are Accountability and Democracy Always Good? Some Necessary Constraints on Beneficiary Control

It is fundamental to our system of prefunded employment-based pension plans that the assets in the plan be invested so as to earn at least the percentage of return on investment used by the plan's actuary in estimating the contributions required to provide the promised benefits. It is also fundamental that an employer may not legally reclaim the assets and earnings so that they remain available to fund the benefits as they become due in the future. In order to retain these fundamental characteristics and the tax-deferral advantages that accompany them, the funds are entrusted to individuals who are subject to strict fiduciary duties to the pension plan's beneficiaries. There is a clear division of responsibilities in this relationship, aimed at the most efficient use of resources to generate the required investment income. Thus, trustees are required to use their discretion in choosing investments and to obtain the necessary expertise to exercise that discretion in the beneficiaries' best interests.

These arrangements suggest that transferring the decision making in this area to beneficiaries implies that they ought to each be provided with the same professional advice and explanation concerning asset classes, diversification, index strategies, and so on as are provided to the trustees prior to their decisions on these topics. This would clearly be an impractical and inefficient use of the beneficiaries' time and the plan's professional resources, however. Thus, practicality, efficiency, and ready access to appropriate professional advice all tilt the scales in favour of restricting certain classes of decisions to trustees. To that extent at least, democracy and accountability are not an unadulterated good, but rather qualities that must be constrained by these considerations.

Making Corporate Governance Work: Reforms Outside of an Accountability Regime

In discussing the issue of accountability to beneficiaries, one must try to keep in mind that one of the justifications for such accountability is its potential to unlock the constraints on corporate governance activity by institutional investors. The reason why corporate governance activity is important is its potential to increase the value of investments in corporate equities for the beneficiaries. It may also generate collateral benefits for them and society by encompassing the potentially infinite capacity for good and harm in the corporate organizational form within a form of accountability to real, rather than abstracted, human beings, whose preferences for corporate social responsibility may then be given a forum in which they can be realized. It will take more than accountability to the beneficiaries to implement such a system, however. It will also require changes to pension, trust, corporate, and securities law in order to make corporate governance at the behest of beneficiaries a workable alternative.

Permitting Trustees to Consider Collateral Benefits

One of the main recommendations from the Canadian Democracy and Corporate Accountability Commission is that pension legislation in the rest of the country be amended to contain a provision such as the following provision from the Manitoba legislation:

> Subject to any express provision in the instrument creating the trust, a trustee that uses non-financial criteria to formulate an investment policy or to make an investment decision does not thereby commit a breach of trust, if in relation to the investment policy or investment decision the trustee exercises the judgment and care that a person of prudence, discretion and intelligence would exercise in administering the property of others.[97]

The Manitoba provision provides statutory clarification of the law of trusts' duty of loyalty by removing any uncertainty that considering collateral benefits would be a breach of that duty. The purpose of adding the provision to legislation in other jurisdictions would not be to change the law but rather to remove an unnecessary impediment to the trustees' development of a corporate governance policy that dealt directly with social responsibility issues. Trustees would no longer be able to claim that they could not take corporate social responsibility into account because to do so would breach their fiduciary duty.

Corporate Law's Balance of Power

One of the reasons cited for institutional investor activism's ambiguous effect on the investment returns of target corporations is the advisory nature of shareholder resolutions. Yet this advisory status is also the essence of the corporate form of business organization, an essence that is captured in corporate law provisions that assign the management and/or supervision of the management of the enterprise to the corporation's board of directors. Thus, corporate governance advocates face a problem similar to that concerning the degree of accountability between pension trustees and beneficiaries. These advocates argue that corporate law allows management to ignore legitimate concerns of its shareholders as expressed in resolutions submitted through the proxy process. But, as one scholar points out, the proxy process is not a corporate law creation but rather a pragmatic solution to the problem of widely dispersed shareholders and the costs of physically attending the annual shareholders' meeting.[98] What are the legitimate complaints of institutional investors with respect to the process? They focus on the control over access to the proxy machinery exercised by management and the attendant costs and impracticality for those dissident shareholders who wish to submit a proposal to a shareholder vote. This control includes agenda control,[99] control over director nominations,[100] and the power to refuse to circulate certain proposals because they are not suitable for the shareholders to vote upon.[101]

Of the matters falling within the purview of corporate law that MacIntosh viewed as reforms necessary to encourage institutional investor activism, only his suggestion of increased communication among shareholders without requiring a dissident proxy circular has been implemented.[102] His suggestion that there be mandatory confidential voting (in order to alleviate the vulnerability to pressure of institutional investors who want to obtain or maintain a business relationship with the target company) has not been adopted in legislation. Some institutional investors had a form of confidential voting in the fact that their shares were held in the name of their investment manager, custodial trust company, or the CDS. If they objected to disclosure of their holdings (and thus became an "objecting beneficial owner," or "OBO"), they could vote confidentially. However, recent changes to the beneficial owner voting regulations in securities legislation now require OBOs to bear the costs of their receipt of proxy materials and submission of their proxy votes. Only NOBOs ("non-objecting beneficial owners," whose identity is disclosed to the corporation) can have the costs of these activities paid by the corporation. Thus, OBOs who wish to retain their confidentiality must now pay for the privilege, or refrain from voting. This does seem to send the wrong message and to be at odds with the *Canada Business Corporations Act* (CBCA) amendments, discussed earlier, that reduced barriers to institutional shareholder corporate governance activism.

Changes in corporate law should be aimed at creating accountability and monitoring capability for institutional shareholders while maintaining the appropriate division between managerial responsibilities and shareholder responsibilities. The International Corporate Governance Network (ICGN), an international organization of large institutional investors, has recognized this division in its statement of institutional shareholder responsibilities: "These ownership responsibilities should be dealt with diligently and pragmatically. This Statement, for instance, encourages the support of good corporate management initiatives, as much as opposition to bad ones. Furthermore, as a general rule, institutional shareholders should not interfere with the day-to-day management of companies."[103] The ICGN has also developed the following list of serious corporate governance concerns that they propose are the proper subject of shareholder monitoring and for which management should be accountable to shareholders:

- The level and quality of transparency;
- The company's financial and operational performance, including significant strategic issues;
- Substantial changes in the financial or control structure of the company;
- The role, independence and suitability of non-executive and/or supervisory directors;
- The quality of succession practices and procedures;
- The remuneration policy of the company;
- Conflicts of interest with large shareholders and other related parties;
- The level and protection of shareholder rights;
- Minority investor protection;
- Proxy voting;
- The independence of third party fairness opinions rendered on transactions;
- The accounting and auditing practices;
- The composition of the audit and remuneration committees;
- The adequacy of internal control systems and procedures;
- The management of environmental, ethical and social risks.[104]

The fact that an organization like the ICGN was able to reach agreement on such an extensive list of common issues is reason for optimism concerning its project of having institutional investors take their "ownership" responsibilities seriously. The addition of what are commonly viewed as non-financial criteria – the environment, ethics, and social policy – is also grounds for optimism about the potential for serious consideration of these criteria in large institutional investors' corporate governance policies. Of course, the degree to which they are considered will depend on the definition of "risks" that the institutional investor is using, but their inclusion does provide a starting point for a discussion of that definition. The list also provides a point from which another important discussion can be initiated, a discussion about changing the status of shareholder proposals from advisory to mandatory, at least with respect to some issues.

One potential reform of corporate law would be to split shareholder proposals into those that are advisory and those that are mandatory. The latter would include proposals dealing with the corporate governance concerns on this ICGN list. This reform would help to clarify the proper division between managers and shareholders, and hopefully provide an impetus for further institutional shareholder activism in these areas while preserving management's discretion to operate the business in a profitable manner.

Some US scholars have suggested that corporate law be changed to allow shareholders direct access to amending the corporate charter in matters of process and structure (inclusive of management incentive compensation) while excluding access to the formulation of the business plan, particularly matters of investment or divestment. The costs of such shareholder initiatives would be shifted to the corporation by making them eligible for inclusion in the corporation's proxy circular for the annual shareholders' meeting. Changing the proxy process rules of the US SEC, rather than amending state corporation law, would effect this change.[105] Another scholar has concluded that empowerment through shareholder voting would be too costly because it would lead to the "cycling" of corporate goals as unstable voting coalitions changed and rent seeking by proponents of proposals.[106] In other words, corporate policies and goals would change with each new coalition of shareholders, much like countries where coalition governments are the norm. As well, shareholders would use their control over policy to obtain rents – economic gains beyond those available in a competitive market – from the corporation. William Bratton and J. McCahery point out that their proposal to limit shareholder access to process and structure issues will not create new rent-seeking opportunities beyond those already implicit in the shareholder vote provisions. In addition, they argue that Arrovian cycling problems are issues only where there are no process tools available to control the problem. They propose a number of rules that would reduce the risk of cycling considerably.[107] In Canada, the scope of these proposals would be constrained by the pattern of stock ownership, in which most of the corporations are majority-owned or controlled.[108] Thus, access to the agenda reforms would have their real impact when the patterns of stock ownership changed so as to allow coalitions of institutional investors to control enough votes to ensure passage of process or structure amendments.

Other issues, such as the nomination process for directors, are primarily issues in the US, where the SEC, after considering whether to permit shareholder nominations to appear on the corporate proxy circular, has decided not to permit it and has even prohibited shareholder proposals to amend the corporations bylaws to permit such nominations.[109] In Canada, shareholder nominations are permitted (subject to a minimum shareholding threshold)[110] and the real issue with respect to this and other corporate governance initiatives is those provisions in securities law that impose restrictions on liquidity or disclosure obligations on control persons.

Distinguishing Between Control and Accountability

The problem with securities regulation is that it has some difficulty in making a distinction between the efforts of institutional investors to align corporate management's interests with those of all shareholders and the hazards of corporations in which a shareholder or shareholder group is in *de facto* control of the corporation. Securities regulation is concerned with protecting the minority investor and the credibility of trading in minority shares in the corporation from situations of block holder "capture" by management. In capture situations, management negotiates a side-deal with the block holder to pay rents in return for a commitment not to accept any tender offers opposed by management.[111] However, this concern may not be well founded with respect to coalitions of shareholders seeking a discrete change to a corporation's process or structure.[112] Although securities regulators in Canada appear to have responded to concerns about unintentional aggregation of shareholdings that are under independent control with respect to the control person designation, they have not made the same exemptions for coalitions or voting agreements among institutional investors. They have made it clear that agreements to nominate, select, or elect directors will not receive the same exemptions.[113] Thus, changes to securities regulations to exempt ad hoc coalitions to make discrete changes to corporate structure or process should be made in order to facilitate this activity by institutional investors. The case for such exemptions with respect to director selection is not as strong without additional safeguards. If the point of selecting the director(s) is to increase accountability to shareholders, there is the danger that the director and those institutional shareholders who participated in the selection would come to view accountability as owed to those who were responsible for the selection. Unless another institution not connected with those institutional investors who participated in the selection becomes the source of that accountability, as proposed by Ronald Gilson and Reinier Kraakman, the justification for regulatory action will remain.[114]

Summary

A number of reforms have been discussed in this chapter, ranging from those concerning trust and pension law to changes to securities regulation. The range of these reforms reflects the reach of the issues involved in achieving accountable corporate governance activity by pension fund trustees and other institutional investors. This range is also illustrative of the complex interaction of legal regimes that comprise our present system regulating the relationships between such investors and the corporations in which they hold shares. Real reform will require a coordinated strategy for simultaneous change, as piecemeal reform will result in no real change to either the incentives influencing pension fund managers and their investment managers or the costs of corporate governance activism to their pension fund. Change is required in both the pension/trust law and the corporate/securities law areas in order to achieve the goal of a beneficiary-accountable pension fund policy for corporate governance activity.

Conclusion: Pension Funds Must Be Accountable to Plan Members for Using Corporate Governance to Enhance Corporate Environmental, Social, and Governance Performance

With some notable exceptions, there is agreement that with the rise of institutional shareholding there is the potential for escape from the Berle and Means dynamic of the widely dispersed shareholder model of corporate governance. Institutional shareholding has concentrated shareholding sufficiently that coordination and cooperation in monitoring and disciplining corporate management is now theoretically feasible. Thus, shareholders are now capable of becoming responsible for corporate governance in a way that was not conceivable after the rise of the large publicly held corporation. Nevertheless, it should not be forgotten that it was not so much the separation of ownership and control that Berle and Means saw as the social problem arising from this situation. Rather, they were concerned that immense power over the economic and social life of everyone in their society was being concentrated in the hands of a few managers who were not responsible to anyone but their shareholders for its exercise. Since the shareholders were not capable of holding the managers responsible, these managers exercised virtually unaccountable power.

By 1962, Adolph Berle was satisfied that a combination of Depression-era legislation requiring public disclosure and a public consensus on appropriate management behaviour that had been incorporated into the psyche of corporate management was capable of exerting sufficient social control over corporate power.[1] Berle was aware of the accumulation of equities in private pension plans that had begun after the Second World War.[2] Although he pointed out that legally the relationship between the pension plan manager and beneficiary was unknown, Berle was of the opinion (although without certainty) that the beneficiary's "'beneficial interest' has been completely, solidly and finally severed from the economic and productive enterprise of the corporation whose shares form the corpus of the trust, on whose success, at long last, he and his fellow beneficiaries depend."[3] Since Berle wrote his 1962 article, the consensus about managerial responsibility has shifted to one of shareholder wealth maximization. This shift does not, however, enable those who are responsible for corporate governance to evade the issue of corporate social responsibility. While shareholder wealth maximization as a goal of corporate activity has an appealing simplicity to it, the simplicity is deceiving. Conceptually, it contains a level of indeterminacy that continues to raise issues of the proper exercise of corporate power, the balance between interests of investors with differing time horizons, and the appropriate concern to be shown to stakeholders other than shareholders by corporate management. In addition, the entry of corporate management, armed with the funds in the corporate treasury, into political life has raised the issue of how the management's choices with respect to the social and political policies they support in the name of the corporation can be legitimized. Their wealth maximization justification may not survive an examination of the heterogeneous political, social, and ethical preferences of the shareholders in whose name political campaign funds are being expended. Finally, the range of options on corporate management's desk rarely involves the following decision pairs: profit, only if socially irresponsible, versus no profit, only if socially responsible. Provided one takes into account all consequences that can reasonably be expected to occur over the foreseeable future; having only these choices before one is rare. These rare choices will be provided only if one is focused solely on the immediate cost and benefit, to the exclusion of all other costs and benefits.

The nature of the choices is highlighted by the climate change debate. As Sir Nicholas Stern points out in his report, each year that action on reducing greenhouse gas emissions is delayed can be measured in the estimated costs to the world of the consequential increase in global temperatures.[4] As mentioned earlier, pension funds as major investors have a role to play in ensuring that their investee companies are prepared to attack the problem of greenhouse gas emissions, have properly disclosed their risks in this area, and are confident that their investors will support them in greenhouse gas emission reductions. Where necessary, pension funds can shift their investment allocations in response to risk disclosure and the rise of new low-emission alternatives. This is certainly an area in which democratic accountability is amply justified in light of the global impact of inaction.

In view of all these factors, it makes little sense to discuss a corporate governance policy for a pension fund without including corporate governance issues that the fund's beneficiaries consider likely to lead to collateral benefits for them. Collateral benefits would include improvements in the quality of their lives or constraints on adverse effects from certain corporate activities. Thus, a corporate governance policy for a pension fund should include a social responsibility component. The component would necessarily be more social than might first appear because the corporate governance policies will only have an impact on corporate behaviour if the efforts of a number of pension funds are combined. Having to coordinate corporate governance goals will increase the likelihood that the collateral benefit being sought will be one that can be enjoyed by the population generally rather than only by the beneficiaries of a single pension plan. The contents of the social responsibility component, together with the other structural and process provisions, would be determined by the beneficiaries in the manner set out in Chapter 6.[5] Beneficiary self-regulation through democratic decision making is preferable to having the same obligations imposed by regulators. Democratic decision making is important because as a society we prefer it to other modes of decision. It provides a process in which the competing concerns of autonomy and order are somewhat reconciled. Individuals are consulted about intended actions that will affect them and their freedoms, and through their consent, autonomy is vindicated while order is imposed.

Democratic decision making is also important because pension fund managers and their delegates are presently subject to counter-incentives to disregard their fiduciary duty to act in the best interests of the beneficiaries with respect to corporate governance. When corporate governance issues arise in a company in which their pension plan has invested, they do not take action to resolve those issues in the beneficiaries' interest. Instead they respond to countervailing pressure from corporate management by voting for management or abstaining (and implicitly supporting management). The target corporate management is able to apply that pressure on two fronts. First, it can threaten to deny continuing or future business to professional fund managers. Second, it can offer an implicit undertaking that the target corporation's pension plan trustees will also support the investing corporation's management in any corporate governance issues with respect to the target corporation plan's investments in the investing corporation. As we have seen, these counter-incentives have been quite effective in causing passivity with respect to corporate governance in private sector pension plans, where they have the most impact. Public sector plans, together with plans where one-half of the trustees are appointed by the trade unions that represent the employees, are not as vulnerable to these counter-incentives.[6] Their activity in corporate governance provides a stark contrast to that of private sector pension funds, whose trustees are appointed solely by the employer. Thus, any reforms adopted to overcome corporate governance passivity must do more than merely enable trustees; it must generate incentives to enter into corporate governance activity that are strong enough to overcome the counter-incentives. Requiring democratic accountability through approval of corporate governance policies and election of trustees may generate enough such incentives.

Mandating democratic decision making, when combined with the other suggested reforms in pension, trust, corporate, and securities law, may also assist in overcoming the problems of collective good, free-riding, and rational apathy ("collective action problems") that attach to the investment in corporate governance activity by institutional investors.[7] These mandatory reforms may also assist by providing positive incentives to professional investment managers to demonstrate success in pursuing the fund's corporate governance strategy. At present, these managers are, at best, indifferent in view of the costs (where they may have cost constraints) and the fact that success will not assist them in meeting their market performance benchmarks, because institutional investors' corporate governance success increases the overall performance of the market.[8]

The one issue that the reform proposals may not address directly, however, is that of the benefits of corporate governance activity. As William Bratton and J. McCahery have pointed out, these benefits are largely assumed rather than concretely calculated.[9] The most recent study does not measure the effects of corporate governance activity directly, but rather compares the performance of companies whose structure resembles the institutional investors' ideal company with the revenues of companies whose structure does not resemble the ideal. The former group significantly outperformed the latter over the decade of the 1990s, but the authors could not determine whether it was the governance structure or some unobserved factor that caused the difference.[10] Roberta Romano noted the lack of any empirical evidence that corporate governance in the form of shareholder proposals has any effect on the targeted firms' performance.[11]

The uncertainty over immediate cash payout, the potentially lengthy time lag between governance initiative and improvement, the fact that some of the benefits will be in harm reduction rather than direct increases in revenue, and the inability to isolate a causal connection between improved performance and corporate governance activity all point towards the vulnerability of these reforms to sudden downturns in pension fund returns. This vulnerability stems from the inability to closely connect the costs and benefits, as well as from the tendency to blame new initiatives for unusual results. Thus, two additional grounds for undertaking the reform should also be emphasized. The first is the value of democracy itself to those participating in that form of decision making. Democracy has its roots in the concept of the equal worth of every human being and, by giving each person an equal vote, it seeks to recognize this equality.

The second reason for preferring democratic accountability for pension funds' corporate governance activity is that our society requires that corporations' useful economic function be properly situated as a means to human fulfillment, not as an end in itself.[12] One means of achieving this is to reintroduce heterogeneous human preferences into policy decisions at the corporate level. Under our present system of corporate law, the only means by which this may be accomplished is to introduce the preferences of the corporation's shareholders, as they are granted the right to make such changes through a democratic vote. Otherwise, directors and managers must construe those preferences from an abstraction of the "typical" shareholder. That typical shareholder's moral and ethical sense is limited to compliance with the formal standards of behaviour enacted or proclaimed in the law. The only information provided to directors and managers about their shareholders is that they expect to profit from their shareholdings. Directors and officers are legally obligated to act in the best interests of the corporation, and that duty has typically been interpreted as maximizing shareholder wealth. How, then, can they be responsible to society, except by deviating from their fiduciary duty to the shareholders in a situation in which profit and the potential for social harm potentially collide?

As one author has reflected, our conception of a responsible individual is bound up with the ability to use moral imagination about consequences in perceiving a course of action; accept that one is free and account for the freely chosen course of action using the moral vocabulary of rights, obligations, and good or bad; and justify one's choice on moral grounds.[13] Providing the beneficiaries of pension plans with an opportunity to express their preferences for a corporate governance policy that includes a corporate social responsibility element through a system of democratic accountability is one means of establishing this sense of responsibility in the corporate sphere. It is also a means of establishing this responsibility in a manner that is internally legitimate in corporate law. Such policy making is consistent with the role of shareholders in corporate law, in which certain policy decisions are made by their democratic vote.[14] It is also consistent with responsibility in the individual sense, inasmuch as such responsibility can be expressed through collective decision making. It is certainly preferable to a regime in which managers and directors attempt to reproduce this exercise of responsible judgment while under a duty to an abstract construct of their shareholders, an abstraction whose only common denominator is a desire for profit. While profit is certainly one of their major points of commonality (and one of the corporation's goals), the shareholders' concept of human communities may include the imposition of limitations on increasing profit on socially responsible grounds. An accountability regime will certainly allow the issues of the relationship between the corporate form, regulation, and social responsibility to be raised in a forum where there is a potential for democratic governance with respect to these matters. It may also provide an opportunity for the exercise of what Amartya Sen has called the exercise of substantive freedoms or capabilities: "to choose a life one has reason to value" through the process of debate and decision on corporate governance policy for the pension plans in which one is involved.[15]

Accountability by pension fund trustees to the pension plan's beneficiaries is not going to replace our need for public policy initiatives by our government acting in the public interest. As I mentioned at the outset of this book, the pursuit of this accountability with respect to pension funds' corporate governance activity is merely a means to allow a broader cross-section of the citizenry access to participation in the decision-making process in our economic system through the markets. Membership in a pension plan does not reflect on an individual's fitness to make choices from among contested claims concerning the appropriate policies for corporations to adopt with respect to the environment, ethical behaviour, or social policy, and neither does one's employment as a corporate pension fund trustee or investment manager. However, an accountability regime will allow these decisions to be made by concretely situated humans who will experience the effects of the decision, rather than by fiduciaries acting within their duty towards an artificially constructed beneficiary/shareholder.

The role of government as protector of the public interest is key to the success of the project. The norms it generates in its governance activity, whether providing basic income support, protecting the environment, or providing a floor of legally acceptable behaviour above which the beneficiaries can seek socially responsible behaviour among their portfolio companies, give shape and scope to the concepts of socially responsible behaviour. In addition, its role in providing a voice for those who are excluded from this accountability model because of their limited participation in the labour market will become even more crucial. Government must play a role in the accountability of multinational enterprises (MNEs) by participating in initiatives that will generate sufficiently reliable and comparable data concerning the effects of MNE activities on the environment and international human, social, and political rights.

For the future, the development of metrics (or clear explanations of alternatives for determining the effects) that connect changes in corporate structures, procedures, or activity with changes in the value of investments in a corporation are clearly an important avenue for research. As part of such a project, a clearer legal basis needs to be developed for the consideration by management and directors of factors that have not traditionally been included in the corporation's balance sheet, such as legally permissible environmental, ethical, and social activity that falls within the penumbra of corporate social responsibility. One method for conceptualizing this consideration is by treating these factors as "risks." One could question whether this conception is too narrow, and whether the concept of opportunity is more appropriate. What is clear is that one way to broaden the consideration of these topics is through the participation of pension fund beneficiaries in a thorough discussion of the appropriate balance in the context of the need for earnings and for a decent social, political, and physical environment in which to enjoy them.

Notes

Introduction

1 Peter F. Drucker, *The Unseen Revolution: How Pension Fund Socialism Came to America* (New York: Harper and Row, 1976).

2 Mark J. Roe, "The Modern Corporation and Private Pensions" (1993) 41 UCLA L. Rev. 75 at 76.

3 Employee Benefit Research Institute, "Equity Holdings of Retirement Plans" in *Facts from EBRI* (2000), online: Employee Benefit Research Institute, http://www.ebri.org/facts/0800fact2.htm. These figures include assets held by insurance companies for the provision of retirement benefits, but exclude individual retirement accounts as these are not considered to have a sufficient connection to the employment relationship.

4 Employee Benefit Research Institute, "Retirement Plan Assets: Year-End 2001" in *Facts from EBRI* (2002), online: Employee Benefit Research Institute, http://www.ebri.org/facts/0902fact.pdf.

5 Statistics Canada, *Quarterly Estimates of Trusteed Pension Funds: First Quarter 2002* (Ottawa: Statistics Canada, 2002) at 4. This figure includes all assets held for retirement purposes in pension plans, including public plans such as the Canada Pension Plan and individual Registered Retirement Savings Plans.

6 *Ibid.*, Table 1 at 5.

7 Gil Yaron, "Canadian Institutional Shareholder Activism in an Era of Global Deregulation" in Janis P. Sarra, ed., *Corporate Governance in Global Capital Markets* (Vancouver: UBC Press, 2003) 111; Yaron reports that these figures exclude pension fund investments in equities through pooled and indexed funds, which are significant portions of their investments.

8 Robert A.G. Monks, *The New Global Investors: How Shareowners Can Unlock Sustainable Prosperity Worldwide* (Oxford: Capstone, 2001) at 92.

9 William H. Simon, "The Prospects of Pension Fund Socialism" (1993) 14 Berkeley J. Emp. & Lab. L. 251.

10 Paul P. Harbrecht, S.J., *Pension Funds and Economic Power* (New York: Twentieth Century Fund, 1959) at 3-4; Adolph A. Berle, *Power without Property: A New Development in American Political Economy* (New York: Harcourt, Brace, 1959) at 52-56.

11 Adolph A. Berle and Gardiner C. Means, *The Modern Corporation and Private Property* (New York: Macmillan, 1932).

12 Simon, *supra* note 9 at 259-65.

13 The ICGN, a multinational organization of large institutional investors, has a "Statement of Institutional Shareholder Responsibilities" in which are listed some of the serious shareholder concerns that are the object of corporate governance activity; see International Corporate Governance Network, "ICGN Statement on Institutional Shareholder Responsibilities" (2003), online: International Corporate Governance Network, http://www.icgn.org/documents/GuidelinesResponsibilities0503.pdf, and proposed "Statement of Principles on Institutional Shareholder Responsibilities" (2007), online: International Corporate

Governance Network, http://www.icgn.org/organisation/documents/src/Statement%20on%20Shareholder%20Responsibilities%202007.pdf.

14 Harbrecht, *supra* note 10 at 233-36; Berle, *supra* note 10 at 54-55.

15 Harbrecht, *ibid.* at 163-90.

16 See the discussion of the issues surrounding "ownership" in the text accompanying notes 17 to 46.

17 Daniel Fischel and John H. Langbein, "ERISA's Fundamental Contradiction: The Exclusive Benefit Rule" (1988) 55 U. Chicago L. Rev. 1105 at 1117: "Employees pay for pension benefits in the form of lower wages"; U.S., Senate Committee on Governmental Affairs, *Statement of Professor John Langbein,* 107th Cong. (24 January 2002) at 99: "Employers offer pension plans as part of the compensation package, as what we call deferred compensation," noting at fn. 17 that the United States federal employee benefit legislation's vesting and benefit accrual rules implement the deferred compensation view of pension benefits.

18 Gordon L. Clark, *Pension Fund Capitalism* (Oxford: Oxford University Press, 2000) at 36.

19 Employee Benefit Research Institute, *supra* note 4 reports that the equity holdings of insurance companies' retirement plan assets were $653.3 billion, while those of trusteed pension plans equalled $2.83 trillion.

20 It should be noted that there is a distinction recognized in applicable statutes between administering a pension plan and administering a pension fund, as in Canada the latter function may be performed for a registered pension plan only by a trust, an insurance company, or a government; see Patrick Longhurst, "Plan Design and Administration" in Raymond Koskie *et al.*, eds., *Employee Benefits in Canada* (Brookfield, MN: International Foundation of Employee Benefit Plans, 2001) 197 at 205. In the United States, the *Employee Retirement Income Security Act,* 29 U.S.C. (1994) (ERISA) requires all employee benefit assets to be held in trust; see John H. Langbein, "The Secret Life of the Trust: The Trust as an Instrument of Commerce" (1997) 107 Yale L.J. 165 at 169. The former function involves determining benefit eligibility, amending the plan, and perhaps retaining actuarial services to determine the cost of present and future benefits and required contribution levels.

21 Harbrecht, *supra* note 10 at 66, notes that some control was maintained as pension trustees may retain a veto over retention of a particular asset in the investment manager's portfolio.

22 Clark, *supra* note 18 at 185-86.

23 Harbrecht, *supra* note 10 at 65; Berle, *supra* note 10 at 105.

24 Roe, *supra* note 2 at 91-94, relating the passivity of pension fund investment managers in the face of hostile takeovers, pressure from the pension plan sponsors' management, and the issuance of a letter from the United States Department of Labor requiring the exercise of proxy votes in the plan participants' interests; Clark, *supra* note 18 at 35; see also Berle, *supra* note 10 at 55, relating the refusal of investment managers to do anything with pension plan voting rights other than support incumbent management.

25 See Larry A. Ribstein, "Market versus Regulatory Responses to Corporate Fraud: A Critique of the Sarbanes-Oxley Act of 2002" (2002) 28 J. Corp. L. 1 at 1-2, arguing that a new round of regulatory intervention in response to the Enron failure is the wrong response since active and vigilant markets are the only cost-effective means to expose fraudulent activity; and Faith Stevelman Kahn, "Bombing Markets, Subverting the Rule of Law: Enron, Financial Fraud and September 11, 2001" (2001-02) 76 Tul. L. Rev. 1579 at 1615-17, noting that the stance of most contemporary academics and practitioners is that of regulatory minimalism and reliance on "governance through markets."

26 See, for example, Claire F.L. Young, *Women, Tax and Social Programs: The Gendered Impact of Funding Social Programs through the Tax System* (Ottawa: Status of Women Canada, 2000), discussing the domino-like effect on women's access to the tax benefits of employment-based pension plans arising from their differential access to and participation in the labour market.

27 Nevertheless, while the entire body of pension plan participants may not be perfectly representative of the gender, economic status, and ethnic makeup of our society, they are certainly far more representative of our society's diversity than the present decision makers, who are pension fund investment managers and corporate officers acting as pension fund trustees.

28 Drucker, *supra* note 1 at 1.

29 Clark, *supra* note 18 at 29, citing data from Deutsche Bank AG, *Aspiring Equity Culture in Germany* (Frankfurt am Main: Deutsche Morgan Grenfell European Equity Research, 1997).

30 U.K., National Statistics Online, "Pensions and National Accounts," online: UK National Statistics Online, http://www.statistics.gov.uk/CCI/nugget.asp?ID=1283&Pos=&ColRank=2&Rank=224.

31 Langbein, *supra* note 20 at 168-69.

32 U.S., Federal Reserve, "Flow of Funds," Tables L.118-L.120, online: Federal Reserve, http://www.federalreserve.gov/releases/z1/Current/z1r-4.pdf.

33 Statistics Canada, "Pension Savings of Canadians," online: Statistics Canada, http://www40.statcan.ca/l01/cst01/labr78.htm. Note that the values are expressed in constant 2003 dollars.

34 Harbrecht, *supra* note 10 at 232, noting that over one-fourth of the net stock purchases of thirty large pension funds were from a list of twenty-five companies, citing the U.S. Senate Committee on Banking and Currency investigation into pension funds in 1955.

35 Clark, *supra* note 18 at 74.

36 Adam Harmes, *Unseen Power: How Mutual Funds Threaten the Political and Economic Wealth of Nations* (Toronto: Stoddart, 2001) provides a number of cases in which he argues that the preferences of mutual fund investment managers for a particular kind of monetary policy and their willingness to transfer investments out of countries that deviate from this policy has led to recent fiscal problems for certain countries or regions.

37 Adolph Berle, *supra* note 10 at 51, wrote the following in 1959 concerning his prediction about the future role of pension fund investment managers: "One estimate nevertheless can be hazarded with some assurance. A relatively small oligarchy of men operating in the same atmosphere, absorbing the same information, moving in the same circles and in a relatively small world knowing each other, dealing with each other, and having more in common than in difference, will hold the reins."

38 This issue was recognized by Drucker, *supra* note 1 at 85-98, in which he reviewed the conflicts inherent in the pension investment management services of large commercial banks and called for new boards of trustees representative of the beneficiaries. Berle also recognized this as a problem that he saw as being resolved through the restraints available from a public consensus on the appropriate behaviour of corporate management being capable of calling on the state to intervene in particular cases of abuse through the mobilization of public opinion; Berle, *supra* note 10 at 98-116; see also Adolph A. Berle, "Modern Functions of the Corporate System" (1962) 62 Colum. L. Rev. 433 at 444.

39 See, for example, Kenneth B. Davis Jr., "Shareholder Liability for Claims by Employees" (1984) 1984 Wis. L. Rev. 741, criticizing the Wisconsin statute imposing joint and several liability for unpaid wages. For a contrary view, see Henry Hansmann and Reinier Kraakman, "Toward Unlimited Shareholder Liability for Corporate Torts" (1991) 100 Yale L.J. 1879, arguing for unlimited shareholder liability for corporate torts, but on a *pro rata* rather than joint and several liability basis.

40 See Simon, *supra* note 9.

Chapter 1: Corporate Investment by Employee Pension Funds

1 Christopher D. Stone, "Corporate Social Responsibility: What It Might Mean, If It Were to Really Matter" (1986) 71 Iowa L. Rev. 557 at 559-60, summarizes what we mean when we talk about individual responsibility as "someone not only law-abiding, but morally reflective," which he argues is reflection in the negative sense – repressing immediate gratification in favour of reflection – and the positive sense – capable of moral imagination and the use of a moral vocabulary in accepting responsibility for the consequences of one's actions and a desire to do the right thing and provide justification for action.

2 Canadian Democracy and Corporate Accountability Commission, "Recommendations" in *The New Balance Sheet: Corporate Profits and Accountability in the 21st Century* (2002), online: http://www.corporate-accountability.ca/pdfs/Recommendations2002.pdf.

3 Douglas M. Branson, "The Very Uncertain Prospect of 'Global' Convergence in Corporate Governance" (2001) 34 Cornell Int'l L.J. 321 at 356, noting that the value of Unilever-Best's production and sales exceeds the GDP of all but about fifty nations.

4 One of the most quoted versions of this norm was that of the Nobel Prize–winning economist Milton Friedman in Milton Friedman, "The Social Responsibility of Business Is to Increase Its Profits" *New York Times* (13 September 1970) 6 at 32.

5 I use the word "accountable" in the sense of being answerable for policy choices or having to provide justifications for one's choices. Clearly, other mechanisms of holding corporations accountable, in the strict financial sense, are available, and corporations will be financially accountable for their debts and torts.

6 Of course, unlike other members of society, shareholders might also want to have management act in a socially irresponsible manner to the extent that they believe such actions would result in a net increase in their utility or welfare notwithstanding the socially negative effects of the decisions. However, the nature of the shareholder interests that are advanced by corporate management are not based upon this kind of individualized decision making about shareholder welfare.

7 Daniel J.H. Greenwood, "Fictional Shareholders: For Whom Are Corporate Managers Trustees, Revisited" (1996) 69 S. Cal. L. Rev. 1021 [Greenwood, "Fictional Shareholders"]; see also *Danaher Corp. v. Chicago Pneumatic Tool Co.,* 635 F.Supp. 246, 55 U.S.L.W. 2022 (S.D.N.Y. 1986) at 250, in which the court held that pension fund trustees must consider the interests of the beneficiaries "in the abstract" and ignore their express wishes when deciding whether or not to tender the plan's shares in the corporate employer to a hostile bidder.

8 Bruce Chapman, "Trust, Economic Rationality and the Corporate Fiduciary Obligation" (1993) 43 U.T.L.J. 547; Lawrence E. Mitchell, *Corporate Irresponsibility: America's Newest Export* (New Haven and London: Yale University Press, 2001).

9 Greenwood, "Fictional Shareholders," *supra* note 7 at 1025-26.

10 Mitchell, *supra* note 8 at 44-45.

11 Robert A.G. Monks, *The New Global Investors: How Shareowners Can Unlock Sustainable Prosperity Worldwide* (Oxford: Capstone, 2001); Greenwood, "Fictional Shareholders," *supra* note 7 at 1103-4.

12 Canadian Democracy and Corporate Accountability Commission, *supra* note 2 at 11. The telephone survey of 2,006 adults was conducted by Vector Research between 28 September and 8 October 2001 (before the facts concerning Enron and related scandals became public knowledge); Vector Research, "Analysis of the Public Opinion Poll Conducted for the Canadian Democracy and Corporate Accountability Commission" (2001), online: http://www.corporate-accountability.ca/pdfs/PollReport.pdf.

13 Gordon L. Clark, *Pensions and Corporate Restructuring in American Industry: A Crisis in Regulation* (Baltimore and London: The Johns Hopkins University Press, 1993).

14 *Ibid.* at 4.

15 *Ibid.* at 75-150, c. 4 and 5.

16 *Ibid.* at 225-26.

17 *Ibid.* at 227-28.

18 *Ibid.* at 253-58; see also the approach in the *Sarbanes-Oxley Act of 2002, An Act To Protect Investors by Improving the Accuracy and Reliability of Corporate Disclosures Made Pursuant to the Securities Laws, and for Other Purposes,* Pub. L. No. 107-204, 116 Stat. 745 (2002), in which criminal penalties were increased and the power of the SEC to bar individuals from acting as directors of public companies was expanded by reducing the threshold for the bar from "substantially unfit" to "unfit."

19 Ronald J. Daniels, "Must Boards Go Overboard? An Economic Analysis of the Effects of Burgeoning Statutory Liability on the Role of Directors in Corporate Governance" (1995) 24 Can. Bus. L.J. 229.

20 These consequences are graphically described in Faith Stevelman Kahn, "Bombing Markets, Subverting the Rule of Law: Enron, Financial Fraud and September 11, 2001" (2001-02) 76 Tul. L. Rev. 1579 at 1615.

21 Janis Sarra, "Corporate Governance Reform: Recognition of Workers' Equitable Investments in the Firm" (1999) 32 Can. Bus. L.J. 384.

22 Milton Friedman and Eli Goldston, "The 'Responsible' Corporation: Benefactor or Monopolist?" Excerpts from their debate in (1973) 56 *Fortune* 88 reprinted in Edward J. Bander, ed., *The Corporation in a Democratic Society* (New York: The H.W. Wilson Company, 1975) at 43-45.

23 *Ibid.* at 44-45.
24 David Sciulli, *Corporate Power in Civil Society: An Application of Societal Constitutionalism* (New York: New York University Press, 2001).
25 Amartya Kumar Sen, *Development as Freedom* (New York: Anchor Books, 1999) at c. 3.
26 Cynthia A. Williams, "The Securities and Exchange Commission and Corporate Social Transparency" (1999) 112 Harv. L. Rev. 1197 at 1296.
27 Jeffrey G. MacIntosh, "Designing an Efficient Fiduciary Law" (1993) 43 U.T.L.J. 425.
28 Ronald J. Daniels, "Stakeholders and Takeovers: Can Contractarianism Be Compassionate" (1993) 43 U.T.L.J. 315.
29 Thomas A. Smith, "The Efficient Norm for Corporate Law: A Neotraditional Interpretation of Fiduciary Duty" (1999) 98 Mich. L. Rev. 214, argues that restricting the duty to maximization of shareholder wealth sanctions inefficient transfers of wealth from other classes of investors to the shareholders.
30 S. Myers and N. Majluf, "Corporate Financing When Firms Have Information that Investors Do Not Have" (1984) 13 Journal of Financial Economics 187; Henry T.C. Hu, "New Financial Products, the Modern Process of Financial Innovation, and the Puzzle of Shareholder Welfare" (1991) 69 Tex. L. Rev. 1273 [Hu, "New Financial Products"] at 1300-3.
31 *Ibid.* at 1280-81.
32 *Ibid.* at 1282-85; Henry T.C. Hu, "Risk, Time and Fiduciary Principles in Corporate Investment" (1990) 38 UCLA L. Rev. 277 [Hu, "Risk, Time and Fiduciary Principles"] at 357-58.
33 Richard A. Booth, "Stockholders, Stakeholders and Bagholders (or How Investor Diversification Affects Fiduciary Duty)" (1998) 53 Bus. Law. 429 at 437-38.
34 Hu, "New Financial Products," *supra* note 30.
35 Greenwood, "Fictional Shareholders," *supra* note 7; Daniel J.H. Greenwood, "Essential Speech: Why Corporate Speech Is Not Free" (1997-98) 83 Iowa L. Rev. 995.
36 U.S., Senate Committee on Governmental Affairs, *Statement of Professor John Langbein,* 107th Cong. (24 January 2002) at 96, fn. 9; see also Robin Blackburn, "The New Collectivism: Pension Reform, Grey Capitalism and Complex Socialism" (1999) 233 New Left Review 3 at 63.
37 Sen, *supra* note 25 at c. 1.
38 Greenwood, "Fictional Shareholders," *supra* note 7 at 1062.
39 Lucian A. Bebchuk, "The Pursuit of a Bigger Pie: Can Everyone Expect a Bigger Slice?" (1979-80) 8 Hofstra L. Rev. 671, challenging Richard Posner's consent justification for using wealth maximization criteria (willingness to pay) to assign common law rights, on the grounds that the rule is irretrievably biased against the poor, and thus Posner cannot use consent as a justification.
40 Kellye Y. Testy, "Linking Progressive Corporate Law with Progressive Social Movements" (2002) 76 Tul. L. Rev. 1227 at 1242-43.
41 John H. Langbein and Richard A. Posner, "Market Funds and Trust-Investment Law" [1976] 1 American Bar Foundation Research Journal 1, and John H. Langbein and Richard A. Posner, "Market Funds and Trust-Investment Law: II" [1977] 1 American Bar Foundation Research Journal 1, set out the rationale supporting this strategy and predicted that it would become mandatory for trustees.
42 See Smith, *supra* note 29, criticizing the notion of exclusive fiduciary duties to shareholders on economic efficiency grounds (rational investors will be diversified across all forms of investment in the firm, and the fiduciary duty is to increase the value of those investments, taken as a whole, not just share value); Gregory Scott Crespi, "Rethinking Corporate Fiduciary Duties: The Inefficiency of the Shareholder Primacy Norm" (2002) 55 SMU L. Rev. 141, supporting the same standard for fiduciary duty on "hypothetical bargain" grounds, which treat fiduciary duties as replications of the *ex ante* agreements that investors would reach with perfect information and zero transaction costs; see also Booth, *supra* note 33 at 454-56.
43 Monks, *supra* note 11 at 105.
44 James P. Hawley and Andrew T. Williams, *The Rise of Fiduciary Capitalism: How Institutional Investors Can Make America More Democratic* (Philadelphia: University of Pennsylvania Press, 2000). The authors present a much more detailed picture of the scope of pension fund investment in the United States, using the concept of "universal owner" to describe the

extent to which these funds own the economy and the incentives for these funds to discourage corporate externalities; see also Stephen Davis, Jon Lukomnik, and David Pitt-Watson, *The New Capitalists: How Citizen Investors Are Reshaping the Corporate Agenda* (Boston: Harvard Business School Press, 2006) at 49-60.

45 Ronald J. Gilson and Reinier Kraakman, "Reinventing the Outside Director: An Agenda for Institutional Investors" (1991) 43 Stan. L. Rev. 863 at 866-67.

46 Julie Froud *et al.*, "Shareholder Value and Financialization: Consultancy Promises, Management Moves" (2000) 29 Economy and Society 80 at 107.

47 Lucian A. Bebchuk, Jesse M. Fried, and David I. Walker, "Managerial Power and Rent Extraction in the Design of Executive Compensation" (2002) 69 U. Chicago L. Rev. 751 at 757-58.

48 Hu, "Risk, Time and Fiduciary Principles," *supra* note 32 at 325.

49 Michel Aglieta, "Shareholder Value and Corporate Governance: Some Tricky Questions" (2000) 29(1) Economy and Society 146 at 155.

50 Froud *et al., supra* note 46 at 107.

51 Aglieta, *supra* note 49 at 156.

52 William Lazonick and Mary O'Sullivan, "Maximizing Shareholder Value: A New Ideology for Corporate Governance" (2000) 29 Economy and Society 13 at 31-32; Aglieta, *supra* note 49 at 152-53.

53 Froud *et al., supra* note 46 at 107-8.

54 Teresa Ghilarducci, "US Pension Investment Policy and Perfect Capital Market Theory" (1994) 37(4) Challenge 4 [Ghilarducci, "US Pension Investment Policy"].

55 Robert A.G. Monks and Allen Sykes, "Shareholder Capitalism Is Damaging Shareholders (The Need to Achieve Effective Ownership)" (2002), online: http://www.ragm.com/library/topics/RagmSykes031502.pdf; see also Hu, "New Financial Products," *supra* note 30 at 1285, citing theoretical models showing how managers can maximize short-term share prices by investing "myopically."

56 Paul Myners, "Institutional Investment in the United Kingdom: A Review" (Report to the Chancellor of the Exchequer, 2001) at 88-89, online: The Corporate Library, http://www.thecorporatelibrary.com/special/myners/myners-review.pdf.

57 Aglieta, *supra* note 49 at 157-58.

58 Teresa Ghilarducci, "Myths and Misinformation about America's Retirement System" in Jeff Madrick, ed., *Unconventional Wisdom: Alternative Perspectives on the New Economy* (New York: Century Foundation, 2000) 69 at 19, online: PDF copy obtained from http://www.nd.edu/~tghilard/.

59 *Ibid.* at 14.

60 Archon Fung, Tessa Hebb, and Joel Rogers, eds., *Working Capital: The Power of Labor's Pensions* (Ithaca and London: Cornell University Press, 2001).

61 Damon Silvers, William Patterson, and J.W. Mason, "Challenging Wall Street's Conventional Wisdom: Defining a Worker-Owner View of Value" in Fung *et al., ibid.* 203 at 206-7.

62 *Ibid.* at 207-8; Marleen O'Connor, "Labor's Role in the Shareholder Revolution" in Fung *et al., supra* note 60, 67 at 86-92. O'Connor reports on the potential for such pension funds to promote long-term value by advancing an agenda requiring investment in human capital and high-performance workplaces.

63 A 401(k) plan is a defined contribution pension plan in which the plan participant is given a choice of investment vehicles. Under US law, it is treated as a participant-directed pension plan and the employer is exempt from any fiduciary obligation with respect to the plan and its investments. More information about these types of plans is provided in the following section, dealing with the Enron pension plans.

64 Silvers *et al., supra* note 61 at 215-16.

65 Ghilarducci, "US Pension Investment Policy," *supra* note 54 at 8.

66 Larry A. Ribstein, "Market versus Regulatory Responses to Corporate Fraud: A Critique of the Sarbanes-Oxley Act of 2002" (2002) 28 J. Corp. L. 1 at 4; see also Hu, "New Financial Products," *supra* note 30, noting price manipulation as one of the dangers of the use of share prices as a measure of fidelity to shareholder interests.

67 The specific information concerning the Enron plan was obtained from U.S., Senate Committee on Governmental Affairs, *Statement of Professor John Langbein,* 107th Cong. (24 January 2002) at 93-94, citing to the plan document "Enron Corp. Savings Plan as Amended and Restated Effective July 1, 1999."

68 U.S., Senate Committee on Governmental Affairs, *Prepared Statement of Professor Susan Stabile,* 107th Cong. (5 February 2002) at fn. 2, citing a Congressional Research Service report: Patrick Purcell, *The Enron Bankruptcy and Employer Stock in Retirement Plans* (CRS Report for Congress, 22 January 2002) at 3.

69 "*Eighty-nine percent of this represents stock purchased by employees* and the rest is attributable to company matching contributions" [emphasis added]; *ibid.*

70 *Ibid.*

71 U.S., Senate Committee on Health, Education, Labor and Pensions, *Prepared Statement of Jan Fleetham,* 107th Cong. (7 February 2002), at 64, online: U.S. Senate, http://frwebgate.access.gpo.gov/cgi-bin/getdoc.cgi?dbname=107_senate_hearings&docid=77-706; *Testimony of Stephen E. Lacey,* 107th Cong. (7 February 2002), at 58 online: U.S. Senate, http://frwebgate.access.gpo.gov/cgi-bin/getdoc.cgi?dbname=107_senate_hearings&docid=77-706.

72 U.S., Senate Committee on Finance, *Statement of Steven A. Kandarian, Executive Director, Pension Benefit Guaranty Corporation,* 107th Cong. (27 February 2002) at 4.

73 *Ibid.*

74 Steven Kandarian testified that the Pension Benefit Guaranty Corporation "is not aware of other ESOP offset plans that have fixed the value of the ESOP stock in computing the offset"; U.S., Senate Committee on Finance, *supra* note 72 at 5.

75 *Ibid.*

76 Christine Dugas, "Enron's Dive Destroys Workers' Pensions" *USA Today* (5 February 2002), online: *USA Today,* http://cgi.usatoday.com/money/energy/2002-02-06-enron-pensions.htm.

77 An article in the *Wall Street Journal* indicated that the legality of the permanent reduction of the pension benefits based on the market price at the time the ESOP Enron stock was released to the participants in 1996-2000 is being questioned, and if the reduction was unlawful, the PBGC might be liable for hundreds of millions of dollars in benefits to the Enron employees: Ellen E. Schultz, "US Taxpayers May Have to Pay Enron's Workers' Pension Benefits" *Wall Street Journal* (27 February 2002).

78 I have provided a more detailed description of these conflicts in Ronald B. Davis, "The Enron Pension Jigsaw: Assembling Accountable Corporate Governance by Fiduciaries" (2003) 36(3) U.B.C. L. Rev. 541

79 Mark J. Roe, "The Modern Corporation and Private Pensions" (1993) 41 UCLA L. Rev. 75 at 78; William M. O'Barr et al., *Fortune and Folly: The Wealth and Power of Institutional Investing* (Homewood, IL: Irwin Professional Publishing, 1992) at 200-01 describe this phenomenon as the "Golden Rule."

80 Gretchen Morgenson, "In a Broker's Notes, Trouble for Salomon" *New York Times* (22 September 2002) Business, reporting the allegations by a former employee about the use of confidential information concerning the vesting date of employee stock option plans administered by brokers to make profitable trades on behalf of other clients; Gretchen Morgenson, "Regulators Find Another Analyst with Questionable Reports" *New York Times* (12 September 2002) Business, reporting that e-mail messages were obtained by securities regulators in which analysts discussed alleged pressure from investment bankers at their firm to maintain optimistic forecasts for certain stocks.

81 Roe, *supra* note 79 at 91-95; see also Edward B. Rock, "The Logic and (Uncertain) Significance of Institutional Shareholder Activism" (1991) 79 Geo L.J. 445 at 470-71 and footnotes therein.

82 These incentives and the corresponding inability of the employee-beneficiaries and the market to exert any controls are described in J.G. MacIntosh, "The Role of Institutional Investors in Canadian Capital Markets" (1993) 31 Osgoode Hall L.J. 371 at 430-33. MacIntosh goes on to report that only a small percentage of private sector pension plans indicated that they would engage in corporate governance activity: *ibid.* at 432, fn. 265, citing Kathryn

E. Montgomery, "Survey of Institutional Shareholders" (1992) 4(4) Corporate Governance Review 5 at 7. See also Monks and Sykes, *supra* note 55 at 8-9.

83 See text accompanying note 9 in Chapter 3.

84 Ronald J. Daniels and Randall Morck, eds., *Corporate Decision-Making in Canada* (Calgary: University of Calgary Press, 1995).

85 Ronald J. Daniels and Randall Morck, "Canadian Corporate Governance: Policy Options" in Daniels and Morck, *ibid.* 661 at 680-82.

86 Michael E. Murphy, "Dispelling Tina's Ghost from the Post-Enron Corporate Governance Debate" (2002) 43 Santa Clara L. Rev. 63 at 94-95.

87 See text accompanying notes 145 to 149 in Chapter 5.

88 For example, a survey of socially responsible investment in Canada in 2006 reported an increase in assets invested according to socially responsible guidelines from $65.46 billion in 2004 to $503.61 billion in 2006, and said that the "vast majority of this increase is due to the recent adoption of socially responsible investment practices by several major pension funds, mostly in the public sector": see Social Investment Organization, *The Canadian Socially Responsible Investment Review 2006* (Toronto: Social Investment Organization, 2007), online: Social Investment Organization, http://www.socialinvestment.ca.

89 United Nations Environment Programme Finance Initiative Asset Management Working Group and the United Kingdom Social Investment Forum Sustainable Pensions Project, *Responsible Investment in Focus: How Leading Public Pension Funds Are Meeting the Challenge* (April 2007), online: United Nations Environment Programme, http://www.unepfi.org/fileadmin/documents/infocus.pdf.

90 Chris Gibben and Matthew Gitsham, *Will UK Pension Funds Become More Responsible? A Survey of Trustees* (Berkhamsted, Herfordshire: Ashridge Centre for Business and Society, 2006) at 13-14, online: UK Social Investment Forum, http://www.uksif.org/cmsfiles/uksif/ukpf2006-justpens.pdf. The survey reported responses from seventy-nine pension funds, 35 percent of which had assets over £1 billion, and 72 percent of which were private sector pension funds.

91 See James Gifford, "Measuring the Social, Environmental and Ethical Performance of Pension Funds" (2003) 53 Journal of Australian Political Economy 139 at 158.

92 Gibben and Gitsham, *supra* note 90 at 6-8, report that UK trustees believe that few social, environmental, or ethical issues will have a positive impact on the market value of investments in the short term, but most believe that they will have at least some positive impact over the longer term (five to ten years).

93 Sir Nicholas Stern, *The Economics of Climate Change* (London: HM Treasury, 2006), online: HM Treasury, http://www.hm-treasury.gov.uk/independent_reviews/stern_review_economics_climate_change/stern_review_report.cfm.

94 Shareholder Association for Research and Education. "2006 Key Proxy Vote Survey," online: Shareholder Association for Research and Education, http://www.share.ca/files/Proxy_Survey_2006_FINAL.pdf.

95 Canada Pension Plan Investment Board, "Responsible Investing: An Investor's Perspective" (Speech by Don Raymond, Senior Vice-President, Public Market Investments to Conference Board of Canada, National CSR Conference, 26 March 2007), online: Canada Pension Plan Investment Board, http://www.cppib.ca/files/PDF/speeches/2007_March26_Don Raymond_CSR.pdf.

96 Bebchuk, Fried, and Walker, *supra* note 47; Lucian A. Bebchuk and Jesse M. Fried, *Pay without Performance: The Unfulfilled Promise of Executive Compensation* (Cambridge and London: Harvard University Press, 2004), argue that executive pay is not set through arm's-length bargains but rather by the exercise of managerial influence over boards of directors, and that this difference imposes substantial costs on shareholders of these corporations.

97 Gretchen Morgenson, "Say-on-Pay Gets Support at Verizon" *New York Times* (19 May 2007), online: *New York Times*, http://www.nytimes.com/2007/05/19/technology/19verizon.html?ex=1181102400&en=d17d1b7f61ca39a7&ei=5070, reporting that a shareholder resolution at Verizon Communications, sponsored by a retiree organization for Bell Telephone workers, had received a majority of the votes cast, as had a similar resolution at Blockbuster and J.C. Penney.

Chapter 2: Pension Fund Assets and Plan Members

1 *McKinney v. University of Guelph*, [1990] 3 S.C.R. 229 (S.C.C), in which the court held that the exclusion, while discriminatory, was justifiable under s. 1 of the *Canadian Charter of Rights and Freedoms* as furthering the structure of pension plans and work opportunities for others built on mandatory retirement.

2 Ontario joined Québec, Alberta, Manitoba, Prince Edward Island, Yukon, Nunavut, and the Northwest Territories in discarding mandatory retirement with the *Ending Mandatory Retirement Statute Law Amendment Act*, S.O. 2005, c. 29, s. 1, amending s. 1(1) definition of "age" in Ontario *Human Rights Code*, R.S.O. 1990, c. H.19; British Columbia has introduced similar legislation: Bill 31, *Human Rights Code (Mandatory Retirement Elimination) Amendment Act, 2007*, 3d Sess., 38th Parl., British Columbia, 2007 (first reading 25 April 2007).

3 Leslie Steeves and Peter Miodonski, "Old Age Security" in Raymond Koskie *et al.*, eds., *Employee Benefits in Canada* (Brookfield, MN: International Foundation of Employee Benefit Plans, 2001) 119 [Steeves and Miodonski, "Old Age Security"] at 119.

4 Human Resources Development Canada, "Overview of the Old Age Security Program," online: Human Resources Development Canada, http://www.Hrdc-Drhc.Gc.Ca/Isp/Oas/Oasind_e.Shtml.

5 Steeves and Miodonski, "Old Age Security," *supra* note 3 at 122.

6 The CPP also provides disability pensions, spousal pensions (for the spouses of deceased plan members), and death benefits: Ari N. Kaplan, "Canada Pension Plan and Quebec Pension Plan: An Overview" in Raymond Koskie *et al.*, eds., *Employee Benefits in Canada* (Brookfield, MN: International Foundation of Employee Benefit Plans, 2001) 75 at 75.

7 Leslie Steeves and Peter Miodonski, "Canada Pension Plan and Quebec Pension Plan Benefits" in Raymond Koskie *et al.*, eds., *Employee Benefits in Canada* (Brookfield, MN: International Foundation of Employee Benefit Plans, 2001) 84 [Steeves and Miodonski, "Canada Pension Plan"] at 86.

8 *Ibid. at* 89.

9 Prior to this decision to invest in equities, the bulk of the CPP fund was lent to various provincial governments at relatively low rates of interest, albeit rates of interest that realistically reflected the "practically no risk" nature of the investments: Federal/Provincial/Territorial CPP Consultations Secretariat, "Strengthening CPP Financing and Reducing CPP Costs" in *An Information Paper for Consultations on the Canada Pension Plan* (1996), online: Department of Finance, http://www.cpp-rpc.gc.ca/summe/summ2e.html#strength.

10 Kaplan, *supra* note 6 at 75 and fn. 3 at 82, citing the federal government's white paper on Bill C-136 (March 1964), in which the objectives of providing a minimum retirement income and relying on private pensions to provide a comfortable income are set out.

11 There are limits, however, to the amount of tax-deferred contributions that can be made on behalf of a particular employee: Andrew J. Hatnay, "Taxation of Pension Benefits" in Raymond Koskie *et al.*, eds., *Employee Benefits in Canada* (Brookfield, MN: International Foundation of Employee Benefit Plans, 2001) 253 at 256.

12 Given the mandatory nature of the CPP, it is not clear why the government accepted its inadequate contribution and benefit levels, other than the fact that there were existing private and public sector pension plans that would have been adversely affected by imposing the larger mandatory CPP contributions needed to generate more than minimum benefits onto a wage structure that already reflected the cost of the non-CPP pension plans.

13 The RRSP plan is locked-in because the contributions and income of an RRSP may not be withdrawn before retirement age without paying substantial tax penalties.

14 Judy Gerwing, "Savings Plans" in Raymond Koskie *et al.*, eds., *Employee Benefits in Canada* (Brookfield, MN: International Foundation of Employee Benefit Plans, 2001) 387 at 392.

15 Paul Myners, "Institutional Investment in the United Kingdom: A Review" (Report to the Chancellor of the Exchequer, 2001) at 4, online: The Corporate Library, http://www.thecorporatelibrary.com/special/myners/myners-review.pdf, points out that, in addition to the public interest in impact on the retirement savings of several million individuals, and the favourable tax treatment, there is also a public policy interest in the capital allocation effects of these investments that influences economic growth and productivity.

16 Vector Research, "Analysis of the Public Opinion Poll Conducted for the Canadian Democracy and Corporate Accountability Commission" (2001), online: http://www.corporate-accountability.ca/pdfs/PollReport.pdf (copy on file with author).
17 The discussion in this section draws upon an earlier publication in which this structure is described in detail: Janis P. Sarra and Ronald B. Davis, *Director and Officer Liability in Corporate Insolvency* (Markham, ON, and Vancouver: Butterworths Canada, 2002) at 147-49.
18 *Ibid.* at 148.
19 Patrick Longhurst, "Plan Design and Administration" in Raymond Koskie *et al.*, eds., *Employee Benefits in Canada* (Brookfield, MN: International Foundation of Employee Benefit Plans, 2001) 197 [Longhurst, "Plan Design"].
20 Patrick Longhurst, "Single Employer Pension Plans (SEPPs)" in Raymond Koskie *et al.*, eds., *Employee Benefits in Canada* (Brookfield, MN: International Foundation of Employee Benefit Plans, 2001) 215 at 219. The issue of "surplus" in a defined contribution plan and the claims on that surplus will be dealt with separately in the text accompanying notes 31 to 45, *infra.*
21 Sarra and Davis, *supra* note17 at 149; Longhurst, "Plan Design," *supra* note 19 at 198.
22 *Schmidt v. Air Products of Canada Ltd.* (1994), 115 D.L.R. (4th) 631 (S.C.C.); vary'g (1992), 89 D.L.R. (4th) 762 (Alta. C.A.), aff'g (1992), 66 D.L.R. (4th) 230 (Alta. Q.B.) [*Schmidt v. Air Products*] at 690; *Bathgate v. National Hockey League Pension Society* (1994), 110 D.L.R. (4th) 609 (Ont. C.A.), varying (1992), 98 D.L.R. (4th) 326 (Ont.Ct.(Gen.Div.)), leave to appeal to S.C.C. refused, (1994), 114 D.L.R. (4th) vii (S.C.C.) at 623-24; *C.U.P.E.-C.L.C., Local 1000 v. Ontario Hydro* (1989), 58 D.L.R. (4th) 552 (Ont. C.A.), rev'g (1987), 36 D.L.R. (4th) 727 (Ont. H.C.J. Div. Ct.), leave to appeal to S.C.C. refused, (1989), 62 D.L.R. (4th) vii (S.C.C.).
23 *Trent University Faculty Association v. Trent University* (1997), 150 D.L.R. (4th) 1 (Ont. C.A.); aff'g (1992), 99 D.L.R. (4th) 451 (O.C.G.D. (Div. Ct.)); *Schmidt v. Air Products, supra* note 22 at 663-64.
24 Gerwing, *supra* note 14 at 387.
25 Kaplan, *supra* note 6 at 75. In Québec, the Québec Pension Plan, administered by the provincial government, provides these benefits and reciprocity with the CPP: *ibid.* at 77.
26 Steeves and Miodonski, "Canada Pension Plan," *supra* note 7 at 84-85.
27 Federal/Provincial/Territorial CPP Consultations Secretariat, *supra* note 9.
28 Steeves and Miodonski, "Old Age Security," *supra* note 3.
29 See MacIntosh, "The Role of Institutional Investors in Canadian Capital Markets" (1993) 31 Osgoode Hall L.J. 371; see also Robert A.G. Monks and Allen Sykes, "Shareholder Capitalism Is Damaging Shareholders (The Need to Achieve Effective Ownership)" (2002) at 8-9, online: http://www.ragm.com/library/topics/RagmSykes031502.pdf.
30 See the case law referred to in notes 22 and 23, *supra.*
31 *Schmidt v. Air Products, supra* note 22 at 659.
32 *Ibid.*
33 Mark Zigler and Ari N. Kaplan, "Pension Plan Surpluses" in Raymond Koskie *et al.*, eds., *Employee Benefits in Canada* (Brookfield, MN: International Foundation of Employee Benefit Plans, 2001) 222 [Pension Surpluses] at 223.
34 Kate Zernike, "Stocks' Slide Is Playing Havoc with Older Americans' Dreams" *New York Times* (14 July 2002) Business.
35 For example, TIAA-CREF's "Mutual Funds Performance Chart" indicated that as of 17 July 2002, its year-to-date return on its equity funds varied between –7.56 percent and –27.72 percent: TIAA-CREF, "Mutual Funds Performance Chart" (2002), online: TIAA-CREF, http://www.tiaa-cref.org/charts/mf-performance.html.
36 Zigler and Kaplan, *supra* note 33 at 223.
37 *Ibid.* at 223.
38 *Schmidt v. Air Products, supra* note 22 at 665-66.
39 It is important to note that deficits in plan funding can arise from factors other than lower than assumed rates of return, including factors such as changes in age at retirement, the rate of salary growth, mortality rates, and employee turnover: see Douglas E. Hyatt and James E. Pesando, "The Distribution of Investment Risk in Defined Benefit Pension Plans" (1996) 51(1) Relations Industrielle 136. Of course, changes in these factors and/or rates of

investment return that are above the assumed levels can generate a surplus in such a plan as well: see Zigler and Kaplan, *supra* note 33 at 223-24.

40 For example, the *Pension Benefits Act,* R.S.O. 1990, c. P.8, as amended (Ontario), provides for amortization periods that vary between fifteen and five years, depending on the source of the funding deficiency.

41 Hyatt and Pesando, *supra* note 39, found evidence that this might be occurring in an analysis of data from large unionized pension plans as well as from responses to a questionnaire by pension specialists about the impact of large deficiencies on future wages and benefits. However, due to the difficulties in isolating all the relevant variables and the absence of large deficiencies resulting from investment performance in the time period for which the data were available, the authors could only conclude that the evidence indicated that the employers' claims of exclusive risk bearing were "overstated." See also Ronald J. Daniels and Randall Morck, "Canadian Corporate Governance: Policy Options" in Ronald J. Daniels and Randall Morck, eds., *Corporate Decision-Making in Canada* (Calgary: University of Calgary Press, 1995) 661 at 680: "It is arguable that there is really no such thing as a 'pure' defined benefit plan, in that in all pension plans employees potentially pay some costs for poor investment performance."

42 See Susan Rowland and Daniel Kingwell, "Plan Wind-up and Deficits" in Raymond Koskie *et al.*, eds., *Employee Benefits in Canada* (Brookfield, MN: International Foundation of Employee Benefit Plans, 2001) 235 at 240, for the limits of the Ontario Pension Benefit Guarantee Fund.

43 For a more detailed discussion of the issue, see Ronald Davis, "Restructuring Proceedings and Pension Fund Deficits: A Question of Risk and Reward" in *Annual Review of Insolvency Law – 2003* (Aurora, ON: Carswell Canada, 2004) 29.

44 Daniel Fischel and John H. Langbein, "ERISA's Fundamental Contradiction: The Exclusive Benefit Rule" (1988) 55 U. Chicago L. Rev. 1105 at 1117, citing this as a fundamental feature of labour economics even where the pension plan does not require any direct contributions from employees.

45 *Ibid.* at 1118-20.

46 *Schmidt v. Air Products, supra* note 22 at 664-65.

47 *Canada Pension Plan Act,* R.S.C. 1985, c. C-5 at s. 108.

48 *Ibid.* at s. 108(4).

49 *Guerin v. R.* (1984), 13 D.L.R. (4th) 321 (S.C.C.).

50 *Canada Pension Plan Investment Board Act,* S.C. 1997, c. 40.

51 Canada Pension Plan Investment Board, "Who We Are" in *CPP Investment Board Investing for Canadians,* online: Canada Pension Plan Investment Board, http://www.cppib.ca/who/index.html.

52 *Canada Pension Plan Investment Board Act, supra* note 50 at s. 5.

53 U.S., Department of Labor, *Interpretive Bulletin Relating to Written Statements of Investment Policy, Including Proxy Voting Policy or Guidelines,* 29 CFR 2509.94-2 (1994). This position has been supported in some district court cases concerning the votes of employee stock ownership plans – *O'Neill v. Davis,* 721 F.Supp. 1013, 1015 (N.D. Ill 1989); *Newton v. Van Otterloo,* 756 F.Supp. 1121 (N.D. Ind. 1991) – but rejected by the Sixth Circuit Court of Appeal in *Grindstaff v. Green,* 133 F.3d 416 (6th Cir. 1998). The Department of Labor position is also supported by the common law of trusts; see American Law Institute, *Restatement (Second) of Trusts,* s. 193, comment a.

54 George P. Dzuro *et al.,* "Pension Funds as Shareholders" in Raymond Koskie *et al.,* eds., *Employee Benefits in Canada* (Brookfield, MN: International Foundation of Employee Benefit Plans, 2001) 286 at 287; and see *Authorson v. Canada (Attorney General)* (2002), 58 O.R. (3d) 417 at 438-39, for discussion of the fundamental nature of the fiduciary's obligation to invest and earn interest on assets entrusted to her. The obligation to utilize a valuable component of the assets in order to advance the beneficiaries' interests would seem to be at least as fundamental an obligation.

55 See, for example, *Pension Benefits Act, supra* note 40 at s. 22.

56 Dzuro *et al., supra* note 54 at 287, and see *Pension Benefits Standards Regulations, 1985,* S.O.R./87-19 (Canada) at s. 7.1(1)(f).

57 Dzuro *et al., supra* note 54 at 287.

58 U.S., Department of Labor, *supra* note 53, takes this position provided the potential effects of the votes of other shareholders on the issue are also taken into account by the fiduciary. I discuss the issue of collective action, free-riding, and rational apathy in the context of the exercise of corporate governance rights by pension fund fiduciaries in Chapter 6.

59 Canada Pension Plan Investment Board, "Frequently Asked Questions" in *Keeping You Informed* [CPP Investment Board, "Frequently Asked Questions"], online: Canada Pension Plan Investment Board, http://www.cppib.ca/info/faqs/index.html ("How will you vote your shares in companies?").

60 *Ibid.,* "Policy on Responsible Investing" (7 February 2007) [CPP Investment Board, "Policy on Responsible Investing"], online: Canada Pension Plan Investment Board, http://www.cppib.ca/files/PDF/policies/policies/Responsible_Investing_Policy.pdf.

61 *Ibid.,* "Social Investing Policy" (2002), online: Canada Pension Plan Investment Board, http://www.cppib.ca/who/policy/Social_Investing_Policy.pdf.

62 *Ibid.,* "Policy on Responsible Investing," *supra* note 60 at 3.

63 *Ibid.,* "Proxy Voting Principles and Guidelines" (7 February 2007) [CPP Investment Board, "Proxy Voting Principles"] at 2, online: Canada Pension Plan Investment Board, http://www.cppib.ca/files/PDF/policies/policies/Proxy_Voting_Guidelines.pdf.

64 There is no shortage of potential measurement tools or criteria, some of which I have discussed in Ronald B. Davis, "Investor Control of Multi-National Enterprises: A Market for Corporate Governance Based on Justice and Fairness?" in Janis Sarra, ed., *Corporate Governance in Global Capital Markets* (Vancouver: UBC Press, 2003). There is no doubt, however, that any attempt to become more explicit would lead to the kind of political, economic, social, and religious debate with which the CPP Investment Board appears not to be comfortable. See, for example, Global Reporting Initiative, "About GRI," online: Global Reporting Initiative, http://www.globalreporting.org/AboutGRI/; Commission of the European Communities, Communication to European Institutions, Member States, Social Partners and Other Concerned Parties, "Communication from the Commission Concerning Corporate Social Responsibility: A Business Contribution to Sustainable Development," COM (2002) 347 final (2 July 2002); Commission of the European Communities, Communication to the Council, the European Parliament and the Economic and Social Committee, "Promoting Core Labour Standards and Improving Social Governance in the Context of Globalization" Communique COM(2001) 416 final (18 July 2001); Kathryn Gordon, "The OECD Guidelines and Other Corporate Responsibility Instruments: A Comparison" in *Working Papers on International Investment No. 2001/5* (2001), online: OECD, http://www.oecd.org/pdf/M00027000/M00027380.pdf.

65 CPP Investment Board, "Frequently Asked Questions," *supra* note 59.

66 Dean Baker and Archon Fung, "Collateral Damage: Do Pension Fund Investments Hurt Workers?" in Archon Fung, Tessa Hebb, and Joel Rogers, eds., *Working Capital: The Power of Labor's Pensions* (Ithaca and London: Cornell University Press, 2001) 13 at 13-22; Teresa Ghilarducci, "Small Benefits, Big Pension Funds, and How Governance Reforms Can Close the Gap" in Fung, Hebb, and Rogers, *ibid.,* 158 at 163; Teresa Ghilarducci, "US Pension Investment Policy and Perfect Capital Market Theory" (1994) 37(4) Challenge 4. For reports that fund managers experience this short-term pressure, see text accompanying note 56 in Chapter 1.

67 CPP Investment Board, "Proxy Voting Principles," *supra* note 63 at 1.

Chapter 3: The Duties of Pension Fund Managers towards Plan Members

1 Gil Yaron, "The Responsible Pension Trustee: Reinterpreting the Principles of Prudence and Loyalty in the Context of Socially Responsible Institutional Investing" (2001) 20 E.T.P.J. 305 at 308, fn. 8, points out that one of the distinguishing features of the pension trust is the absence of a gratuitous transfer, as the employees often contribute to the plan and employer contributions are in consideration of services rendered rather than a gift.

2 John H. Langbein and Richard A. Posner, "Social Investing and the Law of Trusts" (1980) 79 Mich. L. Rev. 72 [Langbein and Posner, "Social Investing"]; James D. Hutchinson and Charles G. Cole, "Legal Standards Governing Investment of Pension Assets for Social and Political Goals" (1980) 128 U. Pa. L. Rev. 1340.

3 Gordon L. Clark, *Pension Fund Capitalism* (Oxford: Oxford University Press, 2000) at 236.
4 *Ibid.* at 273-74.
5 *Ibid.* at 133-54.
6 Mark J. Roe, "The Modern Corporation and Private Pensions" (1993) 41 UCLA L. Rev. 75 at 78.
7 Gretchen Morgenson, "In a Broker's Notes, Trouble for Salomon" *New York Times* (22 September 2002) Business, reporting the allegations by a former employee about the use of confidential information concerning the vesting date of employee stock option plans administered by brokers to make profitable trades on behalf of other clients; Gretchen Morgenson, "Regulators Find Another Analyst with Questionable Reports" *New York Times* (12 September 2002) Business, reporting that e-mail messages were obtained by securities regulators in which analysts discussed alleged pressure from investment bankers at their firm to maintain optimistic forecasts for certain stocks.
8 Roe, *supra* note 6 at 91-95; see also Edward B. Rock, "The Logic and (Uncertain) Significance of Institutional Shareholder Activism" (1991) 79 Geo L.J. 445 at 470-71 and footnotes therein.
9 See Stephen Davis, Jon Lukomnik, and David Pitt-Watson, *The New Capitalists: How Citizen Investors Are Reshaping the Corporate Agenda* (Boston: Harvard Business School Press, 2006) at 67-69, and Klaus Ulrich Schmolke, *Institutional Investors' Mandatory Voting Disclosure: European Plans and US Experience* (New York University Law and Economics Working Papers, Paper 71, 2006) at 18-19, online: New York University School of Law, http://lsr.nellco.org/nyu/lewp/papers/71.
10 *Hewlett v. Hewlett-Packard Company,* 2002 Del. Ch. LEXIS 35. The SEC decision is found at U.S., Securities and Exchange Commission, Administrative Proceeding, Release No. 2160, "In the Matter of Deutsche Asset Management, Inc." (19 August 2003), online: SEC, http://www.sec.gov/litigation/admin/ia-2160.htm.
11 Roberto Tomassini, "Pension Funds and Socially Responsible Investing" in Raymond Koskie *et al.*, eds., *Employee Benefits in Canada* (Brookfield, MN: International Foundation of Employee Benefit Plans, 2001) 316 at 318; Yaron, *supra* note 1 at 311-12.
12 Hutchinson and Cole, *supra* note 2; Maria O'Brien Hylton, "'Socially Responsible' Investing: Doing Good versus Doing Well in an Inefficient Market" (1992-93) 42 Am. U. L. Rev. 1; and Langbein and Posner, "Social Investing," *supra* note 2 confine their analysis to the effect of social screening of investments, although the latter at fn. 9 do comment that social share voting that deflects management from "profit-maximization" is more costly as it imposes a capital loss on the fund.
13 Myron P. Curzan and Mark L. Pelesh, "Revitalizing Corporate Democracy: Control of Investment Managers' Voting on Social Responsibility Proxy Issues" (1980) 93 Harv. L. Rev. 670. The authors point out that the effective control of the proxy votes of pension funds resides with the investment managers and custodial trustees, not the pension fund trustees or the employee-beneficiaries.
14 Tomassini, *supra* note 11 at 325; Stuart A. Baldwin *et al., Pension Funds and Ethical Investment: A Study of Investment Practices and Opportunities – State of California Retirement Systems* (New York: Council on Economic Priorities, 1980).
15 Hylton, *supra* note 12 at 42-43, points out that a socially responsible investment strategy that imposes no or very minimal costs in comparison with a portfolio constructed on purely financial terms will not attract liability for breach of fiduciary duties. She goes on to set out the argument that in view of the mounting evidence that equity markets are inefficient, social investment criteria may be justified as either a proxy for a well-managed company or just another stock-picking strategy: *ibid.* See also Lynn A. Stout, "Are Stock Markets Costly Casinos? Disagreement, Market Failure and Securities Regulation" (1995) 81(3) Va. L. Rev. 611. She provides an in-depth analysis of some possible causes of this inefficiency.
16 For a complete listing of the criteria specified, please see Canada Pension Plan Investment Board, "Social Investing Policy" (2002) [CPP Investment Board, "Social Investing Policy"] at 3, online: Canada Pension Plan Investment Board, http://www.cppib.ca/who/policy/Social_Investing_Policy.pdf; Canada Pension Plan Investment Board, "Frequently Asked Questions" in *Keeping You Informed,* online: Canada Pension Plan Investment Board, http://

www.cppib.ca/info/faqs/index.html; or the text accompanying nn. 59 and 61 in Chapter 2. The rationale offered by the CPPIB for including these factors in the matters to be considered in proxy voting is that they may contribute to "long-term investment returns" of the corporation.

17 Office of the Superintendent of Financial Institutions (Canada), "Guideline for Governance of Federally Regulated Pension Plans" (1998), online: Office of the Superintendent of Financial Institutions, http://www.osfi-bsif.gc.ca/app/DocRepository/1/eng/pension/guidance/govengl3_e.pdf.

18 Langbein and Posner, "Social Investing," *supra* note 2, make this point, albeit only with respect to the aspect of "social investing" concerned with the design of a pension fund's investment portfolio by excluding investments based on social criteria rather than the aspect of voting the shares after they have been acquired based on social criteria. However, they do indicate, at fn. 8, that any voting that deflects management from profit maximization is more costly to the beneficiaries because it causes a capital loss to the fund.

19 *Ibid.* at 98-99.

20 John H. Langbein and Richard A. Posner, "Market Funds and Trust-Investment Law" [1976] 1 American Bar Foundation Research Journal 1 [Langbein and Posner, "Market Funds I"]; *ibid.,* "Market Funds and Trust-Investment Law: II" [1977] 1 American Bar Foundation Research Journal 1 [Langbein and Posner, "Market Funds II"].

21 Josef Lakonishok, Andrei Shleifer, and Robert W. Vishny, "The Structure and Performance of the Money Management Industry" in *Brookings Papers on Economic Activity; Microeconomics* (Washington, DC: Brookings Institution, 1992) 339, cited in Dean Baker and Archon Fung, "Collateral Damage: Do Pension Fund Investments Hurt Workers?" in Archon Fung, Tessa Hebb, and Joel Rogers, eds., *Working Capital: The Power of Labor's Pensions* (Ithaca and London: Cornell University Press, 2001) 13 at 35. See also Hylton, *supra* note 12, noting recent evidence that is inconsistent with the efficient capital markets hypothesis also undermines the economic basis for the critique of social investing utilized by Langbein and Posner in "Social Investing," *supra* note 2.

22 Baldwin *et al., supra* note 14 at 94-95.

23 Edward S. Adams and Karl D. Knutsen, "A Charitable Corporate Giving Justification for the Socially Responsible Investment of Pension Funds: A Populist Argument for the Public Use of Private Wealth" (1995) 80 Iowa L. Rev. 211; see *Steinway v. Steinway & Sons,* 17 Misc. 43, 40 N.Y.S. 718 (1896), corporation using corporate resources to build housing, free library, schools, churches, and free public bath; and *Smith, A.P. Mfg. Co. v. Barlow,* 13 N.J. 145, 98 A.2d 581, 39 ALR.2d 1179, app dismd 346 U.S. 861 (1953), corporation donating large sum of money to Princeton University.

24 Adams and Knutsen, *supra* note 23 at 249-50.

25 The CPPIB principles state the Board's belief that "responsible corporate behaviour – in such matters as the environment, employee practices, stakeholder relations, human rights, respect for domestic and international laws, and ethical conduct – generally contributes to enhanced long-term investment returns": CPP Investment Board, "Social Investment Policy," *supra* note 16.

26 Jeff Frooman, "Socially Irresponsible and Illegal Behavior and Shareholder Wealth: A Meta-Analysis of Event Studies" (1997) 36(3) Business and Society 221. He sets out the results of twenty-seven event studies, from which he concludes that socially irresponsible and illegal corporate behaviour has a negative effect on shareholder wealth.

27 Marc Orlitzky, Frank L. Schmidt, and Sara L. Rynes, "Corporate Social and Financial Performance: A Meta-Analysis" (2003) 24 Organization Studies 403.

28 Yaron, *supra* note 1 at 323-50.

29 Alec Sauchik, "Beyond Economically Targetted Investments: Redefining the Legal Framework of Pension Fund Investments in Low-to-Moderate Income Residential Real Estate" (2001) 28 Fordham Urb. L.J. 1923. Sauchik points out that despite the 1994 promulgation of a regulation by the US Department of Labor supporting the investment of pension funds in economically targeted investments (where both economic and non-economic benefits are considered in the investment decision), the legality of such investments is still hotly contested in the scholarly literature.

30 Baker and Fung, *supra* note 21 at 22-28, review the studies that have sought evidence for the supposed increases in productivity and innovation that have been advanced to justify these activities, and conclude that there is good reason to be skeptical about their existence, while the collateral damage to employees through workforce reductions, reduced pensions and benefits, and a myopic reduction in capital, research, and human capital investments that accompanies a shift from strategic to financial goals has been clearly documented as resulting from such activities.
31 *Cowan v. Scargill,* [1985] 1 Ch. 270 [*Cowan v. Scargill*].
32 *Blankenship v. Boyle,* 329 F.Supp. 1089 (D.C. 1971) [*Blankenship v. Boyle*].
33 *Donovan v. Bierworth,* 680 F.2d 263 (2d Cir. 1982); order modified (2d Cir. 1982) [*Donovan v. Bierworth*].
34 *Cowan v. Scargill, supra* note 31 at 293.
35 *Ibid.* at 295.
36 *Ibid.* at 296.
37 Douglas E. Hyatt and James E. Pesando, "The Distribution of Investment Risk in Defined Benefit Pension Plans" (1996) 51(1) Relations Industrielle 136, recite evidence that the ultimate incidence of "extra" payments to fund deficiencies is borne by the employees in future wage packages.
38 *Cowan v. Scargill, supra* note 31 at 296.
39 *Blankenship v. Boyle, supra* note 32 at 1105-6.
40 *Withers v. Teachers' Retirement System of the City of New York,* 447 F.Supp. 1248 (S.D.N.Y. 1978); aff'd mem 595 F.2d 1210 (2d Cir. 1979) [*Withers*].
41 *Donovan v. Bierworth, supra* note 33.
42 *Ibid.* at 273-75.
43 *Donovan v. Walton,* 609 F.Supp. 1221 (D.C. Fla. 1985); affd. per cur. *Brock v. Walton* 794 F.2d 586 (11th Cir. 1986), reh. denied, 802 F.2d. 1399 (11th Cir. 1986) [*Donovan v. Walton*].
44 *Ibid.* at 1244-45.
45 *Donovan v. Walton, supra* note 43 at 588.
46 *The Board of Trustees of the Employees' Retirement System of the City of Baltimore v. Mayor and Council of Baltimore City,* 562 A.2d 720 (Md. C.A. 1989).
47 *Ibid.* at 85-87; see also the report on the cost of divestment for CalPERS, which reached a similar conclusion as Baldwin *et al., supra* note 14 at 93-118; a recent study by Moshe A. Milevsky, Andrew Aziz, *et al.,* "Cleaning a Passive Index: How to Use Portfolio Optimization to Satisfy CSR Constraints" (Spring 2006) Journal of Portfolio Management 110, demonstrates how portfolio managers can retain a statistically indistinguishable level of diversification while incorporating CSR screens on their portfolio holdings.
48 *Martin v. City of Edinburgh District Council,* [1988] S.L.T. 329 (Court of Session, Outer House) [*Martin v. Edinburgh*].
49 *Ibid.*
50 Yaron, *supra* note 1 at 351.
51 Freya Kodar, *Corporate Law, Pension Law and the Transformative Potential of Pension Fund Investment Activism* (LL.M. Thesis, Graduate Programme in Law, York University, Toronto, 2002) [unpublished].
52 Hutchinson and Cole, *supra* note 2.
53 In terms of the real world of fiduciary duties, one need only ask whether or not Shell Oil's current advertising campaign concerning its protection of the environment during its extraction activities is a breach of Shell's directors' fiduciary duty to act in the best interests of the corporation. It represents a real present cost to the corporation, one that is recorded on its financial statements, but where do the benefits show up in the balance sheet?
54 Benjamin J. Richardson, "Do the Fiduciary Duties of Pension Funds Hinder Socially Responsible Investment?" (2007) 22 B.F.L.R. 145 at 199.
55 Freshfields Bruckhaus Deringer, *A Legal Framework for the Integration of Environmental, Social and Governance Issues into Institutional Investment* (Geneva: UNEP FI AMWG, 2005) at 6.
56 *Ibid.* at 13.
57 Albert J. McClean, "Variation of Trusts in England and Canada" (1965) 43(2) Can. Bar Rev. 181 at 184. He describes them as the "emergency" exception enabling the court to authorize

changes to the trust administration to deal with unforeseen emergencies that threaten the integrity of the trust property, and the "maintenance" exception, in which contingent beneficiaries are provided income from the trust, pending receipt of their benefit.

58 McClean, *supra* note 57 at 194-208.

59 Albert McClean and Sandra McCallum, "Administration of Trusts" in Mark R. Gillen and Faye Woodman, eds., *The Law of Trusts: A Contextual Approach* (Toronto: Emond Montgomery Publications, 2000) 269 at 322.

60 *Withers, supra* note 40, for example, in which retirees challenged the investment of the plan's funds in New York City bonds at a time when the city was virtually bankrupt, on the grounds that the interests of the active employees in continued employment were being preferred by jeopardizing the retirement security of retirees through a risky investment that would impair the continuity of benefit payments if bankruptcy ensued. Although the court found that the investment was not a breach of fiduciary duties because the plan's assets would be dissipated within a decade if the city's contributions were not continued and that the retirees' benefits were at risk from a city bankruptcy, some scholars have claimed that the decision to invest involved a wealth transfer from retirees to younger workers because the money invested in the city's securities would have been used exclusively to pay for their benefits (for a short period) in case of bankruptcy; see Daniel Fischel and John H. Langbein, "ERISA's Fundamental Contradiction: The Exclusive Benefit Rule" (1988) 55 U. Chicago L. Rev. 1105 at 1145-46.

61 *Donovan v. Bierworth, supra* note 33.

62 *Trustee Act,* R.S.O. 1990, c. T.23 at ss. 3 and 4, provides a detailed procedure for the appointment of new trustees, always deferring to the power to appoint new trustees provided in the trust instrument; however, the Ontario Superior Court of Justice is granted an unlimited power to appoint trustees (s. 5).

63 See discussion at notes 39 to 45 in Chapter 2 concerning the ultimate incidence of the cost of pension contributions to employees.

64 As to the contractual basis of a claim to the exclusive benefit of funds held to pay the promised benefits, see *Bathgate v. National Hockey League Pension Society* (1992), 98 D.L.R. (4th) 326 (Ont.Ct.(Gen.Div.)). The lower court decision was varied on grounds unrelated to this issue by the court of appeal: (1994), 110 D.L.R. (4th) 609.

65 For example, the US Department of Labor *Interpretive Bulletin Relating to Written Statements of Investment Policy, Including Proxy Voting Policy or Guidelines,* 29 CFR 2509.94-2 (1994), has not resulted a great increase in enforcement activity with respect to proxy voting activity by that department, perhaps due to a lack of resources.

66 Clark's study of the pension fund investment management industry points out that the asset allocation decision is the most crucial for the fund's long-term return and that, on average, investment managers' returns are less than those of the equity markets, once their fees are taken into account: Clark, *supra* note 3.

67 Keith B. Farquhar, "Recent Themes in the Variation of Trusts" (2001) 20 E.T.P.J. 181 at 183-84; see also Julio Menezes, "Overriding the Trust Instrument" in Gillen and Woodman, *supra* note 59, 165 at 165-67.

68 Langbein and Posner, "Social Investing," *supra* note 2 at 106; see also Hyatt and Pesando, *supra* note 37.

69 A refusal to vote the proxy against a management proposal in the proxy circular (which would be the result of requiring unanimity before the trustees would be bound to follow the beneficiaries' wishes) counts as a vote for the management proposal because the number of votes management needs to win a majority has been reduced, since corporate law requires only a majority of votes cast to carry a proposal.

70 Paul P. Harbrecht, S.J., *Pension Funds and Economic Power* (New York: Twentieth Century Fund, 1959).

71 Eileen E. Gillese, "Pension Plans and the Law of Trusts" (1996) 75 Can. Bar Rev. 221 at 227. In the US, although tax deductibility for pension trusts was implemented in various taxation measures during the 1920s, and irrevocability in 1938, it was not until the passage of the federal *Employee Retirement Income Security Act* in 1974 that there were nationwide regulatory standards that gave employees vesting, participation, and funding rights: Employee

Benefit Research Institute, "History of Pension Plans" in *Facts from EBRI* (1998), online: Employee Benefit Research Institute, http://www.ebri.org/facts/0398afact.htm.

72 For example, *Pension Benefits Act,* R.S.O. 1990, c. P.8, as amended (Ontario) [*Pension Benefits Act*] at s. 37; *British Columbia Pension Benefit Standards Act,* R.S.B.C. 1996, c. 352 [*BC PBSA*] at s. 26.

73 *Pension Benefits Act, ibid.* at s. 42; *BC PBSA, ibid.* at s. 33.

74 Harbrecht, *supra* note 70 at c. 6, records the refusal of many courts in the United States, using this reasoning, to grant status to employees during the 1950s who wished to take legal action about the underfunded state of their employers' pension plans.

75 Gillese, *supra* note 71 at 228.

76 Some of the other variables, such as future wage rates, are also not relevant to this calculation, since there is no ongoing service.

77 *British Columbia Pension Benefits Standards Regulation,* B.C. Reg. 433/93 at s. 38, incorporating the limits of Schedule III of the *Pension Benefits Standards Regulations, 1985,* S.O.R./87-19 (Canada) [S.O.R./87-19 (Canada)], s. 9; *Pension Benefits Act Regulation,* R.R.O. 1990, Reg. 909 [*PBA Regulation*] at s. 79, incorporating the same federal investment limits.

78 See generally Langbein and Posner, "Market Funds I" and "Market Funds II," *supra* note 20, for a detailed analysis of the need to engage in diversification in an efficient capital market in order to comply with trustees' fiduciary duties.

79 Gillese, *supra* note 71 at 243.

80 For example, *PBA Regulation, supra* note 77 at s. 78 requires the preparation of a statement of investment policies and procedures in accordance with the requirements of the federal investment regulations, S.O.R./87-19 (Canada), *supra* note 77.

81 *Pension Benefits Act, supra* note 72 at ss. 29 and 30; *PBA Regulation, supra* note 77 at ss. 45 and 46.

82 See *Pension Benefits Act, supra* note 72 at s. 8.

83 Canada, Standing Senate Committee on Banking, Trade and Commerce, *The Governance Practices of Institutional Investors* (November 1998), online: Parliament of Canada, http://www.parl.gc.ca/36/1/parlbus/commbus/senate/com-e/bank-e/rep-e/rep16nov98-e.htm.

Chapter 4: Corporate Law's Opportunities and Limitations

1 Melvin Aron Eisenberg, "The Structure of Corporation Law" (1989) 89 Colum. L. Rev. 1461.

2 Lawrence E. Mitchell, *Corporate Irresponsibility: America's Newest Export* (New Haven and London: Yale University Press, 2001), is an example of the latter.

3 Eisenberg, *supra* note 1 at 1461.

4 Adolph A. Berle and Gardiner C. Means, *The Modern Corporation and Private Property* (New York: Macmillan, 1932).

5 William W. Bratton, "Berle and Means Revisited at the Turn of the Century" (2001) 26 J. Corp. L. 737 [Bratton, "Berle and Means Revisited"] at 754. He points out that the problem arises because the relationship between the managers and equity investors had split the classic entrepreneurial function that, through the ability of competitive markets to eliminate the greedy and incompetent, had legitimized the private exercise of economic power.

6 *Ibid.,* William W. Bratton, "The New Economic Theory of the Firm: A Critical Perspective from History" (1989) 41 Stan. L. Rev. 1471 at 1489.

7 Robert Yalden, "Competing Theories of the Corporation and Their Role in Canadian Business Law," paper presented in *Current Issues in Securities Regulation and Investor Protection* panel at the Symposium on Shareholders, UBC Faculty of Law January 31, 2003. Yalden questions whether the concepts are helpful or whether they make it more difficult to have a reasoned policy discussion about whether and why "shareholder interests should be privileged"; see also Larry D. Soderquist and Robert P. Vecchio, "Reconciling Shareholders' Rights and Corporate Responsibility: New Guidelines for Management" (1978) 27 Duke L.J. 819, reporting on a survey of shareholders of large publicly held US corporations, the great majority of whom responded that they did not view themselves as owners but rather as investors.

8 Bratton, "Berle and Means Revisited," *supra* note 5 at 761-62, points out that Berle and Means's prescription of enhanced enforcement of fiduciary duties to shareholders provides

no prospect of a remedy for the problems of the harmful effects on the public from the unconstrained exercise of corporate power as follows:

> If unconstrained corporate power creates urgent social problems, then stepped-up enforcement of traditional fiduciary duties holds out no serious prospect of a remedy. Indeed, a "public" coloration does not inevitably follow from the description of a separation of ownership and control. Regardless of the incentive and conflict of interest problems resulting from the separation, management and shareholders retain an overwhelming common "private" interest so far as concerns the competing interests of the rest of the world. Berle and Means elide this point, focusing exclusively on the modern corporation's failure to replicate the single responsible individual of the classical model.

He also points out that Berle had no effective answer to the problem that a duty to the "public" was incoherent and gave management too much power versus a duty to shareholders.

9 Bernard S. Black, "Agents Watching Agents: The Promise of Institutional Investor Voice" (1992) 39 UCLA L. Rev. 811 [Black, "Agents"] at 816, attributes the passivity to a combination of "legal rules, agenda control, conflicts of interest, cultural factors and historical accident."

10 Jack Quarter *et al.*, "Social Investment by Union-Based Pension Funds and Labour-Sponsored Investment Funds in Canada" (2001) 56(1) *Relations Industrielles* 92 at 103.

11 *Ibid.* at 109.

12 Shareholder Association for Research and Education, "About SHARE," online: Shareholder Association for Research and Education, http://www.share.ca/en/about.

13 Social Investment Organization, *The Canadian Socially Responsible Investment Review 2006* (Toronto: Social Investment Organization, 2007), online: Social Investment Organization, http://www.socialinvestment.ca.

14 Alfred F. Conard, "Beyond Managerialism: Investor Capitalism" (1988) 22 U. Mich. J.L. Ref. 117 at 151-52, makes the point that despite the clear evidence that pension funds have apparently exercised their vote against the financial interests of the plan's beneficiaries, it is not surprising that no sanctions have been taken against the trustees, given the plausibility of trustee excuses that the vote was cast to avoid retaliation that would harm beneficiaries in the future and the fact that the harm arising from the vote is too uncertain to form the basis for liability.

15 *Business Corporations Act,* R.S.O. 1990, c. B.16 [*BCA*] at s. 115.

16 *Ibid.* at s. 115(3), requires only that the individual not be an officer or employee of the corporation or an affiliate to be eligible for appointment under this provision; the requirements for independent directors are part of the listing standards in the New York Stock Exchange (NYSE) and NASDAQ, while the Toronto Stock Exchange (TSX) proposes to keep the majority unrelated director provision as a guideline rather than a listing requirement. See Toronto Stock Exchange (TSX), *Comparison of Canadian Equivalents to Recent US Corporate Governance Initiatives* (Toronto: TSX, 2002). In the US, however, the *Sarbanes-Oxley Act of 2002,* Pub. L. No. 107-204, 116 Stat. 745 (2002) at s. 301 prohibits companies whose audit committees are not composed of independent directors from being listed in the stock exchanges. The criteria for an independent director are set out as follows:

> In order to be considered to be independent for purposes of this paragraph, a member of an audit committee of an issuer may not, other than in his or her capacity as a member of the audit committee, the board of directors, or any other board committee
> (i) accept any consulting, advisory, or other compensatory fee from the issuer; or
> (ii) be an affiliated person of the issuer or any subsidiary thereof.

17 *BCA, supra* note 15 at s. 119(4).

18 Indeed, a similar strategy was proposed by the authors in Ronald J. Gilson and Reinier Kraakman, "Reinventing the Outside Director: An Agenda for Institutional Investors" (1991) 43 Stan. L. Rev. 863, as the appropriate corporate governance strategy for institutional investors' indexed portfolios.

19 Both of these problems are considered in the California Public Employees' Retirement System (CalPERS) policy on its involvement in the appointment and nomination of directors:

California Public Employees' Retirement System, "California Public Employees' Retirement System Statement of Policy for Representation on Corporate Board of Directors" (1998), online: CalPERS, http://www.calpers.ca.gov/invest/policies/pdfs/Representation-on-Corporate-Boards-of-Directors.pdf. The policy on direct representation requires the System's representatives to recuse themselves when issues that raise conflicting duties arise. System representatives are permitted to be appointed only where CalPERS is already an insider and is convinced that the benefits outweigh the potentially increased liability.

20 *BCA, supra* note 15 at s. 99(4), allows a shareholder or shareholders to include nominations for the board of directors in a shareholder proposal that must be circulated as part of the management information circular, *but only if the shareholder(s) holds at least 5 percent of the corporation's voting shares.* Any nominations made by holders with less than 5 percent of voting shares must be circulated in a dissident information circular that must be distributed to all shareholders: *ibid.* at s. 112(1).

21 U.S., Securities and Exchange Commission, Division of Corporate Finance, "Staff Report: Review of Proxy Process Regarding the Nomination and Election of Directors" (2003) [SEC, "Review of Proxy Process"] at 5, online: SEC, http://www.sec.gov/news/studies/proxyreport.pdf. It characterizes the expense as "substantial" and points out that most shareholders vote by proxy and therefore a floor nomination "has little chance of receiving sufficient support."

22 *Ibid.* for the staff report. SEC-proposed Rule 14a-11: *ibid.,* "Security Holder Director Nominations" (14 October 2003), online: SEC, http://www.sec.gov/rules/proposed/34-48626.htm.

23 SEC, "Review of Proxy Process," *supra* note 21 at 8-10.

24 Stephen Labaton, "Big Pension Funds Object to Proposal on Proxy Rules" *New York Times* (3 October 2003), business section. According to the article:

> The rules set up a two-year process for selecting new board members. In the first year, some triggering event must occur, like a vote by a majority of shareholders to open an election, or a sizable percentage of shareholders withholding votes for the board's own nominees. In the second year, there would be a contested election pitting the directors selected by the board against one to three directors chosen by the largest block of shareholders.

The challengers would be able to propose one to three directors, depending on the size of the board, SEC officials said. They said that the directors up for election would need to certify that they had no conflicts of interest and no financial relationship with or special ties to the investors who had nominated them.

25 SEC, "Review of Proxy Process," *supra* note 21 at 2-5.

26 Harold S. Bloomenthal and Samuel Wolff, "The Short-Lived SEC Proposal to Give Shareholders Access to the Director Nomination Process" in *Securities and Federal Corporate Law,* 2d ed., looseleaf (Eagan, MN: West Group, 2003), vol. 3E (WL) s. 24:71.21.

27 *Am. Fed'n of State, County & Mun. Employees Pension Plan v. Am. Int'l Group,* 462 F.3d 121 (2d Cir. 2006).

28 U.S., Securities and Exchange Commission, "SEC Announces Roundtable Discussions Regarding Proxy Process" (24 April 2007), online: SEC, http://www.sec.gov/news/press/2007/2007-71.htm.

29 Jane K. Storero, "The HP Letter: SEC Staff Takes No View Position on Shareholder Access Proposal" (2007) 11(2) Wallstreetlawyer.com 1: Securities in an Electronic Age.

30 U.S. Securities and Exchange Commission, SEC Final Rules, "Shareholder Proposals Relating to the Election of Directors" (6 December 2007), online: SEC, http://www.sec.gov/rules/final/2007/34-56914.pdf.

31 Bernard S. Black, "Shareholder Passivity Reexamined" (1990) 89 Mich. L. Rev. 520 at 530-33, summarizes these obstacles as follows: "Yet legal obstacles are especially great for shareholder efforts to nominate and elect directors, even for a minority of board seats. The Proxy Rules [of the US SEC], for example, offer shareholders limited help on some matters, but provide mostly obstacles for director elections. And under the insider trading rules, electing a director has consequences comparable to owning a 10% stake."

32 Gilson and Kraakman, *supra* note 18 at 874-75.

33 *Canada Business Corporations Act,* R.S.C. 1985, c. C-44 [*CBCA*] at s. 122; *BCA, supra* note 15 at s. 134.

34 Lawrence E. Mitchell, "A Theoretical and Practical Framework for Enforcing Corporate Constituency Statutes" (1992) 70 Tex. L. Rev. 579. Mitchell discusses these provisions in depth, together with proposals for a theory and practice for enforcement, despite the statutory absence of standing for any of the stakeholder groups; see also Kent Greenfield, "The Place of Workers in Corporate Law" (1998) 39 B.C.L. Rev. 283 at 305-11. He discusses his contention that the interests of workers serve as an appropriate proxy for the interests of the firm when one is risk-averse with respect to its demise.

35 Yalden, *supra* note 7.

36 *Peoples Department Stores Inc. (Trustee of) v. Wise,* 2004 SCC 68; [2004] 3 S.C.R. 461; [2004] S.C.J. No. 64 (QL).

37 *Ibid.* at para. 43.

38 *Ibid.* at para. 42.

39 *BCA, supra* note 15 at s. 132.

40 *Pension Benefits Act,* R.S.O. 1990, c. P.8, as amended (Ontario) [*Pension Benefits Act*] at s. 22. Concern about conflicts of interest was one of the factors identified by participants in a survey of 100 Canadian institutional investors as a reason they had not sought seats on the board of directors: Kathryn E. Montgomery, "Market Shift – The Role of Institutional Investors in Corporate Governance" (1995-96) 26 Can. Bus. L.J. 189 at 195-96. The survey found that the method was the least favoured method of corporate governance activism.

41 Black, "Agents," *supra* note 9 at 842-44, discusses the use of a minority of the board of directors' being independent directors nominated by institutional investors as a means of monitoring corporate management, but rejects the notion that such directors would represent the public interest or non-shareholder constituencies. He also points out that the insider trading and other legal risks would make direct employees of the institutional investors reluctant to serve.

42 J.A. Grundfest, "Just Vote No: A Minimalist Strategy for Dealing with Barbarians Inside the Gates" (1993) 45 Stan. L. Rev. 857 at 865, explains the process as one in which the portion of the management proxy solicitation in which they seek authorization to vote for the management slate of directors is marked to withhold authority from management to vote for the directors.

43 These requirements were imposed in 1992 changes to the regulations under the *Securities Exchange Act of 1934,* 15 U.S.C. concerning Form 10Q: *ibid.* at 907. Voting "no" does not result in the defeat of management's candidate because there is no one running against the management slate of directors. Therefore, provided that the targeted director receives at least one shareholder vote, the director will be considered to have been elected by a majority of the ballots cast for that director's position. In other words, corporate legislation contemplates either a contest for each director position or else a virtual acclamation. Canadian regulation does not require the corporations to publish the results of shareholder votes.

44 Under Canadian securities regulation, a director is independent if he or she has no direct or indirect material relationship with the issuer, with a material relationship being defined as one that "could, in the view of the issuer's board of directors, be reasonably expected to interfere with the exercise of a member's independent judgement." In British Columbia, the standard for independence is that a reasonable person with knowledge of all of the relevant circumstances would conclude that the individual was independent of management and of any significant security holder. Outside of British Columbia, certain relationships are considered to be material *per se,* such as ex-employees within three years of leaving their employment, or their relatives. See Ontario Securities Commission, National Instrument 58-301, *Disclosure of Corporate Governance Practices* (in effect 12 June 2005) at s. 1.2.

45 *Sarbanes-Oxley Act of 2002, supra* note 16, at s. 301.

46 Victor Brudney, "The Independent Director – Heavenly City or Potemkin Village?" (1982) 95 Harv. L. Rev. 597 at 638, concludes that a combination of judicial deference to directors' decisions under the business judgment rule, the absence of the requirement that

management certify that its accounting and disclosure procedures comply with the legal standards for such procedures, and the lack of meaningful standards for poor performance by directors mean that there is no obligation on a director to be diligent.

47 Gilson and Kraakman, *supra* note 18 at 874.
48 *Ibid.* at 875-76.
49 *Ibid.* at 876.
50 *Ibid.* at 883-87.
51 Edward B. Rock, "The Logic and (Uncertain) Significance of Institutional Shareholder Activism" (1991) 79 Geo. L.J. 445. These agency problems were also recognized in Black, "Agents," *supra* note 9, but with a more optimistic conclusion about the future potential for collective action by institutional investors. See also Conard, *supra* note 14 at 147-48.
52 Rock, *ibid.* at 464.
53 *Ibid.* at 469-72, 480.
54 *Ibid. at* 474.
55 *Ibid.* at 505-6.
56 Jeffrey G. MacIntosh, "The Role of Institutional Investors in Canadian Capital Markets" (1993) 31 Osgoode Hall L.J. 371 [MacIntosh, "Role of Institutional Investors"] at 400-1.
57 See John C. Coffee Jr., "Liquidity versus Control: The Institutional Investor as Corporate Monitor" (1991) 91 Colum. L. Rev. 1277 [Coffee, "Liquidity versus Control"] at 1283-84 and footnotes to text therein, where he points to the lack of mechanisms of accountability, coupled with agency costs as requiring the intervention of the law in order to "correct the market's failure by creating adequate incentives for institutional managers to monitor."
58 Ralph Nader, Mark J. Green, and Joel Seligman, *Taming the Giant Corporation* (New York: Norton, 1976) at 128. In their earlier draft of this work, Ralph Nader, Mark J. Green, and Joel Seligman, *Constitutionalizing the Corporation: The Case for the Federal Chartering of Giant Corporations* (Washington, DC: Corporate Accountability Research Group, 1976) [Nader, Green, and Seligman, *Constitutionalizing the Corporation*] at 203-4, the authors dealt with those institutions where there were no individual beneficial shareholders (such as charitable trusts) and those where the pattern of shareholdings was such that each individual might be a beneficial owner of only a fraction of a share of a corporation (such as pension funds) by suggesting that the latter would elect "representatives" to make voting decisions, since they would be unlikely to spend time studying numerous proxy statements in order to vote their fraction of a share.
59 Conard, *supra* note 14 at 127-28, cites the congressional testimony at fn. 36 and concludes that it is even less likely that the beneficiaries would have any useful ideas about the conduct of the enterprise than would direct shareholders.
60 Ronald J. Daniels and Randall Morck, eds., *Corporate Decision-Making in Canada* (Calgary: University of Calgary Press, 1995).
61 *Ibid.* at 680-82.
62 Michael E. Murphy, "Dispelling Tina's Ghost from the Post-Enron Corporate Governance Debate" (2002) 43 Santa Clara L. Rev. 63 [Murphy, *Dispelling Tina's Ghost*] at 94-95.
63 Coffee, "Liquidity versus Control," *supra* note 57 at 1352-56.
64 *Ibid.* at 1362-66.
65 *BCA, supra* note 15 at s. 99.
66 *Ibid.* at s. 99(5).
67 CBCA, *supra* note 32 at s. 131(1.1)(b)
68 *Ibid.* at s. 150(1.1)-(1.2).
69 *Ibid.* at s. 102(1).
70 Organisation for Economic Co-operation and Development. "OECD Principles of Corporate Governance" (1999) at 27, online: OECD, http://www.oecd.org/pdf/M00008000/M00008299.pdf.
71 Michael J. Whincop, "The Role of the Shareholder in Corporate Governance: A Theoretical Approach" (2001) 25 Melbourne U.L. Rev. 418 at 438-40; see also Jeffrey N. Gordon, "Shareholder Initiative: A Social Choice and Game Theoretic Approach to Corporate Law" (1991) 60 U. Cin. L. Rev. 347.

72 In Murphy's "Dispelling Tina's Ghost" *supra* note 62 at 129, Michael Murphy utilizes the insight of Christopher Stone, in "Corporate Social Responsibility: What It Might Mean, If It Were to Really Matter" (1986) 71 Iowa L. Rev. 557, that there is often a range of options on corporate management's desk in which there is no clear "most profitable" choice, to argue that shareholder democracy would cause corporate decisions to be made in a more open forum and allow the expression of perspectives from other important segments of the public in such circumstances.

73 Roberta Romano, "Less Is More: Making Institutional Investor Activism a Valuable Mechanism of Corporate Governance" (2001) 18 Yale J. on Reg. 174 at 180-81. Of course, I also take issue with the use of stock price as the sole metric of value measurement, as does Henry T.C. Hu in "New Financial Products, the Modern Process of Financial Innovation, and the Puzzle of Shareholder Welfare" (1991) 69 Tex. L. Rev. 1273.

74 Romano, *ibid.* at 224-29.

75 *Ibid.* at 233-41.

76 Jeffrey N. Gordon, "'Just Say Never?' Poison Pills, Deadhand Pills and Shareholder Adopted Bylaws: An Essay for Warren Buffet" (1997) 19 Cardozo L. Rev. 511 [Gordon, "Just Say Never?"] at 546-47, pointed out that the exercise of statutory interpretation soon exhausts itself in circularity due to the statutory language in both provisions in the Delaware corporations statute that make the exercise by either the directors or the shareholders of the bylaw amending power subject to those sections of the statute that grant the power to enact and amend bylaws to another body, such as directors or shareholders.

77 *International Brotherhood of Teamsters General Fund v. Fleming Companies, Inc.,* No. CIV-96-1650-A, 1997 US Dist. LEXIS 2980 (US Dist. W.D. Okla. 24 January 1997). The legal issue as to whether Oklahoma corporate law made the proposed bylaw an unlawful interference in the management of the corporation and whether such an amendment could be passed as a shareholder proposal was then referred by the US Court of Appeal (10th District) to the Oklahoma Supreme Court for determination. The Oklahoma Supreme Court held that neither the proposed bylaw nor its inclusion in the shareholder proposals was contrary to state corporate law: *International Brotherhood of Teamsters General Fund v. Fleming Companies, Inc.* 975 P.2D 907, 1999 Okla. LEXIS 3 (Okla. Sup. Ct. 1999) [*Teamsters v. Fleming Companies* (Okla. Sup. Ct.)].

78 *Teamsters v. Fleming Companies* (Okla. Sup. Ct.), *ibid.*

79 John C. Coffee Jr., "The Bylaw Battlefield: Can Institutions Change the Outcome of Corporate Control Contests"? (1997) 51 U. Miami L. Rev. 605 [Coffee, "Bylaw Battlefield"]; Gordon, *supra* note 76; Jonathan R. Macey, "The Legality and Utility of the Shareholder Rights Bylaw" (1998) 26 Hofstra L. Rev. 835.

80 *Teamsters v. Fleming Companies* (Okla. Sup. Ct.), *supra* note 77 at 912.

81 Macey, *supra* note 79 at 839-56.

82 *Ibid.* at 845-48.

83 *Securities Act,* R.S.O. 1990, c. S.5 [*Securities Act* (Ontario)] at s. 97. The Canadian Securities Administrators (CSA), an organization of all securities regulators in Canada, has issued a proposed national instrument, NI 62-104, *Takeover Bids and Issuer Bids* 2.21-2.23 (issued 28 April 2006), containing similar provisions, which when adopted will implement the prohibition on two-tier bids in all jurisdictions.

84 We care about the free-rider problem because if there is a real potential for free-riding, then there will not be sufficient resources invested in the research of potential takeover targets, and therefore a reduction in the disciplinary incentives that the takeover market generates for managers.

85 Gordon, "Just Say Never?" *supra* note 76 at 522-30.

86 *Ibid.* at 549-50; Coffee, "Bylaw Battlefield," *supra* note 79 at 614-15, offers a similar justification.

87 *CBCA, supra* note 32 at ss. 103, 137; *BCA, supra* note 15 at ss. 99, 116

88 Coffee, "Bylaw Battlefield," *supra* note 79 at 616-19.

89 *Ibid.* at 616.

90 *Ibid.* at 617, citing *American Int'l Rent-A-Car, Inc. v. Cross,* 1984 WL 8204 (Del. Chancery).

91 He cites *USACAFES v. Office,* 1985 WL 44685 (Del. Ch. 1985), as one example.

92 Coffee, "Bylaw Battlefield," *supra* note 79 at 617-18.
93 *Ibid.* at 618-19.
94 Lawrence A. Hamermesh, "Corporate Democracy and Stockholder-Adopted By-laws: Taking Back the Street"? (1998) 73 Tul. L. Rev. 409 at 415-17.
95 See text accompanying note 87, *supra.*
96 *CBCA, supra* note 32 at s. 103(3); *BCA, supra* note 15 at s. 116(3).
97 *BCA, ibid.* at s. 116(4); the *CBCA* contains the same language at s. 103(4).
98 *Teamsters v. Fleming Companies* (Okla. Sup. Ct.), *supra* note 77 at 910.
99 *CBCA, supra* note 32 at s. 103(5); *BCA, supra* note 15 at s. 106(5).
100 *An Act to Amend the Canada Business Corporations Act and the Canada Cooperatives Act and to Amend Other Acts,* S.C. 2001, c. 14.
101 *BCA, supra* note 15 at s. 99(5)(b); *CBCA, supra* note 32 at ss. 137(5)(b), (b.1) and (e).
102 CBCA, *ibid.* at ss. 137(1.1) (minimum shareholding) and 137(5)(a); *BCA, supra* note 15 at s. 99(5)(a).
103 *Michaud v. Banque Nationale du Canada,* [1997] R.J.Q. 547 (Que. S.C.) [*Michaud*]. Although this case involved a corporation incorporated under the *Bank Act,* S.C. 1991, c. 46, the statutory language in that act and the *CBCA* setting out the grounds for excluding shareholder proposals was very similar.
104 *Michaud, ibid.* at paras. 11-13.
105 B.R. Cheffins, "*Michaud v. National Bank of Canada* and Canadian Corporate Governance: A 'Victory for Shareholder Rights'?" (1998) 30 Can. Bus. L.J. 20 at 44-45.
106 *Ibid.* at 25, 36-37.
107 *BCA, supra* note 15 at s. 116(5).
108 Jacob S. Ziegel *et al., Cases and Materials on Partnerships and Canadian Business Corporations,* 3d ed. (Scarborough, ON: Carswell, 1994) at 1024-25.
109 Hamermesh, *supra* note 94 at 432-44.
110 *CBCA, supra* note 32 at s. 153, requires the intermediary (someone who is the registered shareholder where the shares are beneficially owned by another) to seek voting instructions from the beneficial owner for every proxy solicitation the intermediary receives and not to vote the shares without written instructions.
111 See *Verdun v. Toronto-Dominion Bank,* [1996] 3 S.C.R. 550, (1996), 139 D.L.R. (4th) 415 (SCC). This was a case decided before the amendments interpreting a *Bank Act* provision with wording similar to that in the pre-amendment *CBCA.*
112 Ontario Securities Commission, National Instrument 54-101, *Communication with Beneficial Owners of Securities of a Reporting Issuer* (2002), online: Ontario Securities Commission, http://www.osc.gov.on.ca/Regulation/Rulemaking/Current/Part5/rule_20020614_54-101.pdf, sets out the rules. For a clear and concise explanation of how they work, see Jeffrey G. MacIntosh and Christopher C. Nicholls, *Securities Law* (Toronto: Irwin Law, 2002) at 372-76.
113 *CBCA, supra* note 32 at s. 150(1.1).
114 *Ibid.* at s. 150(1.2).
115 Janis P. Sarra, "The Corporation as a Symphony: Are Shareholders First Violin or Second Fiddle?" (2003) 36(3) U.B.C. L. Rev. 403.
116 Ontario Teachers' Pension Plan, News Release, "Institutional Investors Form Coalition to Fight for Improved Corporate Governance" (2002), online: Ontario Teachers' Pension Plan, http://www.otpp.com/web/website.nsf/web/CoalitionforCorpGov.
117 Although the concept of "long term superior returns" is contrasted with "short term behavior" in CalPERS' proxy voting policy, see California Public Employees' Retirement System, "California Public Employees' Retirement System Global Proxy Voting Principles" (2001), online: CalPERS, http://www.calpers-governance.org/principles/global/globalvoting.pdf.
118 These are the Ontario Teachers' Pension Plan and the Ontario Municipal Employees Retirement System.
119 Canadian Coalition for Good Governance, "Mission Statement and Objectives" (2003), online: Canadian Coalition for Good Governance, http://www.ccgg.ca/web/website.nsf/web/ccgghome.

120 *Ibid.*, "Vote Your Proxies" (2003), online: Canadian Coalition for Good Governance, http://www.ccgg.ca/web/website.nsf/web/ccggvoteyourproxies.

121 Janis P. Sarra, "Rose-Coloured Glasses, Opaque Financial Reporting and Investor Blues: Enron as Con and the Vulnerability of Canadian Corporate Law" (2002) 73 St. John's L. Rev. 101.

122 Donald C. Langevoort, "Capping Damages for Open-Market Securities Fraud" (1996) 38 Ariz. L. Rev. 639 at 662-63; James D. Cox, "The Social Meaning of Shareholder Suits" (1999) 65 Brook. L. Rev. 3 at 8-9.

123 Patrick McGeehan, "Sprint Settles Suit with Policy Shift and $50 Million" *New York Times* (20 March 2003) C1. He reports that in a suit concerning the treatment of managers' stock options in failed mergers filed by shareholder Amalgamated Bank (owned by labour unions), Sprint's directors agreed to submit to re-election every year, increase the independence of the directors, and appoint one of the independent directors as a lead director; see also California Public Employees' Retirement System, Press Release, "CalPERS Emerges Victor in Cendant Securities Lawsuit" (1999), online: CalPERS, http://www.calpers-governance.org/news/1999/1207a.asp, reporting that the corporation agreed that its audit, compensation, and nominating committee would be composed of independent directors, as would the majority of the board within two years of the settlement; no stock options would be re-priced without shareholder approval; and shareholders would be given a vote on whether or not to have annual director elections.

124 California Public Employees' Retirement System, "CalPERS and W.R. Grace" (2000), online: CalPERS, http://www.calpers-governance.org/litigation/grace.asp, recording a settlement of a claim of breach of fiduciary duty by W.R. Grace's directors for providing a large termination benefit to the CEO, who resigned after allegations of sexual harassment from several employees. The settlement included the adoption of a sexual harassment policy acceptable to CalPERS, the return of some $4 million of the termination package, and agreement to some corporate governance reforms, including the appointment of independent directors to the nomination, compensation, and audit committees of the board of directors.

125 *Ibid.*, "Case by Case Evaluation Process" (1999), online: CalPERS, http://www.calpers-governance.org/litigation/evaluation.asp.

126 Jill E. Fisch, "Teaching Corporate Governance through Shareholder Litigation" (2000) 34 Ga. L. Rev. 745 at 750-52, sets out these risks.

127 The hostility to derivative litigation in the United States and in Canada was commented on by Stanley M. Beck in "The Shareholders' Derivative Action" (1974) 52 Can. Bar Rev. 159 at 162-63.

128 "Distinguishing Between Direct and Derivative Shareholder Suits," Note (1962) 110 U. Pa. L. Rev. 1147.

129 *Ibid.* at 1147.

130 *Securities Act* (Ontario), *supra* note 83 at ss. 138.1-138.14, creates a new civil liability regime for misrepresentation in the secondary markets.

131 The typical conditions are those set out in the *CBCA, supra* note 32 at s. 239, as follows:

> (1) Subject to subsection (2), a complainant may apply to a court for leave to bring an action in the name and on behalf of a corporation or any of its subsidiaries, or intervene in an action to which any such body corporate is a party, for the purpose of prosecuting, defending or discontinuing the action on behalf of the body corporate.
>
> *Conditions precedent*
>
> (2) No action may be brought and no intervention in an action may be made under subsection (1) unless the court is satisfied that
>
> (*a*) the complainant has given notice to the directors of the corporation or its subsidiary of the complainant's intention to apply to the court under subsection (1) not less than fourteen days before bringing the application, or as otherwise ordered by the court, if the directors of the corporation or its subsidiary do not bring, diligently prosecute or defend or discontinue the action;

> (*b*) the complainant is acting in good faith; and
> (*c*) it appears to be in the interests of the corporation or its subsidiary that the action be brought, prosecuted, defended or discontinued.

132 Brian Cheffins, "The Oppression Remedy in Corporate Law: The Canadian Experience" (1988) 10 U. Pa. J. Int'l Bus. L. 305.

133 (1843), 2 Hare 461, 67 E.R. 189 (V.C.).

134 Edward M. Iacobucci and Kevin E. Davis, "Reconciling Derivative Claims and the Oppression Remedy" (2000) 12 Sup. Ct. L. Rev. 87 at 90.

135 Beck, *supra* note 127 at 164-68, sets out the development of the rule that allowed majority directors to ratify self-interested transactions and bar any suit by minority shareholders unless they could establish an *ultra vires* act, an act that had to be ratified by a special majority of shareholders, a fraud on the minority, or a personal right of action.

136 Jeffrey G. MacIntosh, "The Oppression Remedy: Personal or Derivative?" (1991) 70 Can. Bus. L.J. 29 at 31; see also Beck, *supra* note 127 at 168: "the path to the remedy was narrow and hazardous."

137 Beck, *supra* note 127 at 160-62; see also Cheffins, *supra* note 132 at text accompanying fnn. 45-47, discussing the general understanding that the lack of a market for the minority's shares justifies the interference in corporate operations.

138 Although the analysis of institutional investor trading in Josef Lakonishok, Andrei Shleifer, and Robert W. Vishney, "The Impact of Institutional Trading on Stock Prices" (1992) 32 Journal of Financial Economics 23, indicates that in the ordinary course their trading has little impact on stock price volatility for the stocks of large-capitalization corporations, the authors did find evidence of negative price impact measured on a quarterly basis for smaller-capitalization corporations where the fund managers sold the corporation's stock. The authors said this loss in value could result from either the pressure on prices from the sales or positive feedback trading by institutional investors: *ibid.* at 40-42, Table 6.

139 See discussion regarding the few choices left to those institutional investors, such as pension funds, governed by the restrictions on foreign securities in their portfolios in MacIntosh, "Role of Institutional Investors," *supra* note 56 at 383-84. The restriction on foreign securities applied to tax-exempt investors (such as pension funds and Registered Retirement Savings Plans) and was contained in the *Income Tax Act,* R.S.C. 1985, c. 1 (5th Supp.) at s. 206.

140 Ronald J. Daniels and Jeffrey G. MacIntosh, "Toward a Distinctive Corporate Law Regime" (1991) 29 Osgoode Hall L.J. 863 at 884, point out that based on 1990 data, 85.7 percent of the publicly traded companies on the TSE 300 index had either a single controlling shareholder or a group of shareholders (up to three shareholders) with sufficient shares to exercise effective control over the corporation.

141 The same statutory definition of "complainant" is used for both derivative and oppression claims, and, by way of example, in the *BCA, supra* note 15 at s. 245, is defined as follows:

> "complainant" means,
> (a) a registered holder or beneficial owner, and a former registered holder or beneficial owner, of a security of a corporation or any of its affiliates,
> (b) a director or an officer or a former director or officer of a corporation or of any of its affiliates,
> (c) any other person who, in the discretion of the court, is a proper person to make an application under this Part. ("plaignant")

142 *BCA, supra* note 15 at s. 248 (2).

143 *Ibid.* at s. 248(3).

144 Iacobucci and Davis, *supra* note 134 at 91.

145 *BCA, supra* note 15 at ss. 248 (3)(i) and (j), respectively.

146 MacIntosh, *supra* note 137.

147 Iacobucci and Davis, *supra* note 134 at 90.

148 *Ibid.,* citing *Re Goldstream Resources* (1986), 2 B.C.L.R. (2d) 244 (S.C.); *Goldhar v. Quebec Manitoru Mines Ltd.* (1975), 9 O.R. (2d) 740 (Div. Ct.); and MacIntosh, *supra* note 136.

149 *BCA, supra* note 15 at s. 247(d), allows the court to order the corporation to pay the complainant's legal costs.

150 Iacobucci and Davis, *supra* note 134 at 92-100, develop this analysis of the free-rider problem and compared it with similar free-rider problems in a regime where individual derivative plaintiffs were awarded their damages directly in derivative actions. The free-rider potential in the second regime arises from the lessened costs of subsequent derivative actions concerning the same wrongdoing as a result of the "abuse of process" branch of the issue estoppel doctrine, which would prevent the defendants from contesting the subsequent plaintiffs' claims. Thus, only first movers would bear the legal costs of proving wrongdoing, while subsequent litigants could free-ride on their efforts.

151 Iacobucci and Davis, *ibid.* at 105-10, offer this as the justification for leave requirements in the derivative action and argue that the absence of the indemnity in the oppression remedy justifies the absence of the leave provision, notwithstanding the availability of similar remedies in both provisions.

152 Cheffins, *supra* note 132.

153 *BCA, supra* note 15 at ss. 248(3)(c) and (e), respectively.

154 Cheffins, *supra* note 132 at text accompanying fnn. 26-27. Such problems would include being outvoted by the majority, unless the result was oppressive to the minority.

155 Daniel J. Dykstra, "The Revival of the Derivative Suit" (1967) 116 U. Pa. L. Rev. 74.

156 *Ibid.* at 81-82.

157 Dykstra, *ibid.* at 88-95, notes that many of these reforms occurred between 1944 and 1965.

158 Studies by Romano (1991) and Bradley and Fischel (1986) cited in Cox, *supra* note 122 at 13-16.

159 Cox, *ibid.* at 8-20.

160 *Ibid.* at 22-29.

161 *Ibid.* at 29-38.

162 *Ibid.* at 40-42.

163 *Securities Act* (Ontario), *supra* note 83 at s. 138.3; *Securities Act,* R.S.A. 2000, c. S-4 [*Securities Act* (Alberta)] at s. 211.03.

164 *Securities Act* (Ontario), *supra* note 83 at s. 138.1; *Securities Act* (Alberta), *supra* note 163 at ss. 211.01(h) and 211.07(1) at the greater of $1 million or 5 percent of market capitalization for issuers and $25,000 or 50 percent of aggregate compensation for the twelve months prior to the event.

165 *Securities Act* (Ontario), *supra* note 82 at s. 138.6; *Securities Act* (Alberta), *supra* note 163 at s. 211.06.

166 See discussion of this potential in Mary Condon, "Your Money or Your Life: The Future of Litigation and Enforcement in Ontario Securities Regulation" in *Taking Stock: Challenge and Change in Securities Regulation – Papers Presented at the 12th Queen's Annual Business Law Symposium* (Kingston, ON: Queen's Business Law Symposium, 2006) 221.

167 Harry G. Hutchison, "Presumptive Business Judgment, Substantive Good Faith, Litigation Control: Vindicating the Socioeconomic Meaning of *Harhen v. Brown*" (2001) 26 J. Corp. L. 285 at 292; Jonathan R. Macey and Geoffrey P. Miller, "The Plaintiffs' Attorney's Role in Class Action and Derivative Litigation: Economic Analysis and Recommendations for Reform" (1991) 58 U. Chicago L. Rev. 1 at 36.

168 *Ibid.* at 293.

169 *Ibid.* at 291, fn. 45.

170 This appears to be the standard adopted by the New York state courts; see Macey and Miller, *supra* note 167 at fn. 112, citing *Auerbach v. Bennet,* 47 NY2d 619; 393 NE2d 994.

171 *Zapata Corp. v. Maldonado,* 430 A.2d 779 (Del. Sup. Ct. 1981); Macey and Miller, *supra* note 167 at 39.

172 They include Macey and Miller, *supra* note 167, whose suggestions include holding an auction for derivative claims among plaintiff attorneys, with the cash going into the corporation's treasury in the case of derivative litigation; Cox, *supra* note 122, which includes requiring individual defendants to contribute to the amount of settlements or court awards up a limit of one year's compensation; Hutchison, *supra* note 167, saying that the courts

ought to adopt a substantive review of the claim where self-interested transactions are at issue; John C. Coffee Jr., "Litigation and Corporate Governance: An Essay on Steering Between Scylla and Charybdis" (1984) 52 Geo. Wash. L. Rev. 789 at 826-28, adopting a limitation of damages in derivative claims regarding the breach of the duty of care and proposing that all decisions of special litigation committees concerning litigation of allegations of breaches of the duty of loyalty must be subjected to increased judicial review.

173 Hutchison, *supra* note 167 at 294.

174 Herbert A. Denton, "Differing Approaches to Governance in Portfolio Management Process" (Panel presentation, International Corporate Governance Network Annual Meeting, Amsterdam, 2003).

175 Jeffery G. MacIntosh, "Minority Shareholder Rights in Canada and England: 1860-1987" (1989) 29 Osgoode Hall L.J. 561 at 641; *BCA, supra* note 15 at s. 249(1).

176 *UPM-Kymmene Corp. v. UPM-Kymmene Miramichi Inc.* (2002), 27 B.L.R. 203 (Ont. S.C.J. (Commercial List)), affirmed (2004), 42 B.L.R. (3d) 34 (Ont. C.A.).

177 *Catalyst Fund General Partner I Inc. v. Hollinger Inc.* (2004), 135 A.C.W.S. (3d) 80 (Ont. S.C.J.).

178 *Greenlight Capital Inc. v. Stronach* (2006), 152 A.C.W.S. (3d) 616; 22 B.L.R. (4th) 11 (Ont. S.C.J.).

179 *Ford Motor Co. of Canada v. Ontario Municipal Employees Retirement Board,* [2006] O.J. No. 27, 79 O.R. (3d) 81 (C.A.), varying [2004] O.J. No. 191 (Ont. S.C.J.).

180 Examples include *Danylchuk v. Wolinsky,* [2007] M.J. No. 80 (Man. Q.B.) – trustee of Winnipeg Jets Employee Benefit Plan, one of the applicants, complaining about failure to hold shareholder meetings or disclose financial reports while numerous related party transactions occurred; and *Metropolitan Police Widows and Orphans Fund v. Telus Communications Inc.* (2005), 79 O.R. (3d) 784 (Ont. C.A.), allowing appeal from (2003), 30 B.L.R. (3d) 288 (Ont. S.C.J.), complaining that the corporation's actions in securitizing accounts receivable contravened a protective term in the bondholder trust agreement.

181 Poonam Puri and Stephanie Ben-Ishai, "The Canadian Oppression Remedy Judicially Considered: 1995-2001" (2004) 30 Queen's L.J. 79.

182 *Ibid.* at 108.

183 *Naneff v. Concrete Holdings Limited* (1995), 23 O.R. (3d) 481 (C.A.) at 6-7.

Chapter 5: The Enhancing and Constraining Effects of Securities Regulation

1 These goals are included expressly in some legislation. See, for example, *Securities Act,* R.S.O. 1990, c. S.5 [*Securities Act* (Ontario)] at s. 1.1

2 Alfred F. Conard, "Beyond Managerialism: Investor Capitalism" (1988) 22 U. Mich. J.L. Ref. 117; Victor Brudney, "The Independent Director – Heavenly City or Potemkin Village?" (1982) 95 Harv. L. Rev. 597; Ronald J. Gilson and Reinier Kraakman, "Reinventing the Outside Director: An Agenda for Institutional Investors". (1991) 43 Stan. L. Rev. 863.

3 Jeffrey G. MacIntosh, "The Role of Institutional Investors in Canadian Capital Markets" (1993) 31 Osgoode Hall L.J. 371 [MacIntosh, "Role of Institutional Investors"].

4 *Ibid.* at 390.

5 Conard, *supra* note 2 at 161, citing requirement for "underwriting" of sales by a controlling person in *Securities Act of 1933,* Pub. L. No. 73-22, 48 Stat. 74 at s. 2(11); see also Bernard S. Black, "Shareholder Passivity Reexamined" (1990) 89 Mich. L. Rev. 520 [Black, "Shareholder Passivity"] at 548.

6 Jeffrey G. MacIntosh and Christopher C. Nicholls, *Securities Law* (Toronto: Irwin Law, 2002) at 60-61: a distribution is not legal unless the distributing corporation has prepared the requisite disclosure material in the form of a prospectus and had that material approved by the relevant securities regulators. These requirements applied to trading in the secondary market will definitely constrain the liquidity of that shareholder.

7 *Securities Act,* R.S.O. 1990, c. S.5 [*Securities Act* (Ontario)] at s. 1(1).

8 *Pension Benefits Act Regulation,* R.R.O. 1990, Reg. 909 at ss. 79 and 80, requires the investments of Ontario pension plans to follow the investment regulations of the federal pension statute, *Pension Benefits Standards Regulations, 1985,* S.O.R./87-19 (Canada), Schedule 3 (Permitted Investments) at s. 9.

9 MacIntosh, "Role of Institutional Investors," *supra* note 56, chapter 4 at 390-91.

10 MacIntosh and Nicholls, *supra* note 6 at 178.
11 All of the examples that follow are drawn from those set out in MacIntosh, "Role of Institutional Investors," *supra* note 3 at 392-93.
12 *Ibid.* at 394.
13 MacIntosh and Nicholls, *supra* note 6 at 179, citing Ontario Securities Commission, National Instrument 62-101, *Control Block Distribution Issues,* 23 OSCB 1367 [Ontario Securities Commission, National Instrument 62-101], now repealed and replaced by the exemptions for institutional investors in National Instrument 45-106, *Prospectus and Registration Exemptions* (2005) 28 OSCB Supp-4, online: Ontario Securities Commission, http://www.osc.gov.on.ca/Regulation/Rulemaking/Current/Part4/rule_20050909_45-106_consq_amend.pdf.
14 The definition of "eligible institutional investor" is set out in Ontario Securities Commission, National Instrument 62-103, *The Early Warning System and Related Take-Over Bid and Insider Reporting Issues* [Ontario Securities Commission, National Instrument 62-103] at s. 1.1, online: Ontario Securities Commission, http://www.osc.gov.on.ca/Regulation/Rulemaking/Current/Part6/rule_20000225_62-103fr.jsp, as follows:

"eligible institutional investor" means
(a) a financial institution,
(b) a pension fund that is regulated by either the Office of the Superintendent of Financial Institutions (Canada), a pension commission of a jurisdiction, or a similar regulatory authority,
(c) a mutual fund that is not a reporting issuer,
(d) an investment manager in relation to securities over which it exercises discretion to vote, acquire or dispose without the express consent of the beneficial owner, subject to applicable legal requirements, general investment policies, guidelines, objectives or restrictions, or
(e) an entity referred to in clauses (D) or (F) of Rule 13d-1(b)(1)(ii) under the 1934 Act.

15 Among the proponents of this strategy are Gilson and Kraakman, *supra* note 2; Bernard S. Black, "Agents Watching Agents: The Promise of Institutional Investor Voice" (1992) 39 UCLA L. Rev. 811 [Black, "Agents"] at 839-45; and Edward B. Rock, "The Logic and (Uncertain) Significance of Institutional Shareholder Activism" (1991) 79 Geo. L.J. 445 at 505-6, although he expressed considerable skepticism that it could ever be achieved under the current legal regime.
16 Ontario Securities Commission, National Instrument 45-106 *supra* note 13 at s. 4.1(3)(b).
17 MacIntosh, "Role of Institutional Investors," *supra* note 56, chapter 4 at 395.
18 MacIntosh and Nicholls, *supra* note 6 at 223.
19 MacIntosh, "Role of Institutional Investors," *supra* note 56, chapter 4 at 395-96.
20 MacIntosh and Nicholls, *supra* note 6 at 224-31.
21 The former definition is found in the *Securities Act* (Ontario), *supra* note 7 at s. 1(1) "insider," and the latter definition at s. 76(5) of the same legislation. Section 76(5) incorporates the definition of "insider" in s. 1(1) by reference.
22 This prohibition results from the combined effects of the *Securities Act* (Ontario), *supra* note 7 at ss. 76(1) and (5).
23 MacIntosh, "Role of Institutional Investors," *supra* note 56, chapter 4 at 395-97.
24 Gilson and Kraakman, *supra* note 2 at 881.
25 US securities regulation requires that any profits made from sales of corporate securities within a six-month period of any other purchase or sale of that corporation's securities by anyone who holds 10 percent or more of any class of the corporation's equity must be disgorged to the corporation (the six-month period being characterized as the "short-swing" period).
26 This concern had been raised by Conard in the context of the assumption that the institutional investors would choose one of their employees for the director's position; see Conard, *supra* note 2 at 160-61.
27 Other US scholars are not so sure that deputization was restricted solely to these facts. See Black, "Shareholder Passivity," *supra* note 5 at 546-48; John C. Coffee Jr., "Liquidity versus

Control: The Institutional Investor as Corporate Monitor" (1991) 91 Colum. L. Rev. 1277 [Coffee, "Liquidity versus Control"] at 1346.

28 Gilson and Kraakman, *supra* note 2 at 902-3.

29 MacIntosh, "Role of Institutional Investors," *supra* note 56, chapter 4 at 398-99. In her article reporting on a survey of 100 Canadian institutional investors, Kathryn Montgomery reported that insider trading conflicts are a concern to the large public sector pension funds due to the size of their holdings: Kathryn E. Montgomery, "Market Shift – The Role of Institutional Investors in Corporate Governance" (1995-96) 26 Can. Bus. L.J. 189 at 196-97.

30 Ontario Securities Commission, National Instrument 62-103, *supra* note 14 at s. 5.1.

31 *Ibid.* at s. 5.2.

32 *Ibid.* at s. 5.3.

33 *Ibid.* at s. 1.1(1)

34 MacIntosh, "Role of Institutional Investors," *supra* note 56, chapter 4 at 399-400.

35 Ontario Securities Commission, National Instrument 62-103, *supra* note 14 at ss. 5.1(c)(iii) and 5.2(d)(iii).

36 MacIntosh and Nicholls, *supra* note 6 at 327-28; MacIntosh, "Role of Institutional Investors," *supra* note 56, chapter 4 at 408-9.

37 MacIntosh, *ibid.* at 409-10.

38 Ontario Securities Commission, National Instrument 62-103, *supra* note 14 at s. 9.1 (insider reporting) and ss. 4.1-4.8. (early warning system).

39 Effective control is defined in *ibid.* at s. 2.1.

40 *Ibid.* at ss. 9.1(1)(e) and (f).

41 The potential for this in a regime of institutional investors with effective control is reviewed in Coffee, "Liquidity versus Control," *supra* note 27 at 1334-35, but MacIntosh wonders whether the conflicts are as serious as Coffee claims: MacIntosh, "Role of Institutional Investors," *supra* note 56, chapter 4 at 429, fn. 229.

42 Philip Anisman, "Majority-Minority Relations in Canadian Corporation Law: An Overview" (1986-87) 12 Can. Bus. L.J. 473. The author provides a useful summary of the increasing protection offered to minority shareholders in Canadian law; see also Jeffrey G. MacIntosh, "Minority Shareholder Rights in Canada and England: 1860-1987" (1989) 29 Osgoode Hall L.J. 561.

43 SEC-proposed Rule 14a-11: U.S., Securities and Exchange Commission, "Security Holder Director Nominations" (14 October 2003), online: SEC, http://www.sec.gov/rules/proposed/34-48626.htm, and accompanying text.

44 U.S., Securities and Exchange Commission, SEC Final Rules, "Shareholder Proposals Relating to the Election of Directors" (6 December 2007), online: SEC, http://www.sec.gov/rules/final/2007/34-56914.pdf.

45 MacIntosh, "Role of Institutional Investors," *supra* note 56, chapter 4 at 388-412.

46 Daniels and Morck, *Corporate Decision-Making in Canada* (Calgary: University of Calgary Press, 1995) at 683-84, Policy Implication number 15.

47 John Pound, "Proxy Contests and the Efficiency of Shareholder Oversight" (1988) 20 Journal of Financial Economics 237 at 243-44, discusses the hypothesis that this pressure results from the absence of a requirement that fiduciaries report to beneficiaries the manner in which they voted, together with the ease with which management can identify the votes of particular fiduciaries; after analyzing data from 100 proxy contests, he concludes at 260-61 that the data support the conflict of interest hypothesis. See also James A. Brickley, Ronald C. Lease, and Clifford W. Smith Jr., "Ownership Structure and Voting on Antitakeover Amendments" (1988) 20 Journal of Financial Economics 267 at 276-79, for their analysis of voting patterns that shows pressure-sensitive institutional investors (e.g., banks) voting with management much more often than pressure-insensitive investors (e.g., public pension plans).

48 MacIntosh, "Role of Institutional Investors," *supra* note 56, chapter 4 at 388; for a similar proposal in the US, see Black, "Shareholder Passivity," *supra* note 5 at 607-8. MacIntosh goes on to indicate his opposition to regulations implementing "pass-through" voting, in which intermediaries would have to pass through the votes in a plan's stock to the beneficiaries. He opposes it because the result of a beneficiary's failure to provide instructions is

that the stock is not voted at all. Although he recognized the concern about the intermediary bowing to commercial pressures from the corporation, he felt that it was better for the vote to be exercised than for it to be "sterilized" by a failure of the beneficiary to respond, since this would destroy the benefits of concentrated shareownership by reproducing the Berle and Means universe of dispersed (sharevoters): "Role of Institutional Investors," *supra* note 3 at 446.

49 Conard, *supra* note 2 at 177.

50 Robert A.G. Monks and Allen Sykes, "Shareholder Capitalism Is Damaging Shareholders (The Need to Achieve Effective Ownership)" (2002) at 61-63, online: http://www.ragm.com/library/topics/RagmSykes031502.pdf.

51 U.S., Securities and Exchange Commission, *Disclosure of Proxy Voting Policies and Proxy Voting Records by Registered Management Investment Companies,* 17 CFR 270.30b1-4 (2003). For a more complete description of the rule and the debate about its effects, see text accompanying note 40 in Chapter 6, and following.

52 Ontario Securities Commission, National Instrument 81-106, *Investment Fund Continuous Disclosure,* Part 10 – "Proxy Voting Disclosure for Portfolio Securities Held" (3 June 2005), online: Ontario Securities Commission, http://www.osc.gov.on.ca/Regulation/Rulemaking/Current/Part8/rule_20050603_81-106_if-cont-disc.jsp.

53 U.S., Government Accountability Office, *Report to the Ranking Minority Member, Committee on Health, Education, Labor, and Pensions, US Senate: Pension Plans – Additional Transparency and Other Actions Needed in Connection with Proxy Voting,* GAO-04-749 (August 2004), online: Government Accountability Office, http://www.gao.gov/new.items/d04749.pdf.

54 *Companies Act 2006* (U.K.), 2006, c. 46 at ss. 1277-80.

55 U.K., Department of Trade and Industry, *Implementation of Companies Act 2006: A Consultative Document* (February 2007) c. 2, "Secondary Legislation Under the Act," at paras. 2.16-2.17, online: UK Department of Trade and Industry, http://www.dti.gov.uk/files/file37973.pdf.

56 Klaus Ulrich Schmolke, *Institutional Investors' Mandatory Voting Disclosure: European Plans and US Experience* (New York University Law and Economics Working Papers, Paper 71, 2006), online: New York University School of Law, http://lsr.nellco.org/nyu/lewp/papers/71. The Action Plan is Commission of the European Communities, Communication from the European Commission to the Council and European Parliament, "Modernisation of Company Law and Enhancing Corporate Governance in the European Union – a Plan to Move Forward," COM (2003) 284 final (21 May 2003) at 13, online: Europa, http://eur-lex.europa.eu/LexUriServ/site/en/com/2003/com2003_0284en01.pdf.

57 William J. Carney, "The Legacy of the 'Market for Corporate Control' and the Origins of the Theory of the Firm" (1999) 50 Case W. Res. L. Rev. 215.

58 *Ibid.* at 230.

59 Henry G. Manne, "Some Theoretical Aspects of Share Voting: An Essay in Honor of Adolf A. Berle" (1964) 64 Colum. L. Rev. 1427 at 1430-31; Carney, *supra* note 57 at 234-36.

60 Carney, *ibid.* at 231.

61 Robert A.G. Monks, *The New Global Investors: How Shareowners Can Unlock Sustainable Prosperity Worldwide* (Oxford: Capstone, 2001) at 188.

62 Ronald B. Davis, "Investor Control of Multi-National Enterprises: A Market for Corporate Governance Based on Justice and Fairness?" in Janis Sarra, ed., *Corporate Governance in Global Capital Markets* (Vancouver: UBC Press, 2003) 541.

63 Douglas M. Branson, "Teaching Comparative Corporate Governance: The Significance of 'Soft Law' and International Institutions" (2000) 34 Ga. L. Rev. 669 at 678-79, discusses both regulatory arbitrage and plantation production as some of the less desirable effects accompanying the spread of MNEs.

64 Monks, *supra* note 8, Introduction at 188.

65 Naomi Roht-Arriaza, "Private Voluntary Standard-Setting, the International Organization of Standardization and International Environmental Lawmaking" (1995) 6 Y.B. Int'l Env. L. 107 at 152-53, points out that the ISO 14000 standard requires neither public information on performance nor adherence to any particular standard, merely the implementation of certain management systems. See also Meaghan Shaughnessy, "The United Nations

Global Compact and the Continuing Debate about the Effectiveness of Corporate Voluntary Codes of Conduct" (2001) 12 Colorado Journal of International Environmental Law and Policy: 2000 Yearbook 159, reporting the problem of voluntary codes' lack of a legal mechanism to enforce compliance.

66 Other limits that may also apply are similar to those that apply in the cases of dispersed share ownership among individuals – they will be able to reap only a part of the total increase in the value of the corporation that is proportionate to the percentage of shares they own, and the rest of the benefit will go to other shareholders who did not expend the resources to generate the benefits. See the discussion of "rational apathy" in Jeffrey G. MacIntosh, "Institutional Shareholders and Corporate Governance in Canada" (1996) 26 Can. Bus. L.J. 145 at 152-54.

67 Stéphane Rousseau, "Canadian Corporate Governance Reform: In Search of a Role for Public Regulation" in Janis P. Sarra, ed., *Corporate Governance in Global Capital Markets* (Vancouver: UBC Press, 2003) 3.

68 George A. Akerlof, "The Market for 'Lemons': Quality Uncertainty and the Market Mechanism" (1970) 84 Quarterly Journal of Economics 488 at 490-91.

69 MacIntosh and Nicholls, *supra* note 56, chapter 4 at 139-74 and 253-94.

70 *Securities Act of 1933*, Pub. L. No. 73-22, 48 Stat. 74, ss. 5a and c.

71 However, Rule 135a provides for some exceptions, including a "bare bones" announcement of the proposed offering without identifying the underwriters, which is deemed not to constitute an offer under s. 5 of the 33 Act.

72 These include those communications that, while not an offer, are viewed by the SEC as attempts to condition the market by arousing public interest in the upcoming issue of securities. See *In re Carl M. Loeb, Rhoades & Co.* 38 SEC 843 (1959) and SEC Release 5,180 (16 August 1971), distinguishing public information provided in the ordinary course of business from conditioning the market.

73 These requirements for delivery of the final prospectus apply to subsequent purchasers of the securities unless the exemptions in s. 4(1) (sales by a person who is not an issuer, underwriter, or dealer), or s. 4(3) (sales by a dealer outside the prescribed period during which a sale must be accompanied by a final prospectus) of the 33 Act apply.

74 Various periods are prescribed for the prospectus delivery requirements, depending on the status of the issuer. If the issuer has not previously registered any securities under the 33 Act, then the prescribed period is ninety days; if the issuer has previously registered another issue of securities under the 33 Act, the period is forty days pursuant to the provisions of s. 4(3) of the 33 Act. Rule 174 provides that the period is shortened to twenty-five days when the securities are listed on a securities exchange or traded through NASDAQ.

75 In addition, Rule 408 requires the inclusion of any additional material information required to make the specific information required to be disclosed under the applicable rules "not misleading."

76 Section 17(a) of the 33 Act makes such acts unlawful, and s. 24 makes the willful violation of this provision (and others) a felony.

77 Sections 11 and 12 of the 33 Act impose civil liability for misleading statements. The Commission may also seek civil penalties under s. 20(d) of the 33 Act.

78 *Securities Act* (Ontario), *supra* note 7 at s. 53(1); Mary G. Condon, Anita J. Anand, and Janis P. Sarra, *Securities Law in Canada* (Toronto: Emond Montgomery Publications, 2005) at 229 -30.

79 Condon, Anand, and Sarra, *ibid.* at 250-52.

80 MacIntosh and Nicholls, *supra* note 56, chapter 4 at 263, citing the *Securities Act* (Ontario), *supra* note 7 at s. 88.

81 *Securities Act Regulation 1015,* R.R.O. 1990 at s. 176(1).

82 *Securities Act* (Ontario), *supra* note 7 at s. 143(1) para. 26.

83 MacIntosh and Nicholls, *supra* note 56, chapter 4 at 279-81, reporting on the rejection of the importation of the US common law doctrine of "fraud on the market" by Ontario courts into securities class action proceedings.

84 *Securities Act* (Ontario), *supra* note 7 at ss. 138.1-138.14; *Securities Act,* R.S.A. 2000, c. S-4 at ss. 211.01-211.09.

85 George J. Stigler, "Public Regulation of the Securities Market" (1964) 37(2) Journal of Business 117 at 124, found no effect of regulation after comparing pre-regulation and post-regulation new-issue equity prices. Irwin Friend and Edward S. Herman, "The S.E.C. through a Glass Darkly" (1964) 37(4) Journal of Business 382 at 396-97, corrected what they alleged were data errors in Stigler's comparisons and found that post-SEC market performance was greater than that pre-SEC.

86 George J. Benston, "Required Disclosure and the Stock Market: An Evaluation of the Securities Exchange Act of 1934" (1973) 63(1) American Economic Review 132 (no benefit to investors from mandatory periodic disclosure); Irwin Friend and Randolph Westerfield, "Required Disclosure and the Stock Market: Comment" (1975) 65(3) American Economic Review 467, point out that Benston's comparison of two groups of stocks on the issue of disclosure of sales doesn't account for the fact that both groups disclosed net income during the periods he compared them.

87 Sanford J. Grossman and Joseph E. Stiglitz, "On the Impossibility of Informationally Efficient Markets" (1980) 70(3) American Economic Review 393. The authors submit their proofs that a market that is informationally efficient will disappear because the cost of entering the market will exceed any profits that can be made from trading in such a market.

88 Paul G. Mahoney, "Mandatory Disclosure as a Solution to Agency Problems" (1995) 62 U. Chicago L. Rev. 1047 at 1093-1104.

89 John C. Coffee Jr., "Market Failure and the Economic Case for a Mandatory Disclosure System" (1984) 70 Va. L. Rev. 717 [Coffee, "Market Failure"] at 722-23.

90 *Ibid.* at 725-26.

91 As Stout points out in her interesting analysis of stock-trading behaviour, this is not a popular characterization of such trading as most are content to assume that trading is mutually beneficial to both parties or to deny legitimacy to any inquiry into trades between consenting adults: Lynn A. Stout, "Are Stock Markets Costly Casinos? Disagreement, Market Failure and Securities Regulation" (1995) 81(3) Va. L. Rev. 611 at 613-18; Coffee, "Market Failure," *supra* note 89 at 733-34.

92 Mahoney, *supra* note 88 at 1095-97.

93 Coffee, "Market Failure," *supra* note 89 at 734-37.

94 Stout, *supra* note 91 at 629-34.

95 M. Jensen and W. Meckling, "Theory of the Firm: Managerial Behavior, Agency Costs and Ownership Structure" (1976) 3 Journal of Financial Economics 305.

96 *Ibid.* at 317-19.

97 M. Jensen, "Agency Costs of Free Cash Flow, Corporate Finance and Takeovers" (1986) 76 American Economic Review 323.

98 George Triantis and Ronald J. Daniels, "The Role of Debt in Interactive Corporate Governance" (1995) 83 Cal. L. Rev. 1073 at 1074.

99 Frank Easterbrook and Daniel Fischel, "Mandatory Disclosure and the Protection of Investors" (1984) 70 Va. L. Rev. 669 at 673-77, discuss the use of techniques such as employing audit firms, retaining a large portion of stock in managerial portfolios, having underwriters retain a block of a new issue, and relying on the reputation-destroying effects of managerial slack in the face of the "market for lemons" problems that would arise in an unregulated securities market (see Akerlof, *supra* note 68, for a succinct explanation of the market for lemons). However, Easterbrook and Fischel advanced other reasons why disclosure was justifiable, even though they felt that the arguments on underproduction of information and investor protection were weak.

100 Coffee, "Market Failure," *supra* note 89 at 738-48, also points out that techniques such as the leveraged buyout would result in transfers of wealth from shareholders to managers in a regime without mandatory disclosure.

101 Mahoney, *supra* note 88, argues that the US federal securities laws as originally enacted were intended to deal with this problem and that it was only later rule making by securities regulators that has shifted the emphasis to accuracy enhancement and a focus on predictions of future prospects.

102 Cynthia A. Williams, "The Securities and Exchange Commission and Corporate Social Transparency" (1999) 112 Harv. L. Rev. 1197.

103 *Ibid.* at 1240-46, discussing the congressional record of discussions leading to the passage of the 34 Act and noting the different language used to discuss proxy disclosure and periodic financial disclosure mandated by a different section of the 34 Act.
104 *National Resources Defense Council Inc. v. Securities and Exchange Commission,* 606 F.2d 1031 (4th Circ.1979); Williams, *supra* note 102 at 1256-58.
105 U.S., Securities and Exchange Commission, *Advisory Committee on Corporate Disclosure,* 9 S.E.C. Docket 672 (18 May 1976) (Solicitation of Public Comments) at 2.
106 Williams, *supra* note 102 at 1266-67, citing the US Supreme Court's decision in *Basic Inc. v. Levinson,* 485 U.S. 224 (1988).
107 *Ibid.* at 1265-66.
108 Social Investment Forum, "2001 Report on Socially Responsible Investing Trends in the United States" (2001), online: Social Investment Forum, http://www.socialinvest.org/areas/research/trends/SRI_Trends_Report_2001.pdf.
109 Williams cited statistics from 1999 showing that approximately 9 percent ($1.185 trillion) of funds under professional management in the US were using one or more social "screens" to choose investments and that this sector was growing at a rate of 227 percent between 1997 and 1999: *supra* note 102 at 1268.
110 *Ibid.* at 1269-71, noting that the SEC has also required disclosure of the number of board and committee meetings per year and the names of directors who did not attend at least 75 percent of those meetings.
111 *Ibid.* at 1273.
112 *Ibid.* at 1284-89.
113 These examples were in a memorandum from the SEC Director of Corporate Finance to the Acting SEC Chair, dated 8 May 2001, concerning the material information foreign corporations were required to disclose, cited in Gil Yaron, "Submission to the Canadian Securities Administrators from Shareholder Association for Research and Education on Proposed National Policy 51-201, Disclosure Standards" in *Timely and Material Disclosure* (2001) at 5, online: Shareholder Association for Research and Education, http://www.share.ca/index.cfm/fuseaction/page.inside/pageID/6FE05720-B0D0-157F-F4DAFA83A65BF767/index.cfm.
114 Williams, *supra* note 102 at 1289-93, where she notes that differential access to existing information and incomplete information are also problems in the domestic market that must be addressed by mandatory disclosure.
115 Global Reporting Initiative, "About GRI," online: Global Reporting Initiative, http://www.globalreporting.org/AboutGRI/.
116 Global Reporting Initiative, "Application Levels," online: Global Reporting Initiative, http://www.globalreporting.org/GRIReports/ApplicationLevels/.
117 European Parliament, *Report on EU Standards for European Enterprises Operating in Developing Countries: Towards a European Code of Conduct,* Committee on Development and Cooperation, Number PE 228.198/fin. (17 December 1998), Rapporteur, Richard Howitt.
118 *Ibid.*
119 *Ibid.* at 7, para. 9.
120 Commission of the European Communities, Communication to the Council, the European Parliament and the Economic and Social Committee, "Promoting Core Labour Standards and Improving Social Governance in the Context of Globalization" Communique COM(2001) 416 final (18 July 2001).
121 *Ibid.* at 14.
122 *Ibid.* at 16-17.
123 Commission of the European Communities, *Promoting a European Framework for Corporate Social Responsibility,* Green Paper COM(2001) 366 final (18 July 2001).
124 *Ibid.* at 22.
125 *Ibid.* at 23.
126 Commission of the European Communities, Communication to European Institutions, Member States, Social Partners and Other Concerned Parties, "Communication from the Commission Concerning Corporate Social Responsibility: A Business Contribution to Sustainable Development," COM(2002) 347 final (2 July 2002) [Commission of the European Communities, "A Business Contribution"].

127 *Ibid.* at 5.

128 *Ibid.* at 6.

129 See text accompanying notes 121-23, *supra;* Commission of the European Communities, "A Business Contribution," *supra* note 126 at 22-25.

130 SRI is the acronym for Socially Responsible Investing. *Ibid.* at 17-18; European Parliament, "European Parliament Resolution on the Commission Green Paper on Promoting a European Framework for Corporate Social Responsibility" P5_TA(2002)0278.

131 Commission of the European Communities, Communication from the Commission to the European Parliament, the Council and the European Economic and Social Committee, "Implementing the Partnership for Jobs and Growth: Making a Pole of Excellence on Corporate Social Responsibility," COM(2006) 135 final (22 March 2006).

132 *Occupational Pension Schemes (Investment) Regulation 1996,* (U.K.) S.I. 1996/3127 s. 11A, as amended by S.I. 1999/1849 at s. 2(4).

133 Benjamin J. Richardson, "Do the Fiduciary Duties of Pension Funds Hinder Socially Responsible Investment?" (2007) 22 B.F.L.R. 145 at 191.

134 Chris Gibben and Matthew Gitsham, *Will UK Pension Funds Become More Responsible? A Survey of Trustees* (Berkhamsted, Herfordshire: Ashridge Centre for Business and Society, 2006) at 7-8, online: UK Social Investment Forum, http://www.uksif.org/cmsfiles/uksif/ukpf2006-justpens.pdf.

135 *Ibid.* at 17.

136 Coffee, "Market Failure," *supra* note 89.

137 Mark Anson (Chief Investment Officer, CalPERS), "Corporate Governance Ratings Come of Age" (Speech to International Corporate Governance Network, 2003), reviewed seven major service providers that provide some form of corporate governance rating on a commercial basis and concluded that rating corporate governance was now a fully developed competitive industry.

138 John C. Coffee Jr., "Understanding Enron: 'It's About the Gatekeepers, Stupid'" (2002) 57 Bus. Law. 1403 [Coffee, "Understanding Enron"].

139 *Ibid.* at 1412-14; see also William W. Bratton, "Enron and the Dark Side of Shareholder Value" (2002) 76 Tul. L. Rev. 1275 at 1348-51, describing the phenomenon of auditor "capture" at Enron.

140 Jan van der Poel (Director, Governance Metrics International, University of Amsterdam), "The Coming of Age of Corporate Governance Ratings" (Presentation at the International Corporate Governance Network 9th Annual Conference, 2003), slide no. 2.

141 These changes are summarized in Toronto Stock Exchange (TSX), *Comparison of Canadian Equivalents to Recent US Corporate Governance Initiatives* (Toronto: TSX, 2002).

142 Ontario Securities Commission, National Instrument 51-102, *Continuous Disclosure Obligations,* Form 51-102F2, "Annual Information Form," 5.1(4) (19 January 2007), online: Ontario Securities Commission, http://www.osc.gov.on.ca/Regulation/Rulemaking/Current/Part5/rule_20070119_51-102_unofficial-cons-ni.pdf.

143 Ontario Securities Commission, National Instrument 58-101, *Disclosure of Corporate Governance Practices* (17 June 2005), online: Ontario Securities Commission, http://www.osc.gov.on.ca/Regulation/Rulemaking/Current/Part5/rule_20050617_58-101_disc-corp-gov-pract.jsp.

144 Ontario Securities Commission, National Policy 58-201, *Corporate Governance Guidelines* (17 June 2005), online: Ontario Securities Commission, http://www.osc.gov.on.ca/Regulation/Rulemaking/Current/Part5/rule_20050617_58-201_corp-gov-guidelines.jsp.

145 Carbon Disclosure Project, "About Us," online: Carbon Disclosure Project, http://www.cdproject.net/aboutus.asp.

146 *Ibid.*

147 Principles for Responsible Investment, Media Release, "Principles for Responsible Investment Hit $8 Trillion Mark on First Year Anniversary" (29 April 2007) [PRI, Media Release], online: Principles for Responsible Investment, http://www.unpri.org/media/PRI_media_release_29-04-07.php.

148 Principles for Responsible Investment, "The Principles for Responsible Investment," online: Principles for Responsible Investment, http://www.unpri.org/principles/.

149 Principles for Responsible Investment, Media Release, "Global Investors Get Serious on Environmental, Social and Governance Issues, 'Principles for Responsible Investment' Issues Report on Progress" (4 July 2007), online: Principles for Responsible Investment, http://www.unpri.org/report07/PRI-Media-Release-4-July-2007.pdf.

150 Principles for Responsible Investment, "PRI Report on Progress 2007: Implementation, Assessment and Guidance," online: Principles for Responsible Investment, http://www.unpri.org/report07/PRIReportOnProgress2007.pdf at 12.

151 *Ibid.* at 35.

152 Although the SEC seems to be moving towards holding some of that information material and, in Canada, the Shareholder Association for Research and Education has made submissions to securities regulators seeking mandatory disclosure of similar information, as well as whether foreign exchanges have threatened delisting or evidence of connections between the company and human rights or environmental violations by the host government; see Yaron, *supra* note 113 at 5-6.

Chapter 6: Designing Democratic Corporate Governance Accountability Options

1 Josef Lakonishok *et al.*, "Window Dressing by Pension Fund Managers" (1991) 81(2) American Economic Review 227.

2 "Should the SEC Expand Nonfinancial Disclosure Requirements," Note (2002) 115 Harv. L. Rev. 1433 at 1437-40, again makes the point that corporate law often treats shareholders as an economic abstraction, a point made previously in Daniel J.H. Greenwood, "Fictional Shareholders: For Whom Are Corporate Managers Trustees, Revisited" (1996) 69 S. Cal. L. Rev. 1021.

3 Amartya Kumar Sen, *Development as Freedom* (New York: Anchor Books, 1999). For a contrary view, see Stephen M. Bainbridge, "Corporate Decisionmaking and the Moral Rights of Employees: Participatory Management and Natural Law" (1998) 43 Vill. L. Rev. 741, arguing that the claims that workers want participation and/or that it will make them less alienated are empirically false, that democracy is incompatible with the hierarchical organization of the corporation (the hierarchy being the principal efficiency justification for its existence), and that it is an unjustifiable expansion of the state to use it to mandate worker participation. He does, however, concede that democracy has its place in the shareholders' vote (at 805).

4 Christopher D. Stone, "Corporate Social Responsibility: What It Might Mean, If It Were to Really Matter" (1986) 71 Iowa L. Rev. 557 at 557.

5 *Ibid.* at 558.

6 David L. Engel, "An Approach to Corporate Social Responsibility" (1979-80) 32 Stan. L. Rev. 1 at 7-8.

7 *Ibid.* at 9, fn. 30.

8 Although I characterize his view of the shareholder as an assumption, Engel did have evidence that institutional investors were voting with management with respect to social responsibility proposals at the time he was writing. More recently, however, there has been the increase in social investment mutual funds and in support for what Engel would have characterized as social responsibility proposals, such as a shareholder proposal that the Hudson's Bay Company require its suppliers to conform to the International Labor Organization's minimum standards, which received 36.8 percent support in the second vote on the issue (the first vote received approximately 15 percent of the votes cast): Shareholder Association for Research and Education, News Release, "Record Numbers Support Shareholder Resolution at the Bay on Sweatshops" (23 May 2002), online: Shareholder Association for Research and Education, http://www.share.ca/files/news/02-05-23-HBC.pdf.

9 The *Pension Benefits Act Regulation,* R.R.O. 1990, Reg. 909 [*PBA Regulation*] at s. 22(1) provides as follows: "22(1) The administrator of a pension plan shall exercise the care, diligence and skill in the administration and investment of the pension fund that a person of ordinary prudence would exercise in dealing with the property of another person." See also *Bathgate v. National Hockey League Pension Society* (1994), 110 D.L.R. (4th) 609 (Ont. C.A.), varying (1992), 98 D.L.R. (4th) 326 (Ont. Ct. (Gen. Div.)) leave to appeal to S.C.C. refused, (1994), 114 D.L.R. (4th) vii (S.C.C.) at 624: "Trustees must exercise their powers in

the best interests of all beneficiaries, holding an even hand between different classes of beneficiaries and not acting in a manner prejudicial to the interests of the beneficiaries."

10 For example, the *PBA Regulation, ibid.* at s. 87, provides that the Superintendent of Financial Services may make an order requiring the administrator to take or refrain from taking any action where, in the Superintendent's opinion, the pension plan or fund is not being administered in accordance with the *Regulation.*

11 *Ibid.* at s. 25.

12 *Ibid.* at s. 27.

13 *Ibid.* at s. 29.

14 *Ibid.* at ss. 38 and 40 set out the contents of the mandatory disclosure to beneficiaries.

15 *Ibid.* at s. 45(2)1.

16 *Ibid.* at s. 78.

17 *Pension Benefits Standards Regulations, 1985,* S.O.R./87-19 (Canada) at s. 7.1(1)(f).

18 *Pension Benefits Act,* R.S.O., 1990, c. P.8, as amended (Ontario) at ss. 29(4).

19 International Corporate Governance Network, "ICGN Statement on Institutional Shareholder Responsibilities" (2003), online: International Corporate Governance Network, http://www.icgn.org/documents/GuidelinesResponsibilities0503.pdf, in which accountability to the investor is provided through disclosure of policies and records of corporate governance activity to the beneficiaries.

20 See text accompanying notes 67 to 77 in Chapter 1.

21 *Employee Retirement Income Security Act,* 29 U.S.C. (1994) [ERISA] at s. 1104(a)(1)(C).

22 *Ibid.* at s. 1104(c); Susan Stabile, "Freedom to Choose Unwisely: Congress' Misguided Decision to Leave 401(k) Plan Participants to Their Own Devices" (2002) 11 Cornell J. L. & Pub. Pol'y 361 [Stabile, "Freedom to Choose Unwisely"] at 362-63.

23 Stabile, *ibid.; ibid.,* "Pension Investments in Employer Securities: More Is Not Always Better" (1998) 15 Yale J. on Reg. 61; *ibid.,* "The Behavior of Defined Contribution Plan Participants" (2002) 77 N.Y.U.L. Rev. 71 [Stabile, "Behavior"].

24 Stabile, "Freedom to Choose Unwisely," *supra* note 22 at 378-86.

25 *Ibid.* at 379-80.

26 Stabile, "Behavior," *supra* note 23 at 80-99.

27 *Ibid.* at 86-94.

28 Jayne Elizabeth Zanglein, "Investment without Education: The Disparate Impact on Women and Minorities in Self-Directed Defined Contribution Plans" (2001) 5 Employee Rights and Employment Policy Journal 223.

29 Stabile, "Behavior," *supra* note 23 at 105-6.

30 Edward N. Wolff, *Retirement Insecurity: The Income Shortfalls Awaiting the Soon-to-Retire* (Washington, DC: Economic Policy Institute, 2002) at 26.

31 Louis Uchitelle, "Empty Nest Eggs: Do You Plan to Retire? Think Again" *New York Times* (31 March 2002) Business; Kate Zernike, "Stocks' Slide Is Playing Havoc with Older Americans' Dreams" *New York Times* (14 July 2002) Business; Edward Wyatt, "Pension Change Puts the Burden on the Worker" *New York Times* (5 April 2002) Business; and see Kenneth N. Gilpin, "Waiting for the Green Light on Stocks" *New York Times* (14 July 2002) Business, reporting that since March 2000, $7 trillion of stock wealth had "evaporated."

32 Stabile has recently concluded that these vulnerabilities and the biases justify regulatory intervention in order to protect the "future beneficiaries" of the decisions of participants concerning their retirement savings accounts, utilizing the concept of future beneficiaries as distinct legal persons whose interests may be different from those of present participants: Stabile, "Freedom to Choose Unwisely," *supra* note 22 at 386-91, utilizing similar concepts from trust and bioethics law. She also justifies the regulatory intervention on the grounds that it protects third parties – the US public from shouldering the burden of providing income support, when they have already provided tax subsidies for contributions that were not invested or retained with a view to the public interest in providing adequate retirement income through these private sector savings plans (at 393-96).

33 The obligation is contained in U.S., Department of Labor, *Interpretive Bulletin Relating to Written Statements of Investment Policy, Including Proxy Voting Policy or Guidelines,* 29 CFR 2509.94-2 (1994). For a recent article in which a former Assistant Secretary of Labor cited

the lack of enforcement in the US, see David White, "Interview: Up to Trustees to Make System Work" (Interview with Robert Monks) (2003) 2 Investments and Pensions Europe 28.

34 U.S., Government Accountability Office, *Report to the Ranking Minority Member, Committee on Health, Education, Labor, and Pensions, US Senate: Pension Plans – Additional Transparency and Other Actions Needed in Connection with Proxy Voting,* GAO-04-749 (August 2004) at 22, online: Government Accountability Office, http://www.gao.gov/new.items/d04749.pdf.

35 Tom Croft and Tessa Hebb, "Collaboration between Labor, Academics and Community Activists to Advance Labor/Capital Strategies" in Isla Carmichael and Jack Quarter, eds., *Money on the Line: Workers' Capital in Canada* (Ottawa: Canadian Centre for Policy Alternatives, 2003) at 193.

36 AFL-CIO. "Office of Investment, About Us," online: AFL-CIO, http://www.aflcio.org/corporatewatch/capital/about.cfm.

37 *Ibid.,* "Proxy Voting Guidelines: Exercising Authority, Restoring Accountability" (2003) at 22, online: AFL-CIO, http://www.aflcio.org/corporatewatch/capital/upload/proxy_voting_guidelines.pdf.

38 Trades Union Congress, "Working Capital: Institutional Investment Strategy" (February 2003), online: Trades Union Congress, http://www.tuc.org.uk/pensions/tuc-6269-f0.pdf.

39 Committee on Workers' Capital, "Welcome," online: Committee on Workers' Capital, http://www.workerscapital.org/.

40 The furor surrounding the SEC's proposal to require mutual funds to disclose both their proxy voting policies and votes is a precursor to the types of arguments that might be made by pension fund managers opposed to such a move. Some of these arguments are reviewed in Alan R. Palmiter, "Mutual Fund Voting of Portfolio Shares: Why Not Disclose?" (2002) 23 Cardozo L. Rev. 1419. In the end, the SEC required the disclosure – see U.S., Securities and Exchange Commission, *Disclosure of Proxy Voting Policies and Proxy Voting Records by Registered Management Investment Companies,* 17 CFR 270.30b1-4 (2003) – and Canadian securities regulators followed suit – see Ontario Securities Commission, National Instrument 81-106, *Investment Fund Continuous Disclosure,* Part 10 – "Proxy Voting Disclosure for Portfolio Securities Held" (3 June 2005), online: Ontario Securities Commission, http://www.osc.gov.on.ca/Regulation/Rulemaking/Current/Part8/rule_20050603_81-106_if-cont-disc.jsp. The arguments for disclosure of proxy voting policies, rather than actual votes, are discussed in Jeffrey Larson, "Institutional Investors, Corporate Governance and Proxy Voting Disclosure" in Poonam Puri and Jeffrey Larsen, eds., *Corporate Governance and Securities Regulation in the 21st Century* (Markham, ON: Lexis-Nexis Canada, 2004) c. 6 at 205-15.

41 The disclosure of such policies and votes is not new to some sectors of the pension industry in Canada, particularly the public sector pension plans, such as the Ontario Teachers' Pension Plan; see http://www.otpp.com/web/proxyvot.nsf/proxyvotes?openform.

42 These comments are summarized in the SEC release concerning the final rule 17 CFR 270.30b1-4, *supra* note 40.

43 Palmiter, *supra* note 40 at 1470-72.

44 *Ibid.* at 1474-77.

45 Paul Gompers, Joy Ishii, and Andrew Metrick, "Corporate Governance and Equity Prices" (2003) 118 Quarterly Journal of Economics 107.

46 Palmiter, *supra* note at 1480-83.

47 *Ibid.* at 1484-88.

48 Ronald J. Daniels and Randall Morck, "Canadian Corporate Governance: Policy Options" in Ronald J. Daniels and Randall Morck, eds., *Corporate Decision-Making in Canada* (Calgary: University of Calgary Press, 1995) 661 at 679-81.

49 See text accompanying notes 33 to 45 in Chapter 2.

50 Open-end mutual funds permit their investors to withdraw their investments at any time (in contrast to closed-end mutual funds, which require investors to commit their funds to the mutual fund for a certain length of time).

51 Daniels and Morck, *supra* note 48 at 681-83.

52 However, disclosure of these policies is one of the recommendations for reform in order to increase corporate democracy, in Myron P. Curzan and Mark L. Pelesh, "Revitalizing

Corporate Democracy: Control of Investment Managers' Voting on Social Responsibility Proxy Issues" (1980) 93 Harv. L. Rev. 670 at 688-89; see also Canadian Democracy and Corporate Accountability Commission, "Recommendations" in *The New Balance Sheet: Corporate Profits and Accountability in the 21st Century* (2002), online: http://www.corporate-accountability.ca/pdfs/Recommendations2002.pdf – Recommendation 3, providing that pension plans be required to disclose whether they take corporate social responsibility into account in their investment decisions.

53 One of the most debated issues in the proposal by the SEC that mutual funds disclose their proxy voting records was the cost to the funds' investors of doing so, with fund managers claiming that the costs were substantial and unjustifiable. However, the SEC noted that it had received the following information from those funds that were already voluntarily disclosing their votes in 17 CFR 270.30b1-4, *supra* note 40:

> Finally, with respect to arguments that the disclosure may impose excessive costs, we note that several fund groups that currently provide disclosure of their complete proxy voting records to their shareholders commented that although there are start-up costs for compliance systems, this cost decreases over time, and that the overall costs of the disclosure are minimal. We find these arguments made by funds that are providing this disclosure to be particularly persuasive and continue to believe that the costs of disclosure are reasonable.

54 This is certainly one of the theories underlying the US securities legislation. See Cynthia A. Williams, "The Securities and Exchange Commission and Corporate Social Transparency" (1999) 112 Harv. L. Rev. 1197 at 1209-35, reviewing the intellectual background and legislative history of the legislation to show that one of the purposes of requiring disclosure was to affect the governance of the corporation; controlling agents subject to conflicts of interest is certainly one of the reasons articulated by the SEC in 2003 for requiring disclosure of proxy voting by mutual funds in the following passage from 17 CFR 270.30b1-4, *supra* note 40:

> Further, shedding light on mutual fund proxy voting could illuminate potential conflicts of interest and discourage voting that is inconsistent with fund shareholders' best interests. Finally, requiring greater transparency of proxy voting by funds may encourage funds to become more engaged in corporate governance of issuers held in their portfolios, which may benefit all investors and not just fund shareholders.

55 The trustee will not be willing to do so for no other reason than that the trustees' own organization, the Pension Investment Association of Canada (representing pension fund investment executives of funds with greater than $200 million in assets) has issued corporate governance guidelines that call for pension funds to be active in exercising their proxy votes and to use those votes to further a corporate governance agenda that clearly conflicts with management's agenda; see Pension Investment Association of Canada, "PIAC Corporate Governance Standards" (1998), online: Pension Investment Association of Canada, http://www.piacweb.org/about_corp_gov_standards.cfm.

56 The funds required to fund future pension benefits are not available to be used by beneficiaries until they retire, and then they are available to be used only to provide a pension benefit in the form of equal periodic payments to beneficiaries; even upon termination of employment, the funds may be transferred only to another pension plan or to a locked-in RRSP: *PBA Regulation, supra* note 9 at s. 1 (definition of "pension benefit") 11, 42, and 63. This absence of "exit" is one factor that Daniels and Morck's proposal (*supra* note 48) to allow transfers at will is intended to change; however, unless the proposal would also remove the power to set contribution rates from the employer by introducing minimum standards for such rates, I would be concerned that it would result in a much lower overall level of pension benefits from employment. Defined contribution plans are less costly and time-consuming to administer: see Zanglein, *supra* note 28 at 228-29; moreover, they deliver less pension benefit per dollar of assets in the combined fund because retirees who die shortly after retirement retain the assets in their account, rather than those funds being available to provide benefits to longer-lived retirees.

57 Janis P. Sarra and Ronald B. Davis, *Director and Officer Liability in Corporate Insolvency* (Markham, ON, and Vancouver: Butterworths Canada, 2002), provide a detailed discussion of the oppression remedy's recent treatment in the courts.

58 See Jeffrey G. MacIntosh, "The Shareholder's Appraisal Rights in Canada: A Critical Reappraisal" (1986) 24 Osgoode Hall L.J. 201.

59 *Ibid.*, "Minority Shareholder Rights in Canada and England: 1860-1987" (1989) 29 Osgoode Hall L.J. 561.

60 Henry G. Manne, "Some Theoretical Aspects of Share Voting: An Essay in Honor of Adolf A. Berle" (1964) 64 Colum. L. Rev. 1427 at 1434-36, describes this strategy in the context of cash tender offers for 100 percent of the shares in a control contest.

61 In her article raising concerns about political influence on the corporate governance of public pension funds, Romano suggested that elected representatives of the beneficiaries might counteract the political influence to take on politically attractive but economically unattractive investments because their own retirement savings were involved and increased earnings could generate extra benefits; see Roberta Romano, "Public Pension Fund Activism in Corporate Governance Reconsidered" (1993) 93 Colum. L. Rev. 795 at 821-22 and 841-42.

62 *Canada Business Corporations Act,* R.S.C. 1985, c. C-44 [*CBCA*] at s. 137(5)(b.1).

63 See text accompanying note 112 in Chapter 4 for a brief description.

64 See Donald E. Schwartz, "Towards New Corporate Goals: Co-Existence with Society" (1971-72) 60 Geo. L.J. 57. He discusses the campaign and the role of institutional investors in the resulting vote and notes this consideration at 74 with respect to General Motors' forty-page proxy circular. The particular campaign the author is discussing in this article is GM II, in which the organization sought amendments to the bylaws to allow nomination of director candidates before the proxy circular was sent out (rather than the management proxy seeking approval for candidates to be nominated by the incumbent board), a proposal that each of the employee, franchisee, and customer constituency be allowed to nominate one candidate for director, and a proposal to require disclosure of hiring practices, data concerning air pollution and franchise practices, subject to a finding that the disclosure would not put the corporation at a competitive disadvantage: *ibid.* at 60-61.

65 Curzan and Pelesh, *supra* note 52 at 694, suggest that in addition to the number of beneficiaries in pension plans, issues such as identification of those employees who are entitled to vote and their differing levels of interest in the funds' assets (due to gradual vesting of pension benefits) would make the pass-through voting "impracticable, if not impossible." However, recent Canadian experience with pension surplus distributions in which beneficiaries must vote for or against a surplus distribution proposal indicates that perhaps the impossibility of doing so may have been overblown; see *PBA Regulation, supra* note 9 at s. 8(1)(b), requiring consent from two-thirds of active employees and a sufficient number of retirees and former employees whose benefits are still vested in the pension plan for any surplus distribution from a terminated pension plan.

66 Adolph A. Berle and Gardiner C. Means, *The Modern Corporation and Private Property* (New York: Macmillan, 1932).

67 William W. Bratton, "Berle and Means Revisited at the Turn of the Century" (2001) 26 J. Corp. L. 737 at 753-54.

68 Jeffrey G. MacIntosh, "The Role of Institutional Investors in Canadian Capital Markets" (1993) 31 Osgoode Hall L.J. 371 [MacIntosh, "Role of Institutional Investors"] at 446.

69 Romano argues that capture by political appointees who use the public sector funds' corporate governance activity to increase their personal political capital explains the differing stance of public versus private sector pension funds and the former's lower returns (*supra* note 61).

70 Canada, Standing Senate Committee on Banking, Trade and Commerce, *The Governance Practices of Institutional Investors* (November 1998), online: Parliament of Canada, http://www.parl.gc.ca/36/1/parlbus/commbus/senate/com-e/bank-e/rep-e/rep16nov98-e.htm: "The Committee recommends that individuals appointed to the boards of pension plans should have the necessary knowledge, to enable them to effectively monitor a fund's managers."

71 Romano, *supra* note 61 at 840-41.

72 One of the largest pension funds in the US, CalPERS elects six of its thirteen trustees by a vote of the employees in the relevant division vote on candidates for the position: California Public Employees' Retirement System, "Board Structure," online: CalPERS, http://www.calpers.ca.gov/about/board/structur/structur.htm.

73 Daniels and Morck, *supra* note 48 at 682, Policy Implication 14; Curzan and Pelesh, *supra* note 52 at 698-700; Romano, *supra* note 61 at 854.

74 *Pensions Act, 2004* (U.K.), 2004, c. 35 at ss. 241-43.

75 U.K., Department for Work and Pensions, Press Release, "Timms Backs Socially Responsible Investment" (17 June 2005), online: UK Department for Work and Pensions, http://www.dwp.gov.uk/mediacentre/pressreleases/2005/jun/pens007.asp.

76 Some political promises, such as balanced budgets or the reduction of poverty among our nation's children, can be fulfilled by politicians only through indirect means, i.e., the response of exogenous factors to the political initiatives of the politicians.

77 Curzan and Pelesh, *supra* note 52 at 694.

78 *Pension Benefits Act,* R.S.O. 1990, c. P.8, as amended (Ontario) at s. 37.

79 *Ibid.* at ss. 1 and 31, provides the definition of members and *PBA Regulation, supra* note 9 at ss. 8 and 10, sets out the requirements for member support for surplus withdrawals.

80 Daniels and Morck, *supra* note 48 at 679-81, Policy Implication 12.

81 Bratton, *supra* note 67 at 754.

82 See Palmiter, *supra* note 40 at 1471-73, in which he summarizes studies of the behaviour of mutual fund investors as follows:

> This imagined story of market responsiveness, though attractive, suffers at a number of levels. Recent studies and investor behavior suggests that fund investors' sensitivity to fund performance is uni-directional and shallow. Mutual fund investors, though they readily move into well-performing funds, fail to withdraw from funds following unfavorable fund performance or increases in expense ratios. Mutual fund investors also regularly approve increased advisory fee rates even as fund assets are growing. Even if net performance were all that mattered to mutual fund investors, market behavior suggests investors are insufficiently sensitive to obtuse or inefficient fund governance activities. In short, funds that adopt high-cost or ineffectual voting/governance policies seem largely immune from market discipline.

He concludes that there is virtually no differentiation based on governance policies among mutual funds, although funds that promise low-expense indexing implicitly reject a more active monitoring and governance program for their investors.

83 Jeffrey N. Gordon, "Employees, Pensions and the New Economic Order" (1997) 97 Colum. L. Rev. 1519 at 1521-22, summarizes the problems as follows:

> Because of the volatility of stock markets, employees are rationally (as well as often irrationally) concerned about equity investments in retirement accounts, in particular, about the possibility of a stock market trough at the time of their retirement. Defined benefit plans have provided a form of "intertemporal risk hedging" that defined contribution plans have not, because the structure of the defined payment builds upon a salary scale that increases over time, aggregates contributions from multiple age cohorts of workers, and is guaranteed by an entity, the firm, that presumptively exists over time. In refashioning a pension system that will depend increasingly on contributory plans, what is needed are capital market instruments, supported by appropriate regulatory changes, that would make it easy for employees to lay off this intertemporal risk on financial intermediaries.

Gordon suggests that the employee can purchase a pension equity "collar," in which a guaranteed rate of return is received from the vendor of the "collar" and in return the vendor receives all of the earnings on the equity investment above the guaranteed rate.

84 As to the limits of even pension funds' abilities to deal with the weaknesses of the stock market as its major source of investment earnings see, Henry T.C. Hu, "Faith and Magic: Investor Beliefs and Government Neutrality" (2000) 78 Tex. L. Rev. 777. He makes the important point that the capital market instrument ("collar") that Gordon suggests is

required (Gordon, *supra* note 83) has not been offered in the real world and suggests that it is because there is no "hedge" available against this risk: Hu, *ibid.* at 812-14.

85 Uchitelle, *supra* note 31; Zernike, *supra* note 31; Wolff, *supra* note 30; Wyatt, *supra* note 31; and Gilpin, *supra* note 31, reporting that since March 2000, $7 trillion of stock wealth has "evaporated."

86 A similar package of reforms was recently promoted as being the necessary conditions for the creation of a market for corporate governance; see Robert A.G. Monks and Allen Sykes, "Shareholder Capitalism Is Damaging.Shareholders (The Need to Achieve Effective Ownership)" (2002) at 53, online: http://www.ragm.com/library/topics/RagmSykes031502.pdf.

87 U.S., Department of Labor, *Interpretive Bulletin Relating to Written Statements of Investment Policy, Including Proxy Voting Policy or Guidelines,* 29 CFR 2509.94-2 (1994).

88 White, *supra* note 33; Monks and Sykes, *supra* note 86 at 59, speaking of "decades of neglect in enforcing trust and fiduciary law" and suggesting that a regulator be given an express mandate to enforce the obligation to exercise corporate governance rights in the interests of the beneficiaries.

89 Monks and Sykes, *ibid.* at 48.

90 *Pension Benefits Act, supra* note 78 at s. 109, makes it an offence to contravene a provision of the *Act,* and s. 110 gives the courts the power to impose fines up to $100,000 for a first offence.

91 *Ibid.* at s. 87 provides the Superintendent of Financial Services (Ontario) with the power to order pension trustees to take any action necessary to comply with their obligations under the *Act* (the problem being, defining what compliance means).

92 In Ontario, the *Rules of Civil Procedure,* R.R.O. 1990, Reg. 194, Rule 14.05, provides a mechanism to bring a simplified court proceeding (an "application") regarding the administration of a trust, including a pension trust, and the *Class Proceedings Act,* S.O. 1992, c. 6, allows a single beneficiary to bring an application as a representative for all beneficiaries.

93 Jonathan R. Macey and Geoffrey P. Miller, "The Plaintiffs' Attorney's Role in Class Action and Derivative Litigation: Economic Analysis and Recommendations for Reform" (1991) 58 U. Chicago L. Rev. 1; Theresa A. Gabaldon, "Free Riders and the Greedy Gadfly: Examining Aspects of Shareholder Litigation as an Exercise in Integrating Ethical Regulation and Laws of General Applicability" (1988) 73 Minn. L. Rev. 425.

94 William W. Bratton and J.A. McCahery, "Regulatory Competition, Regulatory Capture and Corporate Self-Regulation" (1995) 73 N.C.L. Rev. 1861 at 1871, fn. 22, noting the significant costs of deterrent strategies and the labour- and resource-intensive nature of court proceedings. On the uncertainty regarding payoffs from corporate governance activity, see Paul Myners, "Institutional Investment in the United Kingdom: A Review" (Report to the Chancellor of the Exchequer, 2001) at 89, online: The Corporate Library, http://www.thecorporatelibrary.com/special/myners/myners-review.pdf, which discusses the weakening incentive for investment managers to undertake active corporate governance generated by haziness over timescales for judging performance by trustees and the managers' belief that the timescales are short (three to six months). See also Monks and Sykes, *supra* note 86 at 47-48, and Romano, *supra* note 61 at 177-92, reviewing finance economics literature that reports little or no significant price effects and arguing that the explanation is that there is no correlation between corporate governance activism and improved financial performance.

95 Bratton and McCahery, *ibid.* at 1870, fn. 21.

96 Monks and Sykes, *supra* note 86 at 54, suggest that a requirement to vote, without specifying in whose interests, would lead to almost automatic votes in favour of the portfolio company's management's proposals "regardless of merit."

97 Canadian Democracy and Corporate Accountability Commission, *supra* note 52 at 25, citing the Manitoba *Trustee Act,* C.C.S.M. c. T160 at s. 79.1.

98 Melvin Aron Eisenberg, "Access to the Corporate Proxy Machinery" (1969-70) 83(7) Harv. L. Rev. 148 at 1490-92, with respect to the connection between geographic dispersion and the need for proxy machinery and the absence of proxy solicitation regulation in state corporate law.

99 Bratton and McCahery, *supra* note 94 at 1930-32, explain agenda control as the ability of corporate management to control what items come before shareholders for mandatory votes. Shareholders can only vote on resolutions that have been approved for submission to them by the directors. If management controls the board, it merely needs to ensure that no resolution submitting the issue to the shareholders is approved by the board.

100 In the US, direct shareholder nominations can be undertaken only by also undertaking the cost of a dissident proxy circular.

101 Many of these suitability provisions were removed in the recent amendments to the *Canada Business Corporations Act,* R.S.C. 1985, c. C-44 [*CBCA*], *An Act to Amend the Canada Business Corporations Act and the Canada Cooperatives Act and to Amend Other Acts,* S.C. 2001, c. 14, and are no longer part of the corporate law in Ontario; *Business Corporations Act,* R.S.O. 1990, c. B.16 [*BCA*] at s. 131. However, they remain a part of the SEC's administrative rules with respect to its supervision of the proxy process.

102 MacIntosh, "Role of Institutional Investors," *supra* note 68 at 388-89; the recent amendments to the *CBCA* permit increased communication in the manner suggested by MacIntosh in this article.

103 International Corporate Governance Network, *supra* note 19 at 3.

104 *Ibid.* at 3-4.

105 Bratton and McCahery, *supra* note 94 at 1925-29.

106 Jeffrey N. Gordon, "'Just Say Never?' Poison Pills, Deadhand Pills and Shareholder Adopted Bylaws: An Essay for Warren Buffet" (1997) 19 Cardozo L. Rev. 511.

107 Bratton and McCahery, *supra* note 94 at 1941-47.

108 Ronald J. Daniels and Paul Halpern, "Too Close for Comfort: The Role of the Closely Held Public Corporation in the Canadian Economy and the Implications for Public Policy" (1995-96) 26 Can. Bus. L.J. 11.

109 See text accompanying note 30 in Chapter 4 for the multi-year saga of this on-again, off-again proposal.

110 *CBCA, supra* note 101 at s. 137(4); *BCA, supra* note 101 at s. 99(4), granting the right to include nominations in a proposal if shareholdings are equal to or greater than 5 percent of the voting stock.

111 In Bratton and McCahery, *supra* note 94 at 1921-22, the authors discuss the potential for such capture of an individual block owner, and the lower likelihood that capture could occur in a voting coalition of institutional shareholders because "cross-monitoring, reputational interests, and contestability of guardianship provides a circumstantial guarantee that participants will remain faithful to the shareholder interest."

112 MacIntosh, *supra* note 68 at 394, uses the evidence that investors have a difficult time "beating the market" to demonstrate that regulators ought not to apply the control person designation to ad hoc coalitions because the basis for that regulation – access to confidential information – obviously does not apply; see also Bratton and McCahery, *supra* note 94 at 1941-42, where the authors argue that reputational motivation for proponents serves to constrain management capture of institutional investors.

113 See text accompanying notes 14 to 17 in Chapter 5.

114 Ronald J. Gilson and Reinier Kraakman, "Reinventing the Outside Director: An Agenda for Institutional Investors" (1991) 43 Stan. L. Rev. 863, proposed that institutional investors would support candidates for director chosen from a pool of professional directors who had been vetted by a commercial agency that charged all of the institutional investors for the rating.

Conclusion

1 Adolph A. Berle, "Modern Functions of the Corporate System" (1962) 62 Colum. L. Rev. 433 at 438.

2 He was Paul Harbrecht's doctoral thesis supervisor at Columbia University Law School; see Paul Harbrecht, S.J., *Pension Funds and Economic Power* (New York: Twentieth Century Fund, 1959).

3 Berle, *supra* note 1 at 448. This was because, in his view, the capital markets merely allocated wealth, not investment capital, which he argued was almost entirely generated by

retained earnings rather than securities sales. Since 1962, many corporations have undergone "restructuring" such that they are highly leveraged and no longer retaining earnings at the same rate.

4 Sir Nicholas Stern, *The Economics of Climate Change* (London: HM Treasury, 2006) at xv, online: HM Treasury, http://www.hm-treasury.gov.uk/independent_reviews/stern_review_economics_climate_change/stern_review_report.cfm.

5 See Mary Condon, "Gendering the Pension Promise in Canada: Risk, Financial Markets and Neoliberalism" (2001) 10(1) Social and Legal Studies 83 at 93-94 and 99, for discussion of the potential for, and the rejection by the federal government of, a more democratic regime of accountability for the CPP Investment Fund.

6 These funds' trustees also have reputational incentives, beyond merely complying with their fiduciary duty, and these incentives also energize their corporate governance activities. See William W. Bratton and J.A. McCahery, "Regulatory Competition, Regulatory Capture and Corporate Self-Regulation" (1995) 73 N.C.L. Rev. 1861 at 1914-16.

7 See Edward B. Rock, "The Logic and (Uncertain) Significance of Institutional Shareholder Activism" (1991) 79 Geo. L.J. 445 at 453-63, for a description of the "collective action problems" with respect to corporate governance activity by shareholders.

8 Bratton and McCahery, *supra* note 6 at 1905. If the market goes up, so does their benchmark.

9 *Ibid.* at 1871.

10 Paul Gompers, Joy Ishii, and Andrew Metrick, "Corporate Governance and Equity Prices" (2003) 118 Quarterly Journal of Economics 107.

11 Roberta Romano, "Less Is More: Making Institutional Investor Activism a Valuable Mechanism of Corporate Governance" (2001) 18 Yale J. on Reg. 174 at 177-79.

12 Kent Greenfield, "New Principles for Corporate Law" (2005) 1 Hastings Business Law Journal 87 suggests that corporations should be regulated on the principle that their activities must further society's well-being.

13 Christopher D. Stone, "Corporate Social Responsibility: What It Might Mean, If It Were to Really Matter" (1986) 71 Iowa L. Rev. 557 at 559-60.

14 The vote can be on either a shareholder resolution, bylaw amendment, or choice of directors.

15 Amartya Kumar Sen, *Development as Freedom* (New York: Anchor Books, 1999) at c. 3.

Bibliography

Legislation

An Act to Amend the Canada Business Corporations Act and the Canada Cooperatives Act and to Amend Other Acts, S.C. 2001, c. 14.

An Act to Protect Investors by Improving the Accuracy and Reliability of Corporate Disclosures Made Pursuant to the Securities Laws, and for Other Purposes, Pub. L. No. 107-204, 116 Stat. 745 (2002) (*"Sarbanes-Oxley Act of 2002"*).

Bank Act, S.C. 1991, c. 46.

British Columbia Pension Benefit Standards Act, R.S.B.C 1996, c. 352.

British Columbia Pension Benefits Standards Regulation, B.C. Reg. 433/93.

Business Corporations Act, R.S.O. 1990, c. B.16 (Ontario).

Canada Business Corporations Act, R.S.C. 1985, c. C-44.

Canada Pension Plan Act, R.S.C. 1985, c. C-5.

Canada Pension Plan Investment Board Act, S.C. 1997, c. 40.

Class Proceedings Act, S.O. 1992, c. 6 (Ontario).

Companies Act 2006 (U.K.), 2006, c. 46.

Employee Retirement Income Security Act, 29 U.S.C. (1994) (ERISA).

Ending Mandatory Retirement Statute Law Amendment Act, S.O. 2005, c. 29.

Human Rights Code, R.S.O. 1990, c. H.19

Income Tax Act, R.S.C. 1985, c. 1 (5th Supp.).

Occupational Pension Schemes (Investment) Regulation 1996, (U.K.) S.I. 1996/3127 s. 11A, as amended by S.I. 1999/1849.

Pension Benefits Act, R.S.O. 1990, c. P.8, as amended (Ontario).

Pension Benefits Act Regulation, R.R.O. 1990, Reg. 909.

Pension Benefits Standards Regulations, 1985, S.O.R./87-19 (Canada).

Pensions Act, 2004 (U.K.), 2004, c. 35.

Securities Act, R.S.A. 2000, c. S-4 (Alberta).

Securities Act, R.S.O. 1990, c. S.5 (Ontario).

Securities Act, Regulation 1015, R.R.O. 1990.

Trustee Act, C.C.S.M. c. T160 (Manitoba).

Trustee Act, R.S.O. 1990, c. T.23 (Ontario).

Jurisprudence

Canada

Authorson v. Canada (Attorney General) (2002), 58 O.R. (3d) 417.

Bathgate v. National Hockey League Pension Society (1994), 110 D.L.R. (4th) 609 (Ont. C.A.), varying (1992), 98 D.L.R. (4th) 326 (Ont.Ct.(Gen.Div.)), leave to appeal to S.C.C. refused, (1994), 114 D.L.R. (4th) vii (S.C.C.).

C.U.P.E.-C.L.C., Local 1000 v. Ontario Hydro (1989), 58 D.L.R. (4th) 552 (Ont. C.A.), rev'g (1987), 36 D.L.R. (4th) 727 (Ont. H.C.J. Div. Ct.), leave to appeal to S.C.C. refused, (1989), 62 D.L.R. (4th) vii (S.C.C.).

Catalyst Fund General Partner I Inc. v. Hollinger Inc. (2004), 135 A.C.W.S. (3d) 80 (Ont. S.C.J.).

Danylchuk v. Wolinsky, [2007] M.J. No. 80 (Man. Q.B.).

Dylex Ltd. (Trustee of) v. Anderson (2003), 63 O.R. (3d) 659 (SCJ).

Ford Motor Co. of Canada v. Ontario Municipal Employees Retirement Board, [2006] O.J. No. 27, 79 O.R. (3d) 81 (C.A.), varying [2004] O.J. No. 191 (Ont. S.C.J.).

Goldhar v. Quebec Manitoru Mines Ltd. (1975), 9 O.R. (2d) 740 (Ont. H.C.J. (Div. Ct.)).

Greenlight Capital Inc. v. Stronach (2006), 152 A.C.W.S. (3d) 616; 22 B.L.R. (4th) 11 (Ont. S.C.J.).

Guerin v. R. (1984), 13 D.L.R. (4th) 321 (S.C.C.).

McKinney v. University of Guelph, [1990] 3 S.C.R. 229 (S.C.C.).

Metropolitan Police Widows and Orphans Fund v. Telus Communications Inc. (2005), 79 O.R. (3d) 784 (Ont. C.A.).

Michaud v. Banque Nationale Du Canada, [1997] R.J.Q. 547 (Que. S.C.).

Naneff v. Concrete Holdings Limited (1995), 23 O.R. (3d) 481 (C.A.).

Peoples Department Stores Inc. (Trustee of) v. Wise, 2004 SCC 68; [2004] 3 S.C.R. 461; [2004] S.C.J. No. 64 (QL).

Re Goldstream Resources (1986), 2 B.C.L.R. (2d) 244 (S.C.).

Schmidt v. Air Products of Canada Ltd. (1994), 115 D.L.R. (4th) 631 (S.C.C.); vary'g (1992), 89 D.L.R. (4th) 762 (Alta. C.A.), aff'g (1992), 66 D.L.R. (4th) 230 (Alta. Q.B.).

Trent University Faculty Association v. Trent University (1997), 150 D.L.R. (4th) 1 (Ont. C.A.); aff'g (1992), 99 D.L.R. (4th) 451 (O.C.G.D. (Div. Ct.)).

UPM-Kymmene Corp. v. UPM-Kymmene Miramichi Inc. (2002), 27 B.L.R. 203 (Ont. S.C.J. (Commercial List)), affirmed (2004), 42 B.L.R. (3d) 34 (Ont. C.A.).

Verdun v. Toronto-Dominion Bank, [1996] 3 S.C.R. 550, (1996), 139 D.L.R. (4th) 415 (SCC).

United States

Am. Fed'n of State, County & Mun. Employees Pension Plan v. Am. Int'l Group, 462 F.3d 121 (2d Cir. 2006)

American Int'l Rent-A-Car, Inc. v. Cross, 1984 WL 8204 (Del. Chancery).

Blankenship v. Boyle, 329 F.Supp. 1089 (D.C. 1971).

Danaher Corp. v. Chicago Pneumatic Tool Co., 635 F.Supp. 246, 55 U.S.L.W. 2022 (S.D.N.Y. 1986).

Donovan v. Bierworth, 680 F.2d 263 (2d Cir. 1982); order modified (2d Cir. 1982).

Donovan v. Walton, 609 F.Supp. 1221 (D.C. Fla. 1985); affd. per cur. *Brock v. Walton* 794 F.2d 586 (11th Cir. 1986), reh. denied, 802 F.2d. 1399 (11th Cir. 1986).

Grindstaff v. Green, 133 F.3d 416 (6th Cir. 1998).

Hewlett v. Hewlett-Packard Company, 2002 Del. Ch. LEXIS 35.

In re Carl M. Loeb, Rhoades & Co. 38 SEC 843 (1959).

International Brotherhood of Teamsters General Fund v. Fleming Companies, Inc., 975 P.2D 907, 1999 Okla. LEXIS 3 (Okla. Sup. Ct. 1999).

International Brotherhood of Teamsters General Fund v. Fleming Companies, Inc., No. CIV-96-1650-A, 1997 US Dist. LEXIS 2980 (US Dist. W.D. Okla. 24 January 1997).

National Resources Defense Council Inc. v. Securities and Exchange Commission, 606 F.2d 1031 (4th Cir. 1979).

Newton v. Van Otterloo, 756 F.Supp. 1121 (N.D. Ind. 1991).

O'Neill v. Davis, 721 F.Supp. 1013, 1015 (N.D. Ill 1989).

Smith, A.P. Mfg. Co. v. Barlow, 13 N.J. 145, 98 A.2d 581, 39 ALR.2d 1179, app dismd 346 U.S. 861 (1953).

Steinway v. Steinway & Sons, 17 Misc. 43, 40 N.Y.S. 718 (1896).

The Board of Trustees of the Employees' Retirement System of the City of Baltimore v. Mayor and Council of Baltimore City, 562 A.2d 720 (Md. C.A. 1989).

USACAFES v. Office, 1985 WL 44685 (Del. Ch. 1985).

Withers v. Teachers' Retirement System of New York City, 447 F.Supp. 1248 (S.D.N.Y. 1978); aff'd mem 595 F.2d 1210 (2d Cir. 1979).

Zapata Corp. v. Maldonado, 430 A.2d 779 (Del. Sup. Ct. 1981).

United Kingdom

Cowan v. Scargill, [1985] 1 Ch. 270 (Ch. Div.).

Martin v. City of Edinburgh District Council, [1988] S.L.T. 329 (Court of Session, Outer House).

Books, Articles, Reports, and Theses

Adams, Edward S., and Karl D. Knutsen. "A Charitable Corporate Giving Justification for the Socially Responsible Investment of Pension Funds: A Populist Argument for the Public Use of Private Wealth" (1995) 80 Iowa L. Rev. 211.

Aglieta, Michel. "Shareholder Value and Corporate Governance: Some Tricky Questions" (2000) 29(1) Economy and Society 146.

Akerlof, George A. "The Market for 'Lemons': Quality Uncertainty and the Market Mechanism" (1970) 84 Quarterly Journal of Economics 488.

Anisman, Philip. "Majority-Minority Relations in Canadian Corporation Law: An Overview" (1986-87) 12 Can. Bus. L.J. 473.

Bainbridge, Stephen M. "Corporate Decisionmaking and the Moral Rights of Employees: Participatory Management and Natural Law" (1998) 43 Vill. L. Rev. 741.

Baker, Dean, and Archon Fung. "Collateral Damage: Do Pension Fund Investments Hurt Workers?" in Archon Fung, Tessa Hebb, and Joel Rogers, eds., *Working Capital: The Power of Labor's Pensions* (Ithaca and London: Cornell University Press, 2001) 13.

Baldwin, Stuart A., *et al. Pension Funds and Ethical Investment: A Study of Investment Practices and Opportunities – State of California Retirement Systems* (New York: Council on Economic Priorities, 1980).

Bebchuk, Lucian A. "The Pursuit of a Bigger Pie: Can Everyone Expect a Bigger Slice?" (1979-80) 8 Hofstra L. Rev. 671.

Bebchuk, Lucian A., and Jesse M. Fried. *Pay without Performance: The Unfulfilled Promise of Executive Compensation* (Cambridge and London: Harvard University Press, 2004).

Bebchuk, Lucian A., Jesse M. Fried, and David I. Walker. "Managerial Power and Rent Extraction in the Design of Executive Compensation" (2002) 69 U. Chicago L. Rev. 751.

Beck, Stanley M. "The Shareholders' Derivative Action" (1974) 52 Can. Bar Rev. 159.

Benston, George J. "Required Disclosure and the Stock Market: An Evaluation of the Securities Exchange Act of 1934" (1973) 63(1) American Economic Review 132.

Berle, Adolph A. "Modern Functions of the Corporate System" (1962) 62 Colum. L. Rev. 433.

–. *Power without Property: A New Development in American Political Economy* (New York: Harcourt, Brace, 1959).

Berle, Adolph A., and Gardiner C. Means. *The Modern Corporation and Private Property* (New York: Macmillan, 1932).

Black, Bernard S. "Agents Watching Agents: The Promise of Institutional Investor Voice" (1992) 39 UCLA L. Rev. 811.

–. "Shareholder Passivity Reexamined" (1990) 89 Mich. L. Rev. 520.

Blackburn, Robin. "The New Collectivism: Pension Reform, Grey Capitalism and Complex Socialism" (1999) 233 New Left Review 3.

Bloomenthal, Harold S., and Samuel Wolff. "The Short-Lived SEC Proposal to Give Shareholders Access to the Director Nomination Process" in *Securities and Federal Corporate Law,* 2d ed., looseleaf (Eagan, MN: West Group, 2003), vol. 3E (WL).

Booth, Richard A. "Stockholders, Stakeholders and Bagholders (or How Investor Diversification Affects Fiduciary Duty)" (1998) 53 Bus. Law. 429.

Branson, Douglas M. "Teaching Comparative Corporate Governance: The Significance of 'Soft Law' and International Institutions" (2000) 34 Ga. L. Rev. 669.

–. "The Very Uncertain Prospect of 'Global' Convergence in Corporate Governance" (2001) 34 Cornell Int'l L.J. 321.

Bratton, William W. "Berle and Means Revisited at the Turn of the Century" (2001) 26 J. Corp. L. 737.
–. "Enron and the Dark Side of Shareholder Value" (2002) 76 Tul. L. Rev. 1275.
–. "The New Economic Theory of the Firm: A Critical Perspective from History" (1989) 41 Stan. L. Rev. 1471.
Bratton, William W., and J.A. McCahery. "Regulatory Competition, Regulatory Capture and Corporate Self-Regulation" (1995) 73 N.C.L. Rev. 1861.
Brickley, James A., Ronald C. Lease, and Clifford W. Smith Jr. "Ownership Structure and Voting on Antitakeover Amendments" (1988) 20 Journal of Financial Economics 267.
Brudney, Victor. "The Independent Director – Heavenly City or Potemkin Village?" (1982) 95 Harv. L. Rev. 597.
Carney, William J. "The Legacy of the 'Market for Corporate Control' and the Origins of the Theory of the Firm" (1999) 50 Case W. Res. L. Rev. 215.
Chapman, Bruce. "Trust, Economic Rationality and the Corporate Fiduciary Obligation" (1993) 43 U.T.L.J. 547.
Cheffins, Brian R. "*Michaud v. National Bank of Canada* and Canadian Corporate Governance: A 'Victory for Shareholder Rights'?" (1998) 30 Can. Bus. L.J. 20.
–. "The Oppression Remedy in Corporate Law: The Canadian Experience" (1988) 10 U. Pa. J. Int'l Bus. L. 305.
Clark, Gordon L. *Pension Fund Capitalism* (Oxford: Oxford University Press, 2000).
–. *Pensions and Corporate Restructuring in American Industry: A Crisis in Regulation* (Baltimore and London: The Johns Hopkins University Press, 1993).
Coffee, John C. Jr. "Liquidity versus Control: The Institutional Investor as Corporate Monitor" (1991) 91 Colum. L. Rev. 1277.
–. "Litigation and Corporate Governance: An Essay on Steering Between Scylla and Charybdis" (1984) 52 Geo. Wash. L. Rev. 789.
–. "Market Failure and the Economic Case for a Mandatory Disclosure System" (1984) 70 Va. L. Rev. 717.
–. "The Bylaw Battlefield: Can Institutions Change the Outcome of Corporate Control Contests?" (1997) 51 U. Miami L. Rev. 605.
–. "Understanding Enron: 'It's About the Gatekeepers, Stupid'" (2002) 57 Bus. Law. 1403.
Conard, Alfred F. "Beyond Managerialism: Investor Capitalism" (1988) 22 U. Mich. J.L. Ref. 117.
Condon, Mary. "Gendering the Pension Promise in Canada: Risk, Financial Markets and Neoliberalism" (2001) 10(1) Social and Legal Studies 83.
–. "Your Money or Your Life: The Future of Litigation and Enforcement in Ontario Securities Regulation" in *Taking Stock: Challenge and Change in Securities Regulation – Papers Presented at the 12th Queen's Annual Business Law Symposium* (Kingston, ON: Queen's Business Law Symposium, 2006) 221.
Condon, Mary G., Anita J. Anand, and Janis P. Sarra, *Securities Law in Canada* (Toronto: Emond Montgomery Publications, 2005).
Cox, James D. "The Social Meaning of Shareholder Suits" (1999) 65 Brook. L. Rev. 3.
Croft, Tom, and Tessa Hebb. "Collaboration between Labor, Academics and Community Activists to Advance Labor/Capital Strategies" in Isla Carmichael and Jack Quarter, eds. *Money on the Line: Workers' Capital in Canada* (Ottawa: Canadian Centre for Policy Alternatives, 2003).
Crespi, Gregory Scott. "Rethinking Corporate Fiduciary Duties: The Inefficiency of the Shareholder Primacy Norm" (2002) 55 SMU L. Rev. 141.
Curzan, Myron P., and Mark L. Pelesh. "Revitalizing Corporate Democracy: Control of Investment Managers' Voting on Social Responsibility Proxy Issues" (1980) 93 Harv. L. Rev. 670.
Daniels, Ronald J. "Must Boards Go Overboard? An Economic Analysis of the Effects of Burgeoning Statutory Liability on the Role of Directors in Corporate Governance" (1995) 24 Can. Bus. L.J. 229
–. "Stakeholders and Takeovers: Can Contractarianism Be Compassionate" (1993) 43 U.T.L.J. 315.

Daniels, Ronald J., and Paul Halpern. "Too Close for Comfort: The Role of the Closely Held Public Corporation in the Canadian Economy and the Implications for Public Policy" (1995-96) 26 Can. Bus. L.J. 11.

Daniels, Ronald J., and Jeffrey G. MacIntosh, "Toward a Distinctive Corporate Law Regime" (1991) 29 Osgoode Hall L.J. 863.

Daniels, Ronald J., and Randall Morck. "Canadian Corporate Governance: Policy Options" in Ronald J. Daniels and Randall Morck, eds., *Corporate Decision-Making in Canada* (Calgary: University of Calgary Press, 1995) 661.

–, eds. *Corporate Decision-Making in Canada* (Calgary: University of Calgary Press, 1995).

Davis, Ronald B. "Investor Control of Multi-National Enterprises: A Market for Corporate Governance Based on Justice and Fairness?" in Janis Sarra, ed., *Corporate Governance in Global Capital Markets* (Vancouver: UBC Press, 2003) 541.

–. "Restructuring Proceedings and Pension Fund Deficits: A Question of Risk and Reward" in *Annual Review of Insolvency Law – 2003* (Aurora, ON: Carswell Canada, 2004) 29.

–. "The Enron Pension Jigsaw: Assembling Accountable Corporate Governance by Fidicuaries" (2003) 36(3) U.B.C. L. Rev. 541.

Davis, Kenneth B. Jr. "Shareholder Liability for Claims by Employees" (1984) 1984 Wis. L. Rev. 741.

Davis, Stephen, Jon Lukomnik, and David Pitt-Watson. *The New Capitalists: How Citizen Investors Are Reshaping the Corporate Agenda* (Boston: Harvard Business School Press, 2006).

Deutsche Bank AG. *Aspiring Equity Culture in Germany* (Frankfurt am Main: Deutsche Morgan Grenfell European Equity Research, 1997).

"Distinguishing Between Direct and Derivative Shareholder Suits," Note (1962) 110 U. Pa. L. Rev. 1147.

Drucker, Peter F. *The Unseen Revolution: How Pension Fund Socialism Came to America* (New York: Harper and Row, 1976).

Dugas, Christine. "Enron's Dive Destroys Workers' Pensions" *USA Today* (5 February 2002), online: *USA Today,* http://cgi.usatoday.com/money/energy/2002-02-06-enron-pensions.htm.

Dykstra, Daniel J. "The Revival of the Derivative Suit" (1967) 116 U. Pa. L. Rev. 74.

Dzuro, George P., *et al.* "Pension Funds as Shareholders" in Raymond Koskie *et al.*, eds., *Employee Benefits in Canada* (Brookfield, MN: International Foundation of Employee Benefit Plans, 2001) 286.

Easterbrook, Frank, and Daniel Fischel. "Mandatory Disclosure and the Protection of Investors" (1984) 70 Va. L. Rev. 669.

Eisenberg, Melvin Aron. "Access to the Corporate Proxy Machinery" (1969-70) 83(7) Harv. L. Rev. 1489.

–. "The Structure of Corporation Law" (1989) 89 Colum. L. Rev. 1461.

Engel, David L. "An Approach to Corporate Social Responsibility" (1979-80) 32 Stan. L. Rev. 1.

Farquhar, Keith B. "Recent Themes in the Variation of Trusts" (2001) 20 E.T.P.J. 181.

Fisch, Jill E. "Teaching Corporate Governance through Shareholder Litigation" (2000) 34 Ga. L. Rev. 745.

Fischel, Daniel, and John H. Langbein. "ERISA's Fundamental Contradiction: The Exclusive Benefit Rule" (1988) 55 U. Chicago L. Rev. 1105.

Freshfields Bruckhaus Deringer. *A Legal Framework for the Integration of Environmental, Social and Governance Issues into Institutional Investment* (Geneva: UNEP FI AMWG, 2005).

Friedman, Milton. "The Social Responsibility of Business Is to Increase Its Profits" *New York Times* (13 September 1970) 6 at 32.

Friedman, Milton, and Eli Goldston. "The 'Responsible' Corporation: Benefactor or Monopolist?" Excerpts from debate in (1973) 56 *Fortune* 88 (November) reprinted in Edward J. Bander, ed., *The Corporation in a Democratic Society* (New York: The H.W. Wilson Company, 1975) at 43-45.

Friend, Irwin, and Edward S. Herman. "The S.E.C. through a Glass Darkly" (1964) 37(4) Journal of Business 382.

Friend, Irwin, and Randolph Westerfield. "Required Disclosure and the Stock Market: Comment" (1975) 65(3) American Economic Review 467.

Frooman, Jeff. "Socially Irresponsible and Illegal Behavior and Shareholder Wealth: A Meta-Analysis of Event Studies" (1997) 36(3) Business and Society 221.

Froud, Julie, *et al.* "Shareholder Value and Financialization: Consultancy Promises, Management Moves" (2000) 29 Economy and Society 80.

Fung, Archon, Tessa Hebb, and Joel Rogers, eds. *Working Capital: The Power of Labor's Pensions* (Ithaca and London: Cornell University Press, 2001).

Gabaldon, Theresa A. "Free Riders and the Greedy Gadfly: Examining Aspects of Shareholder Litigation as an Exercise in Integrating Ethical Regulation and Laws of General Applicability" (1988) 73 Minn. L. Rev. 425.

Gerwing, Judy. "Savings Plans" in Raymond Koskie *et al.*, eds., *Employee Benefits in Canada* (Brookfield, MN: International Foundation of Employee Benefit Plans, 2001) 387.

Ghilarducci, Teresa. "Myths and Misinformation about America's Retirement System" in Jeff Madrick, ed., *Unconventional Wisdom: Alternative Perspectives on the New Economy* (New York: Century Foundation, 2000) 69.

–. "Small Benefits, Big Pension Funds, and How Governance Reforms Can Close the Gap" in Archon Fung, Tessa Hebb, and Joel Rogers, eds., *Working Capital: The Power of Labor's Pensions* (Ithaca and London: Cornell University Press, 2001) 158.

–. "US Pension Investment Policy and Perfect Capital Market Theory" (1994) 37(4) Challenge 4.

Gifford, James. "Measuring the Social, Environmental and Ethical Performance of Pension Funds" (2003) 53 Journal of Australian Political Economy 139.

Gillese, Eileen E. "Pension Plans and the Law of Trusts" (1996) 75 Can. Bar Rev. 221.

Gilpin, Kenneth N. "Waiting for the Green Light on Stocks" *New York Times* (14 July 2002) Business.

Gilson, Ronald J., and Reinier Kraakman. "Reinventing the Outside Director: An Agenda for Institutional Investors" (1991) 43 Stan. L. Rev. 863.

Gompers, Paul, Joy Ishii, and Andrew Metrick. "Corporate Governance and Equity Prices" (2003) 118 Quarterly Journal of Economics 107.

Gordon, Jeffrey N. "Employees, Pensions and the New Economic Order" (1997) 97 Colum. L. Rev. 1519.

–. "'Just Say Never?' Poison Pills, Deadhand Pills and Shareholder Adopted Bylaws: An Essay for Warren Buffet" (1997) 19 Cardozo L. Rev. 511.

–. "Shareholder Initiative: A Social Choice and Game Theoretic Approach to Corporate Law" (1991) 60 U. Cin. L. Rev. 347.

Greenfield, Kent. "The Place of Workers in Corporate Law" (1998) 39 B.C.L. Rev. 283.

–. "New Principles for Corporate Law" (2005) 1 Hastings Business Law Journal 87.

Greenwood, Daniel J.H. "Essential Speech: Why Corporate Speech Is Not Free" (1997-98) 83 Iowa L. Rev. 995.

–. "Fictional Shareholders: For Whom Are Corporate Managers Trustees, Revisited" (1996) 69 S. Cal. L. Rev. 1021.

Grossman, Sanford J., and Joseph E. Stiglitz. "On the Impossibility of Informationally Efficient Markets" (1980) 70(3) American Economic Review 393.

Grundfest, J.A. "Just Vote No: A Minimalist Strategy for Dealing with Barbarians Inside the Gates" (1993) 45 Stan. L. Rev. 857.

Hamermesh, Lawrence A. "Corporate Democracy and Stockholder-Adopted By-Laws: Taking Back the Street?" (1998) 73 Tul. L. Rev. 409.

Hansmann, Henry, and Reinier Kraakman. "Toward Unlimited Shareholder Liability for Corporate Torts" (1991) 100 Yale L.J. 1879.

Harbrecht, Paul P., S.J., *Pension Funds and Economic Power* (New York: Twentieth Century Fund, 1959).

Harmes, Adam. *Unseen Power: How Mutual Funds Threaten the Political and Economic Wealth of Nations* (Toronto: Stoddart, 2001).

Hatnay, Andrew J. "Taxation of Pension Benefits" in Raymond Koskie *et al.*, eds., *Employee Benefits in Canada* (Brookfield, MN: International Foundation of Employee Benefit Plans, 2001) 253.

Hawley, James P., and Andrew T. Williams. *The Rise of Fiduciary Capitalism: How Institutional Investors Can Make America More Democratic* (Philadelphia: University of Pennsylvania Press, 2000).

Hu, Henry T.C. "Faith and Magic: Investor Beliefs and Government Neutrality" (2000) 78 Tex. L. Rev. 777.

–. "New Financial Products, the Modern Process of Financial Innovation, and the Puzzle of Shareholder Welfare" (1991) 69 Tex. L. Rev. 1273.

–. "Risk, Time and Fiduciary Principles in Corporate Investment" (1990) 38 UCLA L. Rev. 277.

Hutchinson, James D., and Charles G. Cole, "Legal Standards Governing Investment of Pension Assets for Social and Political Goals" (1980) 128 U. Pa. L. Rev. 1340.

Hutchison, Harry G. "Presumptive Business Judgment, Substantive Good Faith, Litigation Control: Vindicating the Socioeconomic Meaning of *Harhen v. Brown*" (2001) 26 J. Corp. L. 285.

Hyatt, Douglas E., and James E. Pesando. "The Distribution of Investment Risk in Defined Benefit Pension Plans" (1996) 51(1) Relations Industrielle 136.

Hylton, Maria O'Brien. "'Socially Responsible' Investing: Doing Good Versus Doing Well in an Inefficient Market" (1992-93) 42 Am. U. L. Rev. 1.

Iacobucci, Edward M., and Kevin E. Davis. "Reconciling Derivative Claims and the Oppression Remedy" (2000) 12 Sup. Ct. L. Rev. 87.

Jensen, M. "Agency Costs of Free Cash Flow, Corporate Finance and Takeovers" (1986) 76 American Economic Review 323.

Jensen, M., and W. Meckling. "Theory of the Firm: Managerial Behavior, Agency Costs and Ownership Structure" (1976) 3 Journal of Financial Economics 305.

Kahn, Faith Stevelman. "Bombing Markets, Subverting the Rule of Law: Enron, Financial Fraud and September 11, 2001" (2001-02) 76 Tul. L. Rev. 1579.

Kaplan, Ari N. "Canada Pension Plan and Quebec Pension Plan: An Overview" in Raymond Koskie *et al.*, eds., *Employee Benefits in Canada* (Brookfield, MN: International Foundation of Employee Benefit Plans, 2001) 75.

Labaton, Stephen. "Big Pension Funds Object to Proposal on Proxy Rules" *New York Times* (3 October 2003) Business.

Lakonishok, Josef, *et al.* "Window Dressing by Pension Fund Managers" (1991) 81(2) American Economic Review 227.

Lakonishok, Josef, Andrei Shleifer, and Robert W. Vishney. "The Impact of Institutional Trading on Stock Prices" (1992) 32 Journal of Financial Economics 23.

–. "The Structure and Performance of the Money Management Industry" in *Brookings Papers on Economic Activity; Microeconomics* (Washington, DC: Brookings Institution, 1992) 339.

Langbein, John H. "The Secret Life of the Trust: The Trust as an Instrument of Commerce" (1997) 107 Yale L.J. 165.

Langbein, John H., and Richard A. Posner. "Market Funds and Trust-Investment Law" [1976] 1 American Bar Foundation Research Journal 1.

–. "Market Funds and Trust-Investment Law: II" [1977] 1 American Bar Foundation Research Journal 1.

–. "Social Investing and the Law of Trusts" (1980) 79 Mich. L. Rev. 72.

Langevoort, Donald C. "Capping Damages for Open-Market Securities Fraud" (1996) 38 Ariz. L. Rev. 639.

Larson, Jeffrey. "Institutional Investors, Corporate Governance and Proxy Voting Disclosure" in Poonam Puri and Jeffrey Larsen, eds., *Corporate Governance and Securities Regulation in the 21st Century* (Markham, ON: Lexis-Nexis Canada, 2004) c. 6.

Lazonick, William, and Mary O'Sullivan. "Maximizing Shareholder Value: A New Ideology for Corporate Governance" (2000) 29 Economy and Society 13.

Longhurst, Patrick. "Plan Design and Administration" in Raymond Koskie *et al.*, eds., *Employee Benefits in Canada* (Brookfield, MN: International Foundation of Employee Benefit Plans, 2001) 197.

–. "Single Employer Pension Plans (SEPPs)" in Raymond Koskie *et al.*, eds., *Employee Benefits in Canada* (Brookfield, MN: International Foundation of Employee Benefit Plans, 2001) 215.

Macey, Jonathan R. "The Legality and Utility of the Shareholder Rights Bylaw" (1998) 26 Hofstra L. Rev. 835.

Macey, Jonathan R., and Geoffrey P. Miller. "The Plaintiffs' Attorney's Role in Class Action and Derivative Litigation: Economic Analysis and Recommendations for Reform" (1991) 58 U. Chicago L. Rev. 1.

MacIntosh, Jeffrey G. "Designing an Efficient Fiduciary Law" (1993) 43 U.T.L.J. 425.

–. "Institutional Shareholders and Corporate Governance in Canada" (1996) 26 Can. Bus. L.J. 145.

–. "Minority Shareholder Rights in Canada and England: 1860-1987" (1989) 29 Osgoode Hall L.J. 561.

–. "The Oppression Remedy: Personal or Derivative?" (1991) 70 Can. Bus. L.J. 29.

–. "The Role of Institutional Investors in Canadian Capital Markets" (1993) 31 Osgoode Hall L.J. 371.

–. "The Shareholder's Appraisal Rights in Canada: A Critical Reappraisal" (1986) 24 Osgoode Hall L.J. 201.

MacIntosh, Jeffrey G., and Christopher C. Nicholls. *Securities Law* (Toronto: Irwin Law, 2002)..

Mahoney, Paul G. "Mandatory Disclosure as a Solution to Agency Problems" (1995) 62 U. Chicago L. Rev. 1047.

Manne, Henry G. "Some Theoretical Aspects of Share Voting: An Essay in Honor of Adolf A. Berle" (1964) 64 Colum. L. Rev. 1427.

McClean, Albert J. "Variation of Trusts in England and Canada" (1965) 43(2) Can. Bar Rev. 181.

McClean, Albert, and Sandra McCallum. "Administration of Trusts" in Mark R. Gillen and Faye Woodman, eds., *The Law of Trusts: A Contextual Approach* (Toronto: Emond Montgomery Publications, 2000) 269.

McGeehan, Patrick. "Sprint Settles Suit with Policy Shift and $50 Million" *New York Times* (20 March 2003) C1.

Menezes, Julio. "Overriding the Trust Instrument" in Mark R. Gillen and Faye Woodman, eds., *The Law of Trusts: A Contextual Approach* (Toronto: Emond Montgomery Publications Limited, 2000) 165.

Milevsky, Moshe A., Andrew Aziz, *et al.* "Cleaning a Passive Index: How to Use Portfolio Optimization to Satisfy CSR Constraints" (Spring 2006) Journal of Portfolio Management 110.

Mitchell, Lawrence E. *Corporate Irresponsibility: America's Newest Export* (New Haven and London: Yale University Press, 2001).

–. "A Theoretical and Practical Framework for Enforcing Corporate Constituency Statutes" (1992) 70 Tex. L. Rev. 579.

Monks, Robert A.G. *The New Global Investors: How Shareowners Can Unlock Sustainable Prosperity Worldwide* (Oxford: Capstone, 2001).

Monks, Robert A.G., and Allen Sykes. "Shareholder Capitalism Is Damaging Shareholders (The Need to Achieve Effective Ownership)" (2002), online: http://www.ragm.com/library/topics/RagmSykes031502.pdf.

Montgomery, Kathryn E. "Market Shift – The Role of Institutional Investors in Corporate Governance" (1995-96) 26 Can. Bus. L.J. 189.

–. "Survey of Institutional Shareholders" (1992) 4(4) Corporate Governance Review 5.

Morgenson, Gretchen. "In a Broker's Notes, Trouble for Salomon" *New York Times* (22 September 2002) Business.

–. "Regulators Find Another Analyst with Questionable Reports" *New York Times* (12 September 2002) Business.

–. "Say-on-Pay Gets Support at Verizon" *New York Times* (19 May 2007), online: *New York Times,* http://www.nytimes.com/2007/05/19/technology/19verizon.html?ex=1181102400&en=d17d1b7f61ca39a7&ei=5070.

Murphy, Michael E. "Dispelling Tina's Ghost from the Post-Enron Corporate Governance Debate" (2002) 43 Santa Clara L. Rev. 63.

Myers, S., and N. Majluf. "Corporate Financing When Firms Have Information that Investors Do Not Have" (1984) 13 Journal of Financial Economics 187.

Nader, Ralph, Mark J. Green, and Joel Seligman. *Constitutionalizing the Corporation: The Case for the Federal Chartering of Giant Corporations* (Washington, DC: Corporate Accountability Research Group, 1976).

–. *Taming the Giant Corporation* (New York: Norton, 1976).

O'Barr, William M. et al., *Fortune and Folly: The Wealth and Power of Institutional Investing* (Homewood, IL: Irwin Professional Publishing, 1992).

O'Connor, Marleen. "Labor's Role in the Shareholder Revolution" in Archon Fung, Tessa Hebb, and Joel Rogers, eds., *Working Capital: The Power of Labor's Pensions* (Ithaca and London: Cornell University Press, 2001) 67.

Orlitzky, Marc, Frank L. Schmidt, and Sara L. Rynes. "Corporate Social and Financial Performance: A Meta-Analysis" (2003) 24 Organization Studies 403.

Palmiter, Alan R. "Mutual Fund Voting of Portfolio Shares: Why Not Disclose?" (2002) 23 Cardozo L. Rev. 1419.

Pound, John. "Proxy Contests and the Efficiency of Shareholder Oversight" (1988) 20 Journal of Financial Economics 237.

Puri, Poonam, and Stephanie Ben-Ishai. "The Canadian Oppression Remedy Judicially Considered: 1995-2001" (2004) 30 Queen's L.J. 79.

Quarter, Jack, *et al.* "Social Investment by Union-Based Pension Funds and Labour-Sponsored Investment Funds in Canada" (2001) 56(1) R.I. 92.

Ribstein, Larry A. "Market versus Regulatory Responses to Corporate Fraud: A Critique of the Sarbanes-Oxley Act of 2002" (2002) 28 J. Corp. L. 1.

Richardson, Benjamin J. "Do the Fiduciary Duties of Pension Funds Hinder Socially Responsible Investment?" (2007) 22 B.F.L.R. 145.

Rock, Edward B. "The Logic and (Uncertain) Significance of Institutional Shareholder Activism" (1991) 79 Geo L.J 445.

Roe, Mark J. "The Modern Corporation and Private Pensions" (1993) 41 UCLA L. Rev. 75.

Roht-Arriaza, Naomi. "Private Voluntary Standard-Setting, the International Organization of Standardization and International Environmental Lawmaking" (1995) 6 Y.B. Int'l Env. L. 107.

Romano, Roberta. "Less Is More: Making Institutional Investor Activism a Valuable Mechanism of Corporate Governance" (2001) 18 Yale J. on Reg. 174.

–. "Public Pension Fund Activism in Corporate Governance Reconsidered" (1993) 93 Colum. L. Rev. 795.

Rousseau, Stéphane. "Canadian Corporate Governance Reform: In Search of a Role for Public Regulation" in Janis P. Sarra, ed., *Corporate Governance in Global Capital Markets* (Vancouver: UBC Press, 2003) 3.

Rowland, Susan, and Daniel Kingwell. "Plan Wind-up and Deficits" in Raymond Koskie *et al.*, eds., *Employee Benefits in Canada* (Brookfield, MN: International Foundation of Employee Benefit Plans, 2001) 235.

Sarra, Janis P. "Corporate Governance Reform: Recognition of Workers' Equitable Investments in the Firm" (1999) 32 Can. Bus. L.J. 384.

–. "Rose-Coloured Glasses, Opaque Financial Reporting and Investor Blues: Enron as Con and the Vulnerability of Canadian Corporate Law" (2002) 73 St. John's L. Rev. 101.

–. "The Corporation as a Symphony: Are Shareholders First Violin or Second Fiddle?" (2003) 36(3) U.B.C. L. Rev. 403.

Sarra, Janis P., and Ronald B. Davis. *Director and Officer Liability in Corporate Insolvency* (Markham, ON, and Vancouver: Butterworths Canada, 2002).

Sauchik, Alec. "Beyond Economically Targetted Investments: Redefining the Legal Framework of Pension Fund Investments in Low-to-Moderate Income Residential Real Estate" (2001) 28 Fordham Urb. L.J. 1923.

Schmolke, Klaus Ulrich. *Institutional Investors' Mandatory Voting Disclosure: European Plans and US Experience* (New York University Law and Economics Working Papers, Paper 71, 2006), online: New York University School of Law, http://lsr.nellco.org/nyu/lewp/papers/71.

Schultz, Ellen E. "US Taxpayers May Have to Pay Enron's Workers' Pension Benefits" *Wall Street Journal* (27 February 2002).
Schwartz, Donald E. "Towards New Corporate Goals: Co-Existence with Society" (1971-72) 60 Geo. L.J. 57.
Sciulli, David. *Corporate Power in Civil Society: An Application of Societal Constitutionalism* (New York: New York University Press, 2001).
Sen, Amartya Kumar. *Development as Freedom* (New York: Anchor Books, 1999).
Shaughnessy, Meaghan "The United Nations Global Compact and the Continuing Debate about the Effectiveness of Corporate Voluntary Codes of Conduct" (2001) 12 Colorado Journal of International Environmental Law and Policy: 2000 Yearbook 159.
"Should the SEC Expand Nonfinancial Disclosure Requirements," Note (2002) 115 Harv. L. Rev. 1433.
Silvers, Damon, William Patterson, and J.W. Mason. "Challenging Wall Street's Conventional Wisdom: Defining a Worker-Owner View of Value" in Archon Fung, Tessa Hebb, and Joel Rogers, eds., *Working Capital: The Power of Labor's Pensions* (Ithaca and London: Cornell University Press, 2001) 203.
Simon, William H. "The Prospects of Pension Fund Socialism" (1993) 14 Berkeley J. Emp. & Lab. L. 251.
Smith, Thomas A. "The Efficient Norm for Corporate Law: A Neotraditional Interpretation of Fiduciary Duty" (1999) 98 Mich. L. Rev. 214.
Soderquist, Larry D., and Robert P. Vecchio. "Reconciling Shareholders' Rights and Corporate Responsibility: New Guidelines for Management" (1978) 27 Duke L.J. 819.
Stabile, Susan J. "Freedom to Choose Unwisely: Congress' Misguided Decision to Leave 401(k) Plan Participants to Their Own Devices" (2002) 11 Cornell J. L. & Pub. Pol'y 361.
–. "Pension Investments in Employer Securities: More Is Not Always Better" (1998) 15 Yale J. on Reg. 61.
–. "The Behavior of Defined Contribution Plan Participants" (2002) 77 N.Y.U.L. Rev. 71.
Steeves, Leslie, and Peter Miodonski. "Canada Pension Plan and Quebec Pension Plan Benefits" in Raymond Koskie *et al.*, eds., *Employee Benefits in Canada* (Brookfield, MN: International Foundation of Employee Benefit Plans, 2001) 84.
–. "Old Age Security" in Raymond Koskie *et al.*, eds., *Employee Benefits in Canada* (Brookfield, MN: International Foundation of Employee Benefit Plans, 2001) 119.
Stigler, George J. "Public Regulation of the Securities Market" (1964) 37(2) Journal of Business 117.
Stone, Christopher D. "Corporate Social Responsibility: What It Might Mean, If It Were to Really Matter" (1986) 71 Iowa L. Rev. 557.
Storero, Jane K. "The HP Letter: SEC Staff Takes No View Position on Shareholder Access Proposal" (2007) 11(2) Wallstreetlawyer.com.
Stout, Lynn A. "Are Stock Markets Costly Casinos? Disagreement, Market Failure and Securities Regulation" (1995) 81(3) Va. L. Rev. 611.
Testy, Kellye Y. "Linking Progressive Corporate Law with Progressive Social Movements" (2002) 76 Tul. L. Rev. 1227.
Tomassini, Roberto. "Pension Funds and Socially Responsible Investing" in Raymond Koskie *et al.*, eds., *Employee Benefits in Canada* (Brookfield, MN: International Foundation of Employee Benefit Plans, 2001) 316.
Toronto Stock Exchange (TSX). *Comparison of Canadian Equivalents to Recent US Corporate Governance Initiatives* (Toronto: TSX, 2002).
Triantis, George, and Ronald J. Daniels. "The Role of Debt in Interactive Corporate Governance" (1995) 83 Cal. L. Rev. 1073.
Uchitelle, Louis. "Empty Nest Eggs: Do You Plan to Retire? Think Again" *New York Times* (31 March 2002) Business.
Whincop, Michael J. "The Role of the Shareholder in Corporate Governance: A Theoretical Approach" (2001) 25 Melbourne U.L. Rev. 418.
White, David. "Interview: Up to Trustees to Make System Work" (Interview with Robert Monks) (2003) 2 Investments and Pensions Europe 28.

Williams, Cynthia A. "The Securities and Exchange Commission and Corporate Social Transparency" (1999) 112 Harv. L. Rev. 1197.

–. "Corporate Social Responsibility in an Era of Economic Globalization" (2002) 35 U.C. Davis L. Rev. 705

Wolff, Edward N. *Retirement Insecurity: The Income Shortfalls Awaiting the Soon-to-Retire* (Washington, DC: Economic Policy Institute, 2002).

Wyatt, Edward. "Pension Change Puts the Burden on the Worker" *New York Times* (5 April 2002) Business.

Yaron, Gil. "Canadian Institutional Shareholder Activism in an Era of Global Deregulation" in Janis P. Sarra, ed., *Corporate Governance in Global Capital Markets* (Vancouver: UBC Press, 2003) 111.

–. "The Responsible Pension Trustee: Reinterpreting the Principles of Prudence and Loyalty in the Context of Socially Responsible Institutional Investing" (2001) 20 E.T.P.J. 305.

Young, Claire F.L. *Women, Tax and Social Programs: The Gendered Impact of Funding Social Programs through the Tax System* (Ottawa: Status of Women Canada, 2000).

Zanglein, Jayne Elizabeth. "Investment without Education: The Disparate Impact on Women and Minorities in Self-Directed Defined Contribution Plans" (2001) 5 Employee Rights and Employment Policy Journal 223.

Zernike, Kate. "Stocks' Slide Is Playing Havoc with Older Americans' Dreams" *New York Times* (14 July 2002) Business.

Ziegel, Jacob S., *et al. Cases and Materials on Partnerships and Canadian Business Corporations,* 3d ed. (Scarborough, ON: Carswell, 1994).

Zigler, Mark, and Ari N. Kaplan. "Pension Plan Surpluses" in Raymond Koskie *et al.,* eds., *Employee Benefits in Canada* (Brookfield, MN: International Foundation of Employee Benefit Plans, 2001) 222.

Reports, Government Documents, and Other Materials

AFL-CIO. "Office of Investment, About Us," online: AFL-CIO, http://www.aflcio.org/corporatewatch/capital/about.cfm.

–. "Proxy Voting Guidelines: Exercising Authority, Restoring Accountability" (2003), online: AFL-CIO, http://www.aflcio.org/corporatewatch/capital/upload/proxy_voting_guidelines.pdf.

American Law Institute. *Restatement (Second) of Trusts,* s. 193, comment a.

Anson, Mark (Chief Investment Officer, CalPERS). "Corporate Governance Ratings Come of Age" (Speech to International Corporate Governance Network, 2003).

California Public Employees' Retirement System. "Board Structure," online: CalPERS, http://www.calpers.ca.gov/about/board/structur/structur.htm.

–. "California Public Employees' Retirement System Global Proxy Voting Principles" (2001), online: CalPERS, http://www.calpers-governance.org/principles/global/globalvoting.pdf.

–. "California Public Employees' Retirement System Statement of Policy for Representation on Corporate Board of Directors" (1998), online: CalPERS, http://www.calpers.ca.gov/invest/policies/pdfs/Representation-on-Corporate-Boards-of-Directors.pdf.

–. "CalPERS and W.R. Grace" (2000), online: CalPERS, http://www.calpers-governance.org/litigation/grace.asp.

–. "Case by Case Evaluation Process" (1999), online: CalPERS, http://www.calpers-governance.org/litigation/evaluation.asp.

–. Press Release, "CalPERS Emerges Victor in Cendant Securities Lawsuit" (1999), online: CalPERS, http://www.calpers-governance.org/news/1999/1207a.asp.

Canada, Standing Senate Committee on Banking, Trade and Commerce. *The Governance Practices of Institutional Investors* (November 1998), online: Parliament of Canada, http://www.parl.gc.ca/36/1/parlbus/commbus/senate/com-e/bank-e/rep-e/rep16nov98-e.htm.

Canada Pension Plan Investment Board. "Frequently Asked Questions" in *Keeping You Informed,* online: Canada Pension Plan Investment Board, http://www.cppib.ca/info/faqs/index.html.

–. "Investment Statement" (2002), online: Canada Pension Plan Investment Board, http://www.cppib.ca/who/policy/Investment_Statement.pdf.

–. "Policy on Responsible Investing" (7 February 2007), online: Canada Pension Plan Investment Board, http://www.cppib.ca/files/PDF/policies/policies/Responsible_Investing_Policy.pdf.

–. "Proxy Voting" in *How We Invest: Public Market Investments,* online: Canada Pension Plan Investment Board, http://www.cppib.ca/how/publicmarket/proxy_voting.html.

–. "Proxy Voting Principles and Guidelines" (7 February 2007), online: Canada Pension Plan Investment Board, http://www.cppib.ca/files/PDF/policies/policies/Proxy_Voting_Guidelines.pdf.

–. "Responsible Investing: An Investor's Perspective" (Speech by Don Raymond, Senior Vice-President, Public Market Investments to Conference Board of Canada, National CSR Conference, 26 March 2007), online: Canada Pension Plan Investment Board, http://www.cppib.ca/files/PDF/speeches/2007_March26_DonRaymond_CSR.pdf.

–. "Social Investing Policy" (2002), online: Canada Pension Plan Investment Board, http://www.cppib.ca/who/policy/Social_Investing_Policy.pdf.

–. "Who We Are" in *CPP Investment Board Investing for Canadians,* online: Canada Pension Plan Investment Board, http://www.cppib.ca/who/index.html.

Canadian Coalition for Good Governance. "Vote Your Proxies" (2003), online: Canadian Coalition for Good Governance, http://www.ccgg.ca/web/website.nsf/web/ccggvoteyourproxies.

–. "Mission Statement and Objectives" (2003), online: Canadian Coalition for Good Governance, http://www.ccgg.ca/web/website.nsf/web/ccgghome.

Canadian Democracy and Corporate Accountability Commission. "Recommendations" in *The New Balance Sheet: Corporate Profits and Accountability in the 21st Century* (2002), online: http://www.corporate-accountability.ca/pdfs/Recommendations2002.pdf.

–. *The New Balance Sheet: Corporate Profits and Responsibility in the 21st Century* (2002), online: http://www.corporate-accountability.ca/pdfs/FullReport2002.pdf.

Carbon Disclosure Project. "About Us," online: Carbon Disclosure Project, http://www.cdproject.net/aboutus.asp.

Commission of the European Communities. Communication from the Commission to the European Parliament, the Council and the European Economic and Social Committee, "Implementing the Partnership for Jobs and Growth: Making a Pole of Excellence on Corporate Social Responsibility," COM(2006) 135 final (22 March 2006).

–. Communication from the European Commission to the Council and European Parliament, "Modernisation of Company Law and Enhancing Corporate Governance in the European Union – a Plan to Move Forward," COM (2003) 284 final (21 May 2003), online: Europa, http://eur-lex.europa.eu/LexUriServ/site/en/com/2003/com2003_0284en01.pdf.

–. Communication to European Institutions, Member States, Social Partners and Other Concerned Parties, "Communication from the Commission Concerning Corporate Social Responsibility: A Business Contribution to Sustainable Development," COM(2002) 347 final (2 July 2002).

–. Communication to the Council, the European Parliament and the Economic and Social Committee, "Promoting Core Labour Standards and Improving Social Governance in the Context of Globalization" Communique COM(2001) 416 final (18 July 2001).

–. *Promoting a European Framework for Corporate Social Responsibility,* Green Paper COM(2001) 366 final (18 July 2001).

Committee on Workers' Capital. "Welcome," online: Committee on Workers' Capital, http://www.workerscapital.org/.

Denton, Herbert A. "Differing Approaches to Governance in Portfolio Management Process" (Panel presentation, International Corporate Governance Network Annual Meeting, Amsterdam, 2003).

Employee Benefit Research Institute. "Equity Holdings of Retirement Plans" in *Facts from EBRI* (2000), online: Employee Benefit Research Institute, http://www.ebri.org/facts/0800fact2.htm.

–. "History of Pension Plans" in *Facts from EBRI* (1998), online: Employee Benefit Research Institute, http://www.ebri.org/facts/0398afact.htm.

–. "Retirement Plan Assets: Year-End 2001" in *Facts from EBRI* (2002), online: Employee Benefit Research Institute, http://www.ebri.org/facts/0902fact.pdf.

European Parliament. "European Parliament Resolution on the Commission Green Paper on Promoting a European Framework for Corporate Social Responsibility" P5_TA(2002) 0278.

Federal/Provincial/Territorial CPP Consultations Secretariat. "Strengthening CPP Financing and Reducing CPP Costs" in *An Information Paper for Consultations on the Canada Pension Plan* (1996), online: Department of Finance, http://www.cpp-rpc.gc.ca/summe/summ2e.html#strength.

Gibben, Chris, and Matthew Gitsham. *Will UK Pension Funds Become More Responsible? A Survey of Trustees* (Berkhamsted, Herfordshire: Ashridge Centre for Business and Society, 2006), online: UK Social Investment Forum, http://www.uksif.org/cmsfiles/uksif/ukpf2006-justpens.pdf.

Global Reporting Initiative. "About GRI," online: Global Reporting Initiative, http://www.globalreporting.org/AboutGRI/.

–. "Application Levels," online: Global Reporting Initiative, http://www.globalreporting.org/GRIReports/ApplicationLevels/.

Gordon, Kathryn. "The OECD Guidelines and Other Corporate Responsibility Instruments: A Comparison" in *Working Papers on International Investment No. 2001/5* (2001), online: OECD, http://www.oecd.org/pdf/M00027000/M00027380.pdf.

Howitt, Richard. Rapporteur, *Report on EU Standards for European Enterprises Operating in Developing Countries: Towards a European Code of Conduct,* Committee on Development and Cooperation, European Parliament, Number PE 228.198/fin. (17 December 1998).

International Corporate Governance Network. "ICGN Statement on Institutional Shareholder Responsibilities" (2003), online: International Corporate Governance Network, http://www.icgn.org/documents/GuidelinesResponsibilities0503.pdf.

–. "Statement of Principles on Institutional Shareholder Responsibilities" (2007), online: International Corporate Governance Network, http://www.icgn.org/organisation/documents/src/Statement%20on%20Shareholder%20Responsibilities%202007.pdf.

Kodar, Freya. *Corporate Law, Pension Law and the Transformative Potential of Pension Fund Investment Activism* (LL.M. Thesis, Graduate Programme in Law, York University, Toronto, 2002) [unpublished].

Myners, Paul. "Institutional Investment in the United Kingdom: A Review" (Report to the Chancellor of the Exchequer, 2001), online: The Corporate Library, http://www.thecorporatelibrary.com/special/myners/myners-review.pdf.

Office of the Superintendent of Financial Institutions (Canada). "Guideline for Governance of Federally Regulated Pension Plans" (1998), online: Office of the Superintendent of Financial Institutions, http://www.osfi-bsif.gc.ca/app/DocRepository/1/eng/pension/guidance/govengl3_e.pdf.

Ontario Securities Commission. National Instrument 51-102, *Continuous Disclosure Obligations,* Form 51-102F2, "Annual Information Form," 5.1(4) (19 January 2007), online: Ontario Securities Commission, http://www.osc.gov.on.ca/Regulation/Rulemaking/Current/Part5/rule_20070119_51-102_unofficial-cons-ni.pdf.

–. National Instrument 54-101, *Communication with Beneficial Owners of Securities of a Reporting Issuer* (2002), online: Ontario Securities Commission, http://www.osc.gov.on.ca/en/Regulation/Rules/rules.html.

–. National Instrument 58-101, *Disclosure of Corporate Governance Practices* (17 June 2005), online: Ontario Securities Commission, http://www.osc.gov.on.ca/Regulation/Rulemaking/Current/Part5/rule_20050617_58-101_disc-corp-gov-pract.jsp.

–. National Instrument 58-301, *Disclosure of Corporate Governance Practices* (in effect 12 June 2005), online: Ontario Securities Commission, http://www.osc.gov.on.ca/Regulation/Rulemaking/Current/Part5/rule_20050617_58-101_disc-corp-gov-pract.jsp.

–. National Instrument 45-106, *Prospectus and Registration Exemptions* (2005) 28 OSCB Supp-4, online: Ontario Securities Commission, http://www.osc.gov.on.ca/Regulation/Rulemaking/Current/Part4/rule_20050909_45-106_consq_amend.pdf.

–. National Instrument 62-103, *The Early Warning System and Related Take-Over Bid and Insider Reporting Issues,* online: Ontario Securities Commission, http://www.osc.gov.on.ca/Regulation/Rulemaking/Current/Part6/rule_20000225_62-103fr.jsp.

–. National Instrument 62-104, *Takeover Bids and Issuer Bids* 2.21-2.23 (issued 28 April 2006).

–. National Instrument 81-106, *Investment Fund Continuous Disclosure,* Part 10 – "Proxy Voting Disclosure for Portfolio Securities Held" (3 June 2005), online: Ontario Securities Commission, http://www.osc.gov.on.ca/Regulation/Rulemaking/Current/Part8/rule_20050603_81-106_if-cont-disc.jsp.

–. National Policy 58-201, *Corporate Governance Guidelines* (17 June 2005), online: Ontario Securities Commission, http://www.osc.gov.on.ca/Regulation/Rulemaking/Current/Part5/rule_20050617_58-201_corp-gov-guidelines.jsp.

Ontario Teachers' Pension Plan. News Release, "Institutional Investors Form Coalition to Fight for Improved Corporate Governance" (2002), online: Ontario Teachers' Pension Plan, http://www.otpp.com/web/website.nsf/web/CoalitionforCorpGov.

Organisation for Economic Co-operation and Development. "OECD Principles of Corporate Governance" (1999), online: OECD, http://www.oecd.org/pdf/M00008000/M00008299.pdf.

Pension Investment Association of Canada. "PIAC Corporate Governance Standards" (1998), online: Pension Investment Association of Canada, http://www.piacweb.org/about_corp_gov_standards.cfm.

Principles for Responsible Investment. Media Release, "Principles for Responsible Investment Hit $8 Trillion Mark on First Year Anniversary" (29 April 2007), online: Principles for Responsible Investment, http://www.unpri.org/media/PRI_media_release_29-04-07.php.

–. "The Principles for Responsible Investment," online: Principles for Responsible Investment, http://www.unpri.org/principles/.

Shareholder Association for Research and Education. "2006 Key Proxy Vote Survey," online: Shareholder Association for Research and Education, http://www.share.ca/files/Proxy_Survey_2006_FINAL.pdf.

–. "About SHARE," online: Shareholder Association for Research and Education, http://www.share.ca/en/about.

–. News Release, "Record Numbers Support Shareholder Resolution at the Bay on Sweatshops" (23 May 2002), online: Shareholder Association for Research and Education, http://www.share.ca/files/news/02-05-23-HBC.pdf.

Social Investment Forum. "2001 Report on Socially Responsible Investing Trends in the United States" (2001), online: Social Investment Forum, http://www.socialinvest.org/areas/research/trends/SRI_Trends_Report_2001.pdf.

Social Investment Organization. *The Canadian Socially Responsible Investment Review 2006* (Toronto: Social Investment Organization, 2007), online: Social Investment Organization, http://www.socialinvestment.ca.

Statistics Canada. "Pension Savings of Canadians," online: Statistics Canada, http://www40.statcan.ca/l01/cst01/labr78.htm.

Stern, Sir Nicholas. *The Economics of Climate Change* (London: HM Treasury, 2006), online: HM Treasury, http://www.hm-treasury.gov.uk/independent_reviews/stern_review_economics_climate_change/stern_review_report.cfm.

TIAA-CREF. "Mutual Funds Performance Chart" (2002), online: TIAA-CREF, http://www.tiaa-cref.org/charts/mf-performance.html.

Trades Union Congress, "Working Capital: Institutional Investment Strategy" (February 2003), online: Trades Union Congress, http://www.tuc.org.uk/pensions/tuc-6269-f0.pdf.

U.K., Department for Work and Pensions. Press Release, "Timms Backs Socially Responsible Investment" (17 June 2005), online: UK Department for Work and Pensions, http://www.dwp.gov.uk/mediacentre/pressreleases/2005/jun/pens007.asp.

U.K., Department of Trade and Industry. *Implementation of Companies Act 2006: A Consultative Document* (February 2007) c. 2, "Secondary Legislation Under the Act," online: UK Department of Trade and Industry, http://www.dti.gov.uk/files/file37973.pdf.

U.K., National Statistics Online. "Pensions and National Accounts," online: UK National Statistics Online, http://www.statistics.gov.uk/CCI/nugget.asp?ID=1283&Pos=&ColRank =2&Rank=224.

United Nations Environment Programme Finance Initiative Asset Management Working Group and the United Kingdom Social Investment Forum Sustainable Pensions Project. *Responsible Investment in Focus: How Leading Public Pension Funds Are Meeting the Challenge* (April 2007), online: United Nations Environment Programme, http://www.unepfi.org/fileadmin/documents/infocus.pdf.

U.S., Department of Labor. *Interpretive Bulletin Relating to Written Statements of Investment Policy, Including Proxy Voting Policy or Guidelines,* 29 CFR 2509.94-2 (1994).

U.S., Government Accountability Office. *Report to the Ranking Minority Member, Committee on Health, Education, Labor, and Pensions, US Senate: Pension Plans – Additional Transparency and Other Actions Needed in Connection with Proxy Voting,* GAO-04-749 (August 2004), online: Government Accountability Office, http://www.gao.gov/new.items/d04749.pdf.

U.S., Federal Reserve. "Flow of Funds," Tables L.118-L.120, online: Federal Reserve, http://www.federalreserve.gov/releases/z1/Current/z1r-4.pdf.

U.S., Securities and Exchange Commission. Administrative Proceeding, Release No. 2160, "In the Matter of Deutsche Asset Management, Inc." (19 August 2003), online: SEC, http://www.sec.gov/litigation/admin/ia-2160.htm.

–. *Advisory Committee on Corporate Disclosure,* 9 S.E.C. Docket 672 (18 May 1976) (Solicitation of Public Comments).

–. *Disclosure of Proxy Voting Policies and Proxy Voting Records by Registered Management Investment Companies,* 17 CFR 270.30b1-4 (2003).

–. "SEC Announces Roundtable Discussions Regarding Proxy Process" (24 April 2007), online: SEC, http://www.sec.gov/news/press/2007/2007-71.htm.

–. "Security Holder Director Nominations" (14 October 2003), online: SEC, http://www.sec.gov/rules/proposed/34-48626.htm.

U.S., Securities and Exchange Commission, Division of Corporate Finance. "Staff Report: Review of Proxy Process Regarding the Nomination and Election of Directors" (2003), online: SEC, http://www.sec.gov/news/studies/proxyreport.pdf.

U.S., Senate Committee on Finance. *Statement of Steven A. Kandarian, Executive Director, Pension Benefit Guaranty Corporation,* 107th Cong. (27 February 2002).

U.S., Senate Committee on Governmental Affairs. *Prepared Statement of Professor Susan Stabile,* 107th Cong. (5 February 2002), online: U.S. Senate, http://hsgac.senate.gov/020502stabile.htm.

–. *Statement of Professor John Langbein,* 107th Cong. (24 January 2002), online: U.S. Senate, http://hsgac.senate.gov/012402langbein.htm.

U.S., Senate Committee on Health, Education, Labor and Pensions. *Prepared Statement of Jan Fleetham,* 107th Cong. (7 February 2002), online: U.S. Senate, http://frwebgate.access.gpo.gov/cgi-bin/getdoc.cgi?dbname=107_senate_hearings&docid=77-706.

–. *Testimony of Stephen E. Lacey,* 107th Cong. (7 February 2002), online: U.S. Senate, http://frwebgate.access.gpo.gov/cgi-bin/getdoc.cgi?dbname=107_senate_hearings&docid=77-706.

van der Poel, Jan. "The Coming of Age of Corporate Governance Ratings" (Presentation at the International Corporate Governance Network 9th Annual Conference, 2003).

Vector Research. "Analysis of the Public Opinion Poll Conducted for the Canadian Democracy and Corporate Accountability Commission" (2001), online: http://www.corporate-accountability.ca/pdfs/PollReport.pdf.

Yalden, Robert. "Competing Theories of the Corporation and Their Role in Canadian Business Law" Paper presented in *Current Issues in Securities Regulation and Investor Protection* panel at the Symposium on Shareholders, held at UBC Faculty of Law, 31 January 2003.

Yaron, Gil. "Submission to the Canadian Securities Administrators from Shareholder Association for Research and Education on Proposed National Policy 51-201, Disclosure Standards" in *Timely and Material Disclosure* (2001), online: Shareholder Association for Research and Education, http://www.share.ca/index.cfm/fuseaction/page.inside/pageID/6FE05720-B0D0-157F-F4DAFA83A65BF767/index.cfm.

Index

Printed and bound in Canada by Friesens
Set in Stone by Artegraphica Design
Copy editor: Francis Chow
Indexer: Adrian Mather